Interpreting American History:

The New South

INTERPRETING AMERICAN HISTORY

Brian D. McKnight and James S. Humphreys, series editors

THE AGE OF ANDREW JACKSON
Edited by Brian D. McKnight and James S. Humphreys

THE NEW DEAL AND THE GREAT DEPRESSION
Edited by Aaron D. Purcell

RECONSTRUCTION
Edited by John David Smith

THE NEW SOUTH
Edited by James S. Humphreys

INTERPRETING AMERICAN HISTORY

THE NEW SOUTH

Edited by

JAMES S. HUMPHREYS

The Kent State University Press

Kent, Ohio

© 2018 by The Kent State University Press, Kent, Ohio 44242
ALL RIGHTS RESERVED
Library of Congress Catalog Card Number 2017016130
ISBN 978-1-60635-315-8
Manufactured in the United States of America

LIBRARY OF CONGRESS CATALOGING-IN-PUBLICATION DATA
Names: Humphreys, James Scott, 1963- editor of compilation.
Title: Interpreting American history : the new South / edited by James S.
    Humphreys.
Description: Kent, Ohio : Kent State University Press, [2017] | Series:
    Interpreting American history series | Includes bibliographical
    references and index.
Identifiers: LCCN 2017016130 | ISBN 9781606353158 (pbk.) | ISBN
    9781631013027 (epub) | ISBN 9781631013034 (epdf)
Subjects: LCSH: Southern States--History--1865-1951. | Woodward, C.
    Vann (Comer Vann), 1908-1999. Origins of the new South, 1877-1913. |
    Southern States--Historiography. | Southern States--Social conditions.
Classification: LCC F215 .I58 2017 | DDC 975--dc23
LC record available at https://lccn.loc.gov/2017016130

22 21 20 19 18   5 4 3 2 1

To Joy

Contents

Foreword

Interpreting American History Series

Of all the history courses taught on college campuses, historiography is one of the most challenging. The historiographic essays most often available are frequently too specialized for broad teaching and sometimes too obtuse for the average undergraduate student. Every day, frustrated scholars and students search for writings that offer both breadth and depth in their approach to the historiography of different eras and movements. As young scholars grow more intellectually mature, they remain wedded to the lessons taught within the pages of historiographic studies. As graduate students prepare for seminar presentations, comprehensive examinations, and dissertation work, they often wonder why that void has remained. Then, when they complete the studies and enter the profession, they find themselves less intellectually connected to those ideas of which they once showed a mastery, and they again ask about the lack of meaningful and succinct studies of historiography . . . and the circle continues.

Within the pages of this series, innovative young scholars discuss the different interpretations of the important eras and events of history, not only focusing on the intellectual shifts that have taken place, but on the various catalysts that drove these shifts. It is the hope of the series editors that these volumes fill those aforementioned intellectual voids and speak to the young scholars in a way that will supplement their other learning; that the same pages that speak to undergraduate students will also remind the established scholar of his or her historiographic roots; that a difficult subject is made more accessible to curious minds; that ideas are not lost among the details offered within the classroom.

BRIAN D. MCKNIGHT, The University of Virginia's College at Wise
JAMES S. HUMPHREYS, Murray State University

Acknowledgments

I greatly appreciate the assistance I received in bringing this book of essays on New South historiography to fruition. Editors at the Kent State University Press, Will Underwood and Joyce Harrison, offered much needed guidance and encouragement throughout the course of this project. Although they demonstrated an abundance of patience, they also urged me when necessary to work harder to see this book through to completion. My sincere thanks go to both of them. I am grateful for copyeditor Will Moore's painstaking efforts to enhance the quality of this book when it was in manuscript form. Will's expertise made the finished volume far better than it otherwise would have been. The eleven scholars who contributed chapters have my deepest admiration for the thoughtfulness and exertion they invested in their writing. They all taught me a great deal. Brian D. McKnight, coeditor of the Interpreting American History series, always supported this project and provided helpful insights into how to improve it. Working with such a gifted group of editors and historians was a pleasure and an honor. Finally, I thank my wife, Joy, for enduring along with me the challenges of writing and editing. Joy's love and support have made those challenges less daunting.

Introduction

The concept of the "New South" has elicited fierce debate among historians since the mid-twentieth century. At the heart of the argument is the question of whether the post-Civil War South transformed into something genuinely new or held firm to patterns of life established before 1861. The South did change in significant ways after the war ended, but many of its enduring trademarks—the most prominent being white supremacy—remained constant well into the twentieth century. Scholars have yet to meet the vexing challenge of proving or disproving the existence of a New South. Even in the twenty-first century, amid the South's sprawling cities, expanding suburbia, and high-tech environment, vestiges of the Old South remain.

Bringing order out of the voluminous canon of writing on the New South poses a challenge. The essays here trace the lineaments of historical debate on the most important questions related to the South's history since 1865 and how that argument has changed over time as modernity descended on Dixie. *Interpreting American History: The New South* consists of essays written by noted scholars who address topics relating to the New South, such as the Populist era, the Great Depression, and the civil rights movement, and emerging fields, such as Reconstruction in a global context, New South environmental history, and southern women. Each contributor explains clearly and succinctly the winding path historical writing has taken on each of the topics.

Andrew Zimmerman, in his essay, argues that Reconstruction in the United States was not an isolated event, but instead had transnational repercussions. Zimmerman illumines aspects of Reconstruction in the United States that were similar to events unfolding simultaneously in other regions of the world. For example, the switch from slave to free labor and the subsequent restrictions to capital placed on the newly freed people during Reconstruction occurred likewise in the Caribbean after British emancipation. Zimmerman also asserts that European colonial leaders adopted practices used in the New South to control blacks socially and economically. German officials, for instance, in building their cotton industry in West Africa, subjected blacks to forms of discrimination first employed in the American South after the Civil War. Rarely have historians viewed Reconstruction in the transnational light Zimmerman provides.

Connie L. Lester examines the history of Populism in an essay that explores what scholars have written about the characteristics of Americans attracted to Populist politics in the late nineteenth century and whether they adhered to traditionalist or modernist thinking. She also analyzes historians' views on the legacy of Populism to American politics. Many historians, Lester points out, believe Populism's influence lingered well into the twentieth century. The policies of progressive stalwarts, such as President Woodrow Wilson and President Franklin Delano Roosevelt, resembled those of the Populists. Few social and political movements have left such an indelible stamp on American life as Populism.

In a searching essay on racial violence, Sarah L. Silkey reminds readers of what was probably the most shocking aspect of the New South, lynching—a practice, she asserts, employed to produce a pliant black workforce and to reinforce white supremacy following the disruption to the southern economy by the Civil War. Silkey explores a century of both popular and scholarly writing in charting the unfolding of the historiography of lynching. Reform organizations, such as the National Association for the Advancement of Colored People, gathered information and statistics related to lynching in the early twentieth century. Historians next began writing monographs on the subject, and then, over the last several decades, scholarly studies on lynching burgeoned to include not only lynching in the South, but in other regions of the country and to focus not only on the crime's impact on black males, but also black women, and other targets of lynching, such as Mexicans and Asians. Silky explains that historians now portray lynching as not simply a southern phenomenon, but one that occurred in other regions of the United States and in other countries.

Rebecca Montgomery's essay sheds light on the ways in which historians have evaluated women's impact on public life in the New South. Montgomery examines, for example, the debate over female suffrage and the efforts that southern women undertook to win the vote. The issue of suffrage rights for women revealed underlying racial tensions, because granting voting rights to African American women would transform them into significant political actors. Southern women, historians have also shown, exerted their influence over not only political developments, but also social matters, by joining church groups, enrolling in temperance organizations, and engaging in labor activism. Scholars, Montgomery points out, now realize that women actively, not passively, pursued necessary reforms, which, women believed, constituted a semblance of equality with men.

In his essay, Robert H. Zieger charts historical writing addressing the rise and decline of labor unions in the South. As unionization proceeded in other regions of the United States in the late nineteenth and early twentieth centuries, he explains, it struggled to take root in the South; but after World War II, it gained momentum there, reaching its apex around 1990. Just as the South began to mirror other parts of the country in terms of unionization, it succumbed to a business model antithetical to unions, represented most prominently by the Walmart corporation. This model, which offered consumers low prices and workers paltry wages and benefits, spread to other sections of the country. It now seemed, ironically, that the South had become a trendsetter, not a laggard. So weak have unions become in the South that Zieger expresses doubt that they have a viable future in the region. Zieger posits that in the South today, laborers—many of whom are immigrants—face the difficult challenge of making unionization relevant again in a hostile economic and social environment.

Stephanie A. Carpenter, in her chapter, views as incomplete the historiography of the South during the Great Depression. She examines the historiography of the subject through the lenses of four distinct genres—histories of the South, histories of the Great Depression, histories of the South during the Great Depression, and the histories of the individual. Carpenter contends that both the positive and negative impacts of the New Deal on life in the South have not been explored adequately. Carpenter challenges scholars to engage in more thorough and more revisionist studies of the Great Depression South.

Jennifer E. Brooks opens her essay on World War II's role in changing racial paradigms in the New South with an examination of Gunnar Myrdal's pathbreaking *An American Dilemma: The Negro Problem and Modern Democracy* (1944). Myrdal viewed World War II as a sea change in the history of southern race relations, one that rapidly would expand the rights of blacks. While Brooks accords Myrdal the credit he deserves for *An American Dilemma,* she points out that scholars who followed Myrdal argued over the effect of the war on race relations in the South and continue to debate the issue.

Three periods, says Brooks—the civil rights era, the commemorative era, and the millennial era—serve as useful vehicles in understanding what historians have written about changes in the New South's race pattern as a result of the Second World War. During each era, scholars ruminated over whether World War II exerted a profound influence over race relations and black rights; the answer to the question became less clear and more complex the further away historians were from 1945.

Michael Bertrand examines the voluminous historiography relating to the civil rights movement by placing it under the categories of top-down or bottom-up history—or some combination of both. As Bertrand writes in his chapter, the top-down approach, which focused on chipping away at racial segregation through legal and political means, permeated the thinking of the early historians of the civil rights movement. Scholars next began to view the civil rights movement from a bottom-up approach, which highlighted the efforts of non-elites to engender positive changes in race relations in the South. Historians later combined both perspectives in penning studies of the civil rights movement that illumined the actions of both political figures and average folk, and explored the nexus between legal efforts and social activism. The civil rights movement, Bertrand declares, fulfilled the promises born during the Reconstruction era after the Civil War, ending a century of struggle for the rights of African Americans. Bertrand eloquently concludes that by the mid-twentieth century black southerners as well as many white ones decided that they had within their power the means to alter the course of history by striving to build a more just and enlightened society, and their effort largely succeeded.

Michael Bowen explores historians' views on the rise of the Republican Party in the South from World War II to the present. Historians and political scientists, Bowen explains in his chapter, cite numerous causes for the growth of the Republican Party in a region where before the Second World War the party had been extremely weak. Scholars emphasize three causes: a backlash among whites against the gains made by African Americans as a result of the civil rights movement, the appeal of conservative economic policies to middle-class, suburban whites, and support for traditional social values espoused by Republican Party leaders from white evangelicals, whose numbers grew substantially in the 1980s. As Bowen writes, scholars, while hotly debating which factor is most important, see a connection between all three causes. Because interpretations of modern southern politics are in substantial flux, making consensus among historians difficult to reach, few definitive conclusions may be drawn from the historical scholarship on the role of the Republican Party in the modern South.

Mark D. Hersey and James C. Giesen's essay explores a relatively young field in the study of the New South: environmental history. Hersey and Giesen explain that until the 1980s, southern historians' interest in matters related to class, race, and gender dwarfed their concern for the influence of the environment on the direction of southern history. Few courses in the South's environmental history—much less entire graduate programs in the subject—were offered forty years ago in the curriculum of universities in the South.

The subject was given short shrift, but not completely neglected; southern agriculture, for instance, received ample attention. However, scholars of southern agriculture considered themselves historians writing about the environment, rather than environmental historians. As Hersey and Giesen point out, southern environmental history emerged as a field within southern history during the last two decades of the twentieth century. Scholars identifying themselves as environmental historians and often having graduated from newly established doctoral programs in the subject explored long-neglected issues related to the South's natural world and the interaction of humans with it. The field of environmental history then burgeoned into a multifaceted discipline, often focusing on geographical regions, such as southern Appalachia, the Mississippi Delta, and the Chesapeake Bay. Hersey and Giesen concede that while studies related to class, race, and gender still take center stage in the study of the history of the American South, environmental history has attracted a corps of superb scholars and includes an impressive canon of writing, which continues to grow.

The American South has been a fertile field of study for over a century, with the civil rights movement having exerted an especially important influence on the study of the region. The discipline of southern history has become multidimensional since the mid-twentieth century. Today, books on the South address a myriad of topics, including race, politics, gender, economics, ecology, public history, and the environment. Little wonder, then, that southern history continues to command ample scholarly attention. The chapters in this volume reflect the eclecticism that now characterizes the historiography of the New South.

CHAPTER ONE

New South Historiography

JAMES S. HUMPHREYS

The history of the "New South" maintains a firm grip on the interest of scholars and the imagination of the public. Despite the hardship, tragedy, and pathos that have plagued them since the Civil War, white and black southerners over the past century exorcised many of the demons that once made their home a quagmire of backwardness, poverty, and racism. New South historiography illuminates the process through which southerners became modern, especially in their attitudes concerning race and gender. Academic and popular writing on the subject, not surprisingly, changed over time, but during each phase it reflected the impact of events occurring in the South, in other regions of the United States, and in other parts of the world. It originally mirrored the nostalgia and provincialism of the nineteenth-century white South; it then grew into a more academic pursuit in the late nineteenth and early twentieth centuries; and finally blossomed into a full-fledged academic discipline after World War II. In each iteration, the novices and scholars who delved into, argued over, and wrote about the New South provided the next group of researchers a foundation on which to build a richer and deeper understanding of a region that often defied explanation.

Perhaps the significant questions concerning the New South have been answered. The process of standardization, promoted by

radio and television, that began sweeping over the United States after World War II undermined the idea of the South as a distinctive
region within the country; however, a century and half ago, the
burning questions related to the fate of a region decimated by civil
war seemed endless.

New South Historiography from 1865 to 1920

The most important genre of writing to emerge in the South after
the Civil War consisted of memoirs and histories written by southern civilians and ex-Confederate military and political figures, who
offered their versions of the issues related to the war and the roles
they fulfilled during the fighting. An especially significant partisan
account penned during the postwar era was Confederate president
Jefferson Davis's massive apologia, *The Rise and Fall of the Confederate Government* (1881).[1] Not all Confederates, like Davis, held firm
to their belief in the rightness of the "rebel" cause after the fighting
ceased. Ironically, the author of *The Lost Cause* (1866) and *The Lost
Cause Regained* (1868), Edward A. Pollard, reevaluated his faith in
traditional southern values during the Reconstruction era.[2] Jack P.
Maddex Jr. explains that Pollard's views on secession, race, and slavery became more nuanced and critical as the period unfolded. Pollard, Maddex argues, dispensed after the war with his ardent faith
in the Confederate cause; rejected secession as a viable alternative
to the sectional disputes of the antebellum era; and jettisoned the
notion of the Confederate war effort as a holy struggle to protect
the South from Union barbarism. Pollard lambasted Jefferson Davis
as a poor wartime leader and questioned whether the Confederates
should have fought to protect slavery. Maintaining his faith in white
supremacy, he nevertheless supported suffrage rights for blacks and
yearned for the development of a coalition between moderates in
the North and the South as a bulwark against Radical Reconstruction.[3] Maddex refers to Pollard, after his conversion, as "one of the
most advanced Southern conservatives of his day."[4] Many white
southerners, however, remained unrepentant.

Pollard's change of heart failed to prevent the Lost Cause mentality from sweeping over the South. Adherents of the Lost Cause view cherished their memories of the Confederacy and its attempt, in their estimation, to protect the slaveholding South from northerners intent on destroying the "peculiar institution" and foisting notions of black equality and capitalist economics on white southerners. Lost Cause advocates viewed the Confederate war effort as a necessary struggle to protect white southerners' way of life and attributed its collapse to a lack of manpower as well as the vicious methods of warfare practiced by its enemies. Slavery played only a small role as a rationale for war among many southern whites in the late nineteenth and early twentieth centuries. The most significant reason for fighting, they claimed, was to defend the honor of southern civilization from an onslaught of an alien society tainted by the decadent notions of abolitionism, black equality, and free labor. The numerous commemorations held, the massive monuments dedicated, and the eloquent paeans delivered in an effort to memorialize Confederate values all attested to the power with which the Lost Cause mentality gripped the imagination of many white southerners in the late nineteenth and early twentieth centuries.[5]

Ex-Confederate officers wrote voluminous works on the war in an attempt to vindicate the Confederate cause and to burnish their own reputations in the face of criticism from white southerners smarting from the sting of defeat. Among these writings were James B. Avirett's *The Memoirs of General Turner Ashby and His Compeers* (1867); James Longstreet's *From Manassas to Appomattox* (1896); John B. Gordon's *Reminiscences of the Civil War* (1903); and Alexander E. Porter's *Military Memoirs of a Confederate* (1907). Southern civilians also wrote at length about the war, leaving such portraits of the Old South and Civil War years as Mary Boykin Chesnut's *A Diary from Dixie* (1905) and Phoebe Pember's *A Southern Woman's Story* (1879).[6]

The writings of Confederates officials, civil and political, and the memoirs of "rebel" citizens offered a window on the way in which southern partisans thought about the war and reacted to defeat;

they did not, however, provide readers with an objective rendering of the history of their times. More scholarly works on the Civil War and Reconstruction would come later as the passage of time enabled historians to view the era with more objectivity than their predecessors and as the study of history developed into a scholarly discipline.

The study of history in the United States became more professional at the close of the nineteenth century, evidenced, for example, by the founding in 1884 of the American Historical Association (AHA). Not only history, but also other academic fields experienced a similar transformation as a result of the Progressive era's emphasis on the training of elites to combat the serious ills besetting American society in the late nineteenth and early twentieth centuries. The field of history in the United States underwent a shift during the Progressive era from one dominated by amateurs to one led by professionals.[7]

Referring to a historian as an "amateur" does not mean that he or she lacked academic talent. It indicates instead that the amateur possessed little formal academic training in history. Boston businessman James Ford Rhodes, who penned a multivolume history of the United States that American readers greatly admired, and President Theodore Roosevelt, author of a multivolume work titled *The Winning of the West* (1889-99) as well as other writings, both qualified as amateurs.[8] Professional historians—that is, those with ample academic training in the subject—eclipsed the amateurs in influence as the Progressive era unfolded. Many of these professional historians, such as scholar and diplomat George Bancroft, University of Chicago professor William Edward Dodd, and Columbia University professor William Archibald Dunning, took part of their education in Germany, where progressive thought permeated the academy and other areas of German society more thoroughly than it did in the United States. At the University of Berlin, students absorbed Leopold von Ranke's practices of scientific history, which stressed the need for in-depth research in primary sources, emphasized an unbiased reading of documents, and espoused the belief that historical truth was attainable through a diligent quest for historical accuracy. The study of history in universities in the United States soon reflected a German influence.[9]

The most significant scholarly work to appear at this time derived from the efforts of Professor William Archibald Dunning, a northerner, and a collection of his graduate students, most of whom were southerners. The "Dunning School" of Reconstruction portrayed the Radical Republicans' plan for reconstructing the South as harsh and vindictive toward ex-Confederates. According to the Dunning scholars, the Radicals erred in placing faith in the ability of blacks to participate in politics and to serve in public offices. Thus the southern state governments run by blacks, northerners, and white unionists consistently committed acts of mismanagement, fraud, and overspending. Ex-Confederates, according to the Dunning School, had no choice but to engage in an all-out-effort to overthrow the Republican-led governments and to replace them with Democratic regimes.[10]

A number of Dunning's southern students penned state studies of Reconstruction. James W. Garner wrote *Reconstruction in Mississippi,* published in 1901; Joseph Gregoire de Roulhac Hamilton's *Reconstruction in North Carolina* appeared in 1914; and C. Mildred Thompson's *Reconstruction in Georgia* (1915) came out a year later. A number of other states—Arkansas, Texas, and Florida—also received similar treatment by students of Dunning. The state studies varied in quality and objectivity, but were usually critical of Radical Reconstruction. Dunning's books on Reconstruction showed more professionalism, but still portrayed the Radical plan for the South as a misguided, dictatorial scheme bound to fail because it attempted to dismantle white supremacy as a basis for governing the South.[11] The Dunning School of Reconstruction stood out as the first comprehensive explanation of the era and, through the first half of the twentieth century, would guide historical writing on the period after the Civil War.

As the nineteenth century came to a close, the two leading institutions for the study of the South were Columbia University, in New York City, and Johns Hopkins University, located in Baltimore. Dunning, as mentioned earlier, made significant contributions to

the field at Columbia, while Herbert Baxter Adams, also a northerner, promoted the study of the subject at Johns Hopkins. The curriculum at John Hopkins eventually included southern history
courses. Dunning and Adams exerted a direct influence over scholarship related to the history of the South through the efforts of
many of their students, who after completing their graduate studies
dedicated their careers as academics to the advancement of southern history.[12]

Columbia and Johns Hopkins may have dominated the study of
the South, but the discipline was also growing in Dixie. For example, a student of Adams's, George Petrie, secured a job at Alabama's
Auburn University, where he taught the future scholars Frank L.
Owsley, Herman Clarence Nixon, and Walter Lynwood Fleming.
Courses were developed at Auburn stressing Alabama history and
other southern topics. Also, the Alabama Department of Archives
and History came to fruition through the assiduous efforts of a
lawyer, Thomas M. Owen. Officials in other states copied Owen's
work in building their archives.[13]

Another of Adams's students, Franklin L. Riley, provided the impetus behind what historian W. Conrad Gass referred to as Mississippi's "great historical renaissance."[14] Riley began teaching at
the University of Mississippi in 1897. He edited the *Publications of
the Mississippi Historical Society* from 1898 to 1914; oversaw graduate
and undergraduate education in the history department; and spear-
headed the development of the Mississippi Department of Archives
and History.[15]

John Spencer Bassett arrived at North Carolina's Trinity College,
now Duke University, after studying under Adams at John Hopkins.
Bassett stressed greater impartiality in writing about the South, arguing that the reminiscences of Confederate officers and other nostalgic southerners should no longer pass for history. While teaching
at Trinity, his undergraduate and graduate students began studying
North Carolina history through the analysis of primary sources,
and the library's holdings in southern history grew. In addition, the
university came out with two new publications, the *Historical Papers*

of the Trinity College Historical Society in 1897 and the *South Atlantic Quarterly* five years later. Bassett played a major role in all of these developments at Trinity.[16]

The field of southern history clearly experienced growth in the early twentieth century. As Wendell Stephenson has explained, "By 1913 six colleges and universities were offering courses in the history of the South; the number had increased to thirty or forty by the 1920s, and to nearly a hundred by 1940."[17] Emphasis on southern history also increased within the American Historical Association. Although the influence of northeastern historians permeated the AHA, the presence of William Dunning, who played a prominent role in the organization, made it easier for southern historians to join. At least twice prior to the 1920s, AHA officials chose southern cities, New Orleans and Charleston, as sites for the organization's annual meetings. Pressure to hold the 1903 gathering in New Orleans came from Dunning, who served as president of the organization when it met in Charleston in 1913.[18] Having begun as a field dominated by partisans and nonspecialists, the study of southern history had developed into a more scientific discipline by the early twentieth century.

NEW SOUTH HISTORIOGRAPHY FROM 1920 TO 1950

The South's backwardness became a topic of growing interest in the 1920s to scholars in the fields of sociology, public health, political science, anthropology, and history. A salient example of this scholarly attention was the development, starting in 1924, of the Institute for Research in Social Science at the University of North Carolina at Chapel Hill. The institute stemmed from the work of sociologist Howard W. Odum, who aimed to build a research center focusing on the study of the ills afflicting the South—poverty, lynching, poor health care, inadequate education, and a host of other troubles. Odum yearned not only to illuminate these problems, but also to suggest ways to combat them. In the 1920s, the

American South sorely needed clear-eyed, scholarly approaches to ameliorating its afflictions in order to shake off the doldrums in which it had wallowed since Reconstruction.[19]

The first two studies produced by the institute in Chapel Hill came from the pen of Odum and his research assistant Guy B. Johnson. Published in 1925 and 1926, these works explored the songs sung by blacks in order to better understand black folklife.[20] As the institute's role expanded and gained more attention, so did the number of scholars carrying out research under its auspices. Professors from numerous departments at Chapel Hill and from other universities engaged in research for the institute. Among Odum's cadre of professors were a number of historians whose scholarship plowed new terrain in the study of the American South. Officials of the University of North Carolina Press published William S. Jenkins's *Pro-Slavery Thought in the Old South* in 1935, and Guion Griffis Johnson's researches resulted in a major study, published in 1930, titled *A Social History of the Sea Islands of South Carolina and Georgia, with Special References to St. Helena Island, South Carolina.* Especially pathbreaking was the work of sociologist Arthur F. Raper, who shed light on one of the South's greatest horrors in a 1933 work, *The Tragedy of Lynching,* and three years later produced a study examining the lives of rural blacks in Georgia titled *Preface to Peasantry: A Tale of Two Black Belt Counties* (1936).[21] The hundreds of studies emanating from the institute in the coming decades demonstrated that Odum and the scholars who contributed to his work achieved their goal of generating writings that were both scholarly and useful. The Institute for Research in Social Science outlived its founder, who passed away in 1954. It is now known as the Howard W. Odum Institute for Research in Social Science.

The second influence on the study of southern history coming from Chapel Hill originated in 1930, when Joseph Gregoire de Roulhac Hamilton founded the Southern Historical Collection. Hamilton had been a student of William Dunning at Columbia University, where he wrote a dissertation that served as the basis of his *Reconstruction in North Carolina,* a book that took a jaundiced view toward Radical Reconstruction. Thanks to his efforts, the Southern Historical Collection ranks today as a major research center for the history of the South.[22]

The crucible of the Great Depression clearly gave rise to a myriad of challenges to traditional scholarly notions concerning social matters, economics, and politics. The 1930s witnessed the flowering of several new genres of historical writing. Social history, such as Guion Griffis Johnson's sea island study, gained a wider audience among historians; and even the Dunning School of Reconstruction, having been attacked for several decades by black scholars, came under scrutiny from two white historians: Francis Butler Simkins and Robert Hilliard Woody. Simkins and Woody's *South Carolina during Reconstruction* (1932) stands out as the most thorough examination of Reconstruction published up to that time; it was also noteworthy for the authors' refusal to fixate on the political events of Reconstruction at the expense of other aspects of the era. Developments in South Carolina related to the economy, to religion, to agriculture, and to other areas of life in the state received in-depth attention from the authors.[23]

Simkins and Woody's monograph challenged the Dunning School's claim that Radical Reconstruction had been an abject failure by citing positive developments occurring in the decade after the Civil War for blacks. For example, the emergence of sharecropping, a system that later became exploitive, initially offered black croppers greater independence from whites than they had experienced under slavery, as did the development of all-black churches. African Americans also gained political experience by voting, joining Republican organizations, and holding political office. In contrast to the traditional view of blacks who participated in Reconstruction politics as venal incompetents, Simkins and Woody demonstrated that many of them diligently carried out their public duties. Officials of the American Historical Association rewarded the authors with the John H. Dunning Prize in 1932 for their contribution to Reconstruction history.[24] Furthermore, as the historian David Levering Lewis points out, the conclusions put forth in *South Carolina during Reconstruction* significantly influenced a black scholar who, in 1935, published an iconoclastic account of the Reconstruction era.[25]

W. E. B. Du Bois's magnum opus bore the title *Black Reconstruction: An Essay toward a History of the Part Which Black Folk Played in the Attempt to Reconstruct Democracy in America, 1860–1880.*[26] The Dunning School, Du Bois argued, presented a narrow interpretation reeking of white racism, and it violated the methods of scientific history the Dunningites claimed to be following. Du Bois applied Marxist theory to his interpretation of Reconstruction, resorting to terms such as "general strike" to describe slavery's decline as a result of black resistance efforts during the Civil War.[27] More than previous scholars, Du Bois credited blacks with seizing opportunities to undermine slavery during the war and lauded their later efforts to win the rights to vote and own property. Powerful white elites, seeing that poor whites also sought such privileges, employed racist propaganda to steer poor whites away from an alliance with African Americans. The proletarian revolution then died, when a combination of northern and southern financial interests arose to dominate the South and return blacks to a condition similar to slavery. Bourgeoisie society, declared Du Bois, made no room for black equality.[28] Historians would later recognize Du Bois's study as a watershed in Reconstruction historiography.

Comer Vann Woodward, another historian trained at the University of North Carolina, traced the life of the Georgia politician Tom Watson in a biography that also employed the Marxist interpretation. *Tom Watson, Agrarian Rebel* was published by officials of the Macmillan Company in 1938. The Bourbon Democrats who attempted to modernize the South after the Civil War stand out as the villains of Woodward's study. Watson, a congressman, U.S. senator, and vice-presidential candidate for the Populist Party in 1896, struggled but failed to defend the farmers from the ravages of the predatory policies championed by the capitalist-minded Bourbons, who colluded with northern business interests in order to control the southern economy while ignoring the desperate plight of the farmers. Frustrated by his political failures, Watson transformed himself from a racial progressive to a racist demagogue; but the powerful forces of capitalism nevertheless defeated him.[29] *Tom Watson, Agrarian Rebel,* one of the first great biographies of an influential southern politician and a study that put forth a new and controversial thesis regarding the Bourbons, earned the reputation of a classic work in southern history and placed its author on the path to becoming the most influential scholar of the New South.

The impact of the Second World War altered race relations for the better in the United States. Prejudice against blacks appeared more egregious after the war in the light of Nazi atrocities. Condemning the Nazis for racism against Jews, Slavs, and other European minorities while treating blacks as second-class citizens made white Americans appear hypocritical. Furthermore, "scientific racism" was no longer considered intellectually or morally defensible, since it had served as a rationale for the Holocaust. By providing opportunities for blacks in military and civilian life, the experience of World War II fostered hope and confidence in the African American community that blacks would not remain oppressed forever. Little wonder, then, that the civil rights movement began coalescing after the war ended in 1945.[30]

The year 1941 saw the publication of two books of importance to understanding white southern thought at the beginning of World War II. The two works were penned not by academics, but by a newspaperman, Wilber J. Cash, and a scion of a powerful planter family, William Alexander Percy. In *The Mind of the South,* Cash put forth a memorable rendering of southern history based, not on scholarly research, but on his experiences living in the piedmont regions of North Carolina and South Carolina.[31]

Cash, who honed his gift as a writer on the staff of the *Charlotte Observer,* viewed the South as a region impervious to change despite the many enormities through which it had passed. Cash argued that southern history had been one continuous march, with each era being more similar than different: "The South . . . is a tree with many age rings, with its limbs and trunk bent and twisted by all the winds of the years, but with its tap root in the Old South."[32] The patterns of life and thought established in the South during the eighteenth and early nineteenth centuries, Cash asserted, remained dominant in the twentieth century. Individualism, hierarchy, paternalism, and white supremacy had defined the southern social and political order in every era of the South's past. Cash, who followed with great foreboding the outbreak of war in Europe, suggested that the longstanding southern pattern might crumble "in [the] face of the forces sweeping over the world in the fateful year of 1940," and his prophecy soon came to fruition.[33]

Writing more autobiographically than Cash, William Alexander Percy also illuminated a traditional view of the South in *Lanterns on the Levee: Reflections of a Planter's Son.* Scholars of the American South know well the many roles Percy inhabited: southern poet; son of a U.S. senator; uncle and stepfather of the renowned novelist, Walker Percy; and the epitome of white elitism. In *Lanterns on the Levee,* Percy traced the unfolding of his life, beginning with his Mississippi boyhood and spanning his college years in Sewanee, Tennessee; law school at Harvard; service in combat during World War I; and, finally, his return to the South, where he maintained his family heritage as the master of Trail Lake Plantation, a lawyer, and a writer. Throughout his narration of these events Percy provides insight, sometimes trenchant and occasionally banal, into a world he believed to be in steep decline. "Leveling down's the fashion now," he lamented.[34]

Percy's paternalistic views on race reflected those of the white southern upper classes, who blamed violence against blacks on rowdy, uneducated whites and considered blacks to be inferior to whites and in need of guidance from them. Percy condemned what he saw as a decline of morality and decency in both races and perceived that old patterns of living were being tested as modern ideas on race and society made inroads into southern culture. Unrelenting loneliness, both individual and cosmic, so engulfed him that it became the prism through which he saw the world. Little wonder, then, that the novels written by his nephew and stepson, Walker, featured characters struggling to overcome their existential despair. Brilliant and eccentric, perceptive and quixotic, *Lanterns on the Levee* offers readers a window on the life and thought of a white southerner, steeped in the traditions of his region, trying to make sense of a rapidly changing world. Other memoirs followed Percy's, such as Ben Robertson's nostalgic rendering of life in the South Carolina

upcountry, *Red Hills and Cotton: An Upcountry Memoir* (1942), published one year after *Lanterns on the Levee,* and Katherine Du Pre
Lumpkin's *The Making of a Southerner* (1946), which came out five
years after Percy's book.[35]

C. Vann Woodward's study of Tom Watson may have been one
of the early political biographies in New South historiography, but
it was certainly not the last. In 1944, officials of the Louisiana State
University Press published Francis Simkins's *Pitchfork Ben Tillman,
South Carolinian.* Simkins portrayed Tillman, governor of South Carolina and later U.S. senator, as the embodiment of the aspirations of
white, struggling South Carolina farmers, who overthrew Bourbon
rule in the state. Tillman was progressive in the areas of agricultural
education, women's education, regulation of the alcohol industry,
and economic development, but he despised blacks and spared no
effort in vilifying them. Although few politicians bore as much guilt
as Tillman for inflaming white race hatred, declared Simkins, the
South Carolina governor and senator possessed redeeming qualities
that made him an effective politician and a respectable individual.
Simkins's well-researched and elegantly crafted biography revealed
the many sides, positive and negative, of a complex politician.[36]

John Hope Franklin, a young black scholar, accused Simkins of
glossing over Tillman's vitriolic racism. In a review published in
the *Journal of Negro Education,* Franklin portrayed Tillman as a vile
politician, whose prejudice against blacks and willingness to foment
racial violence branded him as a brute rather than a statesman. An
individual as hateful as Tillman merited no respect from civilized
Americans. The racial animosity Tillman stoked so adroitly, Franklin lamented, remained alive in the 1940s.[37]

Both prolific writers, Simkins and Franklin wrote textbooks relevant to the field of southern studies in 1947. Simkins's *The South, Old
and New: A History of the South, 1820-1947* was among the first textbooks on the subject, and Franklin's *From Slavery to Freedom: A History of Negro Americans* became a classic work. Franklin's study has
gone into numerous editions and remains the best single volume
on the history of black Americans. Simkins's southern history textbook went through four editions, the last one published in 1972.[38]

Perhaps it was only fitting that at the conclusion of a decade during which race attitudes began to change a memoir was published casting southern segregation as a deleterious system damaging to both blacks and whites. Lillian Smith's *Killers of the Dream* (1949) portrayed southern society as a place torn by racial injustice and constantly tense about its ability to maintain time-honored customs, laws, and values in the face of modernization. Smith despised the southern pattern of race relations for its destructiveness, and longed for its collapse.[39]

NEW SOUTH HISTORIOGRAPHY FROM 1950 TO 1990

The study of history in the United States showed signs of a world being transformed after World War II. The number of minority scholars among the ranks of professional historians grew, and many scholars of both races sought through their writing and often through direct social action to promote greater equality for African Americans. These developments made much of what white historians had written about the South before World War II appear parochial, provincial, and often racist. The alterations wrought by the war engendered in the historical profession an interest in the way in which historical writing might be employed to promote social justice in the United States and other parts of the world. This interest burgeoned during the 1960s and remains strong today within the historical guild.[40]

C. Vann Woodward penned a work in 1954 that became a watershed interpretation of New South history. *Origins of the New South, 1877-1913* put forth controversial views of southern history spanning the era from the end of the Civil War to the eve of World War I. Woodward argued that the Civil War greatly reduced the prestige of the slaveholding elite, giving rise to a new urban class that had not been a part of the slaveholding aristocracy prior to the war. Central to his argument once again was the Bourbons' union with northern business interests. Bourbon reign, which, in Woodward's telling, focused mainly on increasing the wealth of the Redeemers and their business-minded followers, ended in the 1890s as a result of a vast revolt of disgruntled farmers who had benefited little from Bourbon economic policies. The revolt toppled the Bourbons and brought to power racist politicians who subjugated blacks through support for disfranchisement, lynching, and Jim Crow legislation. The failure of the Bourbons and later the Populists to remedy the South's economic ills, especially those affecting farmers, led to an explosion of racial animosity against blacks, who earlier had reason to believe they might be given a semblance of equality with whites. It also precipitated the rise of the Jim Crow system of strict racial segregation in southern society.[41]

A striking feature of *Origins of the New South* was its author's willingness to face the difficulties of the southern past candidly and unromantically. "Inevitably," William B. Hesseltine posited, "Professor Woodward's first task was to clear away the rubbish which has been said about the South by partisan attackers, vigorous apologists, and ill-informed historians. Perhaps this is the greatest contribution of the book." Hesseltine viewed *Origins of the New South* as undoubtedly "the most valuable book that has been written about the South in these years" and proclaimed that it "clearly establishes the author's primacy among the scholars of the 'New South' (a term which he righteously deplores.)"[42] Woodward had expected reviewers of his book to be severe in their evaluation; however, instead of "[being] fallen upon and beaten to a pulp by the critics," as he feared, Woodward received unstinting praise.[43] Woodward's revisionism, declared Roger W. Shugg, dispensed with "all the common coinage of historical thinking about the modern South" and "for the first time . . . brings order out of the apparent confusion of southern history since Reconstruction." Shugg predicted that "this book will surely be recognized as one of the masterpieces of our historical literature."[44] He probably failed to realize how correct he was in his prediction.

One year after publishing *Origins of the New South* and in the same year that white thugs murdered Emmett Till in Mississippi, officials of the Oxford University Press published Woodward's *The Strange Career of Jim Crow* (1955). "The people of the South,"

Woodward asserted, "should be the last Americans to expect indefinite continuity of their institutions and social arrangements."[45] In *Strange Career,* Woodward expanded on his contention that the strict separation of the races in southern society was a relatively new development, one that arose out of the economic discontent that roiled the South in the late nineteenth century. To support his thesis, he cited examples of cooperation between blacks and whites in earlier decades. After the Civil War, for instance, whites allowed African Americans access to many public places and competed for their votes at the polls. The 1890s, however, saw the rise of a new and harsh racial pattern, as southern legislatures disfranchised blacks and passed laws restricting their use of public facilities, such as railroad cars and schools. Woodward noted that the degree of separation existing among the races by the early 1900s stunned whites who remembered an earlier time, when blacks enjoyed more tolerant treatment. Jim Crow laws, therefore, represented a departure from southern legal thought and social custom that had prevailed until the 1890s.[46]

Woodward's point was clear: If Jim Crow legislation was a relatively new development and because earlier examples of interracial cooperation demonstrated southern history could have taken a different path, the strict separation of the races could be removed more easily than more traditional scholars had argued. So influential was Woodward's study of the Jim Crow South that Martin Luther King Jr. praised it as "the historical Bible of the Civil Rights Movement."[47] Like several other works by Woodward, *The Strange Career of Jim Crow* ranks as a classic in the historiography of the New South.

The writing of southern history received a boost from the civil rights movement, when intense national attention came to rest on the South. Two especially significant works written during this time were George B. Tindall's *The Emergence of the New South, 1913-1945* (1967) and Paul Gaston's *The New South Creed: A Study in Southern Mythmaking* (1970).[48] Reviewers lauded Tindall's work as a tour de force, a felicitously written study astounding for its thoroughness and depth of research.[49] Vast changes in almost every aspect of life in the South markedly altered the region from 1913 to 1945. Tindall expertly traced these developments—in agriculture, politics, literature, religion, and race relations—engendered by the enormities of the First World War, the Great Depression, and the Second World War. By the end of World War II, although the South's backwardness had not disappeared completely, the region's future looked brighter than its past.

Paul Gaston questioned whether the New South embodied change or continuity. He regarded the New South ethos as a facade created by southern politicians and businessmen to mask serious social and economic ills with false notions about the South's burgeoning economic potential and improving race relations. As southern leaders trumpeted the arrival of a new era, one in which the South teemed with new opportunities for business, industry, and agriculture, their region remained mired in a backwardness that had been its dismal trademark for five decades. By the era of the Great Depression, Gaston concluded, the South retained mostly old rather than new characteristics. The question of whether a new South had come into existence in the late nineteenth century would continue to perplex historians.

The scholarly assault on the Dunning interpretation begun during the World War II era intensified as the civil rights movement swept over the United States. One of the most prominent critics of the Dunning School during the 1960s was University of California-Berkeley professor Kenneth Milton Stampp, who in *The Era of Reconstruction* (1965) conceded that the Dunning School had "made a deep and lasting impression on American historians" and that "much of what Dunning's disciples have said about reconstruction is true." It was, however, the biases of the Dunning School that disturbed Stampp. "The Dunningites," he declared, "are guilty of distortion by exaggeration, by a lack of perspective, by superficial analysis, and by overemphasis. They make corruption a central theme of their narratives, but they overlook constructive accomplishments," such as ratification of the Fourteenth and Fifteenth amendments, which granted citizenship to blacks and voting rights to African American males. "Indeed," he asserted, "without radical reconstruction, it would be impossible to this day for the federal government to protect Negroes from legal and political discrimination."[50]

Stampp found no vindictiveness in Radical Reconstruction, pointing out that "the generosity of the federal government's terms [toward the ex-Confederates] were quite remarkable." He cited rampant racism in the North and the South as well as the perceived threat of large numbers of immigrants coming into the United States in the decades after the Civil War as reasons for the enduring popularity of the Dunning School throughout the United States during the late nineteenth and early twentieth centuries.[51] Along with Stampp, other prominent scholars, such as John Hope Franklin and Eric McKitrick, also penned works favorable to Radical Reconstruction in the 1960s.[52]

The decades following the height of the civil rights movement witnessed an outpouring of academic writing on the New South. Prominent issues, seminal events, and important historical figures received scrutiny and reevaluation from historians, who by the late twentieth century were able to write more dispassionately than their predecessors, being farther removed from the events about which they wrote and benefiting from the scholarship of earlier generations of scholars. Reconstruction, the Lost Cause, the industrialization of the South, southern agriculture, the politics of the South, and southern biography were all treated with a greater breadth and depth than ever before. With the notion of the New South a century old, studies synthesizing research on different eras of New South history became easier to write. In 1982, Daniel Joseph Singal shed light on the intellectual history of the South from the end of World War I to the completion of World War II. In 1988, Eric Foner argued that Reconstruction had not yet ended and that the main issues of the post–Civil War period continued to resonate in the late twentieth century. Reconstruction, he said, was "America's unfinished revolution." In the 1990s, John Egerton explored "the generation before the Civil Rights Movement in the South"; Numan Bartley illuminated the New South period from 1945 to 1980; and Edward L. Ayers provided a history of the entire New South era. By century's end, writing about the region had experienced a revolution, one that deeply enriched the subject, but one that remained nevertheless "unfinished."[53]

Recent Trends

The study of the New South has grown richer and more nuanced in recent decades because of the attention granted to new fields of inquiry: the role of women in the New South, the environmental history of the region, and the global influence of the New South. Gerda Lerner's *The Grimké Sisters: Rebels against Slavery* (1967) stands out as a classic in women's history.[54] Numerous presses rejected the book in the 1960s, telling Lerner that women's history would not sell well. Officials of the Houghton Mifflin Company, however, accepted the manuscript and saw their gamble pay off. The book remains in print. Editors at Oxford University Press, in 1998, and at the University of North Carolina Press, in 2004, came out with new editions of Lerner's book under the same title but with a different subtitle.[55] In deft prose, Lerner traced the rise of the Grimkè sisters from a powerful slaveholding family in Charleston, South Carolina, to outspoken critics of slavery and the subjugation of women. The sisters left the South and through their assiduous efforts became prominent abolitionists and women's rights advocates. Since both sisters had died by 1880, the study of their lives dealt mainly with the antebellum and Civil War years, with some attention being given to their last years after the war.

A second major work in women's southern history is Anne Firor Scott's *The Southern Lady: From Pedestal to Politics, 1830-1930* (1970). In it, Scott argued that, before the Civil War, women attempted to fulfill idealized standards of behavior by being submissive wives and mothers and by refusing to participate in activities outside their homes. These demands, Scott explained, changed as a result of the Civil War, with many duties once fulfilled by men being left to women. Southern women proved to be versatile in their abilities, as they managed plantations, tended to the needs of their children, served as nurses in military hospitals, taught school, and performed other roles necessary to maintaining a semblance of order within their families and the larger society. The necessity of seizing duties fulfilled by men before the war; the gender imbalance resulting from the massive death toll suffered by Confederate troops; and the large number of men who returned to their homes with debilitating injuries all combined to diminish southern men while emboldening southern women. As Scott wrote, "It was in the Reconstruction period that the first foreshadowing of a new style of woman began to appear," and the upward trajectory women's opportunities continued into the late nineteenth and early twentieth centuries.[56] The achievement of women's suffrage in 1920 with the passage of the Nineteenth Amendment, which won the ratification of four southern state legislatures, marked the culmination of an arduous battle for women's voting rights by dedicated suffragists in the United States. By 1930, Scott declared, so much greater were the opportunities in southern society for women than in 1830 that the change constituted a revolution in women's rights.[57]

Recently, Anya Jabour examined the issues Scott broached fifty years ago and put forth somewhat different conclusions. In *Scarlett's Sisters: Young Women in the Old South* (2007), Jabour offered a window on the world of young southern women who grew to adulthood during the Civil War. More specifically, her study focused on these women from their teenage years to their mid-twenties. Jabour argued that the young women viewed their status in southern society differently from older southern women. The young women, beset by both feelings of youthful rebellion and intense emotions engendered by the trauma of war, were either unable or unwilling to fulfill expectations to become dutiful wives and mothers with few opportunities beyond the home. Jabour suggested that young women's refusal to cooperate in seeking a life of domesticity paralleled, on a smaller scale, the Confederate rebellion against the authority of the U.S. government.[58]

Jabour also argued that older southern women, by the time the war erupted, had already imbibed deeply the Old South ethic for women and therefore accepted their fate more stoically than did their younger counterparts. She conceded Anne Firor Scott's point that the war expanded opportunities for women, but she also asserted that the women, who came of age during the antebellum period, carried over their thinking about the roles of women and ex-slaves to the New South era. The younger women, who matured during the war years, brought a more enlightened attitude into the postwar era, an attitude that played a role in planting the seeds for the growth of feminism in the New South. In Jabour's thinking, age exerted a profound influence over how women thought about both race and women's issues in the New South.[59]

Many other aspects of southern womens' lives have received attention in the recent collection of works in New South history. The best study of the women's suffrage movement in the South is Elna Green's *Southern Strategies: Southern Women and the Woman Suffrage Question* (1997). In *Southern Strategies,* Green argued that the differences among women who favored female suffrage and those who opposed it were few, but significant. Urban areas tended to produce more suffragists, progressive-minded women of white-collar families with few ties to the South's powerful planters and industrialists. Antisuffragist women often emerged from the South's upper classes with greater wealth and economic and political power than the middle-class suffragists. According to Green, prejudice against blacks exerted less influence over the two groups' views toward women's voting rights than economic and class concerns.[60]

The lives of women residing in rural areas of the South now constitutes an important area of historical inquiry. Examples of works about rural women are *Mama Learned Us to Work: Farm Women in the New South* (2002) by Lu Ann Jones; *All We Knew Was to Farm: Rural Women in the Upcountry South, 1919-1941* (2000) by Melissa Walker; and *Linoleum, Better Babies, and the Modern Farm Woman, 1890-1930* (2006) by Marilyn Irvin Holt. Studies dealing with the education of southern women also merit scrutiny. Amy T. McCandless's *The Past in the Present: Women's Higher Education in the Twentieth-Century American South* (1999), addressed the education of college-age southern women, while Rebecca S. Montgomery's *The Politics of Education in the New South: Women and Reform in Georgia, 1890-1930*

(2008), analyzed women's roles in Progressive measures dealing with education for women below the college and university level.[61] The history of southern women received almost no agency in historical writing a century ago. It moved to the fringes of southern historiography in the decades after World War II and then to the center of the historiographical debate in the late twentieth and early twenty-first centuries.

The growing interest in the environmental history of the New South stems from the central position that environmental issues, once considered on the fringe of academic and political discourse, now occupies in the academy and the larger society. Actually, southern environmental history has existed for many decades in the guise of agricultural history, as Mark D. Hersey and James C. Giesen point out in their chapter on the historiography of southern environmental history in this volume. Among the notable scholars of southern agricultural history are Charles S. Aiken, Pete Daniel, Jack Temple Kirby, and Gilbert C. Fite. In *The Cotton Plantation South since the Civil War* (1998), Charles Aiken, professor of geography at the University of Tennessee, stripped away the myths and half-truths that often permeated the study of the American South in order to trace accurately the evolution of the cotton plantation system from Reconstruction to the present. His study focused on Georgia, Alabama, and Mississippi, because in these states the system was more firmly entrenched than in other areas of the country. During what Aiken termed the "New South" era, lasting from 1880 to 1940, tenant farming arose, and a change from a nucleated living pattern to a dispersed pattern on the plantation developed. Blacks initially welcomed these changes, Aiken explained, but the tenant system degenerated into an exploitive system that trapped African Americans in debt and despair. The process of stripping them of legal rights and denying them suffrage through poll taxes and literacy tests also burdened blacks during the New South era. The plantation system declined after 1910 for numerous reasons, such as increased rates of absentee landlordism and the devastating effects of the boll weevil.[62]

During the period from 1940 to 1970, the plantation system again underwent changes that resulted in profound demographic and political shifts. The mechanization of agriculture coupled with the impact of white racism, for instance, accelerated the migration of blacks to the North. For those African Americans who did not leave, life in the plantation South improved by 1970 and would continue to get better. Aiken cited the Voting Rights Act of 1964 as an important catalyst for the enhancement of black political power, because the law led to an increase in black voter registration and hence to greater political clout for southern blacks. Aiken viewed the act as a transformative law in the realm of African American political power.[63]

The pioneers of the South's environmental history had earlier investigated topics similar to the ones Aiken explored in the 1990s. Pete Daniel's *Breaking the Land: The Transformation of Cotton, Tobacco, and Rice Cultures since 1880* (1985), Gilbert Fite's *Cotton Fields No More: Southern Agriculture 1865-1980* (1984), and Jack Temple Kirby's *Rural Worlds Lost: The American South, 1920-1960* (1987) all chronicled the transformation that swept over southern agriculture in the twentieth century and provided a foundation on which future scholars of the environmental history of the South would build.[64]

Southern environmental history has matured in the last fifteen years to the point that it now commands great respect among scholars of the South and within university history departments. Historians today seem particularly interested in the Appalachian Mountain region. General histories of the area include John Alexander Williams's *Appalachia: A History* (2002), Richard B. Drake's *A History of Appalachia* (2001), and Ronald D. Eller's *Uneven Ground: Appalachia since 1945* (2008). Among the studies that focus on more specific topics related to the environmental history of the region are Ronald L. Lewis's *Transforming the Appalachian Countryside: Railroads, Deforestation, and Social Change in West Virginia* (1998), Suzanne Marshall's *Lord, We're Just Trying to Save Your Water: Environmental Activism and Dissent in the Appalachian South* (2002), Shannon Elizabeth Bell's *Our Roots Run Deep as Ironweed: Appalachian*

Women and the Fight for Environmental Justice (2013), and Donald Davis's *Where There Are Mountains: An Environmental History of the Southern Appalachians* (2000).[65] Considering the intense impact of the environment on life in Appalachia, the environmental history of the region promises to be a fertile topic for scholars, and studies in southern environmental history in general continue to be published at a swift pace.

Andrew Zimmerman's elegantly written and diligently researched *Alabama in Africa: Booker T. Washington, the German Empire, and the Globalization of the New South* (2010) stands out as an an example of historians' burgeoning interest in the influence of the South on other parts of the world. Zimmerman argued that German authorities followed Booker T. Washington's strategies to educate blacks at Alabama's Tuskegee Institute as a guide in their attempt to dominate workers who were needed to build a cotton industry in Togo from the 1880s to 1914. Togo was a German protectorate, and representatives from Tuskegee arrived there in 1901 to oversee the Germans' efforts to produce a profitable business in cotton. The Germans not only employed cotton-growing methods used in Alabama, but also subjected black Togolese workers to forms of racism rampant in the Deep South. They applied a wide range of patronizing stereotypes popular among southern whites to the Togolese workers, arguing that Africans, like southern blacks, were especially well suited for cotton growing, had little concern for liberal arts education, and were sexually ravenous. The German experience in Togo provided a successful example of how the subordination of blacks on two continents served European colonial interests.[66]

Alabama did not remain untouched by events in West Africa. According to Zimmerman, Booker T. Washington, before collaborating with the Germans, promoted the study of the liberal arts at Tuskegee to a greater degree than after contact with West Africa. Zimmerman hinted that Washington's earlier emphasis on industrial arts education constituted a facade, masking from whites his students' diligent effort to learn languages, history, and literature. Zimmerman regarded Washington's decision to focus more intently on industrial education as one that narrowed his students' ability to escape a cotton economy and culture. So damaging was Washington's shift in focus that Zimmerman accused him of preparing blacks for reintegration into a system similar to slavery.[67]

Numerous other works address the role of the South in the international realm. Several excellent collections of essays have been published on the subject. They include *The U.S. South and Europe: Transatlantic Relations in the Nineteenth and Twentieth Centuries* (2013), edited by Cornelis A. van Minnen and Manfred Berg; *The American South in the Global World* (2015), edited by James L. Peacock, Harry L. Watson, and Carrie R. Matthews; and *The American South and the Atlantic World* (2013), edited by Brian Ward, Martyn Bone, and William A. Link.[68] Along with their interest in gender and the environment, southern historians' attention to the New South's global influence has expanded significantly the scope of their scholarship.

The writing of New South history has undergone a revolution in the last century and a half. Once the province of nonspecialists, it was increasingly dominated by trained historians as the discipline of history became professionalized in the early twentieth century. As the century progressed, it more and more reflected the changing political, economic, and social conditions in the South. While subjects dealing with politics, war, and biography occupied the interests of New South historians until well after World War II, these "traditional" topics now share room with a wide range of subjects related to race, gender, the environment, and the South's place in the larger world. Thus scholars of the New South possess a richer and more nuanced understanding of their field than did their predecessors. Future scholarship on the New South promises to open new avenues of historical inquiry that will allow historians to see a region's past, once considered inscrutable, more clearly.

NOTES

1. Jefferson Davis, *The Rise and Fall of the Confederate Government* (New York: D. Appleton and Company, 1881).

2. Edward A. Pollard, *The Lost Cause: A New Southern History of the War of the Confederates: Compromising a Full and Authentic Account of the Rise and*

Progress of the Late Southern Confederacy—the Campaigns, Battles, Incidents, and Adventures of the Most Gigantic Struggle of the World's History (New York: E. B. Treat and Company, 1866); Pollard, *The Lost Cause Regained* (New York: C. W. Carleton and Company, 1868).

3. Jack P. Maddex Jr., *The Reconstruction of Edward A. Pollard: A Rebel's Conversion to Postbellum Unionism* (Chapel Hill: Univ. of North Carolina Press, 1974), 1-9, 23, 30-33, 46-47, 52, 66-67, 74-76.

4. Ibid., 76.

5. For in-depth studies of the Lost Cause movement in the South, see Charles Reagan Wilson, *Baptized in Blood: The Religion of the Lost Cause, 1865-1920* (Athens: Univ. of Georgia Press, 1980); Gaines M. Foster, *Ghosts of the Confederacy: Defeat, the Lost Cause, and the Emergence of the New South 1865 to 1913* (New York: Oxford Univ. Press, 1985).

6. James B. Avirett, *The Memoirs of General Turner Ashby and His Compeers* (Baltimore: Shelby and Dulany, 1867); James Longstreet, *From Manassas to Appomattox* (Philadelphia: J. B. Lippincott Company, 1896); John B. Gordon, *Reminiscences of the Civil War* (New York: Charles Scribner's Sons, 1903); Alexander E. Porter, *Military Memoirs of a Confederate* (New York: Charles Scribner's Sons, 1907); Mary Boykin Miller Chesnut, *A Diary from Dixie* (New York: D. Appleton and Company, 1905); Phoebe Yates Pember, *A Southern Woman's Story* (New York: G. W. Carleton and Company, 1879).

7. Peter Novick, *That Noble Dream: The "Objectivity Question" and the American Historical Profession* (New York: Cambridge Univ. Press, 1988), 21, 47-60.

8. James Ford Rhodes's history consisted of nine volumes by 1928. James Ford Rhodes, *History of the United States from the Compromise of 1850 to the End of the Roosevelt Administration,* 9 vols., new ed. (New York: The Macmillan Company, 1928); Theodore Roosevelt, *The Winning of the West,* 4 vols. (New York: G. P. Putnam's Sons, 1889-99).

9. James S. Humphreys, "William Archibald Dunning: Flawed Colossus of American Letters," in *The Dunning School: Historians, Race, and the Meaning of Reconstruction,* ed. John David Smith and J. Vincent Lowery (Lexington: Univ. Press of Kentucky, 2013), 79-81; Novick, *That Noble Dream,* 21-40, 47-60.

10. Humphreys, "William Archibald Dunning," 77-105.

11. James W. Garner, *Reconstruction in Mississippi* (New York: Macmillan, 1901); Joseph Gregoire de Roulhac Hamilton, *Reconstruction in North Carolina* (Gloucester, Mass.: Smith, 1914); C. Mildred Thompson, *Reconstruction in Georgia: Economic, Social, and Political 1865-1877* (New York: Columbia Univ. Press, 1915); Thomas Starling Staples, *Reconstruction in Arkansas, 1862-1874* (New York: Columbia Univ. Press, 1923); Charles W. Ramsdell, *Reconstruction in Texas* (New York: Columbia Univ. Press, 1910); William W. Davis, *The Civil War and Reconstruction in Florida* (New York: Columbia Univ. Press, 1913); Humphreys, "William Archibald Dunning," 82-84.

12. Raymond J. Cunningham, "Herbert Baxter Adams," in *Dictionary of Literary Biography,* vol. 47, *American Historians, 1866-1912,* ed. Clyde N. Wil-

son (Detroit: Gale Research, 1983), 30; Anne W. Chapman, "William Dunning," in *Dictionary of Literary Biography: Twentieth Century-American Historians,* ed. Clyde Wilson, vol. 17 (Detroit: Gale Research, 1983), 151; Wendell H. Stephenson, "A Half Century of Southern Historical Scholarship," *Journal of Southern History* 11 (Feb. 1945): 4-8.

13. Stephenson, "Half Century of Southern Historical Scholarship," 15-16, 31.

14. W. Conrad Gass, "Franklin L. Riley and the Historical Renaissance in Mississippi, 1897-1914," *Journal of Mississippi History* 32 (May 1970): 195-227.

15. Gass, "Franklin L. Riley," 196, 201, 208, 216.

16. Stephenson, "Half Century of Southern Historical Scholarship," 8-10.

17. Ibid., 7.

18. Chapman, "William Dunning," 152-53.

19. Guy Benton Johnson and Guion Griffis Johnson, *Research in Service to Society: The First Fifty Years of the Institute for Research in Social Science at the University of North Carolina* (Chapel Hill: Univ. of North Carolina Press, 1980), xi, 5-6, 18-22, 26-27, 29-31, 43-45.

20. Howard W. Odum and Guy B. Johnson, *The Negro and His Songs* (Chapel Hill: Univ. of North Carolina Press, 1925); Howard W. Odum and Guy B. Johnson, *Negro Workaday Songs* (Chapel Hill: Univ. of North Carolina Press, 1926).

21. Johnson and Johnson, *Research in Service to Society,* 133-35; William S. Jenkins, *Pro-Slavery Thought in the Old South* (Chapel Hill: Univ. of North Carolina Press, 1935); Guion Griffis Johnson, *A Social History of the Sea Islands of South Carolina and Georgia, with Special Reference to St. Helena, South Carolina* (Chapel Hill: Univ. of North Carolina Press, 1930); Arthur F. Raper, *The Tragedy of Lynching* (Chapel Hill: Univ. of North Carolina Press, 1933); Raper, *Preface to Peasantry: A Tale of Two Black Belt Counties* (Chapel Hill: Univ. of North Carolina Press, 1936).

22. "Southern Historical Collection: About," The Louis Round Wilson Library Special Collections, http://library.unc.edu/Wilson/shc/about/ (accessed January 31, 2016).

23. Francis Butler Simkins and Robert Hilliard Woody, *South Carolina during Reconstruction* (Chapel Hill: Univ. of North Carolina Press, 1932), vii-viii.

24. Simkins and Woody, *South Carolina during Reconstruction,* vii-ix, 66-67, 101-2, 381-85, 406-43; "Historical News," *North Carolina Historical Review* 9 (Apr. 1932): 220.

25. David Levering Lewis, *The Fight for Equality and the American Century, 1919-1963* (New York: Henry Holt, 2000), 363, 367-68.

26. W. E. Burghardt Du Bois, *Black Reconstruction: An Essay toward a History of the Part Which Black Folk Played in the Attempt to Reconstruct Democracy in America, 1860-1880* (New York: Harcourt, Brace, and Company, 1935).

27. Ibid., 55, 711-14, 717-25.

28. Ibid., 17, 55, 381-430.

29. C. Vann Woodward, *Tom Watson, Agrarian Rebel* (New York: Macmillan, 1938).

30. Merton L. Dillon, *Ulrich Bonnell Philips: Historian of the Old South,* Southern Biography Series (Baton Rouge: Louisiana State Univ. Press, 1985), 141. For an exploration of the changes wrought in the South by the Second World War, see Neil R. McMillen, ed., *Remaking Dixie: The Impact of World War II on the American South* (Jackson: Univ. Press of Mississippi, 1997).

31. W. J. Cash, *The Mind of the South* (1941; repr., New York: Vintage Books, 1991).

32. Ibid., L.

33. Ibid., 429.

34. William Alexander Percy, *Lanterns on the Levee: Recollections of a Planters' Son* (1941; repr., Baton Rouge: Louisiana State Univ. Press, 1994), 283.

35. Ben Robertson, *Red Hills and Cotton: An Upcountry Memoir* (New York: Alfred A. Knopf, 1942); Katherine Du Pre Lumpkin, *The Making of a Southerner* (New York: Alfred A. Knopf, 1946).

36. Francis Butler Simkins, *Pitchfork Ben Tillman, South Carolinian* (Baton Rouge: Louisiana State Univ. Press, 1944); James S. Humphreys, *Francis Butler Simkins: A Life* (Gainesville: Univ. Press of Florida, 2008), 171-78.

37. John Hope Franklin, "Demagoguery—Southern Style," review of *Pitchfork Ben Tillman, South Carolinian,* by Francis Butler Simkins, *Journal of Negro Education* 15 (Autumn 1946): 654-55.

38. Francis Butler Simkins, *The South, Old and New: A History of the South, 1820-1947* (New York: Alfred A. Knopf, 1947); John Hope Franklin, *From Slavery to Freedom: A History of Negro Americans* (New York: Alfred A. Knopf, 1947); Simkins and Charles Pierce Roland, *A History of the South,* 4th ed. (New York: Alfred A. Knopf, 1972).

39. Lillian Smith, *Killers of the Dream* (New York: W. W. Norton, 1949).

40. Novick, *That Noble Dream,* 48-60.

41. C. Vann Woodward, *Origins of the New South, 1877-1913* (Baton Rouge: Louisiana State Univ. Press, 1951), 6, 142-55, 211-12, 289-92, 351-53, 431-32.

42. William B. Hesseltine, review of *Origins of the New South, 1877-1913,* by C. Vann Woodward, *American Historical Review* 57 (July 1952): 994.

43. C. Vann Woodward to Simkins, September 13 and September 22, 1948, "Correspondence U-Z," in Francis Butler Simkins Papers, Special Collections, Greenwood Library, Longwood Univ., Farmville, Va.

44. Roger W. Shugg, review of *Origins of the New South, 1877-1913,* by C.Vann Woodward, *Mississippi Valley Historical Review* 39 (June 1952): 411-12.

45. C. Vann Woodward, The *Strange Career of Jim Crow,* commemorative ed. (New York: Oxford Univ. Press, 2002), 3.

46. Woodward, *Strange Career of Jim Crow,* 31-44, 53-59, 64-65, 67-109.

47. Martin Luther King Jr., quoted in William S. McFeely, "Afterword," in Woodward, *Strange Career of Jim Crow,* 221.

48. George B. Tindall, *The Emergence of the New South, 1913-1945* (Baton Rouge: Louisiana State Univ. Press, 1967); Paul M. Gaston, *The New South Creed: A Study in Southern Mythmaking* (New York: Alfred A. Knopf, 1970).

49. For exceptionally positive reviews of Tindall's book, see David M. Potter, "The Emergence of the New South: An Essay Review," review of *The Emergence of the New South, 1913-1945,* by George B. Tindall, *Journal of Southern History* 34 (Aug. 1968): 420-24; Bennett H. Wall, review of *The Emergence of the New South, 1913-1945,* by George B. Tindall, *American Historical Review* 74 (June 1969): 1741-42.

50. Kenneth M. Stampp, *The Era of Reconstruction, 1865-1877* (1965; repr., New York: Vintage Books, 1965), 3-13, 6, 9, 11, 13.

51. Ibid., 9-23, 11.

52. John Hope Franklin, *Reconstruction after the Civil War* (Chicago: Univ. of Chicago Press, 1961); Eric L. McKitrick, *Andrew Johnson and Reconstruction* (New York: Oxford Univ. Press, 1960).

53. Daniel Joseph Singal, *The War Within: From Victorian to Modernist Thought in the South, 1919-1945* (Chapel Hill: Univ. of North Carolina Press, 1982); Eric Foner, *Reconstruction: America's Unfinished Revolution, 1863-1877* (New York: Harper and Row, 1988); John Egerton, *Speak Now against the Day: The Generation before the Civil Rights Movement in the South* (New York: Alfred A. Knopf, 1994); Numan V. Bartley, *The New South, 1945-1980: The Story of the South's Modernization* (Baton Rouge: Louisiana State Univ. Press, 1995); Edward L. Ayers, *The Promise of the New South: Life after Reconstruction* (New York: Oxford Univ. Press, 1992).

54. Gerda Lerner, *The Grimkè Sisters of South Carolina: Rebels against Slavery* (Boston: Houghton Mifflin, 1967).

55. For the difficulty Lerner experienced in the 1960s in getting her book published, see Gerda Lerner, "Introduction," in *The Grimké Sisters from South Carolina: Pioneers for Women's Rights and Abolition* (Chapel Hill: Univ. of North Carolina Press, 2004), xv-xix; Lerner, *The Grimké Sisters of South Carolina: Pioneers for Women's Rights and Abolition* (New York: Oxford Univ. Press, 1998).

56. Anne Firor Scott, *The Southern Lady: From Pedestal to Politics, 1830-1920* (Chicago: Univ. of Chicago Press, 1970), 4-21, 78-102.

57. Ibid., 165-84, 227-31.

58. Anya Jabour, *Scarlett's Sisters: Young Women in the Old South* (Chapel Hill: Univ. of North Carolina Press, 2007), 1-15, 239-70.

59. Ibid, 280-83.

60. Elna C. Green, *Southern Strategies: Southern Women and the Woman Suffrage Question* (Chapel Hill: Univ. of North Carolina Press, 1997), xv-xvi.

61. Lu Anne Jones, *Mama Learned Us to Work: Farm Women in the New South* (Chapel Hill: Univ. of North Carolina Press, 2002); Melissa Walker, *All We Knew Was to Farm: Rural Women in the Upcountry South, 1919-1941* (Baltimore: Johns Hopkins Univ. Press, 2000); Marilyn Irvin Holt, *Linoleum, Better*

Babies, and the Modern Farm Woman, 1890-1930 (Lincoln: Univ. of Nebraska Press, 2006); Amy T. McCandless, *The Past in the Present: Women's Higher Education in the Twentieth-Century American* South (Tuscaloosa: Univ. of Alabama Press, 1999); Rebecca S. Montgomery, *The Politics of Education in the New South: Women and Reform in Georgia, 1890-1930* (Baton Rouge: Louisiana State Univ. Press, 2008).

62. Charles S. Aiken, *The Cotton Plantation South since the Civil War* (Baltimore: Johns Hopkins Univ. Press, 1998), 10, 22, 71, 81-82, 208, 337.

63. Ibid., xii, 10, 64, 168, 171, 210, 219, 221, 223.

64. Pete Daniel, *Breaking the Land: The Transformation of Cotton, Tobacco, and Rice Cultures since 1880* (Urbana: Univ. of Illinois Press, 1985); Gilbert Fite, *Cotton Fields No More: Southern Agriculture, 1865-1980* (Lexington: Univ. Press of Kentucky, 1984); and Jack Temple Kirby, *Rural Worlds Lost: The American South, 1920-1960* (Baton Rouge: Louisiana State Univ. Press, 1987).

65. John Alexander Williams, *Appalachia: A History* (Chapel Hill: Univ. of North Carolina Press, 2002); Richard B. Drake, *A History of Appalachia* (Lexington: Univ. Press of Kentucky, 2001); Ronald D. Eller, *Uneven Ground: Appalachian since 1945* (Lexington: Univ. Press of Kentucky, 2008); Ronald L. Lewis, *Transforming the Appalachian Countryside: Railroads, Deforestation, and Social Change in West Virginia, 1880-1920* (Chapel Hill: Univ. of North Carolina Press, 1998); Suzanne Marshall, *Lord We're Just Trying to Save Your Water: Environmental Activism and Dissent in the Appalachian South* (Gainesville: Univ. Press of Florida, 2002); Shannon Elizabeth Bell, *Our Roots Run Deep as Ironweed: Appalachian Women and the Fight for Environmental Justice* (Urbana: Univ. of Illinois Press, 2013); Donald Davis, *Where There Are Mountains: An Environmental History of the Southern Appalachians* (Athens: Univ. of Georgia Press, 2000).

66. Andrew Zimmerman, *Alabama in Africa: Booker T. Washington, the German Empire, and the Globalization of the New South* (Princeton, N.J.: Princeton Univ. Press, 2010), ix-x, 1-19, 130-44, 250.

67. Ibid., 52-65, 248-50.

68. Cornelis A. van Minnen and Manfred Berg, eds., *The U.S. South and Europe: Transatlantic Relations in the Nineteenth and Twentieth Centuries* (Lexington: Univ. Press of Kentucky, 2013); James L. Peacock, Harry L. Watson, and Carrie R. Matthews, eds., *The American South in the Global World* (Chapel Hill: Univ. of North Carolina Press, 2005); Brian Ward, Martyn Bone, and William A. Link, eds., *The American South and the Atlantic World* (Gainesville: Univ. Press of Florida, 2013).

CHAPTER TWO

Reconstruction along the Global Color Line

Slavery, International Class Conflict, and Empire

ANDREW ZIMMERMAN

Among the most important periods in U.S. history, Reconstruction might appear too narrowly national to reward an international approach.[1] But viewed from such a perspective, Reconstruction appears as a particularly influential instance in a number of interrelated worldwide processes of the nineteenth century. These include (1) the shift of much agricultural production away from unfree labor, especially slavery in the Americas and serfdom in Eastern Europe; (2) the shift of manufacturing from self-employed craft labor to hired industrial labor; (3) a renewed importance of race, racial hierarchies, and white supremacy, even after the end of slavery, in the organization of economic production and political power at the local, national, and supranational levels; and (4) a resumption of colonial expansion, especially in Africa and the Pacific islands. While all four processes resulted in new concentrations of power and wealth, elites did not simply impose them on a passive world; these processes were rather crossproducts of popular struggles for democracy and autonomy with opposing elite struggles for state power and capital accumulation. Taken together, the four processes made up a new phase in the history of global capitalism—not capitalism as imagined in economics textbooks, but capitalism as lived in workshops and factories, on farms and plantations. They helped create the world we still live in today, structured by what W. E. B. Du Bois identified as "the problem of the color line, the question as to how far differences of race . . . will hereafter be made the basis of denying to over half the world the right of sharing to their utmost ability the opportunities and privileges of modern civilization."[2]

Historians interested in studying phenomena extending beyond the boundaries of the nation-state now have at least three options. The oldest is *international history,* which looks at contacts among nation-states, especially through diplomacy and war. Somewhat more recent is *global history,* which seeks to discern processes affecting people in every nation, including environmental change, technological innovations, and even cultural and intellectual transformations. The most recent is *transnational history.* This looks at processes on many different scales, some confined to nations, some specific only to subnational groups like classes or races, some broadly global, and some narrowly regional. Transnational history does not operate in a predefined geography, as do national and global history, but rather follows its subjects wherever they may go. It is impossible to research any one of these types of history in isolation from the other two. Nonetheless, this essay on Reconstruction will take a more transnational approach. Its losses in geographic and temporal boundedness will be recouped, I hope, by new approaches to U.S. history that it opens.

Viewing Reconstruction as a contested set of global political and economic processes dissolves many of the boundaries that commonly define Reconstruction as a twelve-year period in the history of the U.S. South. The final withdrawal of federal troops from the former Confederacy in 1877, the moment commonly deemed the end of Reconstruction, marked a major shift in, but by no means brought to a halt, the contest over capitalism, democracy, and racial hierarchies in the United States or around the world. We might also trace the search for a postslavery capitalist world order as far back as the founding of Liberia in 1822 as a place to settle manumitted U.S. slaves. Popular struggles against slavery and other forms of political and economic domination emerged even earlier in Europe, Africa, and the Americas. Historians Peter Linebaugh and Marcus Rediker have characterized this broad set of movements as a "many-sided struggle against confinement—on ships, in workshops, in prisons, or even in empires—and the simultaneous search for autonomy."[3] Studying the end of slavery as a component of this broader set of popular struggles challenges conventional approaches to labor history that take free white craft and wage workers as the norm and cast enslaved black workers or indentured Asian workers as challenges to—rather than as participants in their own right in—working-class politics. At issue in global Reconstruction was not only the existence of slavery, but also the meaning of freedom in a world in which a broadly defined democracy stood against dominant plans for economic development.

Reconstruction, viewed transnationally, was thus not only an incomplete transition to freedom in the United States, what Eric Foner called "America's unfinished revolution," but also a deep conflict about what freedom would mean regionally, nationally, and globally.[4] Many groups, above all the formerly enslaved, had far different visions from economic and political elites of what economic, social, and political order might follow the destruction of slave society. At every turn, they contested racial stratification and the concentration of production in hierarchical plantations and firms dominated by the wealthy. Many slaves in the United States fought for a type of freedom for which slaves elsewhere in the Americas and many formally free workers also struggled: economic independence and personal autonomy.[5] The enslaved of the Americas, whether in Haiti, Santo Domingo, Jamaica, Cuba, Brazil, or the United States, sought this independence not simply in legal freedom but also in independent smallhold farms, sometimes carved out of the plantations of their erstwhile masters.[6] Many whites in the United States similarly pursued homesteads as an escape from wage dependency.[7] A variety of socialisms popular in Europe and the United States likewise promised ways of organizing production on an individual or a cooperative basis that would free workers from the dependency of wage labor.[8] In the antebellum period, the division of the U.S. working class between free white workers and enslaved black workers masked these common aspirations, which extended back to popular democratic Atlantic traditions. Reconstruction would begin to reawaken them.

Former slaves and former slaveholders had struggled over the meaning of emancipation in other parts of the Americas well before Civil War broke out in the United States. The movement of freedpeople in the Americas toward autonomous farming prompted plantation owners to devise methods of compelling them to perform for wages the work they had performed as slaves. Historians have produced a rich comparative picture of these coercive, postemancipation labor regimes.[9] Perhaps the best-known example was the short-lived "apprenticeship system" applied in the British West Indies after the passage of the British Emancipation Act in 1833. The act bound former slaves as "apprentices" to their former masters for a period of four to six years. These ex-slaves had worked for years on the plantations to which they were apprenticed, and the function of the act was not to train them in any particular skill but rather to continue coercion after slavery. A combination of labor actions by former slaves in the West Indies and sympathetic protests by abolitionists in Britain brought the apprenticeship system to an end in 1838.[10] For governments considering how to manage abolition, as well as for historians studying this process, the British apprenticeship system has remained a paradigm.[11]

Emancipation did not occur against a static political and economic background, and former slaves were just one of the groups that had to work out their fate in the face of an increasingly all-encompassing system of capitalist production. Capitalist production rests on a separation between those who own the means of production, like factories and farmland, and those who, because they do not own the means of production, even to provide for their own subsistence, must work for these owners.[12] This system was new enough in the mid-nineteenth century that historian Eric Hobsbawm has dubbed the period the "age of capital" and noted that even the word "capitalism" only came into regular use in the 1860s.[13] At the beginning of the nineteenth century, in both Europe and the United States, manufacturing occurred on such a small scale that many white workers could aspire to own their own shops, making the compulsion to work for wages only a passing phase in the life of an individual. The growth of the scale of industry meant that the dream of economic independence remained unattainable for nearly all workers, who now faced the prospect of a lifetime of labor under the supervision of an employer.[14] This process of proletarianization concerned many groups, from workers dismayed by their declining independence to elites repulsed by urban squalor and political radicalization. A wealth of comparative work puts the American Civil War and Reconstruction in the center of this widespread political-economic reorientation.[15]

The racial self-conceptions of many white workers and the most basic political ideas of the United States depended on denying an increasingly obvious similarity—but not identity—between proletarianized and enslaved workers.[16] Well before the wage system compelled free workers to serve employers, enslaved individuals had been compelled to work for owners of the means of production. For this reason, many historians consider plantation slavery, at least in the nineteenth century, to be a form of capitalism. The highly organized labor of the plantation preceded and even prefigured the highly organized labor of the modern factory.[17] President Abraham Lincoln, in his first annual message to Congress, acknowledged the problematic similarity of slavery and wage labor when he rejected the view that economic conditions meant that most Americans would have to become "either hired laborers, or what we call slaves."[18] The diminishing prospects of economic independence for the majority in an expanding capitalist economy troubled not only those directly affected by proletarianization, but also those who praised the independent yeoman farmer and craftsman as the foundation of a republican social order. The perceived similarities of wage, or "hireling," labor and slave labor also threatened racial distinctions between white and black workers. Many working-class whites responded to this perceived threat to their racial status with antiblack racism. Some historians have also detected white working-class identification with their enslaved black counterparts.[19]

A common struggle against slavery in the United States temporarily united groups with fundamentally opposed views of wage labor. Many of the European immigrants who joined the fight against
slavery in the decade before the Civil War were political refugees
who had responded to the declining independence of craft workers by flocking to the growing communist and socialist movements
and taking part in the unsuccessful revolutions of 1848–49.[20] They
would become important leaders and rank-and-file members of the
Union army and of the radical labor movement, thus intertwining
the European with the U.S. response to capitalism.[21] Many blacks
looked to longer Atlantic traditions of economic self-sufficiency
and autonomy. Against these two traditions, many elite opponents
of slavery came to praise wage labor—that is, work for an employer
expected to exercise control and management—as an alternate to
slavery. In doing so, they rejected the older connection of slave and
wage labor as forms of dependent labor. This was in part a defense
against proponents of slavery who pointed to the miserable condition of northern wage workers to argue that slavery was a more
humane form of dependency.[22] Many abolitionists in the United
States thus made an argument that would have great consequences
not only for Reconstruction and the lives of freedpeople, but for all
American workers: they argued that wage labor, rather than threat-
ening individual freedom, was in fact basic to human freedom.[23] In
doing so, some may have intended only to condemn slavery in the
age of capitalism, but they also threatened many other visions of
economic freedom that might have been more beneficial to black
and white workers alike.[24]

It was the anti-wage-labor branch of antislavery that informed
what was perhaps the first great account of this period, *Black Reconstruction* (1935), by the African American historian W. E. B. Du
Bois.[25] For Du Bois, emancipation began with a "general strike" of
enslaved "black workers" against their own bondage. He recounted
how, with the approach of Union soldiers, thousands of slaves
brought about their own emancipation by ceasing to work for slaveholders, fleeing their plantations to Union lines, and eventually tak-

ing up arms against slavery in the United States Colored Troops. He thus challenged common presentations of emancipation as something granted to slaves from above by the federal government. Few historians today would deny that state policy played an important role in emancipation, but most have also accepted some version of what scholars now call the self-emancipation thesis put forward by Du Bois. Du Bois characterized emancipation as a type of political action with which readers in the militant days of the labor movement in the 1930s would have been familiar: the general strike. Du Bois would join the Communist Party of the United States later in his life, but already in the 1930s he, like many, saw Marxism and Communism as welcome allies in the long struggle against racism in the United States and imperialism abroad. If he perhaps spoke too enthusiastically when he called Reconstruction "one of the most extraordinary experiments of Marxism that the world, before the Russian revolution, had seen," his assessment does reflect what was at stake for many in the overthrow of slavery in the United States.[26] By placing emancipation in the context of the labor movement, Du Bois inserted it in a broader democratic struggle of workers, white and black, enslaved and free. Indeed, the radical labor context from which Du Bois wrote *Black Reconstruction* was itself one of the outcomes of the multiracial labor movement that had lain dormant in the antebellum United States and that had been reawakened in the Civil War.

The sharecropping system that emerged in much of the South after the Civil War, though not entirely original to the United States, became an influential model around the world. Even with all its obviously oppressive features, it represented a kind of compromise between the demands of planters for gangs of wage workers and the demands of freedpeople for the economic independence of small landholdings. In this system, plantations were divided into small farms, much as freedpeople had demanded. Farmers were not, however, granted title to this land, which remained the property of former masters. Sharecroppers were thus subjected to a rental agreement that did not simply take a share of the yearly produce, but subjected growers to highly coercive systematic management and extraordinary economic exploitation.[27] Agrarian capitalists from eastern Germany to colonial Africa gradually embraced this combination of landlord supervision with family farming, for it gave a sense of autonomy to farmers, prevented the proletarianization that many feared would lead to more radical politics, and still rendered agricultural surpluses to landlords. In some cases southern sharecropping was an explicit model for foreign economic thinkers and policy makers.[28]

For all the limitations of the freedom won by the enslaved in the postwar U.S. South, Du Bois's example of the massive worker uprising that led to emancipation also offered encouragement and inspiration to predominantly white labor movements in the United States and in Europe. Socialists and other labor radicals around the world had paid close attention to the progress of the American Civil War, concerned as they were with the fate of one of the world's only democratic republics; interested in the war against slaveholders as a kind of proxy battle against their own aristocracy; and opposed to slavery as a grievous injury to workers, both enslaved and free. Karl Marx and Friedrich Engels, living in exile in London, followed the Civil War closely and wrote extensively about the American conflict.[29] Many of their socialist comrades, having been forced into exile in the United States, participated in the Civil War on the side of the Union. Organized workers also arguably kept Britain from intervening to support the Confederacy, and no other European power would have dared offer support to secession on its own.[30] This working-class intervention in British foreign policy, as well as the victories of the Union against Confederate slaveholders, gave working-class radicals in Europe new confidence. In 1864 they founded the International Working Men's Association, with Karl Marx as its intellectual leader.[31] Today known as the First International, the organization brought together British trade unionists with the many radical workers already living in exile in London. Its purpose was to help coordinate the activities of socialist, anarchist, and trade unionist movements in Europe and the United States. Marx's most thorough analysis of capitalism, *Capital* (1867), contained numerous references to the American Civil War. Its preface also declared that the American conflict had "sounded the alarm bell" for the "European working class."[32] Emancipation in the United States gave hope to many that other forms of exploitative labor, including wage labor, might also be abolished. As Marx offered in his inaugural address to the First International, "Like slave labour, like serf labour, hired labour is but a transitory and inferior form, destined to disappear before associated labour plying its toil with a willing hand, a ready mind, and a joyous heart."[33]

The postwar U.S. labor movement, and especially the movement for the legal limitation of the working day to eight hours without a corresponding decrease in wages, also inspired European socialists and trade unionists. As historian David Montgomery has emphasized, the war to end slavery gave way to a U.S. labor movement that, on the one hand, continued the struggle against inequality that antislavery had begun, but, on the other hand, challenged the support for wage labor that prevailed in Reconstruction policy.[34] White workers in the United States continued to express many of their class anxieties in racist terms and often remained violently hostile to black competitors, but an ideal of interracial class solidarity emerged from the war that, according to historian David Roediger, had not existed in the antebellum period.[35] Many advocated the eight-hour day in order to limit the control of employers over the entire waking lives of their employees, much as slaveholders had claimed control over the entire lives of their human chattel. The eight-hours movement achieved some victories in state law and a national victory in 1868 when Congress granted the eight-hour day to all federal employees.

Yet, while the Civil War, emancipation, and the postwar U.S. labor movement inspired Marx and other European working-class and socialist revolutionaries, no mass socialist party emerged in the United States to match those in Europe. A National Labor Union (NLU), founded in 1866, became a political labor party, the National Labor Reform Party, but it collapsed in the 1870s. In Europe, meanwhile, workers and their political allies founded labor and socialist parties in the 1870s and 1880s, slightly later but also with much greater longevity than the NLU.[36] There were chapters of the First International inside the United States, but conflicts between working-class and often foreign-born revolutionaries, on the one hand, and middle-class reformers for whom socialist politics had less appeal, on the other, hindered their success.[37] In 1906, the German sociologist Werner Sombart posed one of the longest-standing puzzles of comparative history: Why is there no socialism in the United States?[38] Though this question has prompted important research, it is also, as Eric Foner has argued, somewhat misleading, because there has in fact been a great deal of resistance to the power of the bourgeoisie in the United States, even if this has rarely employed the rhetoric of socialism or taken the form of a labor party.[39] Still, U.S. emancipation may have exercised a greater influence on international socialist and labor movements than it did in the U.S. labor movement itself.

If the Civil War seemed in retrospect to have been a bourgeois revolution, it was because of the partial victory of liberals in defining the postwar U.S. political scene, not because of anything inherent in the end of slavery itself. If many workers and their political leaders considered the eight-hour movement, other legal protections for workers, and the growing international union and socialist movements as fruits of the northern victory, many bourgeois, including erstwhile radicals, considered the labor movement as a threat to the economic freedom for which they thought the war had been fought.[40] The United States thus experienced what European historians refer to as a "split of proletarian and bourgeois democracy," one that typically emerged on the continent earlier in the nineteenth century.[41] Their opposed positions on the legally mandated eight-hour day illustrate the incompatibility between bourgeois-liberal and working-class attitudes toward the legacy of the Civil War and toward democracy more broadly. Workers and their political allies argued that limitations to the working day continued the process of emancipation by helping to free wage laborers from domination by their employers. Liberals, by contrast, interpreted emancipation as a blow against outside interference over individual economic freedom. They thus rejected attempts by the state to regulate the hours of labor or virtually any other aspect of private business, whether through legislation or through collective bargaining, as a continuation of an economic slavery. It was a great victory for these liberals when the Fourteenth Amendment, designed originally to protect the individual rights of former slaves against political persecution, came to protect the supposed rights of corporations, defined legally as individuals, from much legal regulation.[42]

Liberalism was the bourgeois counterpart of the trade unionism, socialism, and anarchism that emerged as working-class ideologies in the United States and internationally. The Liberal Republican Party, whose candidate, Horace Greeley, unsuccessfully challenged Ulysses S. Grant's reelection in 1872, represented many of the attitudes of U.S. liberals, but liberalism as a political orientation was also much broader and longer lasting than this short-lived party. While contemporary U.S. parlance uses "liberalism" and "leftism" synonymously, no nineteenth-century thinker would have confused the two. Liberals in the United States, as in Europe, considered themselves to be upright men of property and bulwarks against what they perceived as mob rule. Divided responses to the 1871 Paris Commune, a short-lived revolutionary socialist government suppressed violently by the French state, revealed the split of working-class and bourgeois conceptions of democracy in the United States. Leftists in the United States feted the Commune in parades and in the press, while liberals condemned it as an example of the worst excesses of the mob.[43] Many bourgeois elites in the United States also came to look with the same disdain upon the demands of freedpeople in the South for state protection of their freedom as they did upon demands of workers in the North for an eight-hour day and other legal safeguards.[44] European scholars have long looked critically at this elitist form of liberalism whose promises of rights and equality excluded—some would even say depended on excluding—those defined as inferior, often because of their class, race, gender, or all three.[45] This was a liberalism that enthusiastically embraced empire as an opportunity for a supposedly humanitarian elite to impart their self-styled universal values on the world.[46] Like their European counterparts, many bourgeois liberals in the United States came to suspect democracy itself; in New York they even attempted—unsuccessfully in the end—to place property limitations on universal manhood suffrage in city elections.[47]

Whiteness played a role in perhaps every national variant of liberalism, but it played it with particular strength in the United States. Liberalism allowed for a reconciliation between white elites in the North and the South by minimizing emancipation along with a whole range of emancipatory efforts by black and white workers. Historian David W. Blight has analyzed how white elites in the North and the South commemorated the Civil War as a tragic conflict and thereby suggested that black emancipation was secondary or even a mixed blessing.[48] This white bourgeois sectional reconciliation lay at the foundation of an ideology of a so-called New South that presented blacks, not as an awkward reminder of a defunct slave system, but rather as an especially docile and efficient agricultural working class. Racism, as historians beginning perhaps with C. Vann Woodward have shown, was not simply a holdover from slavery, but was rather a development of practices and ideas of race that emerged globally in the wake of slavery.[49] While the Old South elites had justified slavery with reference to racial hierarchies, elites in the New South and in the Gilded Age North made racial hierarchies themselves political and economic institutions. New systems of labor placed various ethnicities, not only people of African descent but also many other groups defined as nonwhite, in various relations of political and economic subordination.[50] As such the United States, or at least the Jim Crow South, for as much as a century after the Civil War, enjoyed the dubious distinction, along with Apartheid South Africa and Nazi Germany, of being a relatively unique racial state. While racism shaped the foreign and domestic economics and politics of many, if not all, European states, whites in these three racial states organized political, social, and economic life around white hegemony and the subordination of those deemed racially inferior by the state and by elite classes.[51]

As the earliest of the three racial states, the New South became a model for many Europeans establishing and expanding colonial empires in the late nineteenth century. To support the proposition that white people should rule not only their own countries, but also much of the globe, political thinkers could turn to the critical narrative of Reconstruction that the political scientist John W. Burgess and the historian William Archibald Dunning crafted at Columbia University. The central tenet of the so-called Dunning School was the proposition that Republicans had erred in allowing African Americans to vote and serve in governments during Reconstruction. To cast doubt on all democratic social change, Dunning even compared Reconstruction to the French Revolution: "The enfranchisement of the freedmen and their enthronement in political power was as reckless a species of statecraft," he explained, as the French Revolution.[52]

John W. Burgess brought such concerns about democracy and race to the fields of political science and international relations when he founded the *Political Science Quarterly* in 1886. In an article that Burgess contributed to the first volume, he warned that legal equality between "the superior race and the inferior"—he specified blacks and Asians as "inferior"—threated the political unity of the state, the very foundation of political science.[53] James Bryce of Oxford University played an especially important role in disseminating Dunning's and Burgess's frankly racist assessments of black political enfranchisement around the world, thereby internationalizing white solidarity against peoples of color, who were seen as potential economic assets as workers but also as political threats to dominant whites.[54] The journal *Foreign Affairs,* today one of the major publications in the United States devoted to the topic, began in 1910 as the *Journal of Race Development.* One of its purposes, as its cofounder George H. Blakeslee explained, was to deal with "the negro problem" in the United States and the similar problems facing European nations colonizing territories of the Pacific Ocean, "inhabited, for the most part, by nations of a more primitive culture than our own."[55] Although it is rarely acknowledged today, the fields of political science and international relations emerged in part from concerns about race and empire prevalent in the United States following Reconstruction.[56]

Such concerns about race and empire also shaped global economic practices, much as they had influenced imperial and international policy. Through the nineteenth century, the large-scale plantation spread from the Americas, where it had been a central component of slave economies, to much of the tropical world; there it became a central component of colonial economies.[57] While these new plantations employed mostly wage labor, they continued to subject their workers, whom they often defined as racially inferior to whites, to high levels of coercion and paid them poorly. Contract laborers from China and India, commonly called "coolies," became one of the most important new plantation labor forces in the age of emancipation. Although Americans tend to remember coolies from China for their work beginning in the 1840s in California, they also worked in the United States on sugar plantations, much as they did in the rest of the world, from Cuba to Samoa. Contracts bound coolies to work far from home for a set number of years. There was a great deal of deception in the contracts, and great privations awaited those workers who signed them. Historian Moon-Ho Jung has studied Chinese coolies who worked in the sugar plantations of Reconstruction Louisiana. Abolitionists had long decried coolie labor as a form of slavery, and supporters of the Chinese Exclusion Act of 1881 equated the measure to earlier prohibitions on the slave trade. At the same time, images of servile Asians helped shore up racial concepts of whiteness in the era of emancipation and wage labor. Even dependent white wage workers seemed free in comparison to servile Asians, while blacks were easily condemned as insolent and unruly when compared to hardworking, docile Asians in this early use of the "model minority" argument.[58]

The global expansion of plantation and other large-scale forms of agriculture also transformed the production and consumption of food staples and raw materials. Both the general expansion of the textile industry and a desire to break the United States's near monopoly of industrial-grade cotton prompted a global expansion of cotton growing. Many of these new cotton efforts followed the example of the New South in its coercive treatment of formally free growers.[59] The ongoing growth of industrial manufacturing also led to a search for global sources for other commodities, including tropical rubber, West African palm oil (which had a range of industrial uses), and even foodstuffs common today like pineapples and bananas.[60] The globalization of agriculture not only brought new supplies of foods and raw materials to powerful nations, but also took these goods from less powerful nations. The expansion of Russian and especially U.S. wheat production challenged Central European agriculture to such an extent that it helped spark the international Panic of 1873.[61] The globalization of agriculture could also have tragic consequences for exporting nations. Scholar Mike Davis has discerned what he calls "late Victorian holocausts" when global traders exported food from areas already suffering from widespread famine, causing millions of deaths in Brazil, India, and elsewhere.[62]

The end of slavery in the Americas, including in the United States, played an important role in the so-called Scramble for Africa, when European powers established colonial states over most of the continent between 1884 and 1914.[63] Africa became the main theater of what historians describe as a new imperialism beginning in the later nineteenth century, a resumption of formal colonial expansion after the loss of the European slave-labor empires founded in the Americas after the sixteenth century. Antislavery, in fact, had played a central role in the colonial conquest of Africa even before the new imperialism. Britain had established Sierra Leone in 1787 to settle manumitted slaves and, after Britain outlawed the slave trade in 1807, so-called recaptives—that is, Africans freed by the British navy from illegal slavers. In 1822, the American Colonization Society (ACS) followed the British example in founding Liberia as a settlement for slaves manumitted in the United States. The members of the ACS acted out of a range of motives, from genuine opposition to slavery to a desire to expel free blacks from the United States. Most black abolitionists and many white abolitionists opposed colonization because they believed it was motivated by racism and by a desire to protect the institution of slavery from the influence of free blacks opposed to human bondage.[64]

Still, some African Americans did detect emancipatory possibilities in Africa that went beyond, or even directly opposed, white

domination and exploitation. In 1859, the African American abolitionist Martin Delany traveled to Abeokuta, in present-day Nigeria,
to establish African American cotton farms that would compete
with, and he hoped undermine, the cotton-producing slave plantations in the United States.[65] Nothing came of this scheme, but the
interesting mix of pan-African solidarity, antislavery, and the prevalent assumption that African Americans could "improve" Africans
reveals important aspects of the fraught relationship between colonialism and antislavery. Such missions of African Americans to
Africa continued throughout the periods of Reconstruction and the
New South and beyond.[66] After the Civil War, African intellectuals
also looked to the postslavery American South, even with all the obvious shortcomings of black life there, as a model of black self-help,
in which people of African descent made their own political and
economic fortunes without waiting for whites to overcome their
own racism. Though the conservative African American educator
and principal of Tuskegee Institute, Booker T. Washington, often
supported European colonial efforts in Africa, many anticolonial
Africans admired him. These included E. W. Blyden of Liberia, J. E.
Casely Hayford of Gold Coast, and John Dube of South Africa.[67]
The Jamaican black nationalist Marcus Garvey had a similarly high
opinion of Tuskegee Institute.[68]

The U.S. federal government also played a direct role in the new
imperialism, especially in the Caribbean and the Pacific.[69] In the
first wave of imperialism, the British had founded, among other
colonies, those in North America that would become the United
States. Imperial expansion in North America continued apace after the Civil War. The United States employed its army, which had
grown massively during the Civil War, in a new wave of conquest of
autonomous Native American nations.[70] Some Native American societies, including the so-called Five Civilized Tribes, held slaves, and
emancipation and birthright citizenship became one of the means
by which the United States diminished Indian sovereignty. Historian Claudio Saunt has highlighted how difficult it is to draw easy
moral or political lessons from this reconfiguration of politics and
economics in westward expansion.[71] Concerns about race, emanci-

pation, and citizenship also shaped U.S. overseas expansion. Often, as historian Eric T. Love has argued, certain forms of antiracism could motivate imperialism as much as forms of racism did.[71] Thus, in his finally unsuccessful efforts to annex Santo Domingo (today the Dominican Republic) to the United States, President Ulysses S. Grant hoped, as he wrote privately, that the island might serve as a refuge for African Americans suffering gross economic, political, and personal oppression. He also speculated that the threat of African American workers relocating to the Caribbean island might prompt whites in the United States to check their own racism. Grant, however, could not make this claim publically, because many whites were loath to do anything that might help African Americans or to expand the United States to include more people of color. The Grant administration negotiated a treaty to annex Santo Domingo in 1870, but the Senate refused to ratify it. Questions about race, emancipation, and the value and purpose of overseas expansion also played important roles in the U.S. occupation of Cuba, Puerto Rico, and the Philippines after the Spanish-American War of 1898 and the gradual acquisition of Hawaii as a U.S. territory in 1900.[73] The decades-long process of locating and building a canal to connect the Caribbean to the Pacific, culminating in the opening of the Panama Canal in 1914, included similar complex entanglements of race, labor, and empire.[74]

Historians incur obvious costs and gain obvious benefits from taking a transnational perspective on Reconstruction. The most obvious cost is that its defining boundaries, like those of nations viewed from outer space, disappear. The transnational history of Reconstruction extends beyond the geographical borders of the United States and outside the temporal limits of 1865-77. Indeed, versions of this essay appear both in this volume, dedicated to the New South, and in another, devoted to Reconstruction. The political movements of the Reconstruction era of the United States blend into long histories of African and African American antislavery; European and Euro-American opposition to wage labor, postemancipation plantation labor regimes, bourgeois liberalism, and overseas colonization. Yet this very breakdown of national distinctions is also an advantage. Without gainsaying the boundaries that define nations and historical periods, these boundaries are porous, and what crosses them is often as important and interesting as what they keep in and keep out.

Those conducting original transnational historical research on Reconstruction, the New South, or any other period would do well to focus on a few, or even just one, of these border crossers, whether individuals, social groups, or commodities.[75] The goal is not to narrow the transnational to a single perspective, but rather to expand the single perspective to the transnational. This will in no way obviate the need for traditionally bounded national and regional studies—indeed, students pursuing transnational history will find themselves all the more grateful for national and regional studies. But transnational history will also provide new insights into traditionally bounded topics, including Reconstruction and the New South.

Notes

A previous version of this chapter was published in 2016 in the Interpreting American History series as "Reconstruction: Transnational History," in *Reconstruction,* ed. John David Smith (copyright © 2016 by The Kent State University Press).

    1. For an exemplary international treatment of Reconstruction, see Mark Smith, "The Past as a Foreign Country: Reconstruction, Inside and Out," in *Reconstructions: New Perspectives on the Postbellum United States,* ed. Thomas J. Brown (New York: Oxford Univ. Press, 2006), 117–40.

    2. Alexander Walters, Henry B. Brown, H. Sylvester Williams, and W. E. B. Du Bois, "To the Nations of the World" (1900), in *An ABC of Color: Selections Chosen by the Author from Over a Half Century of His Writings,* by W. E. B. Du Bois (New York: International Publishers, 1969), 20. On race as a component of capitalism, see esp. Cedric J. Robinson, *Black Marxism: The Making of the Black Radical Tradition,* 2nd ed. (1983; Chapel Hill: Univ. of North Carolina Press, 2000); and David R. Roediger and Elizabeth D. Esch, *The Production of Difference: Race and the Management of Labor in U.S. History* (New York: Oxford Univ. Press, 2012).

    3. Peter Linebaugh and Marcus Rediker, "The Many-Headed Hydra: Sailors, Slaves, and the Atlantic Working Class in the Eighteenth Century," *Journal of Historical Sociology* 3 (Sept. 1990): 225–52, 244. See also their magisterial

The Many-Headed Hydra: Sailors, Slaves, Commoners, and the Hidden History of the Revolutionary Atlantic (London: Verso Books, 2002). The work on popular and working-class revolutionary traditions in the Atlantic world is too rich to cover in a single endnote. One place to start is work on the Haitian Revolution, from C. L. R. James, *The Black Jacobins: Toussaint L'Ouverture and the San Domingo Revolution* (2nd rev. ed. [1938; New York: Vintage, 1963]), to Laurent Dubois, *Avengers of the New World: The Story of the Haitian Revolution* (Cambridge, Mass.: Harvard Univ. Press, 2004). Another place to begin the study of popular politics in the Atlantic world is the literature on Africans in the Americas, perhaps especially J. Lorand Matory, *Black Atlantic Religion: Tradition, Transnationalism, and Matriarchy in the Afro-Brazilian Candomblé* (Princeton, N.J.: Princeton Univ. Press, 2005); Stephan Palmié, *Wizards and Scientists: Explorations in Afro-Cuban Modernity and Tradition* (Durham, N.C.: Duke Univ. Press, 2002); and John Thornton, *Africa and Africans in the Making of the Atlantic World, 1400-1800,* 2nd ed. (New York: Cambridge Univ. Press, 1998).

4. Eric Foner, *Reconstruction: America's Unfinished Revolution, 1863-1877* (New York: Harper and Row, 1988).

5. Barbara Jeanne Fields, *Slavery and Freedom on the Middle Ground: Maryland during the Nineteenth Century* (New Haven, Conn.: Yale Univ. Press, 1985); Julie Saville, *The Work of Reconstruction: From Slave to Wage Laborer in South Carolina, 1860-1870* (New York: Cambridge Univ. Press, 1994); Amy Dru Stanley, *From Bondage to Contract: Wage Labor, Marriage, and the Market in the Age of Slave Emancipation* (New York: Cambridge Univ. Press, 1998).

6. Carolyn Fick, "Emancipation in Haiti: From Plantation Labour to Peasant Proprietorship," *Slavery and Abolition* 21 (Aug. 2000): 11-40; Eric Foner, *Nothing but Freedom: Emancipation and Its Legacy* (Baton Rouge: Louisiana State Univ. Press, 1983); Thomas C. Holt, *The Problem of Freedom: Race, Labor, and Politics in Jamaica and Britain, 1832-1938* (Baltimore: Johns Hopkins Univ. Press, 1992); Stuart B. Schwartz, *Slaves, Peasants, and Rebels: Reconsidering Brazilian Slavery* (Urbana: Univ. of Illinois Press, 1992), esp. chap. 4, "Rethinking Palmares: Slave Resistance in Colonial Brazil," 103-36.

7. Eric Foner, *Free Soil, Free Labor, Free Men: The Ideology of the Republican Party before the Civil War* (New York: Oxford Univ. Press, 1970).

8. For a good introduction to utopian socialisms in the United States, see Daniel Walker Howe, "Pursuing the Millennium," in his *What Hath God Wrought: The Transformation of America, 1815-1848* (New York: Oxford Univ. Press, 2007), 285-327. For a challenging and inspiring approach to artisan socialism in France, see Jacques Rancière, *The Nights of Labor: The Workers' Dream in Nineteenth-Century France* (Philadelphia: Temple Univ. Press, 1989).

9. An excellent introduction to this work is Frederick Cooper, Thomas C. Holt, and Rebecca J. Scott, *Beyond Slavery: Explorations of Race, Labor, and Citizenship in Postemancipation Societies* (Chapel Hill: Univ. of North Carolina Press, 2000).

10. Holt, *Problem of Freedom*. See also the essays collected in Mary Turner, ed., *From Chattel Slaves to Wage Slaves: The Dynamics of Labour Bargaining in the Americas* (Bloomington: Indiana Univ. Press, 1995).

11. Seymour Drescher, *The Mighty Experiment: Free Labor vs. Slavery in British Emancipation* (New York: Oxford Univ. Press, 2002). On the influence of this experiment, and of British abolition more broadly, on U.S. abolition, see Edward Bartlett Rugemer, *The Problem of Emancipation: The Caribbean Roots of the American Civil War* (Baton Rouge: Louisiana State Univ. Press, 2008).

12. The common definition of capitalism as a "market economy" is misleading, since markets are not particular to capitalism or any other system. The nineteenth-century "market revolution" identified by historian Charles Sellers was, as Sellers notes, a consequence of a more fundamental transformation in the way people produced goods in a class society that compelled most people to work for owners of the means of production. See Sellers, *The Market Revolution: Jacksonian America, 1815-1846* (New York: Oxford Univ. Press, 1991).

13. Eric J. Hobsbawm, *The Age of Capital: 1848-1875* (1975; repr., New York: Vintage, 1996), 1.

14. Alfred D. Chandler, *The Visible Hand: The Managerial Revolution in American Business* (Cambridge, Mass.: Harvard Univ. Press, 1977); Sean Wilentz, *Chants Democratic: New York City and the Rise of the American Working Class, 1788-1850* (New York: Oxford Univ. Press, 1984). The southern case was made more complicated by the fact that many in manufacturing were enslaved. For an important study of free white immigrant and enslaved southern urban workers, see Ira Berlin and Herbert G. Gutman, "Natives and Immigrants, Free Men and Slaves: Urban Workingmen in the Antebellum American South," *American Historical Review* 88 (Dec. 1983): 1175-1200. Robert J. Steinfeld has shown how a variety of legal sanctions around the world compelled ostensibly free workers to obey their employers as paternal authorities in a household rather than as partners in a free contract. See Steinfeld, *The Invention of Free Labor: The Employment Relation in English and American Law and Culture, 1350-1870* (Chapel Hill: Univ. of North Carolina Press, 1991), and Steinfeld, *Coercion, Contract, and Free Labor in the Nineteenth Century* (New York: Cambridge Univ. Press, 2001). For the colonial context, see Paul Craven and Douglas Hay, eds., *Masters, Servants, and Magistrates in Britain and the Empire, 1562-1955* (Chapel Hill: Univ. of North Carolina Press, 2004).

15. The greatest comparative study placing the Civil War in the context of bourgeois revolutions and the transition to capitalism remains perhaps Barrington Moore, *Social Origins of Dictatorship and Democracy: Lord and Peasant in the Making of the Modern World* (1966; repr., Boston: Beacon Press, 1993).

16. For a related argument, see John Ashworth, "Towards a Bourgeois Revolution? Explaining the American Civil War," *Historical Materialism* 19, no. 4 (2011): 193-205. This condenses aspects of John Ashworth, *Slavery, Capitalism, and Politics in the Antebellum Republic,* 2 vols. (New York: Cambridge Univ. Press, 1995, 2007).

17. One of the most important works making this case is Sidney W. Mintz, *Sweetness and Power: The Place of Sugar in Modern History* (New York: Viking, 1985). More recently, scholars have begun developing a notion of an especially advanced capitalist "second slavery" in Cuba, Brazil, and the Mississippi Valley. For a good introduction, see Anthony E. Kaye, "The Second Slavery: Modernity in the Nineteenth-Century South and the Atlantic World," *Journal of Southern History* 75 (Aug. 2009): 627-50. The literature on comparative slavery and emancipation is vast. A good place to start is Enrico Dal Lago, *American Slavery, Atlantic Slavery, and Beyond: The U.S. "Peculiar Institution" in International Perspective* (Boulder, Colo.: Paradigm Publishers, 2012). Also important is Peter Kolchin, *A Sphinx on the American Land: The Nineteenth-Century South in Comparative Perspective* (Baton Rouge: Louisiana State Univ. Press, 2003). Most recently, see Walter Johnson, *River of Dark Dreams: Slavery and Empire in the Cotton Kingdom* (Cambridge, Mass.: Harvard Univ. Press, 2013), and Edward E. Baptist, *The Half Has Never Been Told: Slavery and the Making of American Capitalism* (New York: Basic Books, 2014). The journal *Slavery and Abolition* (1980-) remains indispensable.

18. Abraham Lincoln, "Annual Message to Congress," December 3, 1861, in *The Collected Works of Abraham Lincoln,* ed. Roy P. Basler, 8 vols. (New Brunswick, N.J.: Rutgers Univ. Press, 1953), 5:35-53.

19. Noel Ignatiev, *How the Irish Became White* (1995; repr., New York: Routledge, 2009); Eric Lott, *Love and Theft: Blackface Minstrelsy and the American Working Class* (New York: Oxford Univ. Press, 1993); David R. Roediger, *The Wages of Whiteness: Race and the Making of the American Working Class,* rev. ed. (1991; New York: Verso, 1999); Alexander Saxton, *The Rise and Fall of the White Republic: Class Politics and Mass Culture in Nineteenth-Century America* (London: Verso, 2003). For an important critique of the field of whiteness studies, see Eric Arnesen, "Whiteness and the Historians' Imagination," *International Labor and Working-Class History* 60 (2001): 3-32.

20. The greatest study of the European labor movement remains E. P. Thompson, *The Making of the English Working Class* (1964; repr., New York: Vintage, 1966), even if scholars have continued to develop and apply Thompson's insights. For an important study revealing how foundational gender was to class formation, see Anna Clark, *The Struggle for the Breeches: Gender and the Making of the British Working Class* (Berkeley: Univ. of California Press, 1995).

21. On these '48ers in the Civil War, see Alison Clark Efford, *German Immigrants, Race, and Citizenship in the Civil War Era* (New York: Cambridge Univ. Press, 2013); Mischa Honeck, *We Are the Revolutionists: German-Speaking Immigrants and American Abolitionists after 1848* (Athens: Univ. of Georgia Press, 2011); Bruce Levine, *The Spirit of 1848: German Immigrants, Labor Conflict, and the Coming of the Civil War* (Urbana: Univ. of Illinois Press, 1992); Martin W. Öfele, *German-Speaking Officers in the United States Colored Troops, 1863-1867* (Gainesville: Univ. Press of Florida, 2004); Martin W. Öfele, *True Sons of the Republic: European Immigrants in the Union Army* (Westport, Conn.: Praeger,

2008); Andrew Zimmerman, "From the Rhine to the Mississippi: Property, Democracy, and Socialism in the American Civil War," *Journal of the Civil War Era* 5 (Mar. 2015): 3-37.

22. Elizabeth Fox-Genovese and Eugene D. Genovese, *Slavery in White and Black: Class and Race in the Southern Slaveholders' New World Order* (New York: Cambridge Univ. Press, 2008).

23. Marcus Cunliffe, *Chattel Slavery and Wage Slavery: The Anglo-American Context, 1830-1860* (Athens: Univ. of Georgia Press, 1979); Foner, *Free Soil, Free Labor, Free Men.*

24. Jonathan H. Earle, *Jacksonian Antislavery and the Politics of Free Soil, 1824-1854* (Chapel Hill: Univ. of North Carolina Press, 2004).

25. W. E. B. Du Bois, *Black Reconstruction: An Essay toward a History of the Part Which Black Folk Played in the Attempt to Reconstruct Democracy in America, 1860-1880* (1935; repr., New York: Free Press, 1998).

26. Ibid., 319.

27. On sharecropping, see Barbara Jeanne Fields, "The Advent of Capitalist Agriculture: The New South in a Bourgeois World," in *Essays on the Postbellum Southern Economy,* ed. Thavolia Glymph and John J. Kushma (College Station: Texas A&M Univ. Press, 1985), 73-94; Roger L. Ransom and Richard Sutch, *One Kind of Freedom: The Economic Consequences of Emancipation,* 2nd rev. ed. (1977; New York: Cambridge Univ. Press, 2001); and Gavin Wright, *Old South, New South: Revolutions in the Southern Economy since the Civil War* (New York: Basic Books, 1986).

28. Andrew Zimmerman, *Alabama in Africa: Booker T. Washington, the German Empire, and the Globalization of the New South* (Princeton, N.J.: Princeton Univ. Press, 2010).

29. Karl Marx and Friedrich Engels, *The Civil War in the United States,* ed. Andrew Zimmerman (New York: International Publishers, 2016).

30. There has been some debate about the support of British workers for the Union. The consensus is that they did support the Union collectively, although the opinions of individual workers of course varied greatly. See R. J. M. Blackett, *Divided Hearts: Britain and the American Civil War* (Baton Rouge: Louisiana State Univ. Press, 2001).

31. David Fernbach, "Introduction," in *The First International and After,* vol. 3, *Marx's Political Writings,* ed. David Fernbach (1973; London: Verso, 2010), 9-71.

32. Karl Marx, *Capital,* vol. 1, trans. Ben Fowkes (1867; New York: Penguin Classics, 1976), 91 (translation modified).

33. Marx, "Inaugural Address of the Working Men's International Association" (London), September 28, 1864, in Marx and Engels, *Civil War in the United States,* 180.

34. David Montgomery, *Beyond Equality: Labor and the Radical Republicans, 1862-1872* (1967; repr., Urbana: Univ. of Illinois Press, 1981).

35. Roediger, *Wages of Whiteness;* Roediger, *Seizing Freedom: Slave Emancipation and Liberty for All* (Brooklyn, N.Y.: Verso, 2014). For an important

case study, see Eric Arnesen, *Waterfront Workers of New Orleans: Race, Class, and Politics, 1863-1923,* Illini Books ed. (1991; repr., Urbana: Univ. of Illinois Press, 1994).

36. Geoff Ely, *Forging Democracy: The History of the Left in Europe, 1850-2000* (New York: Oxford Univ. Press, 2002).

37. See Robin Blackburn, *An Unfinished Revolution: Karl Marx and Abraham Lincoln* (London: Verso, 2011). Well researched but finally too condemning of the foreign-born sections of the International to serve as a useful introduction is Timothy Messer-Kruse, *The Yankee International: Marxism and the American Reform Tradition, 1848-1876* (Chapel Hill: Univ. of North Carolina Press, 1998).

38. Werner Sombart, *Warum gibt es in den Vereinigten Staaten keinen Sozialismus?* (Tübingen, Germany: J. C. B. Mohr, 1906).

39. Eric Foner, "Why Is There No Socialism in the United States?" *History Workshop* no. 17 (Spring 1984): 57-80.

40. On this individualistic conception of freedom and the limitations it placed on Reconstruction, see Foner, *Free Soil, Free Labor, Free Men.*

41. Gustav Mayer, "Die Trennung der proletarischen von der bürgerlichen Demokratie in Deutschland 1863-1870," in *Radikalismus, Sozialismus und bürgerliche Demokratie,* ed. Hans Ulrich Wehler (Frankfurt am Main, Federal Republic of Germany: Suhrkamp, 1969), 108-78.

42. Amy Dru Stanley, *From Bondage to Contract: Wage Labor, Marriage, and the Market in the Age of Slave Emancipation* (New York: Cambridge Univ. Press, 1998).

43. Philip M. Katz, *From Appomattox to Montmartre: Americans and the Paris Commune* (Cambridge, Mass.: Harvard Univ. Press, 1998).

44. See Nancy Cohen, *The Reconstruction of American Liberalism, 1865-1914* (Chapel Hill: Univ. of North Carolina Press, 2002); Heather Cox Richardson, *The Death of Reconstruction: Race, Labor, and Politics in the Post-Civil War North, 1865-1901* (Cambridge, Mass.: Harvard Univ. Press, 2001); and John G. Sproat, *"The Best Men": Liberal Reformers in the Gilded Age* (New York: Oxford Univ. Press, 1968). Sproat's view has been challenged by Andrew L. Slap, *The Doom of Reconstruction: The Liberal Republicans in the Civil War Era* (New York: Fordham Univ. Press, 2006). For a similar twentieth-century elitist liberalism, see Brett Gary, *The Nervous Liberals: Propaganda Anxieties from World War I to the Cold War* (New York: Columbia Univ. Press, 1999).

45. For a good overview, which begins with a discussion of South Carolinian John C. Calhoun, see Domenico Losurdo, *Liberalism: A Counter-History,* trans. Gregory Elliott (London: Verso Books, 2011).

46. Nobody has analyzed this attitude for the United States better than William Appleman Williams, *The Tragedy of American Diplomacy* (1959; repr., New York: W. W. Norton, 2009). For the European counterpart, see Uday Singh Mehta, *Liberalism and Empire: A Study in Nineteenth-Century British Liberal Thought* (Chicago: Univ. of Chicago Press, 1999). For an especially sophisticated

study connecting liberalism in colony and metropole, see Anne McClintock, *Imperial Leather: Race, Gender, and Sexuality in the Colonial Contest* (New York: Routledge, 1995).

47. Sven Beckert, *The Monied Metropolis: New York City and the Consolidation of the American Bourgeoisie, 1850-1896* (New York: Cambridge Univ. Press, 2001).

48. David W. Blight, *Race and Reunion: The Civil War in American Memory* (Cambridge, Mass.: Harvard Univ. Press, 2001).

49. See C. Vann Woodward, *Origins of the New South, 1877-1913* (1951; repr., Baton Rouge: Louisiana State Univ. Press, 1972), and his *The Strange Career of Jim Crow* (1955; repr., New York: Oxford Univ. Press, 1974). On the historiographical debate following Woodward's work, see John David Smith, *When Did Southern Segregation Begin?* (New York: Bedford/St. Martin's, 2002). See also George M. Fredrickson, *The Black Image in the White Mind: The Debate on Afro-American Character and Destiny, 1817-1914* (New York: Harper and Row, 1971).

50. Roediger and Esch, *Production of Difference.*

51. There has been much interesting comparative work on racisms, and much more needs to be done. See George M. Fredrickson, *White Supremacy: A Comparative Study in American and South African History* (New York: Oxford Univ. Press, 1981); David Theo Goldberg, *The Racial State* (Malden, Mass.: Blackwell Publishers, 2002); and Stanley B. Greenberg, *Race and State in Capitalist Development: Comparative Perspectives* (New Haven, Conn.: Yale Univ. Press, 1980).

52. William Archibald Dunning, "The Process of Reconstruction," in his *Essays on the Civil War and Reconstruction and Related Topics* (New York: Macmillan, 1897), 176-252, 250-51; John David Smith and J. Vincent Lowery, eds., *The Dunning School: Historians, Race, and the Meaning of Reconstruction* (Lexington: Univ. Press of Kentucky, 2013).

53. John W. Burgess, "The American Commonwealth: Changes in Its Relation to the Nation," *Political Science Quarterly* 1 (Mar. 1886): 9-35, 16.

54. Marilyn Lake and Henry Reynolds, *Drawing the Global Colour Line: White Men's Countries and the International Challenge of Racial Equality* (New York: Cambridge Univ. Press, 2008).

55. George H. Blakeslee, "Introduction," *Journal of Race Development* 1 (1910-11): 1-4; quotation, 2.

56. On race and empire and the birth of the field of international relations, see Robert Vitalis, "The Noble American Science of Imperial Relations and Its Laws of Race Development," *Comparative Studies in Society and History* 52 (Oct. 2010): 909-38; Robert Vitalis, *White World Order, Black Power Politics: The Birth of American International Relations* (Ithaca, N.Y.: Cornell Univ. Press, 2015); and the essays in David Long and Brian C. Schmidt, eds. *Imperialism and Internationalism in the Discipline of International Relations* (Albany: State Univ. of New York Press, 2005).

57. Philip D. Curtin, *The Rise and Fall of the Plantation Complex: Essays in Atlantic History* (New York: Cambridge Univ. Press, 1990).

58. Moon-Ho Jung, *Coolies and Cane: Race, Labor, and Sugar in the Age of Emancipation* (Baltimore: Johns Hopkins Univ. Press, 2006).

59. Sven Beckert, "Emancipation and Empire: Reconstructing the Worldwide Web of Cotton Production in the Age of the American Civil War," *American Historical Review* 109 (Dec. 2004): 1405-38; Beckert, *Empire of Cotton: A Global History* (New York: Alfred A. Knopf, 2014); Allen Isaacman and Richard Roberts, eds., *Cotton, Colonialism, and Social History in Sub-Saharan Africa* (Portsmouth, N.H.: Heinemann, 1995); Zimmerman, *Alabama in Africa*.

60. See, for example, Greg Grandin, *Fordlandia: The Rise and Fall of Henry Ford's Forgotten Jungle City* (New York: Metropolitan Books, 2009); Martin Lynn, *Commerce and Economic Change in West Africa: The Palm Oil Trade in the Nineteenth Century* (New York: Cambridge Univ. Press, 1997); Gary Y. Okihiro, *Pineapple Culture: A History of the Tropical and Temperate Zones* (Berkeley: Univ. of California Press, 2009).

61. Scott Reynolds Nelson, *A Nation of Deadbeats: An Uncommon History of America's Financial Disasters* (New York: Alfred A. Knopf, 2012). On U.S. wheat production and exports, see William Cronon, *Nature's Metropolis: Chicago and the Great West* (New York: W. W. Norton, 1991).

62. Mike Davis, *Late Victorian Holocausts: El Niño Famines and the Making of the Third World* (London: Verso, 2001).

63. Kevin Grant, *A Civilised Savagery: Britain and the New Slaveries in Africa, 1884-1926* (New York: Routledge, 2005); Paul E. Lovejoy, *Transformations in Slavery: A History of Slavery in Africa,* 2nd ed. (New York: Cambridge Univ. Press, 2000).

64. On the American Colonization Society, see Eric Burin, *Slavery and the Peculiar Solution: A History of the American Colonization Society* (Gainesville: Univ. Press of Florida, 2005). On abolitionist opposition to the American Colonization Society, see Paul Goodman, *Of One Blood: Abolitionism and the Origins of Racial Equality* (Berkeley: Univ. of California Press, 1998).

65. See Richard Blackett, "Martin R. Delany and Robert Campbell: Black Americans in Search of an African Colony," *Journal of Negro History* 62 (Jan. 1977): 1-25; James T. Campbell, "Redeeming the Race: Martin Delany and the Niger Valley Exploring Party, 1859-60," *New Formations* 45 (Winter 2001-2002): 125-49.

66. For an especially critical perspective, see Tunde Adeleke, *UnAfrican Americans: Nineteenth-Century Black Nationalists and the Civilizing Mission* (Lexington: Univ. Press of Kentucky, 1998). For a broad history, see James T. Campbell, *Middle Passages: African American Journeys to Africa, 1787-2005* (New York: Penguin, 2006). For more specific studies, see James T. Campbell, *Songs of Zion: The African Methodist Episcopal Church in the United States and South Africa* (New York: Oxford Univ. Press, 1995); Kevin K. Gaines, *Uplifting the Race:*

Black Leadership, Politics, and Culture in the Twentieth Century (Chapel Hill: Univ. of North Carolina Press, 1996); and Robert Trent Vinson, *The Americans Are Coming! Dreams of African American Liberation in Segregationist South Africa* (Athens: Ohio Univ. Press, 2012).

67. Imanuel Geiss, *The Pan-African Movement: A History of Pan-Africanism in America, Europe, and Africa* (New York: Africana Publishing, 1974); Zimmerman, *Alabama in Africa;* Frank Andre Guridy, *Forging Diaspora: Afro-Cubans and African Americans in a World of Empire and Jim Crow* (Chapel Hill: Univ. of North Carolina Press, 2010).

68. Judith Stein, *The World of Marcus Garvey: Race and Class in Modern Society* (Baton Rouge: Louisiana State Univ. Press, 1986).

69. For an overview of work on U.S. foreign policy, including imperial policy, at this time, see Jay Sexton, "Toward a Synthesis of Foreign Relations in the Civil War Era, 1848-77," *American Nineteenth Century History* 5 (Fall 2004): 50-73. The classic work remains Williams, *Tragedy of American Diplomacy.* Important recent works include Charles Soutter Campbell, *The Transformation of American Foreign Relations, 1865-1900* (New York: Harper and Row, 1976); Matthew Frye Jacobson, *Barbarian Virtues: The United States Encounters Foreign Peoples at Home and Abroad, 1876-1917* (New York: Hill and Wang, 2000); Jay Sexton, *Debtor Diplomacy: Finance and American Foreign Relations in the Civil War Era, 1837-1873* (Oxford: Clarendon, 2005); and Jay Sexton, *The Monroe Doctrine: Empire and Nation in Nineteenth-Century America* (New York: Hill and Wang, 2011).

70. See especially the powerful account by Steven Hahn, *A Nation without Borders: The United States and Its World in an Age of Civil Wars, 1830-1910* (New York: Viking, 2016).

71. See Claudio Saunt, "The Paradox of Freedom: Tribal Sovereignty and Emancipation during the Reconstruction of Indian Territory," *Journal of Southern History* 70 (Feb. 2004): 63-94. See also Smith, "Past as a Foreign Country," 136-39.

72. Eric T. Love, *Race over Empire: Racism and U.S. Imperialism, 1865-1900* (Chapel Hill: Univ. of North Carolina Press, 2004). See also Amy Kaplan, *The Anarchy of Empire in the Making of U.S. Culture* (Cambridge, Mass.: Harvard Univ. Press, 2002).

73. For an excellent analysis of the complex dynamics of race and empire in the Philippines, see Paul A. Kramer, *The Blood of Government: Race, Empire, the United States, and the Philippines* (Chapel Hill: Univ. of North Carolina Press, 2006). On Santo Domingo, Hawaii, and the Philippines, see Love, *Race over Empire.*

74. Julie Greene, *The Canal Builders: Making America's Empire at the Panama Canal* (New York: Penguin Press, 2009).

75. For an exemplary study of individuals, see James H. Sweet, *Domingos Álvares, African Healing, and the Intellectual History of the Atlantic World* (Chapel Hill: Univ. of North Carolina Press, 2011); of social groups, see Jung, *Coolies and Cane;* of commodities, see the literature cited in notes 59 and 60.

CHAPTER THREE

Populism in the New South

CONNIE L. LESTER

History remembers the day in 1877 when neighbors met at the home of John R. Allen to discuss their mutual problems and develop a plan of action to deal cooperatively with cattle rustling and the purchase of needed farm supplies. Years later, veterans of that meeting returned to the modest Lampasas County, Texas, dwelling to be photographed on the front porch as a way of commemorating the origins of the Farmers' Alliance. The Alliance swept across the South in the 1880s, drawing members from other farm organizations such as the Patrons of Husbandry (Grange) and the Agricultural Wheel, as well as attracting farmers who had been allied with no organizations and some who had worked in other reform efforts, including the Temperance movement and the Greenback Party.

Adopting a nonpartisan program built on cooperativism, the Farmers' Alliance advocated for a capitalist economy based on "the Golden Rule," in which people were valued over money—what historian Norman Pollack has called the "humane economy."[1] The organization developed a set of "demands"—first at Cleburne, Texas, in 1886 and then at Ocala, Florida, in 1890—that agitated for government to take a stronger role in regulating railroads, banks, currency, and taxes and for "the people" to take a stronger role in setting policy through the popular election of U.S. senators. Stymied in their efforts to effect the changes outlined in the Ocala Demands and encouraged by western silver miners, the farmers created a third party—the People's Party, or the Populists—in 1891.

The study of agrarian dissent remains a vibrant scholarly pursuit despite population and economic shifts that have transformed the United States from a largely rural and agricultural society to one that is urban and postindustrial. Today few Americans have direct connections to farm life. Indeed their experiences with food production and the natural world are buffered by layers of processing and the creation of organized landscapes that serve political, economic, and social needs largely removed from that of their nineteenth-century ancestors. Although the origins of agrarian dissent may appear baffling to twenty-first-century readers, the farmers' organizational efforts and their demands informed much of the twentieth century's political and social history, and the study of the Farmers' Alliance and Populism remains an active arena for research by students and academic historians.

Historians have asked three important sets of questions about the Farmers' Alliance and the Populists: First, who were they? Why did some farmers join the organization, but others, with the same challenges, distance themselves from the movement? Second, historians disagree on whether the dissenters were conservative, premodern traditionalists, bent on farming as their fathers had done, or modern, progressive critics of the emerging industrial capitalism, offering an alternative economic future. Finally, historians debate the legacy of the agrarian dissent and Populism. Did it offer a last moment for the democratic ideal that died with the 1896 election, or did Populism shape the twentieth century?

For people who were frequently dismissed, then and now, as "ignorant" farmers, the southern agrarian dissenters and Populists of the late nineteenth century were amazingly self-aware of their place in history. In the books and tracts they wrote explaining their position on the problems of their day, they included historical interpretations of the role of farmers and agriculture in the political and social development of Europe and the United States. Thus, any discussion of Populist historiography should begin with the "official" texts published by the Agricultural Wheel, the Farmers' Alliance, and the Populist Party.[2] Farmers saw themselves as the purveyors of progress, the people who enabled the technological and philo- sophical advances that defined society's advancement through their ability to produce enough food and fiber to support a nonagricul- tural urban society. They proudly pointed to the role of farmers at the "rude bridge" in Concord and counted George Washington as a farmer-president. They noted the actions of French peasants in the events that culminated in the French Revolution. Indeed, their self-conscious identification with earlier revolutions informed their prediction of an "impending" upheaval against what they perceived as an immoral economy that threatened not only their livelihoods, but the very foundations of the republic.

Three twentieth-century historians framed the research on Pop- ulism for the next century: John D. Hicks, Richard Hofstadter, and Lawrence Goodwyn. Writing in the 1930s, Hicks, who had marched "at the tail end of a McKinley-Hobart torchlight procession during the campaign of 1896,"[3] placed agrarian dissent within the context of the rural economic distress and third-party development that characterized the United States of his youth. In his seminal book, *The Populist Revolt: The Farmers' Alliance and the People's Party* (1931), he used the words of the Populists themselves within the context of Frederick Jackson Turner's frontier thesis to explain what he perceived as the rational actions of farmers and their supporters to market changes that did not reward their move to commercial farming and prevented them from continuing in traditional, diver- sified, subsistence agriculture.[4]

If Hicks presented farmers as rational actors in economic hard times, Richard Hofstadter, writing during the post–World War II era of conformity, viewed them as irrational men responding neg- atively to the progressive industrial–urban transformation of the American economy. In *The Age of Reform: From Bryan to FDR* (1955), Hofstadter labeled their actions as indicative of their "status anxi- ety" and dismissed their writings as racist and anti-Semitic.[5] In this view, history left the Populists behind, and Hofstadter had little sympathy for their demands for a cooperative commonwealth.

Two decades later, having witnessed the effect of grassroots organizing on American social and political culture, Lawrence Goodwyn published *Democratic Promise: The Populist Movement in America* (1976), in which he argued that agrarian insurgency and the Populist Party represented a high point in democracy.[6] It was a "moment" built on the culture of reform that emerged from the third-party movements of the late nineteenth century and the cooperative experience shared by farmers in the Farmers' Alliance. In Goodwyn's view, the silver issue and those who supported it represented a "shadow movement" that ultimately destroyed the promise Populism represented.

Whether they argued that Populism was a rational response to hard times, an irrational example of status anxiety, or the high moment of democracy that emerged from the cooperative movement, these historians all agreed that the effect of the agrarian insurgency ended with the 1896 election that elevated the Republican William McKinley to the White House.[7]

In 2007, with the publication of his Bancroft and Saloutos award-winning book, *Populist Vision,* Charles Postel offered a revision of the earlier paradigms.[8] Casting Populism as a national movement, Postel argued that Populists were self-aware modernists who offered an alternative vision for capitalist development. His interpretation suggests that "modern society is not a given but is shaped by men and women who pursue alternative visions of what the modern world should be."[9] Postel's new interpretation of Populism rested on a substantive body of research by a generation of historians who explored social history, labor history, and studies in gender and race in the post-1896 era of agricultural history.[10]

Agrarian dissent existed within the confluence of economic, political, and social changes that transformed the United States from a nation of farmers to an urban–industrial society in which most men worked for wages. The transformation did more than reduce the number of people working the land; it reorganized markets in a way that altered the very fabric of rural life and, many farmers believed, threatened the social and political structure of the nation. Prior to the Civil War, most American farmers operated within a calculus that avoided risk. They practiced a diverse agriculture based on subsistence farming. That is, they planted to provide food and fiber for their families first, and marketed any surplus. Expansion of production awaited either the expansion of family labor, as children developed the strength and skills to contribute to the family economy, or the growth of accumulated savings to procure additional lands or hire farm labor (or in the case of the southern farmers, purchase a slave). The strategy ensured subsistence if not comfort, provided a pathway to potential financial growth, and, most importantly, did not place the land itself at risk. Historically, sons expected to follow their fathers into farming, and the cautious agriculture practices of one generation laid the groundwork for the success of the next.

Post–Civil War farmers in the South and the Plains states faced a new economy that limited the opportunities for following the previously successful strategies, even as agricultural leaders counseled a "live-at-home" philosophy to counter the economic pitfalls of the age. The expansion of farmland in the American West, Australia, western Canada, and eastern Europe drove down the prices of staple commodities at the very moment when many farmers moved from a position of subsistence agriculture to the riskier, market-oriented commercial farming. Southern and western farmers demanded regulation of transportation and communication systems essential to their market needs; purchasing and marketing cooperatives to reduce costs and maximize prices; and banking and currency changes to address the need for farm credit and create a modest inflation to raise commodity prices. Although they initially eschewed partisanship in the pursuit of their goals, resistance to farmers' demands by both political parties laid the foundation for the establishment of the People's (Populist) Party in 1891.

In the South, the physical and fiscal destruction of the war forced small farmers to seek credit for rebuilding in a region with little cash and few lending options. As Ransom and Sutch demonstrated in their seminal work on the postwar South, *One Kind of Freedom: The Economic Consequences of Emancipation* (1977), southern banking had never been as robust as that of the North, and the collapse of the Confederate economy left the region bereft of money and lending institutions.[11] Southern farmers became dependent on merchant credit, in which they mortgaged their future crop in order to obtain tools, fertilizer, clothing, and food at grossly inflated prices in order to survive the year. Merchants demanded the planting of cotton or tobacco as a guarantee for the credit they extended. As the practice spread, states enacted legislation to empower merchants to enforce their claims, resulting in a crop-lien system that impoverished small farmers and prevented newly freed black farmers from rising up the agricultural ladder from sharecropping to land ownership. As David Silkenat argued in his study of North Carolina farmers, "debt stood at the heart of the agrarian critique of American capitalist society . . . [and] many white farmers . . . concluded that their chronic indebtedness amounted to a form of slavery."[12] Seldom able to "pay out" the credit extended, the crop-lien system demanded another year of cotton and credit, with enormous environmental damage and an economy marked by what historian Pete Daniel called "debt peonage."[13]

Southern farmers operated within a social and economic environment changed by war, but also within a national environment transformed by modern industrial economic reorganization. The market threat was multifaceted and not always obvious. A dense web of national rail transportation networks materialized in a brief twenty-year span that increased rail line mileage from 53,000 in 1870 to 207,000 in 1890.[14] The expansion made markets and consumer goods available to all, but it also transformed the process of selling farm commodities from a face-to-face transaction between individuals to an impersonal process that depended on grain elevators, cotton and tobacco warehouses, commodity grading, and futures markets. As William Cronon argued in *Nature's Metropolis: Chicago and the Great West* (1991), this rationalization of the market produced a "second nature" that removed agricultural production from consumption in a manner not previously experienced, with significant consequences for the environment and the organization of farm life.[15] The demand for credit to sustain the transformation to commercial production represented another threat. In the new cash-based economy, manufacturers, distributors, and retailers demanded payment from farmers caught in the vortex of decades of downward-spiraling prices. Economist Anne Mayhew, in her "Reappraisal of the Causes of Farm Protest in the United States" (1972), found the inability of farmers to resist commercial production, as they had done in the past, a primary cause for their protest.[16] Writing two decades later, Cronon recognized the displacement such changes produced, but found a more dynamic, two-way movement of commodities, products, and capital between cities like Chicago and the countryside than other historians had recognized. The economic, social, and environmental implications for agriculture were enormous, but the development of modern systems of finance, production, and distribution were more complex than accounts of the victimization of farmers implied.

Southern farmers had many potential reasons for joining an organization that promised to reduce their costs, raise commodity prices, and push for legislative changes that would favor agricultural interests. Although millions of farmers added their names to the Alliance roles and later joined the People's Party, millions of others ignored the organizations or actively fought against them. Who joined and why? What did the nature of the memberships say about agrarian dissent? Placing the focus on economic and social analysis provides compelling evidence for why farmers cast their lots with the Alliance and the People's Party.

As with many aspects of the history of the New South, C. Vann Woodward provided one of the first interpretative works on southern Populism with the publication of *Tom Watson, Agrarian Rebel* in 1938.[17] Woodward viewed the actions of Watson and the Populists he led as evidence of a break with the Old South. Populist leaders were former Confederates who made common cause with African Americans and former Union soldiers in other parts of the country in order to address mutual concerns. While fully aware of the racism that gained new credence with the implementation of Jim Crow segregation and disfranchisement, he nevertheless focused on the Populist dissent from the reign of Bourbon Democrats to argue that the New South was indeed "new."

In *Democratic Promise,* Lawrence Goodwyn pointed to an economic basis to argue that successful Alliance cooperatives were the best indicator of strong Populist support. Only a few months earlier, Robert C. McMath Jr. had questioned that premise in his book *Populist Vanguard: A History of the Southern Farmers' Alliance* (1975) and suggested that significant numbers of southern farmers had abandoned the Alliance and its cooperatives as unworkable by the time of the rise of the Populist Party in 1891. Unable to operate their farms on a cash basis and unable to withhold their crops for higher prices, they became disenchanted with the promise of cooperativism.[18] For McMath, the answer to the question of who joined the Populists could be found within the social history of the postwar rural South.[19]

The southern historian who most clearly acknowledged the economic roots of agrarian dissent was Steven Hahn. Whereas other scholars of southern Populism focused on the strategy of cooperativism—the Farmers' Alliance's solution to the twin problems of farm prices and credit—Hahn transformed the debate by situating the origins of agrarian dissent within the antebellum and postwar construction of railroads in his award-winning book, *The Roots of Southern Populism: Yeoman Farmers and the Transformation of the Georgia Upcountry, 1850-1890* (1985).[20] He argued that Georgia farmers resisted the market revolution in a struggle that pitted traditional customs of mutuality against the emerging cash nexus. Specifically, his analysis focused on the role of railroads in transforming production toward commercial agriculture and the legislative fights over fence laws and stock laws that challenged traditional livestock practices.

Hahn's work contradicted James Turner's study of Texas Populists and the influence of railroads and the market. Turner concluded that the farmers drawn to Populism were those men most isolated from larger political and economic changes induced by market transformations. Populism was strongest where railroad access and urban markets were weakest. For Turner, men who were marginalized, not men who were stressed by their incorporation into the new economy were those most likely to join the Populist bandwagon.[21]

Explorations of the social networks that sustained rural communities complemented the economic studies of agrarian dissent. As Robert McMath claimed, "Populism developed among people who were deeply rooted in the social and economic networks of rural communities, not . . . among isolated and disoriented individuals."[22] Those social networks included people omitted from earlier studies, including women and African Americans. Social networks also provided a medium for education and religion to impact the development of a culture of dissent.

The Farmers' Alliance allowed, but did not require, female membership. As Annie L. Diggs first noted in her 1892 *Arena* magazine article,[23] farm women, many of whom had been members of the Grange and the Agricultural Wheel, emerged as rural activists who challenged accepted ideas of a "woman's sphere" as they demanded a role in local alliances and pressed for woman suffrage in some areas. Even when their actions followed traditional courses, Alliance women interpreted their behavior within the larger context of Alliance aims.

The scholarship on southern women in agrarian dissent remains small and tied to individual states. Perhaps the most cited article on southern Alliance women is that of Julie Roy Jeffrey, "Women in the Southern Farmers' Alliance: A Reconsideration of the Role and Status of Women in the Late Nineteenth-Century South" (1975), in which she focuses on North Carolina women to argue that they embraced the suffragist demand for the vote.[24] Although Connie Lester found little support for suffrage among Tennessee Alliance women, they nevertheless expressed a determination to be recognized as partners in their family farms and, as such, rightful members of the organization. As the Tennessee Alliance became more involved in politics, the Alliance women disappeared from the public sphere. [25] Marion Barthelme compiled 180 letters written by Texas women to the *Southern Mercury,* the official newspaper of the Texas Alliance and Populist Party, that provide a powerful and insightful view of rural women at the moment of agrarian dissent.[26] Though dealing with women in widely differing southern states, each of the scholars demonstrated the complexity of rural life for farm women and their commitment to reform.

Like women, African American farmers and laborers were often omitted from the political histories of agrarian dissent. In addition, similar to farm women, blacks left little documentary evidence of their actions. Teasing out the history of the Colored Farmers Alliance and black Populism requires considerable research in multiple archives. Gerald H. Gaither wrote the seminal work on black Populism, *Blacks and the Populist Revolt: Ballots and Bigotry in the "New South"* (1977), in which he explored the tension between Populist rhetoric and political expediency. Populist "intellectual and ideological foundations combined . . . the idea of the social gospel and . . . the idea of a social democracy . . . recognizing no race or regional boundaries." However, Populism harbored two distinct racial attitudes: economic and political reform, in which blacks would benefit, and social inequality, in which blacks were inherently morally and intellectually incapable of equality. As white Populists negotiated the conflicts between their ideological positions, they laid the groundwork for the twentieth-century southern doctrine of separate but equal.[27] More recently Omar H. Ali has analyzed black Populism on its own terms and as a vehicle for understanding the "role of African Americans *in* the Populist movement."[28] His research points to earlier fraternal and religious organization among African Americans to argue that black farmers likewise pushed for economic and political reforms and "established third parties alongside white Populists, ran insurgent and independent candidates for office, and created fusion and coalitional campaigns."[29]

The people who joined agrarian dissent and the Populist Party did so through kinship and friendship networks, often as members of the same church. They saw themselves as political and social activists with deep roots in the religious life of the rural South.[30] As Robert McMath noted, "The structures and beliefs of evangelical Protestantism provided crucial elements of the Populists' 'repertoire,' as did other reform and self-help organizations that often knit together in communities by threads of kinship and neighborhood."[31] Alliancemen and Populists used the language of religion to express their dismay with the effects of industrial capitalism, demanding an economy that conformed to the "Golden Rule" and condemning the "booms" that came at the expense of labor. Rural churches provided the physical space for Alliance and Populist meetings, and agrarian rallies were reminiscent of religious revivals and church "dinners-on-the-ground."[32]

Like local churches, rural schoolhouses provided convenient spaces for meetings and rallies. From its inception, the Farmers' Alliance opened membership to rural teachers and mounted a significant campaign to further rural education, fighting for uniform textbooks and courses in agriculture. As Theodore Mitchell observed, the Alliance followed in the footsteps of earlier organizations like the Grange and the Agricultural Wheel in fostering adult education through the activities of local and state lecturers, organizational newspapers and support for Farmers' Institutes. Farmers were versed in new agricultural methods and in civic engagement. They were encouraged to read and to speak publicly in defense of agrarian interests.[33] This early educational organization laid important groundwork for the Country Life movement's educational efforts, the creation of agricultural high schools and extension service work.

Although the Farmers' Alliance adopted a policy of nonpartisanship, offering support to candidates from either major party who measured up to the "Alliance Yardstick," farmers played an increasingly important role in state and national politics. In the 1888 and 1890 elections, alliances elected state legislators, governors and congressmen. As we have already seen, C. Van Woodward interpreted these gains as evidence of discontent with the Bourbon Democrats and the initiation of a New South, while Lawrence Goodwyn saw the political chaos as grassroots democracy in action. However, as a number of state political histories show, despite impressive electoral gains, the ability to enact the list of Alliance reform demands was mixed. In the 1892 elections, Bourbon Democrats worked to oust their opponents from the party and the statehouse. While some Alliancemen willingly moved from the "party of the fathers" to the newly formed People's Party, others renounced their dissent and remained with the Democrats.

Historian James M. Beeby argues that the way "Populism played out on the ground was informed as much by local realities as by lofty political ideals and national platforms."[34] A brief survey of state histories of Populism in the South demonstrates both the importance of local, social, and political circumstances and the universality of southern conflicts over power and race. In 1969, Sheldon Hackney produced a study of Alabama Populists and Progressives that challenged perceived wisdom that "Progressivism was simply Populism that had 'shaved its whiskers, washed its shirt, put on a derby, and moved up into the middle class.'"[35] Instead, Hackney argued that, in Alabama, the two groups of activists were unrelated. Populists engaged in power struggles against the Bourbon Democrats and avoided national issues like railroad rates, while Progressives were more urban "Roosevelt" than rural "Bryan" in their reform activities.

Samuel Webb challenged Hackney's interpretation of Alabama's Populist experience and its legacy. In *Two-Party Politics in the One-Party South* (1997), Webb argues that the conventional view of post–Civil War white southerners as politically wedded to Democratic politics does not apply to Alabama's multiparty system. Focusing on raucous north Alabama, Webb concludes that the collapse of the Populist Party sent dissidents into a reform-minded Republican Party.[36]

Barton C. Shaw's scholarship on Georgia Populists demonstrates the inherent tension within the Alliance political efforts and the People's Party that followed. In order to challenge successfully the structures of power, white farmers had to make common cause with black farmers. However, courting the black vote risked losing potential white support. Populists throughout the South faced the same challenge everywhere that black and white Populists campaigned together. Nevertheless, as the Georgia study shows, Populists, like other white voters, retained their racism and used terror and intimidation to control votes despite their cries for an honest ballot.[37]

Finally, no discussion of state Populism in the South would be complete without mentioning North Carolina, where fusion with Republicans provided a strong statewide reform movement that lasted into the early twentieth century. As Populist historian James

Beeby wrote, "From 1894 to 1897, North Carolina witnessed nothing short of a political revolution, as the reformers liberalized the state election laws, passed a whole host of reform legislation in the state assembly, and elected hundreds of local, state, and federal office-holders."[38] The failure to entrench Populism as a reform alternative in North Carolina politics rested on a complex mix of local factors, but most importantly was influenced by the state Democratic Party's concerted effort to disfranchise African American voters, who had joined with Populists and reform Republicans to capture state government. Populists everywhere recognized the threat that the new laws making their way through southern legislatures posed. Not only were blacks disfranchised, but white votes were reduced dramatically and governance of the South fell into the hands of an elite few.[39]

The most recent generation of historians has dealt with the legacy of Populism. Their scholarship demonstrates the persistence of the Populist "vision" in the progressive reforms of the twentieth century as well as the diversity of Populism's adherents. Having been forcibly ejected from the political process, the tenets of Populism reappeared in the early twentieth century through new agricultural organizations and government agencies. As Connie Lester demonstrated in her study of Tennessee Populists, many joined the more commercial agriculture-minded Farmers' Union after 1905, worked closely with land-grant institutions, accepted positions with the state agricultural regulatory agencies and rose to the highest levels of state agricultural commissions. More regional and national in their efforts, these rural reformers could be found in influential positions in several states over the course of their careers. On the national level, they were appointed to various federal commissions to investigate farm issues, testify before congress, and assist in the development of laws. The persistence of Populist views can be seen in their efforts to effect change, not as elected officials, but as insiders in the new state and federal bureaucracies.[40]

Elizabeth Sanders shows the influence of Populism and Bryan Democracy in the Progressive era more dramatically in her carefully researched study of congressional voting. In *Roots of Reform:*

Farmers, Workers, and the American State 1877-1917 (1999), Sanders
argues that

> agrarian movements constituted the most important political force
> driving the development of the American national state in the half
> century before World War I. And by shaping the form or early
> regulatory legislation and establishing the centrality of the farmer-
> labor alliance to progressive reform and the Democratic Party, the
> agrarian influence was felt for years thereafter.[41]

Sanders connects the demands of the Populists with the legislation of the Progressive era in an accessible and compelling argument. Using the core-periphery model to organize congressional
districts by economic production, she analyzes the votes on key
pieces of legislation on transportation, banking, antitrust, education, and labor. In the case of the Federal Reserve Act, for example,
she argues that the public control and decentralization represented
in the regional banks represented a triumph for agrarian reformers against the greater centralization demanded by capitalist elites.
Sanders acknowledges that agrarians failed to establish the sustain-
able farmer-worker organization they sought, but they continued
to influence legislative action well into the twentieth century and
shaped the regulatory power of the state to maintain decentralized
market conditions that would "yield a more just and broadly pros-
perous society."[42]

With the defeat of William Jennings Bryan in the 1896 presidential election, the future of the Populist Party ended, although
Populists in some southern states continued to run and be elected
to office as independents, fusion candidates, or Republicans. Their
influence as elected representatives quickly waned, but the demands made by Alliancemen and Populists were incorporated into
Progressive-era and New Deal legislation. Historians writing in the
first decade of the twenty-first century built on the voluminous
historiography on Populism to understand the influence of Populism.[43] Together they saw the Populists not as the last gasp of the
nineteenth century, but as shapers of the twentieth century. They

argued from different perspectives—Alliancemen and Populist embedded in agricultural bureaucracies, land-grant universities, and the extension service influenced agricultural policy from inside; U.S. senators from farm states were in a strategic position to influence Progressive era federal legislation; farmers who joined the Colored Farmers Alliance and supported Populism laid important groundwork for black political activism in the face of segregation and disfranchisement; and the intellectual foundations of Populism offered long-term challenges to industrial capitalism. Collectively they argued for a longer view of Populism that did not end in 1896, but rather found its place of influence in the emerging social, intellectual, and political realities of modern America.

NOTES

1. Norman Pollack, *The Humane Economy: Populism, Capitalism, and Democracy* (New Brunswick, N.J.: Rutgers Univ. Press, 1990).

2. N. A. Dunning, *The Farmers' Alliance History and Agricultural Digest* (Washington, D.C.: Farmers' Alliance, 1889); W. Scott Morgan, *History of the Wheel and Alliance and the Impending Revolution* (Hardy, Ark., 1889). Kansan William A. Peffer, one of six Populists elected to the Senate, published his own history of the movement in 1899. William A. Peffer, *Populism: Its Rise and Fall,* ed. Peter H. Argersinger (1899; repr., Lawrence: Univ. Press of Kansas, 1992).

3. Robert C. McMath Jr., "Politics Matters: John D. Hicks and the History of Populism," *Agricultural History* 82, no. 1 (Winter 2008): 2.

4. John D. Hicks, *The Populist Revolt: The Farmers' Alliance and the People's Party* (1931; repr., Minneapolis: Univ. of Minnesota Press, 1955). For critiques of Hicks's book, see Martin Ridge, "Populism Redux: John D. Hicks and the Populist Revolt," *Reviews in American History* 13 (Mar. 1985): 142-54.

5. Richard Hofstadter, *The Age of Reform: From Bryan to FDR* (New York: Vintage, 1955).

6. Lawrence Goodwyn, *Democratic Promise: The Populist Moment in America* (New York: Oxford Univ. Press, 1976).

7. For critiques of Populist historiography, see Robert C. McMath Jr., Peter H. Argersinger, Connie L. Lester, Michael F. Magliari, and Walter Nugent, "Agricultural History Roundtable on Populism," *Agricultural History* 82, no. 1 (Winter 2008): 1-35; Worth Robert Miller, "A Centennial Historiography of American Populism," *Kansas History: A Journal of the Central Plains* 16

(Spring 1993): 54-69; William F. Holmes, "Populism in Search of Context," *Agricultural History* 64 (Fall 1990): 26-58.

8. Charles Postel, *Populist Vision* (New York: Oxford Univ. Press, 2007).

9. Ibid., viii.

10. Among the histories of the Farmers' Alliance and Populism that inform current scholarship, see Bruce Palmer, *"Man Over Money": The Southern Populist Critique of American Capitalism* (Chapel Hill: Univ. of North Carolina Press, 1980); Norman Pollack, *The Humane Economy: Populism, Capitalism and Democracy* (New Brunswick, N.J.: Rutgers Univ. Press, 1990); Michael Kazin, *The Populist Persuasion: An American History* (New York: Basic Books, 1995); Steve Leikin, *The Practical Utopians: American Workers and the Cooperative Movement in the Gilded Age* (Detroit: Wayne State Univ. Press, 2005); Glenda Elizabeth Gilmore, *Gender and Jim Crow: Women and the Politics of White Supremacy in North Carolina, 1896-1920* (Chapel Hill: Univ. of North Carolina Press, 1996); Elisabeth S. Clemens, *The People's Lobby: Organizational Innovation and the Rise of Interest Group Politics in the United States, 1890-1925* (Chicago: Univ. of Chicago Press, 1997); Peter H. Argersinger, *The Limits of Agrarian Radicalism: Western Populism and American Politics* (Lawrence: Univ. Press of Kansas, 1995).

11. Roger Ransom and Richard Sutch, *One Kind of Freedom: The Economic Consequences of Emancipation* (Cambridge: Cambridge Univ. Press, 1977). See also Ransom and Sutch, "Capitalists without Capital: The Burden of Slavery and the Impact of Emancipation," *Agricultural History* 62 (1988): 133-60; Ransom and Sutch, "Debt Peonage in the Cotton South after the Civil War," *Journal of Economic History* 32 (1972): 641-99.

12. David Silkenat, "'Hard Times is the Cry': Debt in Populist Thought in North Carolina," in *Populism in the South Revisited: New Interpretations and New Departures,* ed. James M. Beeby (Jackson: Univ. Press of Mississippi, 2012), 101.

13. Pete R. Daniel, *The Shadow of Slavery: Peonage in the South, 1901-1969* (1972; repr., Urbana: Univ. of Illinois Press, 1990).

14. Statistics from Gary M. Walton and Hugh Rockoff, *History of the American Economy* (Toronto: Nelson Thompson Learning, 2002), 343, derived from *Historical Statistics* (Washington, D.C.: Government Printing Office, 1960), series Q15, 49-50.

15. William Cronon, *Nature's Metropolis: Chicago and the Great West* (New York: W. W. Norton, 1991).

16. Anne Mayhew, "A Reappraisal of the Causes of Farm Protest in the United States, 1870-1900," *Journal of Economic History* 61 (1972): 463-75.

17. C. Vann Woodward, *Tom Watson, Agrarian Rebel* (New York: Macmillan, 1938).

18. Robert C. McMath Jr., *Populist Vanguard: A History of the Southern Farmers Alliance* (Chapel Hill: Univ. of North Carolina Press, 1975).

19. Robert C. McMath Jr., *American Populism: A Social History, 1877-1898* (New York: Hill and Wang, 1978).

20. Steven Hahn, *The Roots of Southern Populism: Yeoman Farmers and the Transformation of the Georgia Upcountry, 1850-1890* (New York: Oxford Univ. Press, 1985).

21. James Turner, "Understanding Populists," *Journal of American History* 67 (1980): 354-73.

22. McMath, *American Populism,* 17.

23. Annie L. Diggs, "The Women in the Alliance Movement," *The Arena* 6 (July 1892): 161-79.

24. Julie Roy Jeffrey, "Women in the Southern Farmers' Alliance: A Reconsideration of Their Role and Status in the Late Nineteenth-Century South," *Feminist Studies* 3 (1975): 72-91.

25. Connie L. Lester, "'Let Us Be Up and Doing': Women in the Tennessee Movements for Agrarian Reform, 1870-1892," *Tennessee Historical Quarterly* 54 (1995): 80-97.

26. Marion K. Barthelme, *Women in the Texas Populist Movement: Letters to the* Southern Mercury (College Station: Texas A&M Univ. Press, 1997).

27. Gerald H. Gaither, *Blacks and the Populist Revolt: Ballots and Bigotry in the "New South"* (Tuscaloosa: Univ. of Alabama Press, 1977), 131-33.

28. Omar H. Ali, "Reconceptualizing Black Populism in the New South," in *Populism in the South Revisited: New Interpretations and New Departures,* ed. James M. Beeby (Jackson: Univ. Press of Mississippi, 2012), 138. See also Ali, *In the Lion's Mouth: Black Populism in the New South, 1886-1900* (Jackson: Univ. Press of Mississippi, 2010); Steven Hahn, *A Nation under Our Feet: Black Political Struggles in the Rural South from Slavery to the Great Migration* (Cambridge, Mass.: Harvard Univ. Press, 2003).

29. Ali, "Reconceptualizing Black Populism in the New South," 136.

30. Joe Creech, *Righteous Indignation: Religion and the Populist Revolution* (Urbana: Univ. of Illinois Press, 2006).

31. McMath, *Populist Vanguard,* 64-76.

32. See Connie L. Lester, *Up from the Mudsills of Hell: The Farmers' Alliance, Populism, and Progressive Agriculture in Tennessee, 1870-1915* (Athens: Univ. of Georgia Press, 2006), chap. 3; Richard C. Goode, "The Godly Insurrection in Limestone County: Social Gospel, Populism, and Southern Culture in the Late Nineteenth Century," *Religion and Culture* (1992): 155-69.

33. Theodore R. Mitchell, *Political Education in the Southern Farmers' Alliance, 1877-1900* (Madison: Univ. of Wisconsin Press, 1987).

34. James M. Beeby, ed., *Populism in the South Revisited: New Interpretations and New Departures* (Jackson: Univ. Press of Mississippi, 2012), ix.

35. Sheldon Hackney, *Populism to Progressivism in Alabama* (Princeton, N.J.: Princeton Univ. Press, 1969), quotation, ix.

36. Samuel L. Webb, *Two-Party Politics in the One-Party South* (Tuscaloosa: Univ. of Alabama Press, 1997).

37. Barton C. Shaw, *The Wool-Hat Boys: Georgia's Populist Party* (Baton Rouge: Louisiana State Univ. Press, 1984).

38. James Beeby, "'[T]he Angels from Heaven Had Come Down and Wiped Their Names off the Registration Books': The Demise of Grassroots Populism in North Carolina," in Beeby, *Populism in the South Revisited*, 179. For other works on North Carolina Populism, see Beeby, *Revolt of the Tar Heels: The North Carolina Populist Movement, 1890-1901* (Jackson: Univ. Press of Mississippi, 2008), and James L. Hunt, *Marion Butler and American Populism* (Chapel Hill: Univ. of North Carolina Press, 2003).

39. For scholarship on disfranchisement, see J. Morgan Kousser, *The Shaping of Southern Politics: Suffrage Restriction and the Establishment of the One-Party South, 1880-1910* (New Haven, Conn.: Yale Univ. Press, 1974), and Michael Perman, *Struggle for Mastery: Disenfranchisement in the South, 1888-1908* (Chapel Hill: Univ. of North Carolina Press, 2001).

40. Lester, *Up from the Mudsills of Hell*, 231-49.

41. Elizabeth Sanders, *Roots of Reform: Farmers, Workers, and the American State, 1877-1917* (Chicago: Univ. of Chicago Press, 1999), 1.

42. Ibid., 4. For more on the labor in the South in the Populist era, see Matthew Hild, *Greenbackers, Knights of Labor, and Populists: Farmer-Labor Insurgency in the Late-Nineteenth Century South* (Athens: Univ. of Georgia Press, 2007).

43. See especially Lester, *Up from the Mudsills of Hell*; Sanders, *Roots of Reform*; Ali, "Reconceptualizing Black Populism in the New South"; Postel, *Populist Vision*.

CHAPTER FOUR

Lynching and Racial Violence in the New South

SARAH L. SILKEY

Following the social and economic devastation of the Civil War, southern leaders sought to court investors and smooth lingering sectional divisions by reinventing their communities. Through their efforts, the former Confederate states were reborn as the "New South," a fertile ground poised to become a vital participant in the national economy. In a period of violent labor conflicts and intense immigration from southern and eastern Europe, New South leaders promised investors a willing, English-speaking labor force for infrastructural and industrial development. To deliver on these promises, they needed to reestablish control of a pliant labor force in the wake of emancipation. Consequently, white southerners employed racial violence coupled with a system of codified segregation to help secure this New South vision.

Racial violence in the New South embraced many forms, ranging from the institutional violence of the convict lease system to individual acts of economic reprisal, sexual assault, beating, arson, torture, and murder. As Herbert Shapiro argues in *White Violence and Black Response: From Reconstruction to Montgomery* (1988), although only a small proportion of incidents were recorded, white supremacist violence and intimidation formed a "central ingredient of the Afro-American experience" that "constituted an ever-present reality in practically every black community."[1] Each act of violence made a direct impact on the individuals targeted, carried repercussions for their friends and families, and served as a warning to the broader community. These methods of direct and indirect coercion reinforced the political, social, and economic boundaries that supported and maintained white supremacy.

Due to the availability of rich sources and the publicity generated by early civil rights activists and antilynching reformers, scholarship on racial violence in the New South has focused primarily on the problem of lynching. Unlike most sexual assaults, beatings, and other forms of individual violent crime, incidents of mob violence received prominent national and international press coverage and frequently revealed the boundaries and tensions between government authority and popular will. While at times such violent social ruptures have been viewed in positive ways, widespread tolerance of mob violence could also threaten to dangerously undercut the authority of the modern state to control "the legitimate use of physical force."[2] To resolve this conflict, Americans popularly adopted the term "lynching" to identify specific acts of mob violence as acceptable forms of extralegal justice, developing a series of narratives to defend their right to operate outside the legal system.

Initially, American apologists argued that lynching was necessitated by the lack of security and established legal systems in frontier communities. In light of the rapid expansion of white settlements throughout the South, Midwest, and West, this romantic notion of "frontier justice" was quickly accepted and permeated American popular culture. While punishments dealt out by "lynch courts" ranged from public humiliation to torture and execution, the authority of the mob hinged on the assertion that its victims were guilty of transgressions against the broader community.[3]

Although romanticized notions of frontier justice continue to persist in American popular culture, by the end of the nineteenth century the term "lynching" became inextricably linked with acts of mob violence targeting African American men accused of raping white women. In order for the public to accept this "lynching for rape" narrative, white southerners established a "new fear, the fear of the Negro as rapist."[4] Criminalizing interracial sexual contact through antimiscegenation laws, they designated white women's sexuality as the sole preserve of white men and perpetuated myths about black inferiority and criminality. The economic benefits of forced labor for state infrastructure projects and private industry provided additional incentives to connect black men with criminality. Southern state legislatures and local communities passed laws criminalizing vagrancy, trespassing, and petty theft with disproportionate fines and sentencing to send a steady supply of cheap black labor into debt peonage and the convict lease system. As Douglas A. Blackmon details in *Slavery by Another Name: The Re-Enslavement of Black Americans from the Civil War to World War II* (2008), American corporations such as U.S. Steel profited greatly from the toil of "thousands of random indigent citizens" captured "under the thinnest chimera of probable cause or judicial process" in waves "attuned to rises and dips in the need for cheap labor."[5] Arrest and conviction rates for black men and teenage boys rose dramatically, further reinforcing the negative stereotypes of black criminality that fed the myth of the "black beast."

Armed with this seemingly irrefutable data, white southerners created the system of Jim Crow segregation laws to "protect" white women by socially and physically isolating them from black men. Depicted as brutes, black men who violated the boundaries of segregation could invoke the wrath of the state or the mob. Thus, through legal and extralegal means, white men claimed to be protectors of white womanhood. But as Jacqueline Dowd Hall observes, there was a "trade-off implicit in the code of chivalry, for the right of the southern lady to protection presupposed her obligation to obey." Black women, in contrast, were not considered delicate enough to warrant the protection of white men and, kept vulnerable by these systems, faced a range of abuses. Overall, segregation served as a useful system for controlling African Americans and educated middle-class white women, inhibiting them from embracing new opportunities for independence realized by their northern counterparts.[6]

Watching their opportunities for advancement close, educated middle-class African Americans fought for full citizenship rights using a wide array of tactics. They asserted their status as respectable ladies and gentlemen by adopting formal titles of address (i.e., Mr., Miss, and Mrs.) and using first-class public transportation; maintained their independence through political engagement and economic self-reliance; and sought justice by pursuing legal remedies to disputes and resorting to armed self-defense when denied protection.[7]

As a newspaper editor and civil rights activist, Ida B. Wells placed herself on the front lines of these struggles. Frequently serving as a lens for observing larger cultural issues and social trends, Wells's life, civil rights activism, and rhetorical attacks on lynching and white supremacy have attracted significant scholarly attention.[8] After losing her press to a Memphis mob in retaliation for her outspoken denunciation of the lynching-for-rape narrative, Wells traveled to England in 1893 and 1894 to cultivate British moral indignation against the lynching of African Americans in the United States. She collected clippings from white newspaper reports and employed statistical analysis to debunk the popular myth that lynching was employed primarily to punish black rapists of white women, demonstrating that southern communities claimed a wide range of motivations for the use of mob violence. Through her newspaper editorials, published pamphlets, and public lectures, Wells redefined lynching as racial violence wielded to solidify white supremacy. She accused white southerners of manipulating the myth of the black beast to hide their true purposes: to eliminate problematic individuals from their communities and to suppress broader African American economic, social, and political advancement. Ultimately, Wells concluded, the terror of mob violence would persist as long as popular sentiment tolerated the practice of denying suspected black offenders due process.[9]

Occurring during the intense social and political upheaval of the 1890s, Wells's activism polarized contemporary public debates about lynching and racial violence through her outspoken rhetoric and transnational tactics. Although other social and political leaders—black and white—worked to suppress mob violence, Wells quickly became the most prominent antilynching campaigner of the late nineteenth century and set the groundwork for future analysis by racializing lynching discourse and employing new social science techniques to support her interpretation.[10] Despite disagreeing with Wells's transnational campaign strategies, James E. Cutler's seminal 1905 study, *Lynch Law: An Investigation into the History of Lynching in the United States,* embraced her framework, defining lynching as "an illegal and summary execution at the hands of a mob or a number of persons, who have in some degree the public opinion of the community behind them," and employing statistical analysis to determine the root causes of lynching.[11] According to Christopher Waldrep, "in basing her approach to lynching on statistics, Wells permanently associated lynching studies with social science positivism" and established a definition of lynching as "community-sponsored murder" that continues to inform modern scholarship.[12]

While her work focused much needed attention on the impact of racial violence on African Americans, Wells's campaign failed to sever the public perception that lynching occurred in response to criminal activity; damaging stereotypes of black-male criminality continued to influence public debates and scholarship in the twentieth century. While Cutler opposed mob violence, he concluded that lynching persisted not because African Americans were denied due process, but because the judicial system had not made "special provision for the control of the negro population in the Southern States" as a "race of inferior civilization."[13] In his 1918 polemic defending mob violence, *The Truth about Lynching and the Negro in the South: In Which the Author Pleads That the South Be Made Safe for the White Race,* Winfield H. Collins argued that southern whites resorted to lynching "as an indirect act of self-defense against" an "abnormally criminal Negro race" that remained immune to punishments delayed by legal due process.[14] The association of lynching with extralegal justice made it difficult to divorce the problem of mob violence from assumptions of black-male criminality. High rates of criminal conviction reinforced these damaging assumptions; however, as Mary Ellen Curtin explains in *Black Prisoners and Their World, Alabama, 1865-1900* (2000), rather than revealing greater levels of criminal behavior, "the extraordinarily high number of black prisoners" reflected the "disproportionate effort to control black citizens" and the inability of those facing fines "to pay their own way out of the system because of severely limited economic opportunity."[15]

Searching for strategies to establish law and order, early twentieth-century social scientists documented lynching incidents and employed statistical analysis to quantify lynching rates and identify contributing factors behind the prevalence of American mob violence. The statistics relied upon by Wells and other antilynching activists from the 1880s until the early 1900s were diligently compiled by the *Chicago Tribune.* After Monroe Work joined its administration in 1908, the Tuskegee Institute surpassed the *Chicago Tribune* as the leading authority on lynching statistics. Frustrated by the unwillingness of local juries to indict and convict lynchers under state laws, the National Association for the Advancement of Colored People (NAACP) began to collect its own statistics to support its campaign to pass federal antilynching legislation.[16] In its 1919 compilation of lynching reports and statistics, *Thirty Years of Lynching in the United States, 1889-1918,* the NAACP built a case for federal intervention, arguing that the crisis of mob violence targeting African Americans in the South continued unabated even as lynching rates declined in the North and West.[17] Using his fair complexion to "pass" for white, Walter White gathered evidence in cases of peonage, lynchings, and race riots as an undercover investigator for the NAACP. In 1929, he published *Rope and Faggot: A Biography of Judge Lynch* based on this research. Echoing Wells's investigation thirty-five years earlier, White provided statistical evidence demonstrating that less than 30 percent of all lynching cases were connected to accusations of sexual assault and concluded that white southerners used mob violence to maintain control of black labor.[18]

In response to a wave of high-profile lynching cases amid the social and economic upheaval of the Great Depression, the Commission on Interracial Cooperation established the Southern Commission on the Study of Lynching, which produced a flurry of sociological studies by southern white scholars in the early 1930s, including James H. Chadbourn's *Lynching and the Law* and Arthur F. Raper's *The Tragedy of Lynching,* both published in 1933. Exploring options for legal recourse against lynchers, Chadbourn's analysis revealed that less than 1 percent of all twentieth-century lynching cases resulted in successful conviction of mob participants. Documenting case studies and statistics on lynching dating back to the 1880s, Raper critiqued southern complicity in mob violence at all levels of society, including law enforcement officials.[19] Mid-century scholars and reformers established a periodization of the phenomenon spanning the early 1880s through the 1930s based on a limited pool of shared lynching data. They identified the 1890s—famously dubbed "the nadir" of race relations by Rayford W. Logan—as the "peak" of the lynching crisis, while the 1930s represented the crucial turning point of modernization and growing public intolerance for the American lynching tradition.[20] The parameters they established shaped the questions pursued by later scholarship.

Reductions in lynching rates in the twentieth century were accomplished in part by resorting to an accelerated form of due process. By expediting the arrest, trial, conviction, and legal execution of black men accused of rape or murder, state and local authorities hoped to circumvent the lynching impulse by demonstrating that successful convictions and executions were assured. In some cases, communities completed the entire process in less than a week.[21] This practice, famously dubbed "legal lynching" by the Communist-backed International Labor Defense (ILD), came under national and international scrutiny during the infamous Scottsboro trials of the 1930s, when the NAACP and ILD transformed the plight of nine black teenage boys accused of raping two transient white women on a freight train into a cause célèbre.[22] The 1931 convictions were followed by more than six years of ensuing appeals, during which the NAACP and ILD competed to represent the "Scottsboro Boys" in both the law courts and the court of public opinion. Scholars have examined the media coverage and larger cultural impacts of the cases as well as the legal precedents set by the Scottsboro appeals and similar cases in other states.[23] Richard C. Cortner sheds light on the federalization of due-process standards with his analysis of the 1934 case of three black sharecroppers arrested for murder, which led to the landmark U.S. Supreme Court ruling, *Brown v.*

Mississippi (1936), prohibiting admission of coerced confessions in state criminal trials. Even when such damaging practices were abandoned and defendants were provided with appropriate due process, the legal system could still be used to enforce racial codes by allowing disproportionate sentencing of black men, as demonstrated by Eric W. Rise's study of the case of seven young black men executed for raping a thirty-two-year-old white woman in Martinsville, Virginia, in 1949.[24] Taken together, these case studies underscore the complex relationships between institutional and mob violence in maintaining white supremacy in the New South.

Successive waves of African American migration to industrial urban centers increased political and economic competition with white residents, creating tensions that sometimes ignited widespread mob violence directed against black communities. By curtailing black political, economic, and social advancement through racial terrorism, these "race riots" served a similar function as lynching in defending white supremacy. Likewise, these large-scale outbreaks of rape, murder, and arson were sometimes justified on the pretense of white outrage over supposed black criminality, particularly the rape or harassment of white women by black men. Determined to crush a successful interracial political coalition between white Populists and black Republicans, white rioters, inflamed by newspaper accounts of an alleged black crime wave, seized control of the streets and local government of Wilmington, North Carolina, prompting fourteen hundred black residents to flee the majority-black city in 1898. Similar exaggerated rumors about attacks by black men on white women inspired the 1906 riot in Atlanta, Georgia. In both cases, the riots ended in the consolidation of white political power, the solidification of segregation, and disruption of black social and economic aspirations.[25] As with lynching, local officials were complicit in some cases of violence. In 1921, while the National Guard disarmed and interned black residents, white residents of Tulsa, Oklahoma, were deputized and armed by local police to suppress a feared "negro uprising." Within twenty-four hours, at least fifty people were dead, most black residents were in custody, and more than one thousand black homes and businesses had burned to the ground in attacks coordinated by airplane.[26]

These patterns spread to communities across the country, with dramatic outbreaks of violence and intimidation following demobilization at the end of both world wars. During the infamous "Red Summer" of 1919, the ease with which dozens of communities embraced the tropes of racist violence demonstrated how fully racism had pervaded national culture. In some cases, race riots served as a form of ethnic or racial cleansing, eliminating thriving black communities, which never fully reformed. White residents then employed restrictive ordinances, threats, and violence to maintain cities and suburbs as all-white communities.[27] Riots in East St. Louis (1917), Chicago (1919), New York (1935), and Detroit (1943) led to official investigations by government-appointed riot commissions, but it required a subsequent wave of urban unrest in the 1960s to draw significant scholarly attention to these earlier outbreaks of racial violence.[28] Recent scholars have sought to assess the impact of race riots on local communities, including the mobilization or suppression of black activism.[29]

Because their efforts left behind substantial evidence, the work of antilynching activists and reform organizations became the subject of the first wave of modern historical scholarship on lynching. In her groundbreaking monograph, *Revolt against Chivalry: Jessie Daniel Ames and the Women's Campaign against Lynching* (1979), Jacqueline Dowd Hall documented the efforts of Jessie Daniel Ames and the Association of Southern Women for the Prevention of Lynching (ASWPL) in their twelve-year campaign to debunk the myth of the black rapist. Ames, who served as the director of woman's work for the Commission on Interracial Cooperation, launched the ASWPL in 1930, encouraging white middle-class southern women to "no longer remain silent in the face of this crime done in their name." Focusing the organization's campaign on the rural south, ASWPL members placed pressure on local law enforcement officials and worked to discourage public tolerance of mob violence on the local level, but eschewed federal intervention, ultimately limiting the scope of their influence.[30] Meanwhile, as Robert L. Zangrando demonstrates, the NAACP increasingly focused its efforts on the pursuit of federal antilynching legislation, making "considerable contributions to interracial justice" and placing "itself simultaneously in the vanguard of black activism and at the center of national affairs."[31]

Due to the challenges of uncovering appropriate sources for broader studies, historians initially turned to case studies of high-profile lynching incidents to analyze the contributing factors and responses to these acts of mob violence. In 1982, James R. McGovern presented the first modern monograph-length analysis of a single lynching, *Anatomy of a Lynching: The Killing of Claude Neal.* Accused of raping and murdering a young white woman, Claude Neal was seized from his jail cell, tortured, and hanged by a well-organized mob in Jackson County, Florida. The NAACP used the 1934 case to rally support for federal antilynching legislation. McGovern argues that "men become violent when they feel justified to do so and when they do not meet effective opposition" from the objects of their brutality. He concludes that the joint forces of urbanization and education in the twentieth century reduced the power of whites over local black populations, increasing the chances of repercussions for extralegal violence.[32] Howard Smead presented a similar case study, examining the 1959 lynching of Mack Charles Parker in Poplarville, Mississippi. Occurring during a period of intensifying civil rights activism and Cold War international scrutiny, the case attracted "an onslaught of adverse national and international publicity," prompting fears of federal intervention that led the citizens of Poplarsville to defiantly support the lynching after the fact. Despite FBI and Justice Department intervention and two grand jury hearings, no indictments or arrests were made. Nevertheless, Smead concludes, rural whites found it "increasingly difficult to get away with vigilante-style violence" by the end of the 1950s.[33] Examining another landmark case, Dominic J. Capeci Jr. argues that the 1942 lynching of Cleo Wright signified an important "transition of the Justice Department's role in civil rights," because it was the first lynching case to prompt federal indictments to prosecute mob participants on the basis of civil rights violations.[34] The work of these historians opened the door for additional explorations of both the local influences that precipitated individual incidents of mob violence and the long-term impact these events had on communities throughout the United States.[35]

Beginning in the 1990s, historians of mob violence increasingly turned their attention to state and regional studies, often relying on quantitative analysis to identify causal factors and establish profiles of counties, states, regions, or subregions that were most likely to experience high rates of lynching. In *The Promise of the New South: Life after Reconstruction* (1992), Edward L. Ayers concludes that lynchings were most likely to occur in rural areas of low population density with proportionately high rates of black population growth and were most likely to target African Americans who were unknown or recent arrivals to the area.[36] W. Fitzhugh Brundage's groundbreaking 1993 comparative study, *Lynching in the New South: Georgia and Virginia, 1880-1930,* examined spatial and temporal variations between Georgia and Virginia as representative Deep South and Upper South states, respectively, with exceptionally high and low rates of lynching. His analysis reveals that lynching "flourished" in plantation districts, "where sharecropping, monoculture agriculture, and a stark line separating white landowners and black tenants existed."[37] In *A Festival of Violence: An Analysis of Southern Lynchings, 1882-1930* (1995), economic historians Stewart E. Tolnay and E. M. Beck empirically tested theories that African Americans were more likely to be lynched when whites felt threatened "economically, politically, or socially." Through rigorous statistical analysis based on a database identifying 2,805 victims of southern lynch mobs killed during the "lynching era" (1880-1930), they dismiss theories that lynchings were motivated by political competition, waned in response to black disfranchisement, or answered perceived failings of the judicial system. Instead, they argue, lynching rates were most clearly tied to economic competition, as demonstrated by the cycles of the cotton market. "Blacks were most vulnerable," they conclude, "when lynching had the potential to benefit most of white society."

When cotton prices fell, lynching rates increased; and when the Great Migration threatened to remove the "supply of cheap and pliant labor" upon which their fortunes rested, elite southern whites rallied to suppress mob violence.[38] The broad trends in mob violence mapped by these scholars reveal that lynching remained an endemic problem of multiple causation. As Brundage concludes, variations in mob size, intent, character, and ritual practices reveal that "the complex and contradictory character of lynching" cannot be adequately explained by a single model.[39] Taken together, state and regional studies provide valuable insight into spatial and temporal variations in mob behavior; consequently, studies of racially targeted mob violence in southern states continue to flourish.[40]

Since statistical analysis cannot reveal the meaning of lynching for participants, scholars turned to cultural studies of racial violence to understand American tolerance and even celebration of lynching. Hall blames the rise of the black-beast mythology on the titillation provided by stories of rape, which supplied an "acceptable folk pornography," while Joel Williamson claims that southern whites cultivated the image of the black beast to alleviate feelings of economic and sexual inadequacy and assert white male supremacy. Trudier Harris argues that black authors sought to "exorcise" this mythology and remove fear from collective memory by replaying lynching violence through their writings. Grace Elizabeth Hale popularized the term "spectacle lynching" to describe ritualized acts of torture and extralegal execution performed in front of crowds of spectators, often numbering in the thousands, and culminating in photographic commemorations and the gruesome collection of artifacts. Hale asserts that these dehumanizing rituals "othered" African Americans to create a collective sense of "whiteness" and "southernness."[41] To establish their position on the white side of the black-white racial binary, European immigrants embraced these lynching rituals, which Orlando Patterson compares to acts of human sacrifice and ritualistic cannibalism.[42]

A series of exhibitions (2000-2002) of James Allen and John Littlefield's collection of lynching photographs and relics brought public and scholarly attention to the production of collective memory through the consumption of lynching artifacts, imagery, and stories.[43] Photography, Shawn Michelle Smith asserts, both documented lynching and "played a role in orchestrating it" by becoming part of the ritual for mob participants. James H. Madison scrutinizes the competing uses and interpretations of an iconic photograph taken after the 1930 lynching of Abe Smith and Tom Shipp, two black teenagers accused of rape and murder in Marion, Indiana. Madison demonstrates how the public gaze in cultural memory shifted from the dead bodies, to the faces of the "shameless" white crowd, to the complicity of American silence against lynching.[44] Dora Apel examines the changing uses and meanings of lynching photographs to reveal how "images that initially evoked white pride" could "come to elicit outrage instead." The dissemination of new technologies like film and audio recording allowed audiences to engage with lynching in new ways. Amy Louise Wood explores the way photography and film influenced the rise and decline of public tolerance for mob violence as representations of lynching shifted from a vicarious celebration of white supremacy to a critical depiction of mob brutality that fueled antilynching activism. Examining media coverage and films depicting racial violence in the 1990s, Jonathan Markovitz argues that lynching continues to serve "as a metaphor for race relations more broadly defined" and as a "lens" for "understanding contemporary race relations."[45]

Seeking to craft a more sophisticated analysis of the problem, historians continue to expand the investigation of lynching by compiling new sources. The scarcity of lynching statistics and reports prior to the twentieth century encouraged many historians to focus initially on lynching as a southern issue after 1880, losing sight of the longer, broader history of mob violence in the United States. George C. Wright brought popular assumptions into question by asserting that lynchings occurred at higher rates during Reconstruction than any other period, including the traditionally accepted "peak" of lynchings during the 1890s. Questioning prevailing assumptions that the lethal targeting of African American victims was a post-Civil War phenomenon, Michael J. Pfeifer likewise advocates for the recovery of data on the lynching of slaves during the antebellum period.[46] Calls have been made to further such lines of inquiry by developing a reliable, comprehensive national database on American lynching.[47]

As the range of sources to investigate expands, historians continue to question why some circumstances led to lethal acts of mob violence while others did not. In some cases, armed resistance mounted by black residents or the intervention of mob participants, local officials, or white residents restrained mob violence. Margaret Vandiver calls for historians to examine such cases of "prevented lynchings" to reveal the full "complexity and contingency of mob violence." Following his previous partnership with Beck, Tolnay teamed up with Amy Kate Bailey to compile a substantial database of demographic profiles on southern lynching victims and comparable populations that were not lynched. While the profiles of lynch victims varied greatly, their analysis concluded that "social marginality *did* make African American men *more susceptible*" to lynching, especially in locations where the rest of the population held strong roots in the community; however, "local context mattered," and the degree of vulnerability experienced by individuals varied greatly. Whether they held low or high status, were well established in the community, or lived on the social margins, African American men were typically safest when they did not stand out from the crowd.[48]

Despite the important insights gained by historians and sociologists, the value of statistical analysis has been questioned because the process by which incidents of lynching were typically identified lacked social scientific rigor. As Waldrep has observed, tabulation of lynching rates relied on local reporters to label particular acts of mob violence as lynchings, press-clipping services to forward these reports, and for the editors at the *Chicago Tribune,* social scientists at the Tuskegee Institute, or activists at the NAACP to have deemed the reports worthy of inclusion. As national and international pressure mounted to eradicate lynching in the early twentieth century, reform organizations with divergent political agendas competed to control the definition of lynching, further complicating the collection of lynching data. Because the meaning of the term has not remained static, Waldrep controversially concludes, "there is no single behavior that can be called 'lynching.'" Therefore, attempts by historians and sociologists to define and quantify lynching as a specific behavior will remain inherently flawed.[49]

Identifying lynching as a rhetorical construct, Waldrep challenged historians to reexamine primary sources to determine how the term "lynching" was used and understood by those who invoked it. Tracing the evolution of lynching rhetoric from its inception in the 1780s through Supreme Court nominee Clarence Thomas's famous 1991 accusation that he was subjected to a "high-tech lynching," Waldrep demonstrates in *The Many Faces of Judge Lynch: Extralegal Violence and Punishment in America* (2002) that "lynching has carried enormous political power," whether used "to indict a whole community or mobilize that community to violence." For example, western vigilance committees promoted lynching as a positive force, acting on behalf of the community to provide safety and justice in districts with weak or corrupt judicial systems. The success of this rhetoric, Waldrep argues, prevented opponents of racial violence from applying the term "lynching" to Ku Klux Klan terrorism during the turmoil of Reconstruction because doing so at that moment would have cast Klan members in a heroic light. Such rhetorical shifts and disconnects have obscured the historical continuities between western and southern practices that historians have been struggling to recover.[50]

Ashraf H. A. Rushdy and Lisa Arellano have expanded on Waldrep's work, examining the rhetoric used to legitimate mob violence, define "what constitutes a lynching," and identify who should be held "responsible" for lynching violence. As public tolerance for spectacle lynchings declined by the 1930s, the NAACP and ASWPL began to debate whether lynching violence had truly diminished or merely transformed into other forms of racial violence. Rushdy argues that activists, public officials, and scholars responding to this shift began to conceptualize the history of lynching as a linear progression, moving inevitably toward a conclusion. In anticipation of that moment, the desire to redeem the honor of the United States by declaring the "last American lynching" won out, and reformers struggled to determine how best to measure the "end of lynching,"

resulting in a narrow definition that largely excluded racially motivated killings and obscured the ongoing problem of racial violence.[51] Arellano focused her analysis on close textual readings of
"official vigilante histories," the work of early western historians,
and Wells's antilynching rhetoric. In order to court broad public support, lynchers depicted themselves as "ideal" vigilantes—upstand-
ing citizens acting on behalf and in defense of their communities in
a hostile environment without effective state support. Nineteenth-
century scholars like Hubert Howe Bancroft, Arellano contends,
consciously supported this positive spin in their interpretations of
western vigilantism. Seeking to dismantle this powerful narrative,
Wells depicted white mobs as "sadistic racists" who "enacted un-
speakable violence on southern black men for the exclusive purpose of expressing their social power." Wells's artful intervention
not only shaped modern understandings of lynching as racialized
violence, Arellano concludes, but also underscored the fundamental
and reinforcing narrative connections between southern and western mob violence.[52]

Recognizing connections between southern and western lynching, historians worked to expand the geographic focus of their investigations to recover the history of lynching and vigilantism in
the West, demonstrate the continuities in mob violence across regions, and broaden the study of lynching victims to include Mexicans, Native Americans, Asian Americans, and whites. William D.
Carrigan's study of the impact of collective memory on public tolerance for lynching in Central Texas demonstrated the importance
of local past experiences in establishing acceptance of vigilante violence as a positive force. Situated on the physical and cultural border between two regions, the historical memory of Central Texas
inherited both the racial tensions from the South and the glorifica-
tion of vigilante violence from the West. Brent M. S. Campney ex-
poses the history of racial violence in Kansas, revealing the array of
expressions of white-on-black violence used to enforce white supremacy and demonstrating that Reconstruction-era political, social, and economic tensions could be felt just as keenly in the West.
In his study of mob violence in California, Ken Gonzales-Day simi-

larly emphasizes the racial dynamics of western lynchings, which targeted Latinos, Native Americans, and Asian Americans in significant numbers.[53] Because the image of western vigilantism as frontier justice presupposes the criminality of the mob's victims, other possible underlying factors frequently have been ignored in discussions of western lynchings. In *Forgotten Dead: Mob Violence against Mexicans in the United States, 1848-1928* (2013), Carrigan and Clive Webb documented the cases of 547 Mexican lynching victims, revealing the racial and ethnic prejudices and economic competition that motivated these attacks, as well as the easily blurred distinctions between mob violence and state actions that led to the loss of countless additional lives. Mexicans resisted these attacks through armed self-defense, collective organization, and political propaganda. However, Carrigan and Webb credit the intervention of the Mexican government as a "decisive factor" in reducing public tolerance for the lynching of Mexicans by the 1920s—a recourse unavailable to their African American counterparts in the South.[54]

Moving beyond regional similarities, scholars have begun to view lynching as a national phenomenon with deep roots in American society. Stretching the periodization of their research to incorporate the colonial roots and national scope of mob violence, Waldrep and Manfred Berg have produced valuable syntheses tracing the evolution of American lynching.[55] Finding similar patterns in the Midwest, South, and West, Pfeifer characterizes late nineteenth-century popular support for "rough justice" as a "revolt against due-process reform" advocated by urban middle-class reformers that threatened to replace the system of legal localism embraced before the Civil War. The rural and working classes criticized the adversarial criminal justice system, with the limitations of codified law and due-process mechanisms. Seeking a compromise, Pfeifer concludes, early twentieth-century officials designed the modern death-penalty system to replace lynching by establishing more rigidly controlled and sanitized execution procedures, while still allowing harsh retribution against racial- and ethnic-minority offenders.[56] In refuting southern exceptionalism, these studies also bring American exceptionalism into question. Scholars have begun to interrogate Cutler's assertion that lynching is "peculiar to the United States" by examining the transmission of lynching rhetoric across national boundaries, transnational opposition to American lynching, and comparing American lynching to mob violence in other nations and historical periods.[57]

Scholars have also begun to examine more closely the role of women as instigators, participants, and apologists as well as victims, witnesses, and opponents of mob violence. Questioning the assumption that black men accused of raping white women were routinely denied due process, Diane Miller Sommerville, Martha Elizabeth Hodes, and Lisa Lindquist Dorr have crafted detailed studies of the complex racial, class, and gender dynamics that shaped legal and extralegal responses to sexual violence and the range of outcomes experienced by both victims and accused.[58] Seeking to challenge the traditional narrative of racial violence that "privileges the plight of African American men at the expense of erasing African American women from the historical record," scholars have examined black women's cultural responses to racial-sexual violence through literature, art, theater, music, and photography.[59] Kerry Segrave compiled a chronology of cases involving female lynching victims, while Julie Buckner Armstrong focused on the lasting cultural importance of Mary Turner, a pregnant twenty-one-year-old black woman whose brutal death and the destruction of her eight-month-old fetus were memorialized by black artists and antilynching activists during the struggle to pass the Dyer Antilynching Bill in 1922. Crystal Feimster's *Southern Horrors: Women and the Politics of Rape and Lynching* (2009) examines the lynching of black and white women against the backdrop of debates over the definition of southern womanhood. Comparing the ways both Wells and famed lynching proponent Rebecca Latimer Felton manipulated rape and lynching narratives, Feimster demonstrates how southern women—black and white—challenged the race and gender boundaries established to maintain white male supremacy in order to increase women's political empowerment.[60]

Although broader studies have noted the sexual abuse, coercion, and assault of black women by white men, the extent of that violence in the New South and the efforts of black women to claim their rights to protection and full citizenship have become the central focus of recent scholarship.[61] To excuse predation on black women and girls, southern slaveholders had routinely asserted that black women could not be raped, not only because they lacked the autonomy for refusal or consent as slaves, but also because they were presumed to be naturally promiscuous. Stereotypes of black hypersexuality persisted after emancipation, excusing white men's continued abuse of black women and the lynching of black men. By claiming respectability and sexual autonomy, black women simultaneously asserted their rights to protection and helped to undermine the myth of the black beast.[62] In *Terror in the Heart of Freedom: Citizenship, Sexual Violence, and the Meaning of Race in Postemancipation America* (2009), Hannah Rosen examines how freedwomen demanded federal recognition "as willful subjects capable of refusal or consent and as honorable women worthy of state protection from sexual abuse" amid the pervasive sexual violence committed by members of the Ku Klux Klan and other supporters of white supremacy during Reconstruction. The developing African American middle-class continued this struggle into the twentieth century. In *Redefining Rape: Sexual Violence in the Era of Suffrage and Segregation* (2013), Estelle B. Freedman traces the changing discourse on rape promoted by parallel black and white feminist movements to achieve full citizenship status in a power structure predicated on white male control over women's sexual availability. Danielle L. McGuire's *At the Dark End of the Street: Black Women, Rape, and Resistance—A New History of the Civil Rights Movement from Rosa Parks to the Rise of Black Power* (2010) traces the important role played by demands for the protection of black women's bodies in mobilizing and shaping the modern civil rights movement.[63]

The diversity of black resistance strategies against racial violence from the origins of the New South to the end of the twentieth century has received increasing scholarly attention. Rebecca N. Hill has traced the intersections between antilynching activism and labor-defense campaigns, revealing the common tactics and rhetorical constructs employed in these movements as well as public attitudes toward popular resistance that limited opportunities for black activism while glorifying white rebellion. In *African Americans Confront Lynching: Strategies of Resistance from the Civil War to the Civil Rights Era* (2009), Waldrep demonstrates the importance of constitutional principles—particularly the "ideal of due process and order promised in the U.S. Constitution"—in black social, political, and legal appeals for government protection against white violence ranging from lynching to hate crimes. In *They Left Great Marks on Me: African American Testimonies of Racial Violence from Emancipation to World War I* (2012), Kidada E. Williams documents the persistent resistance to racial violence that African Americans expressed through individual and collective testimonies presented in correspondence, black newspapers, and legal records. African American resistance assumed many forms, from showing deference to "white-supremacist racial decorum as a means of self-preservation," to open defiance through insolence, migration, armed self-defense, or other public rejections of white supremacy; these same patterns of resistance, Williams argues, were expressed by civil rights activists in the 1950s and 1960s.[64]

Although public tolerance for spectacular displays of racial violence declined dramatically after World War II, acts of racial violence and intimidation persisted. Mid-century racial violence continued the tradition of diffuse acts of physical and sexual violence, murder, economic reprisals, and threats perpetrated by police, mobs, and individuals to reinforce white supremacy. In 1940, the NAACP published a pamphlet, "Lynching Goes Underground: A Report on a New Technique," arguing that concerns over outside scrutiny prompted communities to commit acts of collective violence in secrecy. According to the report, shortly after questioning deductions from his wages, Joe Rodgers disappeared in Canton, Mississippi. When his naked, severely beaten body was later discovered in the Pearl River by authorities, the local press remained silent, concealing the mob murder and shielding the community from criticism.[65] After the kidnapping of fourteen-year-old Emmett Till in 1955, the sheriff conducted a "search along riverbanks and under bridges," customary steps "when something like that happened." Only the persistent efforts of Till's mother, Mamie Till Bradley, brought her son's violent death to the public's attention.[66] The bodies of three black men unexpectedly recovered from rivers in Mississippi during the search for missing civil rights workers James Chaney, Andrew Goodman, and Michael Schwerner in 1964 underscored the persistent threat of racially motivated killings. As Nick Kotz observes, "beyond any question, it was the disappearance of Schwerner and Goodman—the white northerners—that created the national stir," prompting the massive search that led to the discovery of these missing black men. Rather than becoming the victims of ritualized spectacles, African Americans were more likely to be beaten, murdered, or to simply "disappear" in the 1950s and 1960s.[67]

As the civil rights movement gained momentum in the 1960s, white supremacists employed dramatic acts of racial violence that eroded public tolerance, ultimately hastening the demise of segregation. "Substituting dynamite for the rope," white supremacists used explosives to terrorize African Americans in urban areas. Black homes near one white neighborhood were bombed so frequently that the area became known as "Dynamite Hill." In 1963, Ku Klux Klan members bombed the Sixteenth Street Baptist Church, which served as the headquarters for civil rights activism in Birmingham, Alabama. More than all the protests, marches, and demonstrations, Waldrep argues, the tragic deaths of four young girls in the bombing convinced many whites that segregation was immoral.[68] When Klan members murdered three civil rights workers ahead of the Mississippi Freedom Summer campaign the following year, pressure increased on the federal government to intervene. In the mid-1960s, the FBI and Department of Justice took an active interest in cases of terroristic racial violence, and southern juries began to convict perpetrators. Congress reinforced these trends, passing the Civil Rights Act of 1968, which defined most forms of racial violence and intimidation as federal crimes.[69]

By the 1980s, politicians sought to win political capital by introducing hate-crime legislation that treated acts of racial violence as "constitutional violations." By "twisting the old hatreds into new shapes," Waldrep argues, "hate-crime laws" recast lynching in terms of "individual misconduct, not the ills of society." Nevertheless, the transformation of public perceptions of racial violence from community-sanctioned "lynching" into "hate crimes" with individual responsibility opened the door for the prosecution of unsolved attacks on civil rights activists, like the 1994 conviction of Byron de la Beckwith for the 1963 murder of Medgar Evers.[70] Pursuing accountability through other means, Beulah Mae Donald filed a civil suit supported by the Southern Poverty Law Center and NAACP against the Ku Klux Klan for damages resulting from the 1981 murder of her son, Michael; the judgment against the United Klans of America drove the organization into bankruptcy in 1987.[71] Although incapable of addressing larger social structures propagating racial violence, repackaging lynching as hate crimes had opened new legal avenues for the suppression of mob violence.

Despite this progress, the historical culpability of law enforcement officials in tolerating and perpetuating racial violence still raises important questions about the disproportionate sentencing and levels of state-sanctioned violence directed toward African Americans and other minority groups; this disparity has become a defining characteristic of the American experiment in mass incarceration and the death-penalty system. Khalil Gibran Muhammad critiques the statistical "evidence" employed by white social scientists, reformers, and politicians in the early twentieth century to "corroborate their claims regarding black criminality" and "justify a range of discriminatory laws, first targeting blacks, then punishing them more harshly than whites." In *The Condemnation of Blackness: Race, Crime, and the Making of Modern Urban America* (2010), Muhammad concludes that these practices—the selection of racialized narratives to interpret social-scientific data—eventually rendered the racism inherent within the criminal justice system "invisible." As Michelle Alexander argues in *The New Jim Crow: Mass Incarceration in the Age of Colorblindness* (2010), the illusion of colorblind justice cultivated public support for mass incarceration and created a new "racial caste system" in an era when it was "no longer socially permissible" to "explicitly" discriminate on the basis of race. Once people of color have been labeled "criminals," discrimination in housing, employment, education, and social services—even disfranchisement—becomes legal, reinstating many of the restrictions on African American advancement originally imposed under Jim Crow segregation.[72]

While public sentiment has turned slowly away from celebrating open displays of racism, the long history of racial violence remains to be reconciled. A growing number of scholars have advocated for memorialization and the adoption of truth-and-reconciliation processes to come to terms with this difficult history and to heal communities where outbreaks of racial violence occurred.[73] As new scholarship recovers the more pervasive examples of and resistance to racial violence, a more inclusive history will form, shedding light on the myriad ways that violence has shaped the development of American society.

Notes

1. Herbert Shapiro, *White Violence and Black Response: From Reconstruction to Montgomery* (Amherst: Univ. of Massachusetts Press, 1988), xii.

2. Max Weber, *From Max Weber: Essays in Sociology,* ed. H. H. Gerth and C. Wright Mills (London: Routledge, 1991), 78; Manfred Berg and Simon Wendt, *Globalizing Lynching History: Vigilantism and Extralegal Punishment from an International Perspective* (New York: Palgrave Macmillan, 2011), 6-18.

3. On the evolution of lynching narratives, see Christopher Waldrep, *Many Faces of Judge Lynch: Extralegal Violence and Punishment in America* (New York: Palgrave MacMillan, 2002); Sarah L. Silkey, *Black Woman Reformer: Ida B. Wells, Lynching, and Transatlantic Activism* (Athens: Univ. of Georgia Press, 2015).

4. Joel Williamson, *The Crucible of Race: Black-White Relations in the American South since Emancipation* (New York: Oxford Univ. Press, 1984), 184.

5. Douglas A. Blackmon, *Slavery by Another Name: The Re-Enslavement of Black Americans from the Civil War to World War II* (New York: Anchor Books, 2008), 7. See also Pete Daniel, *The Shadow of Slavery: Peonage in the South, 1901-1969* (Urbana: Univ. of Illinois Press, 1972).

6. Jacquelyn Dowd Hall, *Revolt against Chivalry: Jessie Daniel Ames and the Women's Campaign against Lynching* (New York: Columbia Univ. Press, 1979), 151. For a defense of segregation as protection, see Winfield H. Collins, *The Truth about Lynching and the Negro in the South: In Which the Author Pleads That the South Be Made Safe for the White Race* (New York: Neale, 1918), 101-22. For a southern critique of the sex and gender implications of segregation, see Lillian Smith, *Killers of the Dream* (New York: W. W. Norton, 1949).

See also Glenda Elizabeth Gilmore, *Gender and Jim Crow: Women and the Politics of White Supremacy in North Carolina, 1896-1920* (Chapel Hill: Univ. of North Carolina Press, 1996); Crystal Feimster, *Southern Horrors: Women and the Politics of Rape and Lynching* (Cambridge, Mass.: Harvard Univ. Press, 2009); Estelle B. Freedman, *Redefining Rape: Sexual Violence in the Era of Suffrage and Segregation* (Cambridge, Mass.: Harvard Univ. Press, 2013).

7. See Shirley J. Carlson, "Black Ideals of Womanhood in the Late Victorian Era," *Journal of Negro History* 77 (Spring 1992): 61-73; Barbara Y. Welke, *Recasting American Liberty: Gender, Race, Law, and the Railroad Revolution, 1865-1920* (New York: Cambridge Univ. Press, 2001); James West Davidson, *"They Say": Ida B. Wells and the Reconstruction of Race* (New York: Oxford Univ. Press, 2009); Kidada E. Williams, *They Left Great Marks on Me: African American Testimonies of Racial Violence from Emancipation to World War I* (New York: New York Univ. Press, 2012).

8. Wells first attracted scholarly attention with the posthumous publication of her autobiography, Ida B. Wells-Barnett, *Crusade for Justice: The Autobiography of Ida B. Wells,* ed. Alfreda M. Duster (Chicago: Univ. of Chicago Press, 1970). Prominent biographies of Wells include Mildred I. Thompson, *Ida B. Wells-Barnett: An Exploratory Study of an American Black Woman, 1893-1930* (Brooklyn, N.Y.: Carlson Publishing, 1990); Linda O. McMurry, *To Keep the Waters Troubled: The Life of Ida B. Wells* (New York: Oxford Univ. Press, 1998); Patricia A. Schechter, *Ida B. Wells-Barnett and American Reform, 1880-1930* (Chapel Hill: Univ. of North Carolina Press, 2001); Paula Giddings, *Ida: A Sword among Lions* (New York: Amistad, 2008); Mia Bay, *To Tell the Truth Freely: The Life of Ida B. Wells* (New York: Hill and Wang, 2009).

9. Ida B. Wells, *Southern Horrors: Lynch Law in All Its Phases* (New York: New York Age, 1892); Wells, *A Red Record: Tabulated Statistics and Alleged Causes of Lynching in the United States* (Chicago: Donohue and Henneberry, 1895); Wells et al., *The Reason Why the Colored American is Not at the World's Columbian Exposition* (Chicago, 1893).

10. For an example of similar studies, see Robert C. O. Benjamin, *Southern Outrages: A Statistical Record of Lawless Doings* ([Los Angeles], 1894). For scholarship on other contemporary antilynching activists, see David F. Godshalk, "William J. Northen's Public and Personal Struggles against Lynching," in *Jumpin' Jim Crow: Southern Politics from Civil War to Civil Rights,* ed. Jane Dailey, Glenda Elizabeth Gilmore, and Bryant Simon (Princeton, N.J.: Princeton Univ. Press, 2000), 140-61; Christopher Waldrep, "'Raw, Quivering Flesh': John G. Cashman's 'Pornographic' Constitutionalism Designed to Produce an 'Aversion and Detestation,' 1883-1904," *American Nineteenth Century History* 6, no. 3 (Sept. 2005): 295-322.

11. James Elbert Cutler, *Lynch-Law: An Investigation into the History of Lynching in the United States* (London: Longmans, Green, and Co., 1905), 229-30, 276.

12. Christopher Waldrep, "War of Words: The Controversy over the Definition of Lynching, 1899-1940," *Journal of Southern History* 66 (Feb. 2000): 77.

13. Cutler, *Lynch-Law,* 224-25.

14. Collins, *Truth about Lynching,* 70-71.

15. Mary Ellen Curtin, *Black Prisoners and Their World* (Charlottesville: Univ. of Virginia Press, 2000), 80.

16. Waldrep, "War of Words," 78-79.

17. National Association for the Advancement of Colored People, *Thirty Years of Lynching in the United States, 1889-1918* (New York: NAACP, 1919), 8-9.

18. Walter Francis White, *Rope and Faggot: A Biography of Judge Lynch* (New York: A. A. Knopf, 1929).

19. James Harmon Chadbourn, *Lynching and the Law* (Chapel Hill: Univ. of North Carolina Press, 1933); Arthur F. Raper, *The Tragedy of Lynching* (Chapel Hill: Univ. of North Carolina Press, 1933). See also George Fort Milton, *Lynchings and What They Mean: General Findings of the Southern Commission for the Study of Lynching* (Atlanta: Southern Commission for the Study of Lynching, 1931).

20. Rayford W. Logan, *The Negro in American Life and Thought: The Nadir, 1877-1901* (New York: The Dial Press, 1954), 52.

21. For example, see the 1902 hanging of Jim Buchanan in Gary B. Borders, *A Hanging in Nacogdoches: Murder, Race, Politics, and Polemics in Texas's Oldest Town, 1870-1916* (Austin: Univ. of Texas Press, 2006).

22. Waldrep, *Many Faces of Judge Lynch,* 162-63.

23. See Dan T. Carter, *Scottsboro: A Tragedy of the American South* (Baton Rouge: Louisiana State Univ. Press, 1969); James Goodman, *Stories of Scottsboro* (New York: Pantheon Books, 1994); James R. Acker, *Scottsboro and Its Legacy: The Cases That Challenged American Legal and Social Justice* (Westport, Conn.: Praeger, 2008); James A. Miller, *Remembering Scottsboro: The Legacy of an Infamous Trial* (Princeton, N.J.: Princeton Univ. Press, 2009).

24. Richard C. Cortner, *A "Scottsboro" Case in Mississippi: The Supreme Court and* Brown v. Mississippi (Jackson: Univ. Press of Mississippi, 1986); Eric W. Rise, *The Martinsville Seven: Race, Rape, and Capital Punishment* (Charlottesville: Univ. of Virginia Press, 1995).

25. David S. Cecelski and Timothy B. Tyson, eds., *Democracy Betrayed: The Wilmington Race Riot of 1898 and Its Legacy* (Chapel Hill: Univ. of North Carolina Press, 1998), 3-6; H. Leon Prather, *We Have Taken a City: Wilmington Racial Massacre and Coup of 1898* (Madison, N.J.: Fairleigh Dickinson Univ. Press, 1984), 52; Mark Bauerlein, *Negrophobia: A Race Riot in Atlanta, 1906* (San Francisco: Encounter Books, 2001); David Fort Godshalk, *Veiled Visions: The 1906 Atlanta Race Riot and the Reshaping of American Race Relations* (Chapel Hill: Univ. of North Carolina Press, 2005); Gregory Mixon, *The Atlanta Riot: Race, Class, and Violence in a New South City* (Gainsville: Univ. Press of Florida, 2005).

26. Scott Ellsworth, *Death in a Promised Land: The Tulsa Race Riot of 1921* (Baton Rouge: Louisiana State Univ. Press, 1984), 63-66; Alfred L. Brophy, *Reconstructing the Dreamland: The Tulsa Riot of 1921* (New York: Oxford Univ. Press, 2002), 46-47, 50-51, 106.

27. See Elliott Jaspin, *Buried in Bitter Waters: The Hidden History of Racial Cleansing in America* (New York: Basic Books, 2007); James W. Loewen, *Sundown Towns: A Hidden Dimension of American Racism* (New York: New Press, 2005).

28. See William M. Tuttle Jr., *Race Riot: Chicago in the Red Summer of 1919* (New York: Atheneum, 1970); Anthony M. Platt, ed., *The Politics of Riot Commissions, 1917-1970* (New York: Macmillan, 1971); Lee E. Williams and Lee E. Williams II, *Anatomy of Four Race Riots: Racial Conflict in Knoxville, Elaine (Arkansas), Tulsa and Chicago, 1919-1921* (Jackson: Univ. Press of Mississippi, 1972). For more recent comparative studies, see Janet L. Abu-Lughod, *Race, Space, and Riots in Chicago, New York, and Los Angeles* (New York: Oxford Univ. Press, 2007); Ann V. Collins, *All Hell Broke Loose: American Race Riots from the Progressive Era through World War II* (Santa Barbara, Calif.: Praeger, 2012).

29. Examples include Gail Williams O'Brien, *The Color of the Law: Race, Violence, and Justice in the Post-World War II South* (Chapel Hill: Univ. of North Carolina Press, 1999); Nan Elizabeth Woodruff, *American Congo: The African American Freedom Struggle in the Delta* (Cambridge, Mass.: Harvard Univ. Press, 2003); Robert Whitaker, *On the Laps of Gods: The Red Summer of 1919 and the Struggle for Justice that Remade a Nation* (New York: Crown Publishers, 2008); Cameron McWhirter, *Red Summer: The Summer of 1919 and the Awakening of Black America* (New York: Henry Holt, 2011).

30. Hall, *Revolt against Chivalry,* 124, 163-64, 223-24, 252-53.

31. Robert L. Zangrando, *The NAACP Crusade against Lynching, 1909-1950* (Philadelphia: Temple Univ. Press, 1980), 21, 214.

32. James R. McGovern, *Anatomy of a Lynching: The Killing of Claude Neal* (Baton Rouge: Louisiana State Univ. Press, 1982), 155-57.

33. Howard Smead, *Blood Justice: The Lynching of Mack Charles Parker* (New York: Oxford Univ. Press, 1986), xiii, 205.

34. Dominic J. Capeci Jr., *The Lynching of Cleo Wright* (Lexington: Univ. Press of Kentucky, 1998), 192.

35. Notable works include Dennis B. Downey and Raymond M. Hyser, *No Crooked Death: Coatesville, Pennsylvania, and the Lynching of Zachariah Walker* (Urbana: Univ. of Illinois Press, 1991); Harry Farrell, *Swift Justice: Murder and Vengeance in a California Town* (New York: St. Martin's, 1992); Monte Akers, *Flames after Midnight: Murder, Vengeance, and the Desolation of a Texas Community* (Austin: Univ. of Texas Press, 1999); Michael W. Fedo, *The Lynchings in Duluth* (St. Paul: Minnesota Historical Society Press, 2000); Steve Oney, *And the Dead Shall Rise: The Murder of Mary Phagan and the Lynching of Leo Frank* (New York: Pantheon Books, 2003); Patricia Bernstein, *The First Waco Horror: The Lynching of Jesse Washington and the Rise of the NAACP* (College Station: Texas A&M Univ. Press, 2005); Cynthia Carr, *Our Town: A Heartland Lynching, a Haunted Town, and the Hidden History of White America* (New York: Crown Publishers, 2006); Claude A. Clegg III, *Troubled Ground: A Tale of Murder, Lynching, and Reckoning in the New South* (Urbana: Univ. of Illinois Press, 2010).

36. Edward L. Ayers, *The Promise of the New South: Life after Reconstruction* (New York: Oxford Univ. Press, 1992), 153-54, 156-57.

37. W. Fitzhugh Brundage, *Lynching in the New South: Georgia and Virginia, 1880-1930* (Urbana: Univ. of Illinois Press, 1993), 159.

38. Stewart E. Tolnay and E. M. Beck, *A Festival of Violence: An Analysis of Southern Lynchings, 1882-1930* (Urbana: Univ. of Illinois Press, 1995), 232-33, 256-57.

39. Brundage, *Lynching in the New South,* 18-19.

40. Notable works include Walter T. Howard, *Lynchings: Extralegal Violence in Florida During the 1930s* (Selinsgrove, Pa.: Susquehanna Univ. Press, 1995); John Hammond Moore, *Carnival of Blood: Dueling, Lynching, and Murder in South Carolina, 1880-1920* (Columbia: Univ. of South Carolina Press, 2006); Kimberly Harper, *White Man's Heaven: The Lynching and Expulsion of Blacks in the Southern Ozarks, 1894-1909* (Fayetteville: Univ. of Arkansas Press, 2010); Bruce E. Baker, *This Mob Will Surely Take My Life: Lynchings in the Carolinas, 1871-1947* (New York: Continuum, 2008); Terence Finnegan, *A Deed So Accursed: Lynching in Mississippi and South Carolina, 1881-1940* (Charlottesville: Univ. of Virginia Press, 2013).

41. Hall, *Revolt against Chivalry,* 150; Williamson, *Crucible of Race;* Trudier Harris, *Exorcising Blackness: Historical and Literary Lynching and Burning Rituals* (Bloomington: Indiana Univ. Press, 1984); Grace Elizabeth Hale, *Making Whiteness: The Culture of Segregation in the South, 1890-1940* (New York: Pantheon, 1998), 222-39. See also Kristina DuRocher, *Raising Racists: The Socialization of White Children in the Jim Crow South* (Lexington: Univ. Press of Kentucky, 2011).

42. Orlando Patterson, *Rituals of Blood: Consequences of Slavery in Two American Centuries* (Washington, D.C.: Civitas Counterpoint, 1998). See also Robert Zecker, "'Let Each Reader Judge': Lynching, Race, and Immigrant Newspapers," in *Swift to Wrath: Lynching in Global Perspective,* ed. William D. Carrigan and Christopher Waldrep (Charlottesville: Univ. of Virginia Press, 2013), 137-59; Cynthia Skove Nevels, *Lynching to Belong: Claiming Whiteness through Racial Violence* (College Station: Texas A&M Univ. Press, 2007).

43. For background and analysis of the Allen-Littlefield collection exhibitions, see Dora Apel, "On Looking: Lynching Photographs and Legacies of Lynching after 9/11," *American Quarterly* 55, no. 3 (Sept. 2003): 457-78. See also James Allen et al., *Without Sanctuary: Lynching Photography in America* (Santa Fe, N.M.: Twin Palms, 2000).

44. Dora Apel and Shawn Michelle Smith, *Lynching Photographs* (Berkeley: Univ. of California Press, 2007), 16; James H. Madison, *A Lynching in the Heartland: Race and Memory in America* (New York: St. Martin's Press, 2000), 114-17, 153. See also Apel, *Imagery of Lynching: Black Men, White Women, and the Mob* (New Brunswick, N.J.: Rutgers Univ. Press, 2004).

45. Apel and Smith, *Lynching Photographs,* 45; Amy Louise Wood, *Lynching and Spectacle: Witnessing Racial Violence in America, 1890-1940* (Chapel

Hill: Univ. of North Carolina Press, 2009); Jonathan Markovitz, *Legacies of Lynching: Racial Violence and Memory* (Minneapolis: Univ. of Minnesota Press, 2004), xvi-xx.

46. George C. Wright, *Racial Violence in Kentucky, 1865-1940: Lynchings, Mob Rule, and "Legal Lynching"* (Baton Rouge: Louisiana State Univ. Press, 1990), 8-9; Michael J. Pfeifer, *The Roots of Rough Justice: Origins of American Lynching* (Urbana: Univ. of Illinois Press, 2011), 2-3. For the importance of violence during Reconstruction, see Carole Emberton, *Beyond Redemption: Race, Violence, and the American South after the Civil War* (Chicago: Univ. of Chicago Press, 2013).

47. See Michael J. Pfeifer, "At the Hands of Parties Unknown? The State of the Field of Lynching Scholarship," *Journal of American History* 101 (Dec. 2014): 844-45; Margaret Vandiver, "Thoughts on Directions in Lynching Research," *Journal of American History* 101 (Dec. 2014): 854-55.

48. Margaret Vandiver, *Lethal Punishment: Lynchings and Legal Executions in the South* (New Brunswick, N.J.: Rutgers Univ. Press, 2006), 155; Amy Kate Bailey and Stewart E. Tolnay, *Lynched: The Victims of Southern Mob Violence* (Chapel Hill: Univ. of North Carolina Press, 2015), 203-18.

49. Waldrep, *Many Faces of Judge Lynch,* 3, 127-50, 182-83. See also Lisa D. Cook, "Converging to a National Lynching Database: Recent Developments," *Historical Methods* 45 (Apr.-June 2012): 55-63; Michael Ayers Trotti, "What Counts: Trends in Racial Violence in the Postbellum South," *Journal of American History* 100 (Sept. 2013): 375-400.

50. Waldrep, *Many Faces of Judge Lynch,* 11, 66-84. See also Christopher Waldrep, ed., *Lynching in America: A History in Documents* (New York: New York Univ. Press, 2006).

51. Ashraf H. A. Rushdy, *The End of American Lynching* (New Brunswick, N.J.: Rutgers Univ. Press, 2012), 14-17, 97-105, 166-67. Scholars have perpetuated this search to identify the "last" American lynching; see McGovern, *Anatomy of a Lynching;* Smead, *Blood Justice;* B. J. Hollars, *Thirteen Loops: Race, Violence, and the Last Lynching in America* (Tuscaloosa: Univ. of Alabama Press, 2011).

52. Lisa Arellano, *Vigilantes and Lynch Mobs: Narratives of Community and Nation* (Philadelphia: Temple Univ. Press, 2012), 16-18.

53. William D. Carrigan, *The Making of a Lynching Culture: Violence and Vigilantism in Central Texas, 1836-1916* (Urbana: Univ. of Illinois Press, 2004); Brent M. S. Campney, *This Is Not Dixie: Racist Violence in Kansas, 1861-1927* (Urbana: Univ. of Illinois Press, 2015); Ken Gonzales-Day, *Lynching in the West, 1850-1935* (Durham, N.C.: Duke Univ. Press, 2006). Stephen Leonard documented high numbers of white victims in Colorado; see Leonard, *Lynching in Colorado, 1859-1919* (Boulder: Univ. Press of Colorado, 2002).

54. William D. Carrigan and Clive Webb, *Forgotten Dead: Mob Violence against Mexicans in the United States, 1848-1928* (New York: Oxford Univ. Press, 2013), 157-58. Other studies have indicated that diplomatic pressure

provided similar accountability for mob violence targeting Italian immigrants in the South; see the essays by Marco Rimanelli and Giose Rimanelli in Marco Rimanelli and Sheryl L. Postman, eds., *The 1891 New Orleans Lynching and U.S.-Italian Relations: A Look Back* (New York: Peter Lang, 1992); Clive Webb, "The Lynching of Sicilian Immigrants in the American South, 1886-1910," *American Nineteenth Century History* 3, no. 1 (Spring 2002): 45-76.

55. Waldrep, *Many Faces of Judge Lynch;* Waldrep, *Lynching in America;* Manfred Berg, *Popular Justice: A History of Lynching in America* (Chicago: Ivan R. Dee, 2011). See also Michael J. Pfeifer, ed., *Lynching beyond Dixie: American Mob Violence outside the South* (Urbana: Univ. of Illinois Press, 2013). Philip Dray's synthesis focused solely on racial violence in the South; see Dray, *At the Hands of Persons Unknown: The Lynching of Black America* (New York: Random House, 2002).

56. Michael J. Pfeifer, *Rough Justice: Lynching and American Society, 1874-1947* (Urbana: Univ. of Illinois Press, 2004), 94-121, 128-29; Pfeifer, *Roots of Rough Justice.*

57. Cutler, *Lynch-Law,* 1. Transnational and comparative studies include Angelina Snodgrass Godoy, *Popular Injustice: Violence, Community, and Law in Latin America* (Stanford, Calif.: Stanford Univ. Press, 2006); Ivan Thomas Evans, *Cultures of Violence: Lynching and Racial Killing in South Africa and the American South* (Manchester, U.K.: Manchester Univ. Press, 2009); Berg and Wendt, *Globalizing Lynching History;* Robert W. Thurston, *Lynching: American Mob Murder in Global Perspective* (Burlington, Vt.: Ashgate, 2011); William D. Carrigan and Christopher Waldrep, eds., *Swift to Wrath: Lynching in Global Perspective* (Charlottesville: Univ. of Virginia Press, 2013); Silkey, *Black Woman Reformer.*

58. Diane Miller Sommerville, *Rape and Race in the Nineteenth-Century South* (Chapel Hill: Univ. of North Carolina Press, 2004); Martha Elizabeth Hodes, *White Women, Black Men: Illicit Sex in the Nineteenth-Century South* (New Haven, Conn.: Yale Univ. Press, 1997); Lisa Lindquist Dorr, *White Women, Rape, and the Power of Race in Virginia, 1900-1960* (Chapel Hill: Univ. of North Carolina Press, 2004).

59. Evelyn M. Simien, *Gender and Lynching: The Politics of Memory* (New York: Palgrave Macmillan, 2011), 8. Simien joins a broader discussion of literary, theatrical, and artistic responses to lynching, including Sandra Gunning, *Race, Rape, and Lynching: The Red Record of American Literature, 1890-1912* (New York: Oxford Univ. Press, 1996); Jacqueline Goldsby, *A Spectacular Secret: Lynching in American Life and Literature* (Chicago: Univ. of Chicago Press, 2006); Koritha Mitchell, *Living with Lynching: African American Lynching Plays, Performance, and Citizenship, 1890-1930* (Urbana: Univ. of Illinois Press, 2011); Jennie Lightweis-Goff, *Blood at the Root: Lynching as American Cultural Nucleus* (Albany: State Univ. of New York Press, 2011).

60. Kerry Segrave, *Lynchings of Women in the United States: The Recorded Cases, 1851-1946* (Jefferson, N.C.: McFarland, 2010); Julie Buckner Armstrong,

Mary Turner and the Memory of Lynching (Athens: Univ. of Georgia Press, 2011); Feimster, *Southern Horrors*. For an excellent study of turn-of-the-century black and white women's political engagement, see Gilmore, *Gender and Jim Crow.*

61. For examples of discussions in broader studies, see Shapiro, *White Violence and Black Response,* 360-62; Leon Litwack, *Trouble in Mind: Black Southerners in the Age of Jim Crow* (New York: Alfred A. Knopf, 1999), 36-37, 124-25, 342-49; Tera W. Hunter, *To 'Joy My Freedom: Southern Black Women's Lives and Labors after the Civil War* (Cambridge, Mass.: Harvard Univ. Press, 1997), 33-34, 106; Lakisha Michelle Simons, *Crescent City Girls: The Lives of Young Black Women in Segregated New Orleans* (Chapel Hill: Univ. of North Carolina Press, 2015), 82-107.

62. Paula Giddings, *When and Where I Enter: The Impact of Black Women on Race and Sex in America* (New York: Bantam Books, 1984), 31; Litwack, *Trouble in Mind,* 269; Maria Bevacqua, *Rape on the Public Agenda: Feminism and the Politics of Sexual Assault* (Boston: Northeastern Univ. Press, 2000), 18-26. For examples of African American testimony against white rapists and the efforts of early antirape activists, see Gerda Lerner, ed., *Black Women in White America: A Documentary History* (New York: Pantheon Books, 1972), 149-93.

63. Hannah Rosen, *Terror in the Heart of Freedom: Citizenship, Sexual Violence, and the Meaning of Race in Postemancipation America* (Chapel Hill: Univ. of North Carolina Press, 2009), 9; Freedman, *Redefining Rape;* Danielle L. McGuire, *At the Dark End of the Street: Black Women, Rape, and Resistance—A New History of the Civil Rights Movement from Rosa Parks to the Rise of Black Power* (New York: Knopf, 2010). See also Bevacqua, *Rape on the Public Agenda,* 18-26. For the history of the Ku Klux Klan, see Allen W. Trelease, *White Terror: The Ku Klux Klan Conspiracy and Southern Reconstruction* (New York: Harper and Row, 1971); Elaine Frantz Parsons, *Ku-Klux: The Birth of the Klan during Reconstruction* (Chapel Hill: Univ. of North Carolina Press, 2015).

64. Rebecca N. Hill, *Men, Mobs, and Law: Anti-Lynching and Labor Defense in U.S. Radical History* (Durham, N.C.: Duke Univ. Press, 2008); Christopher Waldrep, *African Americans Confront Lynching: Strategies of Resistance from the Civil War to the Civil Rights Era* (Lanham, Md.: Rowman and Littlefield, 2009), 126-27; Williams, *They Left Great Marks on Me,* 236n48. See also Kwando Mbiassi Kinshasa, *Black Resistance to the Ku-Klux Klan in the Wake of the Civil War* (Jefferson, N.C.: McFarland, 2006).

65. National Association for the Advancement of Colored People, "Lynching Goes Underground: A Report on a New Technique," ([New York: NAACP], 1940); Waldrep, *African Americans Confront Lynching,* 87.

66. Stephen J. Whitfield, *A Death in the Delta: The Story of Emmett Till* (New York: Free Press, 1989), 21. See also Devery S. Anderson, *Emmett Till: The Murder That Shocked the World and Propelled the Civil Rights Movement* (Jackson: Univ. Press of Mississippi, 2015).

67. Nick Kotz, *Judgment Days: Lyndon Baines Johnson, Martin Luther King Jr., and the Laws that Changed America* (New York: Houghton Mifflin, 2005), 174.

68. Waldrep, *African Americans Confront Lynching,* 93, 111.

69. Michal R. Belknap, *Federal Law and Southern Order: Racial Violence and Constitutional Conflict in the Post-Brown South* (Athens: Univ. of Georgia Press, 1987), 229–51.

70. Waldrep, *African Americans Confront Lynching,* 125–27. See also Christopher Waldrep, *Racial Violence on Trial* (Santa Barbara, Calif.: ABC-CLIO, 2001); Valerie Jenness and Ryken Grattet, *Making Hate a Crime: From Social Movement to Law Enforcement* (New York: Russell Sage Foundation, 2001).

71. Hollars, *Thirteen Loops,* 143–67.

72. Khalil Gibran Muhammad, *The Condemnation of Blackness: Race, Crime, and the Making of Modern Urban America* (Cambridge, Mass.: Harvard Univ. Press, 2010), 1, 34, 56, 277; Michelle Alexander, *The New Jim Crow: Mass Incarceration in the Age of Colorblindness* (New York: New Press, 2010), 2. For discussions of the connections between lynching and legal executions, see Vandiver, *Lethal Punishment;* Franklin E. Zimring, *The Contradictions of American Capital Punishment* (New York: Oxford Univ. Press, 2003).

73. See Brophy, *Reconstructing the Dreamland;* Sherrilyn A. Ifill, *On the Courthouse Lawn: Confronting the Legacy of Lynching in the Twenty-first Century* (Boston: Beacon Press, 2007); Jack Shuler, *Blood and Bone: Truth and Reconciliation in a Southern Town* (Columbia: Univ. of South Carolina Press, 2012).

CHAPTER FIVE

Women in the New South

REBECCA MONTGOMERY

In 1970, when Anne Firor Scott published her pathbreaking study, *The Southern Lady: From Pedestal to Politics, 1830-1930,* she could not have known that it would be the seminal work in southern women's history for the next forty years. Most subsequent studies did not attempt to emulate Scott's ambitious scope of one hundred years of change, but they did elaborate, and continue to elaborate, on the central themes she identified. Her focus on the significance of the "southern lady" ideal and the impact of the Civil War and Reconstruction on the status of women influenced generations of historians to explore how the construction of white patriarchal authority in slave-owning households shaped gender relations before and after emancipation. The field of southern women's history truly began to blossom in the 1990s, as numerous historians expanded and modified Scott's thesis and began to fill in the gaps by focusing on understudied groups such as working-class, black, and rural women. Although much work remains to be done, in a relatively short period of time an amazingly rich and varied account of the history of southern women has emerged that promises to remake the field of southern history.[1]

Scott was particularly interested in explaining how the southern lady ideal of womanhood masked the realities of women's lives. The ideal, promoted most vociferously by proslavery southerners such as George Fitzhugh, presented middle- and upper-class white women as paragons of virtue and womanly submissiveness. Their social respectability and sexual attractiveness depended upon the cultivation of traits such as piety, modesty, compassion, and emotional sensitivity, which were supposed to counterbalance the aggressive competitiveness of men. In return for their compliance, women were promised protection and a life of relative ease; however, Scott found that the reality could be quite different. Women in slaveholding families faced a life of hard work and considerable responsibility. Slaves represented an intrusion on family privacy and a personal obligation for women who had to train them and supervise their work as well as care for them when they were ill. As white women struggled to remain dutiful in the face of disappointments and marital strife, some came to identify with the status of slaves. They were especially resentful of the sexual double standard that justified white men's sexual exploitation of slave women, and many disagreed with the assumption of female intellectual inferiority that underlay their limited access to education.

The Civil War and emancipation of slaves undercut patriarchal authority and set the stage for the gradual emancipation of women, irrevocably altering the conditions of women's lives. White women's forced self-sufficiency during wartime contradicted notions of feminine dependency, and a dearth of male providers afterwards (due to death, disability, and impoverishment) gave them further impetus to seek educational opportunities and respectable employment. Despite opposition from southerners who feared the demise of the southern lady, the numbers of women in the workforce rapidly increased in southern states between 1870 and 1890. At the same time, the growth of an urban middle class produced a belated women's club movement in towns and cities. Scott argued that the roots of women's political activism lay in Confederate memorial associations, missionary societies, and the Women's Christian Temperance Union (WCTU), which developed female leadership without openly challenging prevailing concepts of respectable womanhood. By the 1890s organized women's interests had expanded to include more overtly political activities such as

civic improvement and social reform. As they became more com-
fortable in their public roles, many women started to believe that
woman suffrage was necessary to achieve their political goals and
gain equality with men.

Scott described a distinctive gender politics in the southern
woman suffrage movement, but she differed from some historians
in her analysis of race. Since many white women as well as men
believed that enfranchisement would destroy the characteristics of
womanhood they cherished, southern suffragists were determined
always to appear as ladies. They hoped to prove that political rights
were compatible with refined womanhood and that they did not
want to become just like men. This strategy, also used by progressive reformers, usually enabled women to gain respectful consideration of their demands even though their actions and goals directly
contradicted antebellum gender roles. Southern suffragists also had
to grapple with the difficult issue of race relations, as opponents
argued that woman suffrage would endanger white supremacy by
enfranchising black women. Scott agreed with historians of the
American woman suffrage movement that southern white women
sometimes presented themselves as allies of white supremacy
whose vote could neutralize black political influence. However, she
argued that this claim was a "minor" part of a "complicated mixture
of real motives and political arguments." As evidence that race was
not suffragists' primary consideration, she noted that in the 1920s
white women became leaders of interracial movements that aided
black voters and publicly opposed lynching.[2]

In the two decades following publication of *The Southern Lady,*
studies of the woman suffrage movement generally supported
Scott's interpretation. Paul Fuller's biography of Laura Clay presented the Kentucky suffragist as a racial moderate, although she
sometimes supported white supremacist political reforms for strategic reasons and regarded the Nineteenth Amendment as a violation
of states' rights. Clay was involved in numerous women's organizations and progressive reform campaigns, illustrating how a desire to
implement political reforms motivated southern women's pursuit
of the vote. This connection is even clearer in the work of A. Eliza-

beth Taylor, whose scholarship was introduced to a new generation of historians with the republication of some of her studies in the 1970s and 1980s. Her examination of the woman suffrage movement in Arkansas, Florida, Georgia, North Carolina, South Carolina, Tennessee, and Texas showed that suffragists' motives mostly derived from the frustration they felt at gender discrimination and resistance to their presence in the public sphere. They sometimes expressed anger and humiliation at being banned from the polls when illiterate blacks (and in Texas, Mexicans) could vote, but southern suffragists also repeatedly argued that women needed the vote to protect their interests as workers, property owners, and citizens as well as to fulfill their obligations to family, community, and nation.[3]

In the 1980s historians began to develop a contrasting picture of the relationship between gender and race for African American women in the South. Their research showed that while black women's lives had many similarities with those of white women of the same class, the burden of race discrimination created critical differences. For privileged black women, this difference was a commitment to race uplift that stemmed from white progressives' neglect of black communities. Educated African Americans who knew that their race would be judged by its lowliest members were determined to promulgate an ethic of self-help and respectability among the working poor. Some historians argued that the urgency of their mission made oppression based on race, rather than gender, the primary concern. Studies by Jacqueline Rouse and Cynthia Neverdon-Morton described black colleges as centers of community service in which the need for racial progress took precedence over gender issues. Jacqueline Jones's sweeping history of working-class women further claimed that black men's relative lack of power due to racial discrimination narrowed the gender gap within African American households. Poor black women were especially vulnerable to gender discrimination, but according to Jones they experienced it most acutely in their relationships with white employers who denied the legitimacy of their labor for their own families and subjected them to sexual harassment. As Dolores Janiewski's examination of tobacco workers revealed, even poor white women were reluctant to make common cause, choosing instead to cling tightly to the limited respectability afforded by race privilege.[4]

As the field of southern women's history matured in the 1990s, consideration of race became better integrated into studies of the origins and nature of women's public activism. Following Scott's lead, historians looked at the role of women's church-based activities in developing female leadership. Elizabeth Hayes Turner's examination of female activism in Galveston, Texas, showed that synagogues and churches were a critical starting point for upper-class white women's institution-building and social reform work. Church membership had even greater significance for Galveston's African American women; just as in their work with colleges, they shaped churches into institutions of self-help that mobilized communities and employed white concepts of respectability in the struggle against racism. Evelyn Brooks Higginbotham argued that black women's church-based social welfare work constituted everyday acts of resistance against discrimination. At times religious belief provided the basis for interracial cooperation, serving as a meeting ground for women concerned about issues impacting home and family.[5]

One such issue was temperance; although slow to take root in the South, it played an influential role in the evolution of women's public activism. Anastatia Sims noted that while the political and economic turmoil associated with the Civil War and Reconstruction delayed North Carolina women's involvement in temperance work, local WCTU chapters proliferated in the 1880s and 1890s. According to Mary Martha Thomas, Alabama women initially favored women's clubs as less radical alternatives to the temperance and suffrage movements, which hindered the growth of WCTU membership in their state until the early 1900s. Marsha Wedell found that temperance organizers in Tennessee also faced difficulties in the 1880s, but by enlisting talented local leaders they were able to build slowly a base of support. In her study of southern suffragists, Elna Green concurred with other historians that while WCTU chapters in the South were more conservative than those in other regions, they nonetheless honed women's organizing and leadership skills. The WCTU's association with Protestant churches helped to ease the transition of southern women, both white and black, from missionary work to political organization.[6]

The inadequacies of women's education also influenced the development of their public activism. Works by Joan Marie Johnson, Amy Thompson McCandless, and Rebecca Montgomery outlined how southern white women's access to education was severely restricted compared to other regions. Many colleges and universities were male-only due to widespread opposition to coeducation, and institutions of higher education for women tended to focus more on inculcating ladylike traits than on widening students' horizons through a rigorous course of study in the liberal arts. As McCandless noted, gender segregation facilitated women's organization by nurturing a distinct women's culture (in contrast to the sense of a common cause that developed among African American men and women in coeducational institutions). Furthermore, those who could afford to go north for a quality education were exposed to alternative and more activist concepts of womanhood. Johnson argued that even though students attending the "Seven Sister" colleges maintained their sense of southernness, they returned home more independent and committed to activism. According to Montgomery, white women's experiences with gender discrimination gave them a personal stake in educational reform. Their leadership in the southern campaign to improve the quality of public schools was motivated not just by their interest in child welfare, but also by their sensitivity to the injustice of limited options.[7]

Scholars seeking to identify the sources and attributes of female political activism continually struggled with how to define southern white women's gender conservatism. This task was complicated by the fact that even women who supported feminist goals often tempered their demands for reform with public displays of respect for antebellum culture. They had a variety of reasons for doing so, some of which were strategic. White women who demonstrated their loyalty to white men by publicly honoring the Confederate dead and outwardly conforming to the southern lady ideal made it more difficult for men to oppose female activism. Judith McArthur described Texas women's ladylike behavior as a tactic designed to disarm male opposition by making them appear as concerned mothers rather than lobbyists in their negotiations with politicians. Ascertaining exactly how much of their conservatism was mere strategy was further complicated by the reality that individual attitudes varied and were not static. Jane Turner Censer's research on elite women in North Carolina and Virginia showed distinct generational changes in women's attitudes and behavior. Women born before 1820 were the most invested in the old order, while the next two generations (born 1820-49 and 1850-69) adapted to postbellum changes more readily and were inclined to embrace the growing opportunities for female independence. As Marjorie Spruill observed, the characteristics of respectable womanhood were in a state of flux. Young white women of privilege were inculcated with a sense of noblesse oblige that in the Old South took the form of local charity, but that in the conditions of the New South inspired them to seek the vote.[8]

In exploring the complicated mix of personal and strategic motives underlying white women's conservatism, historians have highlighted the political implications of their role in shaping public understandings of the past. In her analysis of ladies' memorial associations, LeeAnn Whites argued that women's efforts to honor the Confederate cause had important consequences for both gender and race relations. Women initially formed memorial associations to assist in burying the Civil War dead, but organizational activities soon expanded to include assistance to veterans and their families and ritualized public acknowledgements of their sacrifices. Motivated primarily by their emotional ties with men, association members erased slavery as a causal factor in the war, reconstructing southern manhood by recasting the conflict as a noble defense of home and family. This revisionist narrative helped to ease tensions related to the reversal of the relations of dependency within households—as military defeat had made white men at least temporarily dependent on women—but it also introduced a rhetoric of home protection later used by the Ku Klux Klan to justify oppression of black men. Caroline Janney also identified memorial associations as the origin of Lost Cause mythology, which perpetuated the proslavery view of antebellum whites as benevolent guardians of a backward race who went to war only to preserve their constitutional liberties. Janney emphasized the political nature of the associations' assertion of southern nationalism and its influence on the United Daughters of the Confederacy (UDC).[9]

Research on the UDC has noted how its promotion of a pro-southern version of history also served white supremacist goals. Sarah Gardner provided a detailed overview of white women's written narratives of the Civil War, including histories, memoirs, and fiction, which incorporated the Lost Cause's idealized portrait of the Old South and the sectional conflict. Leaders in the UDC encouraged women to write such narratives and helped to create a market for them as part of the organization's efforts to justify secession and lionize the Confederacy. According to Gardner, the popularization of works such as Margaret Mitchell's *Gone with the Wind* embedded the southern version of events in national culture and, thus, in Americans' historical memory. In her study of the UDC, Karen Cox highlighted the political implications of members' campaigns to insert Lost Cause mythology in public school curricula. Across the South, UDC chapters created history and textbook committees and sponsored scholarships and essay contests to commemorate Confederate heroes. Cox argued that while members were motivated primarily by a desire to restore the honor of their ancestors, their campaign helped to institutionalize a white supremacist version of the Civil War and Reconstruction that was incompatible with racial equality and that perhaps helped fuel the southern white backlash to the *Brown v. Board of Education* decision.[10]

Although conservative women helped to create the rhetoric of home protection that white supremacists used to justify segregation and lynching, the links it created between gender, race, and sex were detrimental to the status of all women in the New South. In her biography of Jessie Daniel Ames, founder of the Association of Southern Women for the Prevention of Lynching, Jacqueline Dowd Hall provided an early analysis of how racial violence was used to reinforce the inferior social position of blacks while also asserting female dependency on men. White men frequently argued that the lynching of black men was necessary to protect white womanhood, and the rituals and language of racial violence accentuated women's physical vulnerability. Martha Hodes's later research on interracial sex documented how policing the separation of the races required policing white women's behavior, as evidenced by Ku Klux Klan attacks on white women sexually involved with black men. If no longer the sexual property of white men, they, like emancipated slaves, no longer were entitled to protection. As Patricia Schechter's biography of activist Ida B. Wells-Barnett explained, black women were acutely aware of the racial sexual politics of lynching. Two recent studies of lynching by Lisa Lindquist Dorr and Diane Miller Sommerville agreed that the late nineteenth-century spike in racial violence represented a backlash to both the political empowerment of African Americans and the growing economic and sexual independence of white women.[11]

Since the ideology that justified lynching defined virtuous womanhood as exclusively white, members of black women's clubs attempted to subvert the southern lady ideal by claiming its mantle of respectability for themselves. Well after the Civil War was over, the antebellum lady stood as an icon of the superiority of the old social order, one in which white women were freed from the heaviest burdens of labor by the enslavement of a supposedly less advanced race. Moreover, southern whites described African American women as tainted by the immorality of female slaves, making sexual respectability and family integrity integral to the struggle for racial equality. Stephanie Shaw documented how middle-class blacks prepared young women for lives of service to their race by encouraging them to be role models, whose appearance and actions were above reproach. African American educators such as Mary McLeod Bethune were convinced that respectable black womanhood was the key to racial progress. Studies addressing this theme modified earlier claims that gender was less important than race. Since white supremacists attacked them not only as African Americans but also as *women,* black women's organizations endorsed high standards of moral behavior and advocated for both gender and racial equality. Black men generally supported these goals as part of the crusade for race uplift, but they sometimes opposed reforms that diminished their own authority. Higginbotham described the emergence of a feminist theology in black Baptist churches that justified a leadership role for women. One result, the creation of separate women's conventions, met with resistance and even hostility at the local level, showing that black women struggled with gender discrimination both inside and outside their own institutions and communities.[12]

The success of the white supremacist campaign for black disfranchisement impacted the struggle for equality for all women by recasting the configurations of power rooted in race and gender. For white women, it changed the struggle for woman suffrage. The studies of Elna Green and Marjorie Spruill explained how the politics of white supremacy divided the movement into distinct phases. In the 1890s the potential advantages of making the case for woman suffrage in racial terms—the need to counterbalance the black male vote—energized southern suffragists. That opportunity largely disappeared when white men chose to disfranchise black men rather than enfranchise white women, and by 1910 suffragists had begun to make their case for the vote based on its value to progressive reform. This change in strategy did not mean that they were immune to the South's conservative political culture. Green observed that while antisuffragists most truly represented the antebellum elite, even suffragists were divided by degrees of conservatism. Some, like Kate Gordon of Louisiana, were white supremacists who staunchly supported a states' rights approach, while others, such as Kentucky's Madeline McDowell Breckinridge, accepted the need for federal legislation. Conflict between the two groups contributed to the defeat of the federal amendment in most southern legislatures, but as Melba Porter Hay's biography showed, Breckinridge was able to secure her state's vote for ratification.[13]

The connections between black disfranchisement and woman suffrage impacted African American women most profoundly. One negative outcome was the limits it placed on interracial cooperation. Rosalyn Terborg-Penn noted that most white suffragists remained silent on the issue of racial discrimination because they feared the injection of race into their campaign would doom it to failure. Even after black disfranchisement, they advocated for whites-only state suffrage initiatives, despite black women's long-standing support of both woman suffrage and progressive reforms. African American women gained the vote anyway with ratification of the Nineteenth Amendment in 1920, but less than a decade later it was taken away from them. According to Glenda Gilmore's study of North Carolina women, this altered but did not destroy black women's political influence. Disfranchisement cleared a space for them in the public sphere by making their presence seem apolitical and nonthreatening; the racial political threat had been quelled and their identities reduced to that of wives and mothers, representatives of homes and families. They became the "diplomats" of their race, and as clients of government services mediated between white officials and black communities.[14]

In her essays on southern black women's political history, Elsa Barkley Brown articulated a different interpretation of African American women's emergence as representatives of their race during the Progressive era. Unlike most southern white women, their activism was not a break with the past, but rather an attempt to recapture the political influence freedwomen had enjoyed after emancipation. During Reconstruction, freed slaves had participated as family groups in political mass meetings, and freedwomen expressed opinions and cast votes at such events both before and after being legally denied the franchise. It was not until white Republicans began to repress popular participation in decision-making in an effort to regain control of the party that black women became marginalized as political actors. As middle-class black men lost political power, they increasingly characterized their rights in terms of manhood, and middle-class women were left with social uplift of the less fortunate as their main source of public authority.[15]

Although few historians have focused on southern white women's political activism after 1920, some have argued for a reinterpretation of that narrative as well. Challenging the usual emphasis on a decline in female activism due to the ineffectualness of the vote and the intransigence of the southern Democratic Party, Lorraine Gates Schuyler countered that the peculiar political climate of the Solid

South gave newly enfranchised female voters the ability to destabilize one-party rule. In local elections with few voters, women could determine the outcome of primaries (which determined officeholders in the absence of second-party challengers), and they did not hesitate to use this power as leverage to get what they wanted from politicians. The League of Women Voters (LWV) further challenged the status quo by opposing measures to limit voter access and by using questionnaires to put candidates' policy positions on record. As Pamela Tyler's research revealed, elite women in New Orleans who mobilized in opposition to populist Huey Long's political machine were able to elect reform candidates to the mayor's office and city council and obtain significant policy changes. Other studies documented white women's role in the creation of a liberal wing in the southern Democratic Party. Minnie Fisher Cunningham of Texas was a leader in the LWV and the Women's Joint Congressional Committee who ran unsuccessfully for the U.S. Senate before serving in the Agricultural Adjustment Administration. According to biographers Judith McArthur and Harold Smith, she rejected the use of appeals to racism and became an outspoken supporter of racial equality. Dorothy Shawhan and Martha Swain detailed how another Roosevelt Democrat, Lucy Somerville Howorth of Mississippi, used political office and her skills as a lawyer to wage a lifelong crusade against gender discrimination in employment.[16]

Other studies detailed how working women also were political actors and not just objects of reform. Nancy Hewitt's history of working-class women in Tampa found that African American, Afro-Cuban, and Anglo-American women were embedded in extensive social networks that included labor unions and political movements as well as mutual aid societies, churches, and women's clubs. The black washerwomen examined by Tera Hunter formed trade organizations, waged strikes, and negotiated with city governments for regulatory reforms to protect them from exploitation and abuse. In addition to engaging in labor activism, the white textile workers in Georgina Hickey's study supported the Atlanta Equal Suffrage Party and collaborated with middle-class reformers in campaigns to influence municipal policy. As Alecia Long demonstrated in her research on the sex trade in New Orleans, even brothel madams and prostitutes used the courts to challenge laws that threatened their livelihoods and infringed on their freedoms. All of these works share a focus on public space as contested terrain. Working women's sexual and economic independence and physical presence in public places conflicted with middle-class notions of what constituted a healthy, safe, and respectable city. When pressured to conform to different models of behavior and appearance, working-class women drew upon the resources of their social networks to develop methods of resistance.[17]

Similar to historians of urban working-class women, scholars of rural women have used the concept of individual agency as an avenue of insight into the larger social importance of women's activities. Although the southern lady ideal rendered the physical labor of less privileged white women invisible, studies by Rebecca Sharpless, Melissa Walker, and Lu Ann Jones revealed their central role in the rural household economy. Sharpless's research on Texas cotton farms operating under the crop-lien system found that women's food production minimized debt while their field labor contributed to household income, in some instances by freeing men for wage labor. Women were not rendered helpless and hopeless by poverty, but instead strove to rise above obstacles of race and class through creative use of limited resources and cultivation of networks of mutual support. As Walker demonstrated in her study of the upcountry South, these skills were especially critical during the Great Depression, when the burden of family and community survival fell mostly on women. They were integral to a flexible family labor system that enabled households to adapt to the commercialization and industrialization of the rural economy, and women carefully chose between the options available to them, including working off-farm or leaving the land completely. In her study of the Upper South, Jones showed that women's expanded sales of chickens and eggs during the Depression not only enhanced their status and increased family income, but also laid the foundations for large-scale poultry production in the South.[18]

While southern rural women's involvement in politics remains an understudied topic, a few works have examined their participation in agrarian organizations. Amy Feely Morsman argued that the Grange and the Farmers' Alliance helped Virginia plantation families adjust to the new gender roles associated with a free-labor economy. Tensions developed in planter households when emancipation narrowed class differences among rural whites by shifting more direct responsibility for domestic labor onto the shoulders of elite women. Whereas tenant and yeoman farm women had always worked in the garden and barnyard, the postbellum necessity that elite women assume these duties served as a constant reminder to their husbands of elite men's military and economic failures. The Grange and Farmers' Alliance included women in local chapters, despite some opposition from men, and alleviated anxiety related to women's new productive role by endorsing mutuality in marriage and the concept of wife as economic partner. Marion K. Barthelme found that this policy of inclusion benefited Populists in Texas, as women there were vital to maintaining grassroots support for the Alliance. Rural women's influence in households and communities made them invaluable allies in membership drives, and cash from their sales of surplus chickens and eggs went to support Alliance projects. Although farm women were divided on the issue of woman suffrage, they were united by their frustration with political corruption and by their belief that cooperation among producers was the answer.[19]

The use of gender analysis to integrate social and political history is one of the lasting contributions that women's history has made to the field of southern history. Previously, southern history monographs centered in feminist theory were scarce and likely to meet with skepticism from reviewers, who doubted that gender had enough explanatory weight to be used as a primary category of analysis. Perceptions have changed as a host of works has integrated gender into the history of the antebellum South, the Civil War and Reconstruction, and the New South. Moreover, recognition that the personal is political—that private and public life are inextricably linked—has focused attention on sexuality and the construction of manhood and womanhood as important aspects of social history that overlap and intersect with political and economic narratives of change. The insights gained from these approaches have become central to our understanding of southern regional identity before and after emancipation.[20]

Another important contribution of women's historians has been their documentation of women's role in the transformation of the state. Whether working as volunteers, professionals (especially educators), or politicians, southern women were generally rooted in a political culture that was distinguished by its commitment to social justice and community. While true of organized women elsewhere, this was remarkable in a region so dedicated to local control. In lobbying for laws to protect women and children from exploitation, female reformers had to directly confront the remnants of antebellum patriarchal authority embedded in economic and political systems. And in working to establish the social infrastructures and public institutions that serve as the foundation of modern towns and cities, they recreated the meaning of community and challenged artificial divisions between private and public. White women's concept of community had its limitations, of course, and as a whole African American women were more committed to truly democratic reform. However, interracial cooperation at the local level and the dynamics of mutual influence it engendered prior to the emergence of the institutionalized efforts of the 1920s has yet to be thoroughly explored.

NOTES

1. Anne Firor Scott, *The Southern Lady: From Pedestal to Politics, 1830-1930* (Chicago: Univ. of Chicago Press, 1970).

2. Ibid., quotation, 182. Scott's position on the role of white supremacy conflicted with Aileen S. Kraditor's treatment of southern suffragists in her intellectual history of the national movement, as Scott explained in her review of Kraditor's book; see Kraditor, *The Ideas of the Woman Suffrage Movement, 1890-1920* (New York: Columbia Univ. Press, 1965); Scott, review, *Journal of Southern History* 31 (Nov. 1965): 472-73.

3. Paul E. Fuller, *Laura Clay and the Woman's Rights Movement* (Lexington: Univ. Press of Kentucky, 1975); A. Elizabeth Taylor, *The Woman Suffrage Movement in Tennessee* (1957; repr., New York: Octagon Books, 1978); Taylor, *Citizens at Last: The Woman Suffrage Movement in Texas,* ed. Ruth Winegarten and Judith N. McArthur, with foreword by Anne Firor Scott (Austin, Tex.: Ellen C. Temple, 1987). See also the following works by Taylor: *The Woman Suffrage Movement in North Carolina* (Raleigh: N.C. State Department of Archives and History, 1961); "The Origin of the Woman Suffrage Movement in Georgia," *Georgia Historical Quarterly* 28 (June 1944): 63-79; "The Woman Suffrage Movement in Arkansas," *Arkansas Historical Quarterly* 15 (Spring 1956): 17-42; "The Woman Suffrage Movement in Florida," *Florida Historical Quarterly* 36 (July 1957): 42-60; "South Carolina and the Enfranchisement of Women: The Early Years," *South Carolina Historical Magazine* 77 (April 1976): 115-26.

4. Jacqueline Anne Rouse, *Lugenia Burns Hope: Black Southern Reformer* (Athens: Univ. of Georgia Press, 1989); Cynthia Neverdon-Morton, *Afro-American Women of the South and the Advancement of the Race, 1895-1925* (Knoxville: Univ. of Tennessee Press, 1989); Jacqueline Jones, *Labor of Love, Labor of Sorrow: Black Women, Work, and the Family, from Slavery to the Present* (New York: Basic Books, 1985); Dolores E. Janiewski, *Sisterhood Denied: Race, Gender, and Class in a New South Community* (Philadelphia: Temple University Press, 1985). Former domestic workers were still angry about being exploited and patronized by white employers when they were interviewed for Susan Tucker's study, *Telling Memories among Southern Women: Domestic Workers and Their Employers in the Segregated South* (Baton Rouge: Louisiana State Univ. Press, 1988).

5. Evelyn Brooks Higginbotham, *Righteous Discontent: The Women's Movement in the Black Baptist Church, 1880-1920* (Cambridge, Mass.: Harvard Univ. Press, 1993); Elizabeth Hayes Turner, *Women, Culture, and Community: Religion and Reform in Galveston, 1880-1920* (New York: Oxford Univ. Press, 1997); Marsha Wedell, *Elite Women and the Reform Impulse in Memphis, 1875-1915* (Knoxville: Univ. of Tennessee Press, 1991).

6. Anastatia Sims, *The Power of Femininity in the New South: Women's Organizations and Politics in North Carolina, 1880-1930* (Columbia: Univ. of South Carolina Press, 1997); Mary Martha Thomas, *The New Woman in Alabama: Social Reforms and Suffrage, 1890-1920* (Tuscaloosa: Univ. of Alabama Press, 1992); Turner, *Women, Culture, and Community;* Wedell, *Elite Women and the Reform Impulse;* Elna C. Green, *Southern Strategies: Southern Women and the Woman Suffrage Question* (Chapel Hill: Univ. of North Carolina Press, 1997).

7. Joan Marie Johnson, *Southern Women at the Seven Sisters Colleges: Feminist Values and Social Activism, 1875-1915* (Athens: Univ. of Georgia Press, 2008); Amy Thompson McCandless, *The Past in the Present: Women's Higher Education in the Twentieth-Century American South* (Tuscaloosa: Univ. of Alabama Press, 1999); Rebecca S. Montgomery, *The Politics of Education in the New South: Women and Reform in Georgia, 1890-1930* (Baton Rouge: Louisiana

State Univ. Press, 2006). See also Johnson, *Southern Women at Vassar: The Poppenheim Family Letters, 1882-1916* (Columbia: Univ. of South Carolina Press, 2002).

8. Judith N. McArthur, *Creating the New Woman: The Rise of Southern Women's Progressive Culture in Texas, 1893-1918* (Urbana: Univ. of Illinois Press, 1998); Jane Turner Censer, *The Reconstruction of White Southern Womanhood, 1865-1895* (Baton Rouge: Louisiana State Univ. Press, 2003); Marjorie Spruill Wheeler, *New Women of the New South: The Leaders of the Woman Suffrage Movement in the Southern States* (New York: Oxford Univ. Press, 1993).

9. LeeAnn Whites, *The Civil War as a Crisis in Gender: Augusta, Georgia, 1860-1890* (Athens: Univ. of Georgia Press, 1995); Whites, "'Stand By Your Man': The Ladies Memorial Association and the Reconstruction of Southern White Manhood," in *Gender Matters: Civil War, Reconstruction, and the Making of the New South* (New York: Palgrave Macmillan, 2005), 85-94; Caroline E. Janney, *Burying the Dead but Not the Past: Ladies' Memorial Associations and the Lost Cause* (Chapel Hill: Univ. of North Carolina Press, 2008).

10. Sarah E. Gardner, *Blood and Irony: Southern White Women's Narratives of the Civil War, 1861-1937* (Chapel Hill: Univ. of North Carolina Press, 2004); Karen L. Cox, *Dixie's Daughters: The United Daughters of the Confederacy and the Preservation of Confederate Culture* (Gainesville: Univ. Press of Florida, 2003). See also Cynthia J. Mills and Pamela H. Simpson, eds., *Monuments to the Lost Cause: Women, Art, and the Landscapes of Southern Memory* (Knoxville: Univ. of Tennessee Press, 2003); John A. Simpson, *Edith D. Pope and Her Nashville Friends: Guardians of the Lost Cause in the Confederate Veteran* (Knoxville: Univ. of Tennessee Press, 2003).

11. Jacquelyn Dowd Hall, *Revolt against Chivalry: Jessie Daniel Ames and the Women's Campaign against Lynching* (New York: Columbia Univ. Press, 1979); Martha Hodes, *White Women, Black Men: Illicit Sex in the Nineteenth-Century South* (New Haven, Conn.: Yale Univ. Press, 1997); Patricia A. Schechter, *Ida B. Wells-Barnett and American Reform, 1880-1930* (Chapel Hill: Univ. of North Carolina Press, 2001); Lisa Lindquist Dorr, *White Women, Rape, and the Power of Race in Virginia, 1900-1960* (Chapel Hill: Univ. of North Carolina Press, 2004); Diane Miller Sommerville, *Rape and Race in the Nineteenth-Century South* (Chapel Hill: Univ. of North Carolina Press, 2004). See also Nancy MacLean, *Behind the Mask of Chivalry: The Making of the Second Ku Klux Klan* (New York: Oxford Univ. Press, 1994).

12. Stephanie J. Shaw, *What a Woman Ought to Be and to Do: Black Professional Women Workers during the Jim Crow Era* (Chicago: Univ. of Chicago Press, 1996); Joyce A. Hanson, *Mary McLeod Bethune and Black Women's Political Activism* (Columbia: Univ. of Missouri Press, 2003); Higginbotham, *Righteous Discontent;* Thomas, *New Woman in Alabama.* See also Darlene Clark Hine and Christie Anne Farnham, "Black Women's Culture of Resistance and the Right to Vote," in *Women of the American South: A Multicultural Reader,*

ed. Christie Anne Farnham (New York: New York Univ. Press, 1997), 204-19; Darlene Clark Hine, "Rape and the Inner Lives of Southern Black Women: Thoughts on the Culture of Dissemblance," in *Southern Women: Histories and Identities,* ed. Virginia Bernhard, Betty Brandon, Elizabeth Fox-Genovese, and Theda Perdue (Columbia: Univ. of Missouri Press, 1992), 177-89; Patricia Morton, *Disfigured Images: The Historical Assault on Afro-American Women* (New York: Greenwood Press, 1991).

13. Green, *Southern Strategies;* Wheeler, *New Women of the New South;* Melba Porter Hay, *Madeline McDowell Breckinridge and the Battle for a New South,* with foreword by Marjorie Julian Spruill (Lexington: Univ. Press of Kentucky, 2009). Both northern and southern women hoped they could exploit the movement for black disfranchisement by portraying the enfranchisement of white women as a less risky proposal.

14. Rosalyn Terborg-Penn, *African American Women in the Struggle for the Vote, 1850-1920* (Bloomington: Indiana Univ. Press, 1998); Glenda Elizabeth Gilmore, *Gender and Jim Crow: Women and the Politics of White Supremacy in North Carolina, 1896-1920* (Chapel Hill: Univ. of North Carolina Press, 1996). See also Ann D. Gordon et al., eds., *African American Women and the Vote, 1837-1965* (Amherst: Univ. of Massachusetts Press, 1997).

15. Elsa Barkley Brown, "To Catch the Vision of Freedom: Reconstructing Southern Black Women's Political History, 1865-1880," in Ann D. Gordon et al., *African American Women and the Vote,* 66-99; Brown, "Negotiating and Transforming the Public Sphere: African American Political Life in the Transition from Slavery to Freedom," in *Women Transforming Politics: An Alternative Reader,* ed. Cathy J. Cohen, Kathleen B. Jones, and Joan C. Tronto (New York: New York Univ. Press, 1997), 343-76.

16. Lorraine Gates Schuyler, *The Weight of Their Votes: Southern Women and Political Leverage in the 1920s* (Chapel Hill: Univ. of North Carolina Press, 2006); Pamela Tyler, *Silk Stockings and Ballot Boxes: Women and Politics in New Orleans, 1920-1963* (Athens: Univ. of Georgia Press, 1996); Judith N. McArthur and Harold L. Smith, *Minnie Fisher Cunningham: A Suffragist's Life in Politics* (Oxford: Oxford Univ. Press, 2003); Dorothy S. Shawhan and Martha H. Swain, *Lucy Somerville Howorth: New Deal Lawyer, Politician, and Feminist from the South* (Baton Rouge: Louisiana State Univ. Press, 2006).

17. Nancy A. Hewitt, *Southern Discomfort: Women's Activism in Tampa, Florida, 1880s-1920s* (Urbana: Univ. of Illinois Press, 2001); Tera W. Hunter, *To 'Joy My Freedom: Southern Black Women's Lives and Labors after the Civil War* (Cambridge, Mass.: Harvard Univ. Press, 1997); Georgina Hickey, *Hope and Danger in the New South City: Working-Class Women and Urban Development in Atlanta, 1890-1940* (Athens: University of Georgia Press, 2003); Alecia Long, *The Great Southern Babylon: Sex, Race, and Respectability in New Orleans, 1865-1920* (Baton Rouge: Louisiana State Univ. Press, 2004). Similarly, Rebecca Sharpless found that domestic cooks relied on informal networks of mutual

aid in their efforts to limit employers' control over them; Sharpless, *Cooking in Other Women's Kitchens: Domestic Workers in the South, 1860-1960* (Chapel Hill: Univ. of North Carolina Press, 2010).

18. Rebecca Sharpless, *Fertile Ground, Narrow Choices: Women on Texas Cotton Farms, 1900-1940* (Chapel Hill: Univ. of North Carolina Press, 1999); Melissa Walker, *All We Knew Was to Farm: Rural Women in the Upcountry South, 1919-1941* (Baltimore: Johns Hopkins Univ. Press, 2000); Lu Ann Jones, *Mama Learned Us to Work: Farm Women in the New South* (Chapel Hill: Univ. of North Carolina Press, 2002). See also Melissa Walker and Rebecca Sharpless, eds., *Work, Family, and Faith: Rural Southern Women in the Twentieth Century* (Columbia: Univ. of Missouri Press, 2006).

19. Amy Feely Morsman, *The Big House after Slavery: Virginia Plantation Families and Their Postbellum Experiment* (Charlottesville: Univ. of Virginia Press, 2010); Marion K. Barthelme, *Women in the Texas Populist Movement: Letters to the* Southern Mercury (College Station: Texas A&M Univ. Press, 1997).

20. See, for example, Nancy Bercaw, ed., *Gender and the Southern Body Politic* (Jackson: Univ. Press of Mississippi, 2000); Victoria Bynum, *Unruly Women: The Politics of Social and Sexual Control in the Old South* (Chapel Hill: Univ. of North Carolina Press, 1992); Catherine Clinton and Nina Silber, eds., *Divided Houses: Gender and the Civil War* (New York: Oxford Univ. Press, 1992); Laura F. Edwards, *Gendered Strife and Confusion: The Political Culture of Reconstruction* (Urbana: Univ. of Illinois Press, 1997); Craig Thompson Friend and Lorri Glover, eds., *Southern Manhood: Perspectives on Masculinity in the Old South* (Athens: Univ. of Georgia Press, 2004); Stephen Kantrowitz, *Ben Tillman and the Reconstruction of White Supremacy* (Chapel Hill: Univ. of North Carolina Press, 2000); Stephanie McCurry, *Masters of Small Worlds: Yeoman Households, Gender Relations, and the Political Culture of the Antebellum South Carolina Low Country* (New York: Oxford Univ. Press, 1995); Nell Irvin Painter, *Southern History across the Color Line* (Chapel Hill: Univ. of North Carolina Press, 2002); Nina Silber, *Gender and the Sectional Conflict* (Chapel Hill: Univ. of North Carolina Press, 2008).

CHAPTER SIX

Historians and Unions in the New South

ROBERT H. ZIEGER

There appears to be a "broken narrative" in southern labor history. A rich tradition of militancy and activism has morphed into apparent acquiescence and, at least for white workers, reluctance to participate in collective action. Indeed, at the heart of recent southern labor historiography lies a paradox. On the one hand, historians have authoritatively dismantled the once-prevalent myth of southern workers' passivity and disinclination to organize. On the other hand, however, a distinctive southern-based industrial-relations regime, featuring neo-paternalism, hostility toward unions, and absence of worker solidarity appears to have become the national norm.[1]

From the 1930s through the 1950s, as unions grew in strength and influence nationally, the South remained exceptional in its successful resistance to organized labor.[2] Its measures of union membership, union density, and labor's political influence consistently trailed those of eastern, middle western, and Pacific Coast regions. Leaders of both national labor federations—the American Federation of Labor (AFL) and the Congress of Industrial Organizations (CIO)—regarded this southern exception as a mortal threat to their hopes of building a strong and influential national labor presence. After World War II both resolved to bring the union cause into the heart of Dixie. Not only would the creation of a potent labor movement in the South serve to buttress union gains in the North, it would help to reshape southern politics. With union organization would come a liberalized electorate and the opportunity to defuse racial conflict and also to break the legislative power of the conservative coalition. Thus, shortly after World War II, it was with high hopes that both labor federations launched ambitious southern organizing drives. "Like a champion fighter," announced the CIO's David McDonald, "we . . . must continue to bore ahead [and] ORGANIZE THE SOUTH!" In fact, however, both the CIO's highly publicized drive, labeled "Operation Dixie," and the AFL's lower-key foray into the South quickly sputtered and eventually folded.[3]

Scholars and other observers posited various explanations for the South's apparent inhospitality toward unions. They pointed to the relative absence of centralized manufacturing, noting, for example, that the South's signature industry, cotton textiles, was diffuse and fragmented. This decentralization made the kinds of strategic organizing campaigns that in the 1930s and 1940s brought U.S. Steel, General Motors, Ford, and other large corporations to the bargaining table problematic in Dixie.[4] Historians also stressed the potent role that race played in dividing southern workers.[5] They noted the cultural insensitivity and even cynicism of northern-based unions, whose efforts to organize in the South ignored or flouted prevailing religious sensibilities and often seemed primarily designed to protect union standards earlier achieved in the North.[6]

Some critics charged that during the heyday of union expansion, the presence of Communists and other secular radicals alienated potential southern members. More recently, however, others have celebrated the success of leftists in building biracial unions and have deplored mainstream labor's strident anticommunism, arguing that it destroyed once-vigorous initiatives. Work by Robert Korstad, Michael Honey, Robin Kelley, Barbara Griffith, Michael Goldfield, and others has posited a missed opportunity, depicting a postwar South rich with possibilities for labor-led, biracial activism until the CIO leadership's purging of pro-Soviet unions destroyed hopes for biracial progressive advance.[7]

Whatever the specific diagnosis, most historians and other commentators once viewed "southern exception" in relation to labor as a temporary phenomenon. F. Ray Marshall, a pioneer chronicler of southern labor, spoke for many when he predicted in 1985 that prospects for union growth in an industrializing South, which was losing its dependence on low-wage industries such as textiles and food processing, were strong. He suggested that the southern economy, and hence the southern labor force, would draw closer in composition to that of other sections. And since unions appeared to be a natural accompaniment of large-scale corporate growth, he speculated, the South would exhibit patterns of union development similar to those prevailing elsewhere.[8]

Indeed, when Marshall wrote, it did appear that southern unionism was on the rise. Thus, in 1990 the proportion of the southern workforce belonging to a union constituted the highest percentage of the national total of union membership in U.S. history. From a perspective that viewed labor union development as a more or less natural concomitant of nonagricultural economic development, it seemed logical that southern patterns would converge toward national norms.[9] With the passage of Title VII of the 1964 Civil Rights Act, mandating equal employment opportunities, and the Voting Rights Act of 1965, so the argument went, one of the great impediments to union growth—racial division and the physical and psychological subordination of the black working class—receded.[10]

Moreover, the post-1960 expansion of unionism in the public sector, with southern workers involved in some of the period's most dramatic organizing initiatives, reinforced the theme of southern convergence. Public sanitation and health-care workers in southern cities waged iconic strikes, linking labor rights with the struggle for racial justice. It was teachers in Florida who in 1968 staged the first statewide school job action in U.S. history. Also in Florida, in the mid-1970s state university faculties gained statewide representation rights, creating a durable union and an ongoing collective bargaining relationship in this "right-to-work" state.[11]

If indeed southern patterns of labor unionism were destined to converge with those elsewhere, it would be necessary to reexamine certain widely prevalent assumptions about the character and even the psychology of southern workers. For some northern-based activists and scholars, the physiological and even mental inferiority of southern white workers was virtually an article of faith. Thus, for example, in attempting to explain the CIO's failure to make headway among cotton mill workers in the 1930s, unionists commissioned the outpatient psychiatric department at the University of North Carolina to create a "Personality Profile of the Textile Worker." The subsequent study found that mill workers were unusually prone to neurotic disorders. Contemporary observers and trade union functionaries often attributed textile workers' rejection of unionism to a pathological lack of energy and thralldom to employers. Thus, in the 1920s, Lois MacDonald, a researcher affiliated with the Young Women's Christian Association (YWCA), found only resignation and hopelessness among the Piedmont women she encountered. "Almost all of them seem to be overworked and prematurely old," she wrote. Textile workers living in employer-dominated villages, MacDonald believed, lacked initiative and insight, believing implicitly that "the boss is the best friend a man has." Disdain and disappointment at the mill workers' seeming lack of sustained commitment to the union cause inflected the observations and reports of organizers who were sent South. Forty years later, historian Dale Newman explained the quiescence and fatalism of textile workers in physiological terms, citing lack of adequate nutrition, absence of medical care, and general physical degeneration in explaining the passivity and hopelessness of the Carolina textile workers she studied.[12]

More recently, however, historians have laid to rest the notion of southern workers' passivity. The cotton textile industry has drawn particular attention in view of its status as the South's leading industrial sector, employing nearly two million workers at its peak in the early 1970s.[13] Historians such as Jacquelyn Dowd Hall, Douglas Flamming, Daniel Clark, Janet Irons, Michelle Brattain, and John Salmond have stressed the distinctive work-culture and community ethos of the men and women who toiled in the Piedmont's mills. Hall's now-classic article, "Disorderly Women: Gender and Labor Militancy in the Appalachian South," has been particularly influential beyond the boundaries of southern labor history, highlighting as it does the theme of women's distinctive forms and idioms of working-class activism. Timothy J. Minchin and James Hodges see textile workers, not as misled victims of bogus paternalism but rather as shrewd calculators of their economic interest, even when they rejected union representation.[14]

The rescue of southern workers from charges of acquiescence and hapless victimhood has not been confined to textiles. In recent decades, a steady stream of publications attesting to the vigor and activism among a wide range of southern workers has emerged. Studies of coal miners, longshoremen, iron and steel workers, food and tobacco workers, railroaders, and timber and lumber workers have spun a rich tapestry of protest and militancy. Brian Kelly, Daniel Letwin, Robert Woodrum, and Karin Shapiro have documented the activism of coal miners in Alabama and Tennessee, spanning the period between the opening of southern mines in the 1870s and the 1950s.[15] Eric Arnesen, Daniel Rosenberg, and Bruce Nelson call attention to the tenacity and militancy of southern dockers.[16] Birmingham's iron, steel, and smelter workers' struggle for union are featured in work by Henry M. McKiven and Horace Huntley.[17] Lumber workers, tobacco workers, shipyard workers, sugar workers, and packinghouse workers have been the subject of extensive investigation by historians over the past two decades.[18]

The role of African Americans in advancing the union cause in the South has drawn particular attention from historians. In the coal mines, so long as unionists avoided gestures of "social equality," blacks gained at least secondary leadership positions in biracial United Mine Workers' locals in Alabama even in the Jim Crow era. Black organizers recruited across the color line and sometimes earned recognition among white miners for their energy and eloquence. During the 1930s and 1940s, it was black workers in the tobacco-processing plants, pulp and paper mills, and shipyards who flocked into the new unions, sometimes to the discomfiture of white leaders and organizers worried that white workers' might perceive the CIO as a black man's union. Similarly, in the 1970s, when African Americans began to find employment in the cotton textile mills, it was they who led in the short-lived revival of union hopes in the industry. The efforts of African American sanitation and hospital workers to rectify their historic subordination and mistreatment through unionism have become legendary.[19]

It is true that among whites, labor activism sometimes took illiberal forms. Eric Arnesen shows how white southern railroad unionists used their unions and their political clout to drive blacks from the high-pay operating trades. South Carolina's textile workers were never so cohesively organized and politically active as when they fought successfully to bar blacks from all but the most menial jobs in the mills. During World War II, white workers in Mobile's shipyards demonstrated particular militancy in the effort to deny African Americans entry into skilled positions. Throughout the postwar civil rights era, white unionists in Alabama, Mississippi, Georgia, and elsewhere mobilized both within their local bodies and against their national leaderships in the crusade against integration. Even in the Alabama coalfields, where biracial unionism had flourished during the depths of Jim Crow and where black miners had been central to the United Mine Workers' rebirth in the 1930s, white unionists employed the race card to the disadvantage of black coworkers in postwar downsizing.[20]

Clearly, race, in the sense of black-white relationships, has been at the center of southern labor historiography from its inception. Historiographical acknowledgment of other aspects of ethnicity, however, have emerged only relatively recently. In a 1987 publication, Gary Mormino and George Pozzetta examined "the immigrant world of Ybor City," a distinctive enclave in Tampa, Florida, that housed a rich multiethic working-class culture, both within the cigar factories and in the community. Since then, the South's Hispanic/Latino/Chicano workers have attracted increasing attention, with historians Emilio Zamora, Zaragosa Vargas, and Max Krochmal exploring the emergence of activist Mexican and Mexican American communities in the Southwest reaching back to the early twentieth century.[21] In tandem with the great expansion of workers from Mexico, Central America, and the Caribbean toward the end of the twentieth century, scholarly interest in the struggles of immigrant and native-born ethnic workers has continued. While most of the Hispanic diaspora has emerged outside the purview of organized labor, struggles on the part of food-processing workers, hospital and adult-care workers, and garment workers have attracted the interest of scholars. Leon Fink analyzed the ultimately unsuccessful efforts of Central American poultry workers to create a union presence in North Carolina, while Bruce Nissen and Melanie Shell-Weiss have brought attention to union-organizing efforts of Caribbean-origin workers in Florida.[22]

Racial and ethnic factors have been particularly significant with respect to agricultural labor. Ethnic and racial subordination have characterized southern agriculture throughout its history and have played critical roles in spurring worker organizing, job actions, and political protest. On the whole, organized labor has paid little attention to the region's agricultural workers, however; most initiatives have emerged directly out of the experiences of agricultural workers themselves, with national unions playing a subsidiary role at best. Agricultural workers, like their counterparts in domestic labor, have often proved inventive and militant in devising strategies with which to confront workplace injustice, giving the term "organized labor" a distinctive meaning in the agricultural sector. Throughout the post-Civil War decades, African Americans, whether as farm tenants or as plantation workers, resorted to strikes and political mobilization in protest over a variety of workplace issues. Efforts of black cotton tenants, sugar workers, and rice plantation workers flared into violent confrontations and left a legacy of protest and activism that periodically resurfaced, eventually feeding into the post-World War II grassroots civil rights movement. Thus M. Langley Biegert chronicles the struggles of cotton workers in southeastern Arkansas dating back to the Civil War to gain equitable treatment at the hands of white plantation owners. Organizing efforts, greeted invariably with violent repression, punctuated the period circa 1861-1934, leading up to the founding in that latter year of the Southern Tenant Farmers Union (STFU). In turn, as chronicled in the work of Donald H. Grubbs and Mark Naison, STFU activists carried forth the legacy of workplace-based biracial activism into the post-World War II era.[23]

As early as the 1910s, but increasingly after the 1930s, agriculture has provided work for large numbers of immigrant workers, both legal and undocumented. Today upward of 80 percent of southern agricultural labor is performed by migrants, mostly from the Caribbean, Mexico, and Central America. As Cindy Hahamovitch has shown in a series of publications, while U.S.-based agricultural workers' unions have been at best ambivalent about the presence of these "guestworkers," the workers themselves have been resourceful in devising informal methods of resisting employers who manipulated workloads, devised incomprehensible payment schemes, and imposed arbitrary disciplinary measures.[24]

The focus on race and ethnicity in the demographics of southern labor relations is also evident when gender is factored in to the equation. Recruitment of white women for work in the cotton textile mills was a key factor in the lily-white employment trajectory of the industry in the South. Meanwhile, African American women's availability as domestic workers enabled white women to take these "outside" jobs. At the same time, African American women could be hired to perform work deemed unsuitable for white women— for example, as leaf stemmers in the tobacco factories. Early in the twentieth century, in the cigar factories of Tampa, the substitution of machinery and nonskilled female workers for skilled, largely male labor occurred during a turbulent period in which immigrant women played a critical role both as workers and as community activists.

From the earliest days of southern industrialism, women were central, both as activists and as supporters of men's efforts, to the story of labor organization. Biracial unionism, writes Daniel Letwin, was possible in the Gilded Age Alabama coalfields in good part because racial segregation in the coal camps precluded possibilities of social interaction outside the worksite and union hall. Since the labor movement, in the South as much as in the North, projected a masculinist ideology, male organizers and activists often regarded women workers as impediments to successful organizing, thus deflecting attention from women's contributions. Even when women marched on picket lines and confronted armed troops, contemporary observers attempted to fit them into demeaning stereotypes of passivity and gentility.[25]

Over the past several decades, however, a clearer and more positive picture of the role of women, black and white, in southern labor struggles has emerged. Nancy Hewitt's work on women's activism in early twentieth-century Tampa, Florida, stresses the role that Italian, Afro-Cuban, and other Hispanic women played in cigar-worker labor and community struggles, both as workers and as frontline supporters of unionism. In the now-classic account of southern mill workers and in a widely cited journal article, Jacquelyn Dowd Hall has investigated the distinctive idioms and strategies of younger women in labor struggles among southern Piedmont textile workers. Michelle Haberland's work on postwar organizing efforts of southern garment workers, the vast majority of them women, further confutes stereotypes of passivity and deference. Recent studies of more contemporary activism among immigrant garment, health-care, and service workers also points to the forceful role gender has been playing in the labor movement's modest organizing successes.[26]

In the immediate post–World War II era, it was widely believed that as the South caught up to the rest of the nation industrially, it would track patterns of union development prevalent elsewhere. Indeed, the establishment or relocation of manufacturing in low-wage southern locales did sometimes bring with it unionization, as evidenced by the early postwar experience of the United Automobile Workers, the United Steelworkers, and other industrial unions. By the 1970s, the extensive southern pulp and paper industry largely operated on a union basis. More common, however, especially over the past thirty years, has been successful resistance to northern-based unions, as evidenced particularly in the lack of success that the United Auto Workers (UAW) has experienced in seeking to organize assembly plants in Kentucky, Tennessee, Alabama, South Carolina, and elsewhere in the South. Indeed, nonunion workers in these states have often embraced company-generated conceptions of workplace relations that express disdain for laborite traditions of solidarity and for the adversarial paradigm implicit in the collective bargaining process.[27] Even in pulp and paper, once a bellwether of southern unionism, as older plants are closed and newer facilities open in rural areas, paper worker unions have struggled with limited success to combat union avoidance.[28] Moreover, the trend of industry moving South has been replaced by the trend of industry *leaving* the American South in quest of even lower wages in Latin America and offshore.[29]

Women's role in the postindustrial southern economy, and its implications for organized labor, have assumed particular importance in understanding what has been termed "the broken narrative of U.S. labor history."[30] Southern employers have pioneered in the development of the new, postindustrial economy, based in good part on flexible work regimes, use of temporary and part-time employees, and a sort of neo-paternalism that projects a familial conception of the workplace and encourages positive identification of employees with the corporation's goals and procedures. A key goal of this emerging employment paradigm has been to resist union organization.[31]

Women workers have been central to the success of Walmart and other southern-based employers in establishing this new labor-relations regime. In *To Serve God and Wal-Mart: The Making of Christian Free Enterprise* (2009), Bethany Moreton combines the themes of women's workplace and community agency, on the one hand, with the company's successful avoidance of unions, on the other. The female workers recruited initially from among working-class and farm families in Walmart's birthplace, northeastern Arkansas, found ways to resist the company's initially masculinist managerial culture and to reshape workplace relations. In the 1970s, the interaction of female floor workers and cashiers with customers, reflecting an ethos of service and female cooperativeness, more or less spontaneously began to define the early stores' shop-floor culture. It was, says Moreton, "a nonmilitant form of worker control."[32] This version of "worker control," which consisted of an unplanned and uncoordinated insinuation of rural and small-town women's sense of neighborliness and female bonding through attitudes toward home, family, consumption, and even religion was a far cry from the "workers' control" celebrated by David Montgomery and other labor historians.[33] But the company's shrewdness in recognizing its value for both sales and promotion of employee loyalty has paid dividends, both tangible and metaphorical.

As the nation's largest employer, Walmart has transcended its southern roots and has helped to establish the current trend in U.S. industrial relations. Low wages, determined union avoidance, and an ideology of common interest between employer and employee have become prevalent. The expectations of post-World War II commentators and observers that the South would converge toward national norms has proven perversely prescient: The southern "exception" has become the national norm.[34]

The current state of labor relations, nationally as well as in the South specifically, poses daunting challenges for historians and others interested in organized labor. Does the documentation of southern workers' historic militancy and union-mindedness have any resonance in the new, postindustrial order? Are there threads of continuity between, on the one hand, the struggles of Alabama coal miners, Carolina cotton mill strikers, and east Texas timber workers and, on the other, the efforts of today's Haitian, Hispanic, and African American poultry, healthcare, and migrant agricultural workers to forge (in Bruce Nissen's words) "a new kind of union"? Union struggles in the South, Timothy J. Minchin reminds us, have invariably been fought "against the odds."[35] There has arisen a critical question, not for historians but for southern workers themselves: Is there room for organized labor in the new New South?

NOTES

1. Robert H. Zieger, "Walmart and the Broken Narrative of US Labor History," *Labor History* 52, no. 4 (Nov. 2011): 563-69. There is an outstanding bibliographical essay in Timothy J. Minchin, *Fighting against the Odds: A History of Southern Labor since World War II* (Gainesville: Univ. Press of Florida, 2005), 187-214. See also Bryant Simon, "Rethinking Why There Are So Few Unions in the South," *Georgia Historical Quarterly* 81, no. 2 (Summer 1997): 465-84.

2. For a challenging perspective on the theme of "southern exceptionalism," see Matthew D. Lassiter and Joseph Crespino, "Introduction: The End

of Southern History," in *The Myth of Southern Exceptionalism,* ed. Lassiter and Crespino (New York: Oxford Univ. Press, 2010), 3-22. See also Michelle Brattain, "The Pursuits of Post-exceptionalism: Race, Gender, Class, and Politics in the New Southern Labor History," in *Labor in the Modern South,* ed. Glenn T. Eskew (Athens: Univ. of Georgia Press, 2001), 1-46.

3. McDonald, quoted in Robert H. Zieger, *The CIO, 1935-1955* (Chapel Hill: Univ. of North Carolina Press, 1995), 233. Historians have devoted more attention to the CIO's "Operation Dixie" than to the more subdued AFL effort. See, for example, Barbara S. Griffith, *The Crisis of American Labor: Operation Dixie and the Defeat of the CIO* (Philadelphia: Temple Univ. Press, 1988); Michael Honey and Solomon Barkin, "'Operation Dixie': Two Views," *Labor History* 31, no. 3 (Summer 1990): 373-85.

4. F. Ray Marshall, *Labor in the South* (Cambridge, Mass.: Harvard Univ. Press, 1967), esp. 344-52.

5. Henry M. McKiven Jr., *Iron and Steel: Class, Race, and Community in Birmingham, Alabama, 1875-1920* (Chapel Hill: Univ. of North Carolina Press, 1995); Bruce Nelson, "Organized Labor and the Struggle for Black Equality in Mobile during World War II," *Journal of American History* 80, no. 3 (Dec. 1993): 952-88; Robert J. Norrell, "Caste in Steel: Jim Crow Careers in Birmingham, Alabama," *Journal of American History* 73, no. 3 (Dec. 1986): 669-94.

6. Elizabeth Fones-Wolf and Ken Fones-Wolf, "Sanctifying the Southern Organizing Campaign: Protestant Activists in the CIO's Operation Dixie," *Labor: Studies in Working-Class History of the Americas* 6, no. 1 (Spring 2009): 5-32; Clete Daniel, *Culture of Misfortune: An Interpretive History of Textile Unionism in the United States* (Ithaca, N.Y.: ILR Press/Cornell Univ. Press, 2001), 144-45; Tami J. Friedman, "'How Can Greenville Get New Industry to Come Here If We Get the Label of a C.I.O. Town?' Capital Migration and the Limits of Unionism in the Postwar South," in *Life and Labor in the New New South: Essays in Southern Labor History since 1950,* ed. Robert H. Zieger (Gainesville: Univ. Press of Florida, 2012), 16-44.

7. Robert Rodgers Korstad, *Civil Rights Unionism: Tobacco Workers and the Struggle for Democracy in the Mid-Twentieth Century South* (Chapel Hill: Univ. of North Carolina Press, 2003); Michael K. Honey, *Southern Labor and Black Civil Rights: Organizing Memphis Workers* (Urbana: Univ. of Illinois Press, 1993); Robin D. G. Kelley, *Hammer and Hoe: Alabama Communists during the Great Depression* (Chapel Hill: Univ. of North Carolina Press, 1990); Griffith, *Crisis of American Labor;* Michael Goldfield, "Was There a Golden Age of the CIO? Race, Solidarity, and Union Growth during the 1930s and 1940s," in *Trade Union Politics: American Unions and Economic Change, 1960s-1990s,* ed. Glenn Perusek and Kent Worcester (Atlantic Highlands, N.J.: Humanities Press, 1995), 78-110; Goldfield, *The Decline of Organized Labor in the United States* (Chicago: Univ. of Chicago Press, 1987), 97n6. See also Patricia Sullivan, *Days of Hope: Race and Democracy in the New Deal Era* (Chapel Hill: Univ. of North Carolina Press, 1996).

8. Ray Marshall, "Southern Unions: History and Prospects," in *Perspectives on the American South: An Annual Review of Society, Politics and Culture,* ed. James C. Cobb and Charles R. Wilson (New York: Gordon and Breach Science Publishers, 1985), 3:163-78.

9. See Goldfield, *Decline of Organized Labor,* 140, table 21.

10. The struggles of black workers to combine union activism with the quest for equal employment opportunity are chronicled in three important books by Timothy J. Minchin: *Hiring the Black Worker: The Racial Integration of the Southern Textile Industry, 1960-1980* (Chapel Hill: Univ. of North Carolina Press, 1999); *The Color of Work: The Struggle for Civil Rights in the Southern Paper Industry, 1945-1980* (Chapel Hill: Univ. of North Carolina Press, 2001); *"Don't Sleep with Stevens!" The J. P. Stevens Campaign and the Struggle to Organize the South, 1963-80* (Gainesville: Univ. Press of Florida, 2005).

11. See, for example, Michael K. Honey, *Going down Jericho Road: The Memphis Strike, Martin Luther King's Last Campaign* (New York: W. W. Norton, 2007); Honey, "Martin Luther King, Jr., the Crisis of the Black Working Class, and the Memphis Sanitation Strike," in *Southern Labor in Transition, 1940-1995,* ed. Robert H. Zieger (Knoxville: Univ. of Tennessee Press, 1997), 146-75; Mark Wilkens, "Gender, Race, Work Culture, and the Building of the Fire Fighters Union in Tampa, Florida, 1943-1985," in Zieger, *Southern Labor in Transition,* 176-204; James Sullivan, "The Florida Teacher Walkout in the Political Transition of 1968," in Zieger, *Southern Labor in Transition,* 205-29; Leon Fink and Brian Greenberg, *Upheaval in the Quiet Zone: A History of Hospital Workers' Union Local 1199* (Urbana: Univ. of Illinois Press, 1989), 129-58. There is no authoritative account of the emergence of the United Faculty of Florida (UFF), but see the interviews with union activists in the Samuel Proctor Oral History Program's UFF collection, University of Florida.

12. Robert H. Zieger, "From Primordial Folk to Redundant Workers: Southern Textile Workers and Social Observers, 1920-1990," in Zieger, *Southern Labor in Transition,* 277-79, 280-81; Dale Newman, "Work and Community in a Southern Textile Town," *Labor History* 19, no. 2 (Spring 1978): 204-25. See also Mariel Rose, "Moving Capital, Moving Workers, and the Mountain Work Ethic," in *Migration and the Transformation of the Southern Workplace since 1945,* ed. Robert Cassanello and Colin J. Davis (Gainesville: Univ. Press of Florida, 2009), 187-90.

13. Harry Boyte, "The Textile Industry: Keel of Southern Industrialization," *Radical America* 6 (March-April 1972): 4-49; Timothy J. Minchin, "Shutdowns in the Sun Belt: The Decline of the Textile and Apparel Industry and the Deindustrialization in the South," in Zieger, *Life and Labor in the New New South,* 258-60; Timothy J. Minchin, *Empty Mills: The Fight against Imports and the Decline of the U.S. Textile Industry* (Lanham, Md.: Rowman and Littlefield, 2012); Robert H. Zieger, "Textile Workers and Historians," in *Organized Labor in the Twentieth-Century South,* ed. Zieger (Knoxville: Univ. of Tennessee Press, 1991), 35-59.

14. Jacqueline Dowd Hall, Robert Korstad, and James Leloudis, "Cotton Mill People: Work, Community, and Protest in the Textile South, 1880-1940," *American Historical Review* 91, no. 2 (April 1986): 245-86; Hall, "Disorderly Women: Gender and Labor Militancy in the Appalachian South," *Journal of American History* 73, no. 2 (Sept. 1986): 354-82; Hall, Leloudis, Korstad, Mary Murphy, Lu Ann Jones, and Christopher B. Daly, *Like a Family: The Making of a Southern Cotton Mill World* (Chapel Hill: Univ. of North Carolina Press, 1987); Douglas Flamming, *Creating the Modern South: Millhands and Managers in Dalton, Georgia, 1884-1984* (Chapel Hill: Univ. of North Carolina Press, 1992); Daniel Clark, *Like Night and Day: Unionization in a Southern Mill Town* (Chapel Hill: Univ. of North Carolina Press, 1997); Janet Christine Irons, *Testing the New Deal: The General Textile Strike of 1934* (Urbana: Univ. of Illinois Press, 2000); Michelle Brattain, *The Politics of Whiteness: Race, Workers, and Culture in the Modern South* (Princeton, N.J.: Princeton Univ. Press, 2001); John A. Salmond, *Gastonia, 1929: The Story of the Loray Mill Strike* (Chapel Hill: Univ. of North Carolina Press, 1995); Salmond, *The General Textile Strike of 1934: From Maine to Alabama* (Columbia: Univ. of Missouri Press, 2002); Melton A. McLaurin, *The Knights of Labor in the South* (Westport, Conn.: Greenwood Press, 1978); McLaurin, *Paternalism and Protest: Southern Cotton Mill Workers and Organized Labor, 1875-1905* (Westport, Conn.: Greenwood Press, 1971); Bryant Simon, *A Fabric of Defeat: The Politics of South Carolina Millhands, 1910-1948* (Chapel Hill: Univ. of North Carolina Press, 1998); Timothy J. Minchin, *What Do We Need a Union For? The TWUA in the South, 1945-1955* (Chapel Hill: Univ. of North Carolina Press, 1997); James A. Hodges, *New Deal Labor Policy and the Southern Cotton Textile Industry, 1933-1941* (Knoxville: Univ. of Tennessee Press, 1986).

15. Brian Kelly, *Race, Class, and Power in the Alabama Coalfields, 1908-21* (Urbana: Univ. of Illinois Press, 2001); Daniel Letwin, *The Challenge of Interracial Unionism: Alabama Coal Miners, 1878-1921* (Chapel Hill: Univ. of North Carolina Press, 1998); Robert H. Woodrum, *"Everybody Was Black Down There": Race and Industrial Change in the Alabama Coalfields* (Athens: Univ. of Georgia Press, 2007); Karin A. Shapiro, *A New South Rebellion: The Battle against Convict Labor in the Tennessee Coalfields, 1871-1896* (Chapel Hill: Univ. of North Carolina Press, 1998); Edwin L. Brown and Colin J. Davis, eds., *It Is Union and Liberty: Alabama Coal Miners and the UMW* (Tuscaloosa: Univ. of Alabama Press, 1999). See also Robert Daniel Ward and William Warren Rogers, *Labor Revolt in Alabama: The Great Strike of 1894* (Tuscaloosa: Univ. of Alabama Press, 1965); Alex Lichtenstein, "Racial Conflict and Solidarity in the Alabama Coal Strike of 1894: New Evidence in the Gutman-Hill Debate," *Labor History* 36, no. 1 (Winter 1995): 63-76.

16. Eric Arnesen, *Waterfront Workers of New Orleans: Race, Class, and Politics, 1863-1923*, Illini Books ed. (1991; repr., Urbana: Univ. of Illinois Press, 1994); Daniel Rosenberg, *New Orleans Dockworkers: Race, Labor, and Unionism, 1892-1923* (Albany: State Univ. of New York Press, 1988); Bruce Nel-

son, "Class and Race in the Crescent City: The ILWU, from San Francisco to New Orleans," in *The CIO's Left-Led Unions,* ed. Steven Rosswurm (New Brunswick, N.J.: Rutgers Univ. Press, 1992), 19-45.

17. McKiven, *Iron and Steel;* Horace Huntley, "The Red Scare and Black Workers in Alabama: The International Union of Mine, Mill, and Smelter Workers, 1945-53," in *Labor Divided: Race and Ethnicity in United States Labor Struggles, 1835-1960,* ed. Robert Asher and Charles Stephenson (Albany: State Univ. of New York Press, 1990), 129-45. But see also Alan Draper, "The New Southern Labor History Revisited: The Success of the Mine, Mill and Smelter Workers Union in Birmingham, 1934-1938," *Journal of Southern History* 62, no. 1 (Feb. 1996): 87-108.

18. William P. Jones, *The Tribe of Black Ulysses: African American Lumber Workers in the Jim Crow South* (Urbana: Univ. of Illinois Press, 2005); Stephen H. Norwood, "Bogolusa Burning: The War against Biracial Unionism in the Deep South, 1919," *Journal of Southern History* 63, no. 3 (Aug. 1997): 591-628; Mark Fannin, *Labor's Promised Land: Radical Visions of Gender, Race, and Religion in the South* (Knoxville: Univ. of Tennessee Press, 2003). See also James R. Green, *Grass-Roots Socialism: Radical Movements in the Southwest, 1895-1943* (Baton Rouge: Louisiana State Univ. Press, 1978). On tobacco workers, see Korstad, *Civil Rights Unionism.* Unionism among food-processing workers is analyzed in Rick Halpern, "The CIO and the Limits of Labor-based Civil Rights Activism: The Case of Louisiana's Sugar Workers, 1947-1966," in Zieger, *Southern Labor in Transition,* 86-112; Halpern, "Interracial Unionism in the Southwest: Fort Worth's Packinghouse Workers, 1937-1954," in Zieger, *Organized Labor in the Twentieth-Century South,* 158-82. Activism among southern shipyard and transport workers is treated in Alex Lichtenstein, "'Scientific Unionism' and the 'Negro Question': Communists and the Transport Workers Union in Miami, 1947-1966," in Zieger, *Southern Labor in Transition,* 58-85; Lichtenstein, "'We at Last Are Industrializing the Whole Ding-busted Party': The Communist Party and Florida Workers in Depression and War," in *Florida's Working-Class Past: Current Perspectives on Labor, Race, and Gender from Spanish Florida to the New Immigration,* ed. Robert Cassanello and Melanie Shell-Weiss (Gainesville: Univ. Press of Florida, 2009), 169-97; Lichtenstein, "Exclusion, Fair Employment, or Interracial Unionism: Race Relations in Florida's Shipyards during World War II," in Eskew, *Labor in the Modern South,* 135-57.

19. Herbert G. Gutman, "The Negro and the United Mine Workers of America," in *The Negro and the American Labor Movement,* ed. Julius Jacobson (Garden City, N.Y.: Anchor Books, 1968), 49-127; Letwin, *Challenge of Interracial Unionism,* 60-63. On pulp and paper, see Robert H. Zieger, *Rebuilding the Pulp and Paper Workers' Union, 1933-1941* (Knoxville: Univ. of Tennessee Press, 1984), 112-14; Zieger, "The Union Comes to Covington: Virginia Paperworkers Organize, 1933-1952," *Proceedings of the American Philosophical Society* 126, no. 1 (Feb. 1982): 51-89. See also Korstad, *Civil Rights Unionism;* Nelson,

"Organized Labor and the Struggle for Black Equality"; Minchin, *Hiring the Black Worker,* 85-86, 241-52; John A. Salmond, *Southern Struggles: The Southern Labor Movement and the Civil Rights Struggle* (Gainesville: Univ. Press of Florida, 2004), 43-44; Max Krochmal, "An Unmistakably Working-Class Vision: Birmingham's Foot Soldiers and Their Civil Rights Movement," *Journal of Southern History* 76, no. 4 (Nov. 2010): 923-60; Honey, "Martin Luther King, Jr., the Crisis of the Black Working Class, and the Memphis Sanitation Strike"; Fink and Greenberg, *Upheaval in the Quiet Zone,* 129-58.

20. Eric Arnesen, *Brotherhoods of Color: Black Railroad Workers and the Struggle for Equality* (Cambridge, Mass.: Harvard Univ. Press, 2001); Eric Arnesen, "'Like Banquo's Ghost, It Will Not Down': The Race Question and the American Railroad Brotherhoods, 1880-1920," *American Historical Review* 99, no. 5 (Dec. 1994): 1601-33; Bryant Simon, *A Fabric of Defeat: The Politics of South Carolina Millhands, 1910-1948* (Chapel Hill: Univ. of North Carolina Press, 1998); Nelson, "Organized Labor and the Struggle for Black Equality"; Alan Draper, *Conflict of Interests: Organized Labor and the Civil Rights Movement in the South, 1954-1968* (Ithaca, N.Y.: ILR Press, 1994); Robert J. Norrell, "Labor Trouble: George Wallace and Union Politics in Alabama," in Zieger, *Organized Labor in the Twentieth-Century South,* 250-72; Robert J. Norrell, "Labor at the Ballot Box: Alabama Politics from the New Deal to the Dixiecrat Movement," *Journal of Southern History* 57, no. 2 (May 1991): 201-34; Robert H. Zieger, "A Venture into Unplowed Fields: Daniel Powell and CIO Political Action in the Postwar South," in Eskew, *Labor in the Modern South,* 158-81; Bruce Nelson, "'CIO Meant One Thing for the Whites and Another Thing for Us': Steelworkers and Civil Rights, 1936-1974," in Zieger, *Southern Labor in Transition,* 113-45. But see also Judith Stein, "Southern Workers in National Unions: Birmingham Steelworkers, 1936-1951," in Zieger, *Organized Labor in the Twentieth-Century South,* 183-222. On the removal of black coal miners, see Woodrum, *"Everybody Was Black Down There,"* 149-50, 157-59, 224-29.

21. Gary Mormino and George E. Pozzetta, *The Immigrant World of Ybor City: Italians and Their Latin Neighbors in Tampa, 1885-1985* (Urbana: Univ. of Illinois Press, 1987); Emilio Zamora, *The World of the Mexican Worker in Texas* (College Station: Texas A&M Univ. Press, 1993); Zaragosa Vargas, *Labor Rights Are Civil Rights: Mexican American Workers in Twentieth-Century America* (Princeton, N.J.: Princeton Univ. Press, 2005); Max Krochmal, "Chicano Labor and Multiracial Politics in Post-World War II Texas: Two Case Studies," in Zieger, *Life and Labor in the New New South,* 133-76.

22. Michael K. Bess, "Obreros in the Peach State: The Growth of Georgia's Working-Class Mexican Immigrant Communities from a Transnational Perspective," in Zieger, *Life and Labor in the New New South,* 214-35; Leon Fink, *The Maya of Morganton: Work and Community in the Nuevo New South* (Chapel Hill: Univ. of North Carolina Press, 2003); Bruce Nissen, "A Different Kind of Union: SEIU Healthcare Florida from the Mid-1990s through 2009," in Zieger, *Life and Labor in the New New South,* 289-313; Melanie Shell-Weiss, "'I Dreamed

I Went to Work': Expanding Southern Unionism in the Mid-Twentieth Century Lingerie Industry," in Cassanello and Shell-Weiss, *Florida's Working-Class Past,* 227-56; Shell-Weiss, "From Minority to Majority: The Latinization of Miami's Workforce, 1940-1980," in Cassanello and Davis, *Migration and the Transformation of the Southern Workplace,* 13-33; Raymond Mohl, "Latinos and Blacks in the Recent American South," in Cassanello and Davis, *Migration and the Transformation of the Southern Workplace,* 81, table 4.1.

23. Robert H. Zieger, *For Jobs and Freedom: Race and Labor in America since 1865* (Lexington: Univ. Press of Kentucky, 2007), 30-36; M. Langley Biegert, "Legacy of Resistance: Uncovering the History of Collective Action by Black Agricultural Workers in Cental East Arkansas from the 1860s to the 1930s," *Journal of Social History* 32, no. 1 (Fall 1998): 73-100; Donald H. Grubbs, *The Cry from the Cotton: The Southern Tenant Farmers' Union and the New Deal* (Chapel Hill: Univ. of North Carolina Press, 1971); Mark D. Naison, "The Southern Tenant Farmers' Union and the CIO," in *"We Are All Leaders": The Alternative Unionism of the Early 1930s,* ed. Staughton Lynd (Urbana: Univ. of Illinois Press, 1996), 102-16. See also Greta de Jong, "'With the Aid of God and the F.S.A.': The Louisiana Farmers' Union and the African America Freedom Struggle in the New Deal Era," *Journal of Social History* 34, no. 1 (2000): 105-39. On domestic workers' organizing efforts, see Tera Hunter, "Domination and Resistance: The Politics of Wage Household Labor in New South Atlanta," *Labor History* 34, nos. 2-3 (Spring-Summer 1993): 205-20; Hunter, "'Work That Body': African-American Women, Work, and Leisure in Atlanta and the New South," *Labor Histories: Class, Politics, and the Working-Class Experience,* ed. Eric Arnesen, Julie Green, and Bruce Laurie (Urbana: Univ. of Illinois Press, 1998), 153-74.

24. Cindy Hahamovitch, "Standing Idly By: 'Organized' Farmworkers in South Florida during the Depression and World War II," in Zieger, *Southern Labor in Transition,* 15-34; Hahamovitch, *The Fruits of Their Labor: Atlantic Coast Farmworkers and the Making of Migrant Poverty, 1870-1945* (Chapel Hill: Univ. of North Carolina Press, 1997); Hahamovitch, *No Man's Land: Jamaican Guestworkers in America and the Global Economy* (Princeton, N.J.: Princeton Univ. Press, 2011).

25. Letwin, *Challenge of Interracial Unionism.* Excellent early surveys of the role of gender in southern labor struggles are found in Mary E. Frederickson, "Heroines and Girl Strikers: Gender Issues and Organized Labor in the Twentieth Century South," in Zieger, *Organized Labor in the Twentieth-Century South,* 84-112; Frederickson, "'I Know Which Side I'm on': Southern Women in the Labor Movement in the Twentieth Century," in *Women, Work and Protest: A Century of U.S. Women's Labor History,* ed. Ruth Milkman (Boston: Routledge and Kegan Paul, 1985), 156-80. See also the citations in note 27, as well as Jacqueline Jones, *American Work: Four Centuries of Black and White Labor* (New York: W. W. Norton, 1998), 229-31; I. A. Newby, *Plain Folk in the New South: Social Change and Cultural Persistence, 1880-1915* (Baton Rouge: Louisiana State

Univ. Press, 1989), 241-44; Dolores E. Janiewski, *Sisterhood Denied: Race, Gender, and Class in a New South Community* (Philadelphia: Temple Univ. Press, 1985), 99-102, 136-41; Korstad, *Civil Rights Unionism,* 2, 14-18; Nancy A. Hewitt, *Southern Discomfort: Women's Activism in Tampa, Florida, 1880s-1920s* (Urbana: Univ. of Illinois Press, 2001); Hall, "Disorderly Women."

26. Hewitt, *Southern Discomfort,* 125-31, 206-11, 243-46; Hall et al., *Like a Family;* Hall, "Disorderly Women"; Michelle Haberland, "After the Wives Went to Work: Organizing Women in the Southern Apparel Industry," in *"Lives Full of Struggle and Triumph": Southern Women, Their Institutions, and Their Communities,* ed. Bruce L. Clayton and John A. Salmond (Gainesville: Univ. Press of Florida, 2003), 283-302; Haberland, "Look for the Union Label: Organizing Women Workers and Women Consumers in the Southern Apparel Industry," in *Entering the Fray: Gender, Politics, and Culture in the New South,* ed. Jonathan Daniel Wells and Sheila R. Phipps (Columbia: Univ. of Missouri Press, 2010), 184-202; Haberland, "'It Takes a Special Kind of Woman to Work Up There': Race, Gender and the Impact of the Apparel Industry on Clarke County, Alabama, 1937-1980," in *Work, Family and Faith: Rural Southern Women in the Twentieth Century,* ed. Melissa Walker and Rebecca Sharpless (Columbia: Univ. of Missouri Press, 2006), 257-82; Shell-Weiss, "'I Dreamed I Went to Work'"; Nissen, "A Different Kind of Union."

27. The historical literature on the UAW's largely unsuccessful recent efforts to organize southern automobile plants is sparse, but see Karsten Hulsemann, "Greenfields in the Heart of Dixie: How the American Auto Industry Discovered the South," in *The Second Wave: Southern Industrialization from the 1940s to the 1970s,* ed. Philip Scranton (Athens: Univ. of Georgia Press), 219-254; Jonathan S. Russ, *Global Motivations: Honda, Toyota, and the Drive toward American Manufacturing* (Lanham, Md.: Univ. Press of America, 2008); Minchin, *Fighting against the Odds,* 152-55.

28. Minchin, *Fighting against the Odds,* 150-52; Timothy J. Minchin, "'Just Like a Death': The Closing of the International Paper Company Mill in Mobile, Alabama, and the Deindustrialization of the South, 2000-2005," *Alabama Review* 59, no. 1 (Jan. 2006): 46-48, 75; Timothy Minchin, "Torn Apart: Permanent Replacements and the Crossett Strike of 1985," *Arkansas Historical Quarterly* 59, no. 1 (Spring 2000): 31-58; Bruce E. Kaufman, "The Emergence and Growth of a Nonunion Sector in the Southern Paper Industry," in Zieger, *Southern Labor in Transition,* 295-329.

29. See Jefferson Cowie, *Capital Moves: RCA's Seventy-Year Quest for Cheap Labor* (Ithaca, N.Y.: Cornell Univ. Press, 1999); Minchin, "Shutdowns in the Sun Belt."

30. Zieger, "Walmart and the Broken Narrative of US Labor History"; Zieger, "Introduction: Southern Workers in a Changing Economy," in Zieger, *Life and Labor in the New New South,* 6-11.

31. Zieger, "Introduction: Southern Workers in a Changing Economy," 7-11; Minchin, *Fighting against the Odds,* 147-81. However, Thomas Jessen

Adams, "Walmart and the Making of 'Postindustrial Society,'" *Labor: Studies in the Working-Class History of the Americas* 8, no. 1 (Spring 2011): 117-25, argues that the distinctively southern component of the postindustrial labor-relations regime has been overemphasized.

32. Bethany Moreton, *To Serve God and Wal-Mart: The Making of Christian Free Enterprise* (Cambridge, Mass.: Harvard Univ. Press, 2009), 76-77. See also Nelson Lichtenstein, *The Retail Revolution: How Wal-Mart Created a Brave New World of Business* (New York: Metropolitan Books/Henry Holt, 2009).

33. David Montgomery, *Workers Control in America: Studies in the History of Work, Technology, and Labor Struggles* (Cambridge: Cambridge Univ. Press, 1979).

34. The spread of the southern labor-relations regime northward has been vividly demonstrated in the largely successful efforts of Republican governors in once union-friendly midwestern states to emulate the southern regime by curtailing public employees' collective bargaining rights and to gain passage of so-called right-to-work legislation. See Mary Beth Schneider and Chris Sikich, "Indiana Becomes Rust Belt's First Right-to-Work State," *USA Today,* February 20, 2012, http://usatoday30.usatoday.com/news/nation/story/2012-02-01/indiana-right-to-work-bill/52916356/1 (accessed October 15, 2012); Thomas J. Sugrue, "Workers' Paradise Lost," *New York Times,* December 14, 2012.

35. Nissen, "A Different Kind of Union"; Minchin, *Fighting against the Odds.*

CHAPTER SEVEN

The Great Depression and the New South

STEPHANIE A. CARPENTER

The "Migrant Mother" (1936) in Dorothea Lange's striking photo-graph and Tom Joad in John Steinbeck's *The Grapes of Wrath* (1939) are iconic representations of the devastation that faced the United States during the 1930s—the Great Depression. Both Lange and Steinbeck presented their characters as emblematic of rural America and its problems at large, rather than as representative of specific regions of the country. These iconic figures evoked an individual, personal experience of the Great Depression that could be shared nationally. Likewise, the classic works of the South during the Great Depression centered on individual experiences that are generalizable, rather than marked as regional. Few scholars have examined the devastation of the era as it distinctly affected the American South. That is not to say that sources do not exist. They do, but the breadth of scholarship regarding the Great Depression and the American South is not comprehensive, and additional work is needed to study fully this pivotal time in terms of regional American history, especially as it relates to southern poverty.

The Great Depression encompassed a period of extreme economic hardship brought about by the stock market crash in 1929 and the ineffective policies of President Herbert Hoover's administration. Hoover failed to recognize initially the overarching completeness of the stock market crash and subsequent depression;

thus his efforts were "too little, too late." With the stock market falling to levels before unseen and the index cut in half within just a few weeks of the Crash, businesses were unprepared for the economic downturn. As businesses failed to meet their economic expenditures, the depression reached all sectors of the economy quickly. The effort to pass high tariffs in 1929 and 1930 seemed like a good fix for the industrial sector—high tariff policy had been used successfully in the nineteenth century. However, the Tariff Act of 1930 (Smoot-Hawley Tariff) did not work as expected. Passed with extremely high rates, Smoot-Hawley put other countries on the defensive, and they retaliated with high tariffs on American goods. And while industry enjoyed a quick influx of cash, the tariff did not sustain the level of income for companies and the industrial sector.

As companies in all economic sectors failed, Americans also felt the economic crunch. By the time of the 1932 election, the U.S. economy had reached its lowest level since the Crash. Unemployment rates and corporate bankruptcies surpassed 25 percent of the population. And with these rates, the numbers of homeless and unemployed men, women, and children reached previously unseen rates. The 1932 presidential election seemed the one bright spot in the overall depressing economy. Governor Franklin D. Roosevelt (D-NY) ran against incumbent president Herbert Hoover (R-CA); and, while the national Republic Party supported President Hoover, the American people did not. Roosevelt won the election with a landslide in the Electoral College (472-59, carrying forty-two states) and by more than 7 million popular votes. Unlike Hoover, FDR had a plan for economic recovery. During the campaign he presented his "New Deal," which gave Americans hope for change. Although scholars of the New Deal are divided on its overall effectiveness, there is no doubt that it did stimulate the economy and provide money to Americans. During this era of "deficit spending," Americans received wages for work, subsidies for agricultural commodities, and payments of support.[1]

The New Deal in the South provided the same benefits to its residents along with relocation, flood control, and economic opportunities. The difference seen in the South during the 1930s, however, was the long-standing issue of poverty and debt. In the South, the Great Depression had been preceded by several decades of poverty in the post-Civil War era. Sharecroppers and tenant farmers had been plagued by surplus and low prices, which led to poverty and a lower standard of living than other regions of the country. And while reformers called for change and modernization during the Progressive era, southern politicians wanted to maintain control and the "simple" life. By the 1920s, Progressive reformers and southern intellectuals became more aggressive in their analyses of the South. Led by academics at southern universities, including the Vanderbilt Agrarians and members of the Institute for Research in Social Science at the University of North Carolina-Chapel Hill, these southern intellectuals critiqued the South with academic rigor, examining the state of the region as well as its social, cultural, and political traditions. As the stock market crashed and the entire nation entered the Great Depression, FDR instituted his New Deal and established hundreds of programs and initiatives. And, while the New Deal did provide economic relief to some, the intellectuals of the South believed the poverty issues of the region would be solved only through scientific and empirical research, through census data and statistics, and through an examination of individual lives.[2]

Southern intellectuals drove the beginnings of southern scholarship about the Great Depression. Their studies can be divided into four distinct genres: histories of the individual, histories of the South, histories of the Great Depression, and histories of the South during the Great Depression. This framework is by no means exhaustive, but points the reader to major historiographical themes and works during this decade. Foremost among these are those classic works of individual history, telling the stories of the sharecropper, the landowner, and the politician through oral histories, census and statistical data, and biographies. As in previous decades of southern historiography, personal accounts and history from the bottom up are prevalent and considered relevant to scholarly investigation.

Like Lange and Steinbeck, James Agee, Walker Evans, and Margaret Jarman Hagood portrayed the face of rural southerners during the 1930s. Their analyses, along with statistical data from the U.S.

government, showed the South to be a poor, destitute place with high levels of unemployment, loss of land, and displaced residents. Biographies of southern politicians, like Pat Harrison and Huey Long, showed the social, political, and cultural sides of the region. In *Let Us Now Praise Famous Men* (1941), journalist James Agee, along with photographer Walker Evans, brought attention to the plight of the southern sharecropper and rural class—too often an invisible part of life in a region where class was all important. Agee and Evans changed that perspective, journeying to Alabama in 1936 and (despite difficulties) recording the story of three Alabama sharecropping families.[3] Like Agee and Evans, Margaret Jarman Hagood also studied the rural southerner in the 1930s—concentrating on the plight of southern white tenant farm women. In researching for *Mothers of the South* (1939) as a sociology doctoral student at the Institute for Research in Social Science at the University of North Carolina-Chapel Hill, Hagood started out to prove (or refute) the high birth rate among southern women. What she found, as she traveled throughout Georgia and Alabama and spoke with hundreds of women, was not just confirmation of a high birth rate, but evidence that women participated in all aspects of southern rural life. In a study rich in social content, Hagood described health care, foods, work systems, social functions, and above all southern poverty. She showed southern women to be "strong, capable, and intelligent," regardless of circumstance.[4] The works of Agee, Evans, and Hagood, documenting the conditions of sharecroppers during the 1930s, have become pivotal sources of the 1930s in the South. At the same time, these personal stories put a face on government data from that era.

Many U.S. governmental agencies assisted the rural population during the 1930s and New Deal. Some provided documentary proof of that study, such as the Farm Security Administration (FSA), National Emergency Council (NEC), and Works Progress/Projects Administration (WPA). The Farm Security Administration, officially absorbing the Resettlement Administration (RA) in 1937, had a history of assisting southerners and attempting to provide for a better way of life. From forced to planned removal projects, the RA/FSA wanted to eradicate southern poverty, and worked to do so. One way that their message reached Americans was through the use of film. Most widely known for *The Plow that Broke the Plains* (1936), the RA/FSA and director Pare Lorentz also produced *The River* (1938), portraying the plight of southern tenant and sharecroppers along the Mississippi River and its tributaries, specifically the Tennessee River. *The River* showed how more than a century of farming practices at the river's edge led to erosion and flooding; the film also championed a solution in addition to the removal of farmers, which was the creation of the Tennessee Valley Authority (TVA). As government propaganda, *The River* fulfilled its role to showcase the New Deal and the TVA.[5] In addition to film, federal agencies, along with many of the southern intellectuals of the 1920s, studied the South and its poverty and issued reports that provided a wealth of primary information to future scholars. The Federal Works Agency of the WPA used cotton plantation surveys conducted in 1934 and 1937 to define southern agriculture, poverty, and the rate of voluntary participation in New Deal programs, specifically the Agricultural Adjustment Administration (AAA). In *The Plantation South, 1934-1937,* William C. Holley, Ellen Winston, and T. J. Woofter Jr. examined 246 surveys as related to the number of families on each farm and acres planted. By 1937, the results indicated that some southern cotton planters had increased acreage to take advantage of New Deal programs and payments.[6] The National Emergency Council also examined southern poverty during the 1930s after receiving a request from President Franklin D. Roosevelt. *The Report on Economic Conditions of the South* (1938) did not focus solely on rural life, but looked to find answers to the region's poverty by looking at several aspects of the region, including education, income, resources, and others.[7] In the end, analyses of these reports were left to future scholars as no real answers or follow-up occurred as the country geared up for World War II.

In addition to the primary sources of the individual, southern historians have long recorded the history of its politicians, specifically Huey Long of Louisiana and Pat Harrison of Mississippi—both Democrats who abandoned FDR in the 1930s, one for being liberal and the other conservative. The two politicians, their lives, and their biographies sum up the South in the 1930s—a democratic region, both progressive and conservative in social, cultural, and political issues. A high point in biographical writing about Long is T. Harry Williams's *Huey Long* (1969), which was awarded a Pulitzer Prize as well as a National Book Award. Long epitomized the southern political machine during the first half of the twentieth century. Even though he swayed from the Democratic Party, his populist ideas made him a favorite in Louisiana, if not in Washington. Williams, a historian at Louisiana State University, spent years researching his subject through interviews, newspapers, and other primary sources, and he told the story of the poor boy that made good, sometimes at the expense of those around him. Long's larger-than-life personality pushed the political envelope, and he used all means to get what he deemed necessary for his constituents. Williams is not alone in his treatment of Long. In *Voices of Protest: Huey Long, Father Coughlin, and the Great Depression* (1982), Alan Brinkley presented Huey P. Long and Father Charles E. Coughlin as leading similar political protest movements of the 1930s. According to Brinkley, these men were committed to defending the individual in an era of big business and expanding government. Brinkley acknowledged the successes and failures of both movements and ultimately the futility in their protests.[8]

In contrast to Long, Pat Harrison, although a conservative, saw himself as a "good" Democrat, one that followed the rules and embraced the New Deal and its programs for his home state of Mississippi. Branded as a "quintessential conservative," however, it was only a matter of time before he was at odds with the New Deal and FDR. Biographer Martha H. Swain followed Harrison's rise in politics and described his split from FDR and his policies. Her portrayal shows the distinction between Harrison and Long: The latter was a modern, progressive, radical populist at odds with the old ways of life in the South; the former remained a conservative politician during a time of great change in the country and region.[9]

The importance of these classic works—histories of the individual—cannot be understated as we examine the South during the

Great Depression. In the years following the reports and primary accounts of the effect of the Great Depression on the region, the scholarship was sparse. Histories of the South and histories of the Great Depression were written, but these analyses did little to combine the two themes into one comprehensive study. Those came later. The initial works, two to three decades following the Depression, concentrated either on the South as a region or the Great Depression as a national economic problem. Histories of the South cover the time frame since the Civil War. Some of the histories include a chapter or section on the Great Depression and New Deal; however, for the most part, these monographs do not focus on one decade, but cover the entire New South in a thematic analysis.[10] Texts that should be examined to set the context of southern economic issues and poverty include Thomas D. Clark and Albert D. Kirwan, *The South since Appomattox: A Century of Regional Change* (1967); Monroe Lee Billington, *The Political South in the Twentieth Century* (1975); Gavin Wright, *Old South, New South: Revolutions in the Southern Economy Since the Civil War* (1986); and Anthony J. Badger, *New Deal/New South: An Anthony J. Badger Reader* (2007).

In *The South since Appomattox,* Clark and Kirwan set the narrative tone by focusing on the tension of tradition versus modernity, change versus status quo, as the South struggled to balance agriculture with industry. A short chapter describes the Great Depression and New Deal with a brief analysis of New Deal programs in labor, agriculture, and industry in the South. This text focuses on the successes of the New Deal and does not analyze the negative issues regarding reform. The "Roosevelt Administration had the courage to force through a program of reform over the opposition of the centers of political power in the region. And while the program fell short in many ways of what the southern situation called for, it nevertheless manifested a profound concern for the needs of the mass of the underprivileged, white and Negro alike."[11]

Likewise, Billington's *The Political South in the Twentieth Century* does not address the New Deal at any length. With only one short chapter in the Great Depression, Billington showed the relationship between state and federal governments.[12] And, while Billington discussed the importance of federal monies to the region, he did not overlook the conservative nature of southern politics and how, as the New Deal progressed, southern politicians distanced themselves from FDR.

In *Old South, New South,* Wright examined southern economic history from the Civil War to the post-World War II era. He placed the South's economy within a global context as he used slavery and sharecropping to describe the southern society, economy, and culture. Wright devoted one chapter to the pre-World War II years, but his analysis of the New Deal and discussion of cotton crop mechanization did not discuss new material, but held to a standard historical interpretation of the period.[13]

In *New Deal/New South,* Badger compiled several of his published and unpublished New Deal and southern-focused manuscripts. Four of the essays examine the 1930s and the New Deal South. Themes include Huey Long and his attack of the New Deal; the New Deal's impact at the local level, specifically with the Agricultural Adjustment Administration, Tennessee Valley Authority, Rural Electrification Administration, and the textile workers strike; southern modernization as a result of World War II rather than the 1930s; FDR's legacy; and southern politicians of the late 1930s, 1940s, and postwar era. The chapter on Huey Long is the most successful, while the others show a lack of focus and direction.[14] Still, these sources do provide the reader not just with the context of the history of the South, but also a chapter (or two) on the New Deal.

One exception to this general focus are histories that concentrate solely on the agriculture of the region. Gilbert Fite, in *Cotton Fields No More: Southern Agriculture, 1865-1980* (1984), traced and analyzed the system of southern agriculture from the advent of sharecropping to the late twentieth century. With Fite's attention mostly dictated by rural and agricultural life, the conditions of the Great Depression and New Deal are an important part of his work. Still, even with an emphasis on agriculture, Fite devoted one chapter to the New Deal and another to the problems faced by tenancy, mechanization, low wages, and strikes.[15] Jeannie M. Whayne also explored the region's agriculture in *A New Plantation South: Land, Labor, and Federal Favor in Twentieth-Century Arkansas* (1996). This work covers issues related to land, labor, and federal programs in an often ignored region of the South; it examines the state's agriculture (corn, cotton, rice, and soybeans) and New Deal programs from the "top-down perspective." In the 1930s, the Arkansas Delta engaged in both class and race divisions/conflicts as New Deal programs favored landowners and the planter class.[16] These two studies emphasize a class conflict in the rural South between landowners and tenants or sharecroppers that, at times, crossed racial lines and reached a culmination in the 1930s.

Like the histories of the South, the histories of the Great Depression also leave the reader wanting more. In this case, it is difficult to find considerable South-related attention and analysis in the general works on the Great Depression.[17] Of the many monographs on the Great Depression (or the stand-alone topic of the New Deal), the following have some southern connection: Robert Golston, *The Great Depression: The United States in the Thirties* (1968); Studs Terkel, *Hard Times: An Oral History of the Great Depression* (1970); Robert S. McElvaine, *Down and Out in the Great Depression: Letters from the "Forgotten Man"* (1983); David E. Hamilton (ed.), *The New Deal* (1999); Harry L. Henderson and David B. Woolner (eds.), *FDR and the Environment* (2005); Harvard Sitkoff, *A New Deal for Blacks: The Emergence of Civil Rights as a National Issue, Volume 1: The Depression Decade* (1978); and Lauren Rebecca Sklaroff, *Black Culture and the New Deal: The Quest for Civil Rights in the Roosevelt Era* (2009). These are texts that share a southern component as part of the overall examination of Great Depression history. Golston's *The Great Depression* is a general history, with minimal information about the South interwoven throughout the text. Golston's strength is his inclusion of New Deal programs that affected American agriculture and labor as well as his attention to the Agricultural Adjustment Administration and the Southern Tenant Farmers Union in the South and the New Deal's impact on sharecroppers.[18] In *Hard Times* Terkel used a practice of the 1930s intellectuals and interviewed Americans regarding their experiences during the Great Depression. Although national in scope (both regionally and thematically), several accounts come from southerners; through their eyes, we glimpse southern life during the Great Depression.[19] Similar to Terkel, McElvaine in *Down and Out in the Great Depression* examined the era with a national focus and utilized the voice of the individual. McElvaine included accounts from almost two hundred people, showcasing a wide variety of lives and giving voice to the experiences of Americans during struggle and poverty. The author set the context for the era, but largely reproduced letters and accounts from Americans, covering a wide variety of topics and issues, including rural life, African Americans, children, conservatives, as well as angry, cynical, and desperate Americans.[20]

With the publication of *Down and Out in the Great Depression,* historians moved from merely retelling the story of the Great Depression to analyzing and revising it. The remaining three authors of histories of the Great Depression provide analysis, revision, and new directions for research. Hamilton's collected volume, *The New Deal,* provides chapters written by prominent historians examining the era. While many of the chapters are national in scope, Pete Daniel's "The New Deal and Southern Agriculture" in particular offers a glimpse of southern agricultural and government programs during the 1930s.[21] Henderson and Woolner's collection of essays in *FDR and the Environment* examine and analyze FDR's position on the environmental issues of the 1930s, including the Tennessee Valley Authority and conservation. Brian Black's essay, "Referendum on Planning: Imaging River Conservation in the 1938 TVA Hearings," maintains that the TVA epitomized FDR's environmental planning in the early 1930s. Reminiscent of his days as governor of New York, Roosevelt's early use of the TVA included flood control, river navigation, electric power, and recreation. Over time, however, the authority found it necessary to change its mission and vision, as shown by the 1938 hearings. While TVA planning may not have been as successful as needed, the practice of governmental regional/environmental planning began in the 1930s, only to reemerge in the 1960s as urban sprawl and other environmental challeges came to bear.[22]

Sitkoff in *A New Deal for Blacks* and Sklaroff in *Black Culture and the New Deal* pushed Great Depression studies in a different direction. Influenced by his own experiences in the 1960s civil rights movement, Sitkoff examined the issues of race and attempts to remove racism from American society. His volume describes the development of civil rights in the 1930s and sets the stage for the movement to come by exploring society and life for African Americans in the South. The decade ended with a feeling of optimism for the time to come. Chapters on New Deal farm policy, legal protection, and southern politics emphasize the South, though the study as a whole is national in scope and purpose.[23] Concerned with the lack of attention given to African Americans during the New Deal, Sklaroff examined the Federal Arts Project, Federal Writers Project, and Federal Theatre Project. Although great attention is given to African Americans within these programs, the same cannot be stated about the analysis of other New Deal programs. Sklaroff maintained that in order not to alienate southern Democrats, Roosevelt and his administration supported the arts, rather than address racial issues within the Agricultural Adjustment Administration and overlooked antilynching legislation.[24] Sklaroff's work, while urban and nationally focused, discusses southern racial conditions and the lack of response by the federal government.

All of the works to this point, while variously within the context of the South or the Great Depression, do not adequately analyze the South during the Great Depression. To do that, we must look at those works that fall within the subcategory of the history of the South during the Great Depression. We can subdivide this theme by looking at those histories written before and after the mid-1980s. Beginning with those written as narrative in the decades following the Depression, we expect a standard version of southern history without revision and without analysis. Of importance in this period are Donald H. Grubbs, *Cry from the Cotton: The Southern Tenant Farmers' Union and the New Deal* (1971); Donald Holley, *Uncle Sam's Farmers: The New Deal Communities in the Lower Mississippi Valley* (1975); Paul E. Mertz, *New Deal Policy and Southern Rural Poverty* (1978); Tom E. Terrill and Jerrold Hirsch (eds.), *Such as Us: Southern Voices of the Thirties* (1978); Douglas L. Smith, *The New Deal and the Urban South: The Advancement of a Southern Urban Consciousness during the Depression Decade* (1988); H. L. Mitchell, *Mean Things Happening in this Land: The Life and Times of H. L. Mitchell, Co-founder of the Southern*

Tenant Farmers Union (1979); John L. Robinson, *Living Hard: Southern Americans in the Great Depression* (1981); North Callahan, *TVA: Bridge over Troubled Waters* (1980); and James A. Hodges, *New Deal Labor Policy and the Southern Cotton Textile Industry, 1933-1941* (1986). These works represent the narrative history of the era that was predominant in the several decades following the 1930s. While these are not primarily analytic, all set the context of time and place and provide the reader with factual information.

The earliest work, Grubbs's *Cry from the Cotton,* is the first scholarly look at the Southern Tenant Farmers' Union (STFU), concentrating on the years of its greatest influence during the 1930s and describing its organizing and successes. Although sympathetic toward the STFU, Grubbs is not complimentary of the federal government and Agricultural Adjustment Administration. Far from unbiased, it does, however, provide a good discussion of southern agriculture and the violence that sharecroppers and tenants (black and white) faced in the 1930s. Grubbs depicted the situation for the southern sharecropper as bleak, with only the STFU to save them after the New Deal failed.[25] In contrast to Grubbs, Holley in *Uncle Sam's Farmers* provides a balanced examination of the influences of federal programs during the New Deal. Concentrating on the lower Mississippi River Valley, Holley described that region's agriculture and its challenges for survival during the Depression. Ravaged by economic hardship, flooding, and drought, the lower Mississippi served as a location for the federal government to "test" several of its social and relocation programs. And while the South as a whole may have been largely ignored by the New Deal, the lower Mississippi had numerous programs of assistance. While some failed, a large number succeeded, which is of importance in this study. Unfortunately, Holley did not present the people's voice in this work or offer much in the way of analysis of New Deal success.[26] In *New Deal Policy and Southern Rural Poverty,* Mertz set the context of the 1930s and southern poverty by describing agriculture, legislation, and the region. Mertz told the story of the rural South through primary manuscripts and a synthesis of secondary sources. The New Deal elevated the nation's poor and radically changed the country's agriculture, industry, and labor; in the South, the rural poor remained the "forgotten man"—without federal assistance and without change. For these, the destitute, the New Deal did not bring prosperity or change. In the end, Mertz concluded the South was inherently poor, rural, and provincial—unable to change. Ultimately, the New Deal administrators did not sufficiently understand the mentality of southern culture and life to bring about the change needed.[27]

Mertz's argument, that the federal government did not understand the South and its peoples, is not unique. Many of the monographs from the late 1970s to mid-1980s advanced a similar thesis. Editors Terrill and Hirsch in *Such as Us* wrote that the South lagged behind the rest of the country in the first half of the twentieth century—even World War II did not change that dynamic. Continuing the work of W. T. Couch in *These Are Our Lives* (1939), Terrill and Hirsch wanted to explore the uniqueness of southern culture and life.[28] As the South moved further from the rest of the country and regionalism became more pronounced, the editors used Federal Writers' Project accounts and analyzed history "from the bottom up" so that *Such as Us* offered a view of southern life, history, and culture forgotten by the rest of the nation. Just as the South lagged behind the rest of the nation by the 1930s, the urban and rural South also seemed at odds. Urban areas saw themselves as progressive and modern, while the rural areas remained conservative and provincial. Smith in "The New Deal and The Urban South" studied four southern cities: Atlanta, Birmingham, Memphis, and New Orleans. These cities represented both the Old and New South and possessed African American populations that were 28-38 percent of total urban population. Smith determined that race concerns in these urban cities seemed less defined than in the rural South. This study served two purposes: first, to provide a narrative of the region during the 1930s, examining the livelihood of its population and the effect that the Depression had on the cities' populations; second, to attempt to measure the impact of the New Deal on the region. Included in these analyses was the idea of urban consciousness and its role in the acceptance (or not) of public social programs, government interaction, and community betterment. Smith examined several aspects of each city and, in the end, determined that the New Deal had a minimum effect on economic recovery in these cities.[29]

The effectiveness of the New Deal is a theme that is present in many of the works that examined the Great Depression in the South. In 1979, Mitchell published his autobiography, *Mean Things Happening in this Land,* which described the state of southern agriculture, sharecroppers and tenants, and southern radicalism. Writing from the "bottom up," Mitchell, a socialist, compared the radicalism of the Southern Tenant Farmers' Union with actions in Oklahoma during the 1910s and in Louisiana with Huey Long in the 1920s and 1930s. Mitchell began his narrative with how he formed his views and ideology in his teens, continued through the founding of the STFU and the post–World War II era, and concluded in the 1970s.[30] In *Living Hard,* with photographs taken by Roy Stryker, Robinson used Federal Writers' Project interviews to tell the human side of the Great Depression in the South. Representing experiences of poverty and rural life, these accounts showed the best and worst of the Great Depression for the South.[31] The effectiveness of the New Deal is epitomized in the success of its programs. Callahan makes this point in his celebratory history of the TVA, showing the importance and necessity of the authority in the region. Without a clear thesis, Callahan's work uses the necessity of flood control for the region in the 1930s as justification for assisting the poverty-stricken. His narrative continues into the 1960s, although there is little analysis regarding the ultimate effectiveness of the program.[32] A final text in this arena of narrative history is Hodges's *New Deal Labor Policy and the Southern Cotton Textile Industry, 1933-1941.* Written later in the 1980s, Hodges missed the opportunity to be a revisionist, instead presenting an old argument—the New Deal did not always work. Although this text is a general history of the southern cotton industry, Hodges discussed both successes and failures within the industry during the 1930s. He paid close attention to describing the industry's workers, their demands for fair labor, and strikes. Although the federal government passed the Wagner Act in 1935, creating the National Labor Relations Board to assist industrial workers, southern culture resisted participation. In the end, while these measures worked for some workers, the southern cotton industrial worker did not achieve economic freedom or collective bargaining. And Hodges's analysis missed a reinterpretation of the time; instead, the text perpetuated the image that the New Deal failed to achieve change in the face of an inflexible southern way of life.[33]

During the 1980s, American historiography took a revisionist turn, as historians reexamined the previous centuries. As a result, histories reevaluated and sought new analyses for traditional conclusions. In the area of the histories of the South during the Great Depression, new interpretations appeared that challenged the likelihood of a "successful" New Deal in the South. Historians still acknowledged that some programs worked and brought advantages to the region, but questioned the cost. It became more important to examine these programs as a greater part of the decade, to determine the benefits while also weighing the failure of federal programs to include minorities and rural poor. Beginning in the mid-1980s, new interpretations appeared in a wide range of works, including James C. Cobb and Michael V. Namorato (eds.), *The New Deal and the South* (1984); Roger Biles, *The South and the New Deal* (1994); Patricia Sullivan, *Days of Hope: Race and Democracy in the New Deal Era* (1996); Janet Irons, *Testing the New Deal: The General Textile Strike of 1934 in the American South* (2000); *Oh Freedom After Awhile: The Missouri Sharecroppers Strike of 1939* (1999), produced by Lynn Rubright, Candace O'Connor, and Steven John Ross; Jarod Roll, *Spirit of Rebellion: Labor and Religion in the New Cotton South* (2010); Erik S. Gellman and Jarod Roll, *The Gospel of the Working Class: Labor's Southern Prophets in New Deal America* (2011); Aaron D. Purcell, *White Collar Radicals: TVA's Knoxville Fifteen, the New Deal, and the McCarthy Era* (2009); and Emily S. Bingham and Thomas A. Underwood (eds.), *The Southern Agrarians and the New Deal: Essays after* I'll Take My Stand (2001).

Cobb and Namorato's *The New Deal and the South* reexamines the New Deal's progress in the fifty years following the first inauguration of Franklin D. Roosevelt, providing the "first comprehensive assessment of the New Deal's impact on the South."[34] The essays, contributed by Numan V. Bartley, Alan Brinkley, Pete Daniel, J. Wayne Flynt, Frank Freidel, Harvard Sitkoff, and others, offer both short- and long-term analyses of the New Deal and its effect on the South as region, on its politics, and on its way of life, specifically looking at race, politics, labor, and agriculture. Published in 1984, this text provided a starting point for historians in their revisionist interpretation of southern history. By focusing on not just the short-term, but also the long-term impact of the New Deal, these historians ushered in a new history of the South during the Great Depression—posing questions for future scholars to explore. In *The South and the New Deal,* Biles presented a sweeping history that examined agriculture in terms of sharecroppers and agribusiness, as well as relief programs, labor issues, race, and politics across the South. While this is a general narrative of the South, Biles still pointed scholars in future directions of study. In contrast to others who see the South as conforming to a traditional conservative way of life, Biles saw the 1930s as the force behind and reason for modernization of the region in the next decade.[35] Biles's work encouraged other historians to look at the South in the 1930s not as conforming to its traditional life, but as attempting—like southern liberal Democrats—to break free of the past.

One work that pushed past the traditional view of the South during the Great Depression and New Deal is Sullivan's *Days of Hope.* Examining both the 1930s and 1940s, Sullivan explored issues of race, politics, and government participation. Beginning with a discussion of southern society in the first years of the twentieth century, she traced the initial enthusiastic response to Roosevelt's New Deal by southern Democrats who supported the influx of dollars and programs to the South. While the white elite and business owners controlled New Deal programs, southern Democrats continued their support of the president; however, as the 1930s progressed and New Deal programs and southern groups like the STFU provided assistance to peoples marginalized by decades of southern politics, conservative southern Democrats withdrew their support. In their place stepped a younger generation of southerners who supported Roosevelt and the message of the New Deal. These young southerners became "sympathetic allies" in Sullivan's account as she examined their relation to the those marginalized in southern society—

African Americans, factory workers, and sharecroppers—and how the latter New Deal programs benefited those groups long ignored by southern democracy.[36] That a division existed between the old guard and young southern Democrats by 1938 is well established, as the text charts the later developments of the Democrats, the South, and then the federal government through the World War II years.

Instead of writing of the larger southern picture, other historians focused on case studies and specific programs or movements within the New Deal. In *Testing the New Deal,* Irons explored the southern Textile Strike of 1934. Using primary accounts, court testimonies, and hearings, Irons used the southern mill strike as a case study of the issues surrounding the industrial worker in the 1930s. The General Textile Strike encompassed the largest strike in southern history and numbered almost 170,000 southern mill workers. With two-thirds of mill workers on strike in five states, southern elites and politicians saw this strike as a threat to their way of life.[37] In the region where the elite voted, politicked, and controlled society, the voice of the southern mill hand was not always heard. As a result, and like their fellow southern sharecroppers, mill workers embraced New Deal policy. Their greatest challenge involved being heard by the union's northern leadership and the federal government. While FDR and the New Deal wanted to support industrial workers, the administration also depended on southern Democrats in Congress, who were tied to the southern elite, not the working class. Irons also concentrated on the aftermath of the strike and the changes brought to the southern mill economy.

Southerners did not just strike in the textile mills, but along the roadsides as well. Probably one of the lesser known strike movements in the South during the 1930s occurred along the highways of Missouri, in a region affectionately known as the "Bootheel." In 1999, Rubright, O'Connor, and Ross's documentary film *Oh Freedom After Awhile* showcased the plight of the twentieth-century southern sharecropper, focusing on the Missouri Bootheel. Long caught in a continual cycle of debt, these black and white sharecropping families took action in the late 1930s and early 1940s to better their lives and working conditions. Long ignored by local and state governments, these farmers hoped for relief from the Agricultural Adjustment Administration and other federal programs, but when that did not occur, they went on strike. Thousands strong, the Sharecroppers' Strike presented a powerful image as they lined the highways to draw attention to their wretched situation. Their organization and protest became the focus of *Oh Freedom After Awhile.* Oral interviews, film clips, historical information, and music strive to show the situation that existed in the region and the means taken to overcome tradition and southern plantation life. This is a complex story, one of economics, politics, society, and southern culture; it passes all social groups as well as race and gender.[38] The film focused the attention of revisionist historians on the sharecroppers. Such is the case with Roll's *Spirit of Rebellion.* Concentrating on the sharecroppers' lives and spirituality, Roll used the Sharecroppers' Strike to show how some southerners tore down barriers in the 1930s. While race had separated the Bootheel sharecroppers as late as World War I, shared evangelical Protestantism and the economic distress of the 1920s and 1930s closed the racial gap. Roll placed special emphasis on the role of the religious revivals of the 1920s and 1930s as the underlying force bringing about racial and economic change, rather than economic injustice.[39] As a group, the Bootheel sharecroppers and tenant farmers realized they had common interests that outweighed their differences, creating an understanding of southern poverty and politics that moved the groups to greater consolidation and cooperation through the National Association for the Advancement of Colored People, Universal Negro Improvement Association, and Southern Tenant Farmers' Union.

The account of the Sharecroppers' Strike is seen in other works that commemorate the individual experience and intellectual culture of the South. Gellman and Roll in *The Gospel of the Working Class* presented accounts of southern labor organizers Owen Whitfield and Claude Williams, two clergymen, who worked to better the lives of their congregations, neighbors, and region. Although Williams, a white man from Arkansas, and Whitfield, a black man from Missouri, may not have lived similar lives, their shared story speaks of the issues that faced poor, rural southerners—be they sharecroppers, industrial workers, or coal miners. These men understood poverty, and their words and actions, as captured by Gellman and Roll, showed how two individuals helped shape the southern way of life in the 1930s.[40] Gellman and Roll are not the only historians to examine the actions of liberal southerners in revisionist history. In *White Collar Radicals*, Purcell examined the Communist Party in Knoxville, Tennessee, during the 1930s and post-World War II, including an analysis of its leadership and members.[41]

One source that epitomized the idea of revisionist history is *The Southern Agrarians and the New Deal*, edited by Bingham and Underwood. This work reexamines the writings of the Southern Agrarians, based at Vanderbilt University, and their contemporaneous critiques of the New Deal. The Agrarians challenged those who supported collective agriculture and "transforming" the southern way of life, which at times meant they opposed both Roosevelt and the work of the Institute for Research in Social Science at the University of North Carolina-Chapel Hill. If the Agrarians challenged FDR and the New Deal, they did so in the effort to reform and revive southern society. The volume includes articles from the 1920s and 1930s that showed the Agrarians wanted to reform governmental policies and create a better society. In the 1930s, the Agrarians seemed far removed from New Deal liberals, but today that gap is not as apparent. The editors included essays by Donald Davidson, Herman Clarence Nixon, Frank Lawrence Owsley, and others.[42]

The South during the Great Depression is a complicated historiographical narrative. Few sources cover the topic exhaustively, but many cover the region and era in a peripheral or secondary manner. Because of this, there is room for additional sources and studies. It is time to reexamine the primary sources of the period (with Bingham and Underwood) and reevaluate, reinterpret, and revise our assumptions and conclusion about the success (or not) of the New Deal in the 1930s. Thus, the sources mentioned above are by no means a complete or exhaustive look at the South in the Great Depression, but a representation of possibilities for scholarship.

NOTES

1. William E. Leuchtenburg, *Franklin Roosevelt and the New Deal, 1932–1940* (New York: Harper and Row, 1963), 17.

2. The Southern Agrarians produced their first work, *I'll Take My Stand: The South and the Agrarian Tradition,* in 1930. Their critique of American society and modernity as spiritually vacuous was not well received. That might have been the end of it, except for the aftershocks of stock market crash, Great Depression, and implementation of the New Deal. In the 1930s, the Agrarians wrote critiques against collective farming, the industrial North, and progressive scholars who claimed to understand the South and its way of life.

3. James Agee and Walker Evans, *Let Us Now Praise Famous Men* (Boston: Houghton Mifflin, 1941).

4. Anne Firor Scott, introduction to Margaret Jarmon Hagood, *Mothers of the South* (New York: W. W. Norton and Company, 1977), vii.

5. *The Plow that Broke the Plains,* directed by Pare Lorentz (U.S. Resettlement Administration/Farm Security Administration, 1936); *The River,* directed by Pare Lorentz (Farm Security Administration, 1938).

6. William C. Holley, Ellen Winston, and T. J. Woofter Jr., *The Plantation South, 1934-1937,* Research Monograph XXII, Division of Research, Federal Works Agency, Works Progress Administration (Washington, D.C.: GPO, 1940). The researchers used T. J. Woofter et al., *Landlord and Tenant on the Cotton Plantation,* Research Monograph 5 (Washington, D.C.: Division of Social Research, Works Progress Administration, 1936), and its study of southern cotton plantations in 1934. To track labor changes, technology use, and economics from 1934, Holley, Winston, and Woofter sought to repeat plantation surveys for the 1937 crop year. Out of the more than 300 plantations/farms the WPA surveyed in the summer of 1938, Holley, Winston, and Woofter matched 246 from the initial survey in 1934. States included North Carolina, Georgia, Mississippi, Arkansas, and Louisiana.

7. The National Emergency Council, *The Report on Economic Conditions of the South* (Washington, D.C.: GPO, 1938).

8. T. Harry Williams, *Huey Long* (New York: Alfred A. Knopf, 1969); Alan Brinkley, *Voices of Protest: Huey Long, Father Coughlin, and the Great Depression* (New York: Alfred A. Knopf, 1982), 3-81, 143-283. See also Brinkley, *Liberalism and Its Discontents* (Cambridge, Mass.: Harvard Univ. Press, 1998), chapter 9; Frank Freidel, *Franklin D. Roosevelt: A Rendezvous with Destiny* (Boston: Little, Brown and Company, 1990), chapter 11. For an in-depth look at Huey P. Long's life and the progression of scholarship, see Huey Pierce Long, *Every Man a King: The Autobiography of Huey P. Long* (1933; repr., Da Capo Press, 1996); Long, *My First Days in the White House* (1935, repr., Stackpole Books, 2013); Long and James J. A. Fortier, *Martyr of the Age* (New Orleans: Louisiana State Museum, 1937); Harnett T. Kane, *Louisiana Hayride:*

The American Rehearsal for Dictatorship, 1928-40 (New York: W. Morrow, 1941); Allan P. Sindler, *Huey Long's Louisiana: State Politics, 1920-1952* (Baltimore: Johns Hopkins Univ. Press, 1956); Henry C. Dethloff, *Huey P. Long: Southern Demagogue or American Democrat?* (Boston: Heath, 1967); T. Harry Williams, *Huey Long* (New York: Alfred A. Knopf, 1969); Henry M. Christman, ed., *Kingfish to America, Share Our Wealth: Selected Senatorial Papers of Huey P. Long* (New York: Schocken Books, 1985); William I. Hair, *The Kingfish and His Realm: The Life and Times of Huey P. Long* (Baton Rouge: Louisiana State Univ. Press, 1991); Glen Jeansonne, *Messiah of the Masses: Huey P. Long and the Great Depression* (New York: HarperCollins College Publishers, 1993); Suzanne LeVert, *Huey Long: The Kingfish of Louisiana* (New York: Facts on File, 1995); Garry Boulard, *Huey Long Invades New Orleans: The Siege of a City, 1934-36* (Gretna, La.: Pelican Publishing, 1998); Garry Boulard, *Huey Long: His Life in Photos, Drawings, and Cartoons* (Gretna, La.: Pelican Publishing, 2003); and Richard D. White Jr., *Kingfish: The Reign of Huey P. Long* (New York: Random House, 2006). Long's life has influenced fictional works as well, with the most recognized being Robert Penn Warren's *All the King's Men* (New York: Harcourt Brace, 1946). This work won the Pulitzer Prize and has been made into film and stage performances.

9. Martha H. Swain, *Pat Harrison: The New Deal Years* (Jackson: Univ. Press of Mississippi, 1978).

10. For those histories of the South that do not address the Great Depression as a topic, but do provide valuable context of the time, see, *Writing Southern History: Essays in Historiography in Honor of Fletcher M. Green,* ed. Arthur S. Link and Rembert W. Patrick (Baton Rouge: Louisiana State Univ. Press, 1965); *Reading Southern History: Essays on Interpreters and Interpretations,* ed. Glenn Feldman (Tuscaloosa: Univ. of Alabama Press, 2001); Paul Harvey, *Freedom's Coming: Religious Culture and the Shaping of the South from the Civil War through the Civil Rights Era* (Chapel Hill: Univ. of North Carolina Press, 2005).

11. Thomas D. Clark and Albert D. Kirwan, *The South since Appomattox: A Century of Regional Change* (New York: Oxford Univ. Press, 1967), 243.

12. Monroe Lee Billington, *The Political South in the Twentieth Century* (New York: Charles Scribner's Sons, 1975).

13. Gavin Wright, *Old South, New South: Revolutions in the Southern Economy Since the Civil War* (New York: Basic Books, 1986).

14. Anthony J. Badger, *New Deal/New South: An Anthony J. Badger Reader* (Fayetteville: Univ. of Arkansas Press, 2007), 1-30.

15. Gilbert Fite, *Cotton Fields No More: Southern Agriculture, 1865-1980* (Lexington: Univ. Press of Kentucky, 1984), 120-62.

16. Jeannie M. Whayne, *A New Plantation South: Land, Labor, and Federal Favor in Twentieth-Century Arkansas* (Charlottesville: Univ. Press of Virginia, 1996), 4, chapter 7.

17. For greater context of the Great Depression, see Amity Shlaes, *The Forgotten Man: A New History of the Great Depression* (New York: Harper Perennial, 2007); Paul K. Conklin, *The New Deal,* 3rd ed. (Wheeling, Ill.: Harlan Davidson, 1992); Anthony J. Badger, *The New Deal: The Depression Years, 1933-1940* (Chicago: Ivan R. Dee, 1989); Michael A. Bernstein, *The Great Depression: Delayed Recovery and Economic Change in America, 1929-1939* (Cambridge: Cambridge Univ. Press, 1987); John A. Garraty, *The Great Depression: An Inquiry into the Causes, Course, and Consequences of the Worldwide Depression in the Nineteen-Thirties, as Seen by Contemporaries and in the Light of History* (San Diego: Harcourt Brace Jovanovich Publishers, 1986); *The Great Depression Revisited,* ed. Karl Brunner (Boston: Martinus Nijhoff Publishing, 1981); Lester V. Chandler, *America's Greatest Depression, 1929-1941* (New York: Harper and Row Publishers, 1970); William E. Leuchtenburg, *Franklin D. Roosevelt and the New Deal, 1932-1940* (New York: Harper and Row, 1963).

18. Robert Golston, *The Great Depression: The United States in the Thirties* (Indianapolis: Bobbs-Merrill Company, 1968).

19. Studs Terkel, *Hard Times: An Oral History of the Great Depression* (New York: Pantheon Books, 1970).

20. Robert S. McElvaine, *Down and Out in the Great Depression: Letters from the "Forgotten Man"* (Chapel Hill: Univ. of North Carolina Press, 1983).

21. Pete Daniel, "The New Deal and Southern Agriculture," in *The New Deal,* ed. David E. Hamilton (Boston: Houghton Mifflin Company, 1999), 120-45.

22. Brian Black, "Referendum on Planning: Imaging River Conservation in the 1938 TVA Hearings," in *FDR and the Environment,* ed. Harry L. Henderson and David B. Woolner (New York: Palgrave Macmillan, 2005), 181-94.

23. Harvard Sitkoff, *A New Deal for Blacks: The Emergence of Civil Rights as a National Issue, Volume 1: The Depression Decade* (New York: Oxford Univ. Press, 1978), see esp. chapters 2, 5, and 9.

24. Lauren Rebecca Sklaroff, *Black Culture and the New Deal: The Quest for Civil Rights in the Roosevelt Era* (Chapel Hill: Univ. of North Carolina Press, 2009), x.

25. Donald H. Grubbs, *Cry from the Cotton: The Southern Tenant Farmers' Union and the New Deal* (Chapel Hill: Univ. of North Carolina Press, 1971).

26. Donald Holley, *Uncle Sam's Farmers: The New Deal Communities in the Lower Mississippi Valley* (Urbana: Univ. of Illinois Press, 1975).

27. Paul E. Mertz, *New Deal Policy and Southern Rural Poverty* (Baton Rouge: Louisiana State Univ. Press, 1978), 253-62.

28. William T. Couch, *These Are Our Lives* (Chapel Hill: Univ. of North Carolina Press, 1939); Tom E. Terrill and Jerrold Hirsch, eds., *Such as Us: Southern Voices of the Thirties* (Chapel Hill: Univ. of North Carolina Press, 1978), xi-xxv.

29. Douglas L. Smith, "The New Deal and The Urban South: The Advancement of a Southern Urban Consciousness during the Depression Decade" (Ph.D. diss., Univ. of Southern Mississippi, 1978).

30. H. L. Mitchell, *Mean Things Happening in this Land: The Life and Times of H. L. Mitchell, Co-founder of the Southern Tenant Farmers Union* (Montclair, N.J.: Allanheld, Osmun and Company Publishers, 1979).

31. John L. Robinson, *Living Hard: Southern Americans in the Great Depression* (Washington, D.C.: Univ. Press of America, 1981).

32. North Callahan, *TVA: Bridge over Troubled Waters* (South Brunswick, N.J.: A. S. Barnes and Company, 1980).

33. James A. Hodges, *New Deal Labor Policy and the Southern Cotton Textile Industry, 1933-1941* (Knoxville: Univ. of Tennessee Press, 1986).

34. James C. Cobb and Michael V. Namorato, eds., *The New Deal and the South* (Jackson: Univ. Press of Mississippi, 1984), 6.

35. Roger Biles, *The South and the New Deal* (Lexington: Univ. Press of Kentucky, 1994).

36. Patricia Sullivan, *Days of Hope: Race and Democracy in the New Deal Era* (Chapel Hill: Univ. of North Carolina Press, 1996), 4.

37. Janet Irons, *Testing the New Deal: The General Textile Strike of 1934 in the American South* (Urbana: Univ. of Illinois Press, 2000), 3-8.

38. *Oh Freedom after Awhile: The Missouri Sharecroppers Strike of 1939,* produced by Lynn Rubright, Candace O'Connor, and Steven John Ross, narrated by Julian Bond (San Francisco: California Newsreel, 1999).

39. Jarod Roll, *Spirit of Rebellion: Labor and Religion in the New Cotton South* (Urbana: Univ. of Illinois Press, 2010).

40. Erik S. Gellman and Jarod Roll, *The Gospel of the Working Class: Labor's Southern Prophets in New Deal America* (Urbana: Univ. of Illinois Press, 2011).

41. Aaron D. Purcell, *White Collar Radicals: TVA's Knoxville Fifteen, the New Deal, and the McCarthy Era* (Knoxville: Univ. of Tennessee Press, 2009).

42. *The Southern Agrarians and the New Deal: Essays after* I'll Take My Stand, ed. Emily S. Bingham and Thomas A. Underwood (Charlottesville: Univ. Press of Virginia, 2001).

CHAPTER EIGHT

Racial Change and World War II in the New South

JENNIFER E. BROOKS

The story of racial change amid the impact of World War II on the American South has yielded a distinctive historiography. Indeed, it defies categorization into traditional schools because its genesis primarily lies in the period after 1965, amid a major transition in American historiography to social and cultural history. Moreover, the question of the war's role in shaping the course of racial change in the Jim Crow South attracted most historians' attention when they started investigating the "long civil rights movement."[1] The focus on this era as a precursor to the civil rights movement also aligned at the time with the impulse in New South historiography to consider the broader impact of World War II on the region.[2] Thus, I categorize the literature of World War II and racial change into three broad groups: the civil rights era, the commemorative era, and the millennial era. Although these divisions are not chronologically hard and fast, nonetheless they roughly embrace three generations of historical scholarship addressing the impact of World War II on race relations in the South. The *civil rights era* starts with works that first began substantively to address this impact during the 1960s and into the early 1980s, alongside the peaks and valleys of the modern civil rights movement itself. The *commemorative era* emerged as the fiftieth anniversaries of World War II arrived in the 1990s, and it percolated throughout the ensuing decade. The *millennial era* refers to those works published in the early twenty-first century. In each era, historians have asked if the war acted mostly as an engine of change, ushering in the modern South and the black civil rights movement, or if the war promulgated tradition by sustaining the foundations of Jim Crow. The following essay explores this theme's journey across these three historiographical eras.

PRECURSOR TO THE CIVIL RIGHTS ERA

A sense that the Second World War might alter the southern home front in important ways emerged even before the conflict had ended. Indeed, World War II generated a flurry of literary interest in southern race relations that only grew in the following decades. Several of these books or articles became staples of the academic and public appetite for assessing the region, such as those by Rayford Logan, Zora Neale Hurston, William Faulkner, Ralph Ellison, Langston Hughes, Lillian Smith, and Katherine Dupre Lumpkin.[3] One of the most famous of these wartime works was Chapel Hill sociologist Howard Odum's *Race and Rumors of Race: The American South in the Early Forties* (1943), which cataloged white fears, suspicions, and conspiracies about black insurrection during the war years.[4]

However, no scholar did more to examine the war's racial impact, nor to predict more provocatively what would follow, than famed Swedish sociologist Gunnar Myrdal.[5] Enlisting a team of researchers to produce *An American Dilemma* in 1944, Myrdal crafted a farsighted analysis of the many winds of racial change unleashed by the war. In so doing, Myrdal struck at the heart of American complacency about its own abysmal racial record, inspiring a generation of liberal civil rights activists and provoking mightily the defenders of Jim Crow. Although his book was published before the war ended, Myrdal nonetheless offered a prescient understanding of the war's contradictory impact. He was not always correct in his predictions, but he mapped out many of the events and developments of the war years that dominated subsequent histories.

Myrdal first pointed to the war's ideological impact on both blacks and whites, noting that justifying America's entry into the war in highly moralistic terms, such as defending democratic values, naturally drew attention to existing racial practices at home. Moreover, the failure of the "close the ranks" strategy pursued by W. E. B. Du Bois during World War I to produce real racial reform primed later African Americans to demand a different outcome this time around. Thus, Myrdal pointed to A. Philip Randolph's March on Washington movement. As president of the Brotherhood of Sleeping Car Porters, an all-black railroad union, Randolph leveraged the beginning of a grassroots civil rights movement—or the threat of one—to target racial discrimination in defense industries and the military. The threat of a mass march on Washington, D.C., in the midst of the war compelled President Franklin D. Roosevelt to issue Executive Order 8802 establishing the Fair Employment Practices Committee (FEPC)—evidence of a new era in black activism touched off by the war.[6] In the face of widespread economic and occupational discrimination in defense industries and the military, black leaders and the press "were not willing cheerfully to postpone their complaints until the war [was] over."[7] Moreover, he found that the black rank-and-file, both North and South, exhibited a bitter cynicism about the war. After all, to most, Myrdal found, "what really matters . . . is his treatment at home, in his own country."[8] Confronted by continued racism, blacks wondered about the meaning of an allegedly democratic war against foreign enemies. As one young black man supposedly related at an Army induction center, "just carve on my tombstone, 'Here lies a black man killed fighting a yellow man for the protection of a white man.'"[9]

Nonetheless, Myrdal also found that even within the pattern of discrimination that persisted, the tremendous economic expansion of the war had, in fact, lifted many boats, even those of black citizens who found more diversity in job opportunities, steady employment, and rising incomes, particularly for migrants who fled the southern countryside. And for those men and women who remained in the South, the war produced some uncomfortable realities that left many whites squirming, often to the delight of southern blacks. As Odum had also delineated in *Race and Rumors of Race,* southern whites were consumed with racial anxiety during the war.[10] White women fretted over the loss of maids and cooks, and planters and employers competed for the first time in a newly opened national labor market.[11] Some black southerners even wondered if a victory of a nonwhite nation, such as Japan, over Deep South "crackers" might not, in fact, be an improvement over living under Jim Crow.[12]

As early as 1942, Myrdal thus had recognized that what the wartime milieu produced in American, and especially southern, race relations above all was tension—and lots of it. On the one hand, as Myrdal states, the "Negro is better prepared than ever before in his history to fight" for his rights; on the other, southern whites feared the racial implications of the war. As a result, racial conflict darkened the horizon, and the North and South appeared increasingly polarized. But ultimately, Myrdal predicted, "there [would] be a change toward equality for the Negro." In ten years, he argued, Americans would look back on the war years as a "temporary interregnum" between a Jim Crow past and a racially progressive future."[13]

Of course, having completed the research for his thoughtful analysis even before the midpoint of World War II, Myrdal missed some key domestic events, including race riots in Harlem and Detroit, hate strikes in New Orleans shipyards, and racial clashes on southern military bases. As a result, Myrdal got a good deal wrong about World War II's racial legacy. But he also got a surprising amount correct.[14] The end of World War II ushered in much of what Myrdal had identified as the markers of racial change to come. The tensions he spoke of during the war only increased with the return of millions of veterans, black and white, to the home front and the reconversion of wartime industries to peacetime production.[15] A spate of postwar lynching in the South, often targeting black veterans, along with the continued pressure exerted by an expanded and energetic National Association for the Advancement of Colored People (NAACP) and a newly empowered black electorate in the North prompted a politically beleaguered President Truman to desegregate the armed forces, appoint a presidential commission on race, and adopt planks for progressive racial reform into the Democratic Party platform. And having won reelection by a razor-thin margin in 1948, only with the help of northern black voters, President Truman seemed poised to direct more federal attention to the cause of racial equality and civil rights in the Jim Crow South.[16] Myrdal seemed almost prophetic.

However, the Cold War intervened, bringing with it a resurgent southern Democratic conservatism, complicating and ultimately stalling the movement for racial reform.[17] Ten years after Pearl Harbor, contrary to Myrdal's prediction, no one was looking back at the war years as a "temporary interregnum." Of course, all of that was about to change, and dramatically so, if not all at once. The *Brown v. Board of Education* Supreme Court decision of 1954 was followed by massive white resistance and federal intervention in Little Rock, Arkansas, and the Montgomery Bus Boycott in Alabama, ushering in the modern phase of the black freedom struggle in the 1950s and 1960s.

CIVIL RIGHTS ERA

Journalists and scholars alike rushed to explain what seemed to be a sudden emergence of a militant, grassroots, direct-action civil rights movement where none had existed before.[18] Scholars soon looked for antecedents and precedents, thereby launching the "civil rights era" period of historiography. One of the first and most notable scholars to assess the racial impact of World War II in the South was George Brown Tindall. He concluded *The Emergence of the New South* (1967), his contribution to Louisiana State University Press's "History of the South" series, with a detailed and insightful analysis of the war's broadly destabilizing impact.[19] Offering a mostly top-down analysis, Tindall emphasized regional and national politics and the demographics of the war's impact; he focused less on the lived experience of black and white southerners, men or women, within the South's war-induced racial milieu. However, whereas Myrdal could only predict how the racial impact of the war ultimately would play out, Tindall drew on primary source evidence to

determine the actual patterns. Tindall highlighted the war as a particularly disruptive event in southern society and politics, one that
heightened both black expectations of positive change and white
dread of impending racial Armageddon.

Not surprisingly, writing in the heat of the modern civil rights
movement, Tindall emphasized the intense southern white backlash to the racial changes wrought by the war. Rather than a "temporary interregnum" before racial reform, as Myrdal had anticipated, Tindall identified a hardening white resistance manifest in
strident southern opposition to the New Deal and any expansion
of federal intervention in racial matters. Nonetheless, Tindall also
pointed to the many ways the war had worked its unexpected racial "magic," stirring up black southerners with hopes of a new day
while also embittering many at the persistence of white resistance
to racial reform. Tindall also listed many of the signature developments of the war years that would feature in one way or another in
virtually every subsequent account of World War II and the South:
the mobility of southerners within the region and to the North and
West; the dramatic but uneven impact of defense industries and
federal spending on the southern economy; rising southern per
capita incomes; chaotic urban growth; booming farms and shrink-
ing farm ownership; Executive Order 8802 and the FEPC; *Smith
v. Allwright,* the Supreme Court decision of 1944 that prohibited
all-white primaries; increasing black protest; and the southern
Democratic assault on the New Deal.[20] Thus, Tindall concluded
by quoting political scientist H. Clarence Nixon, who remarked
in 1944 that the South "emerged from the war . . . with more social change and more unfinished business than any other part of
the country."[21] Indeed, no shared vision existed among black and
white southerners, whether rank-and-file or the region's leaders,
about what the war's legacy would, or should, be. But Tindall made
a convincing case that the war was a signature event in the United
States and the South—particularly to southern race relations—even
if he stopped short of declaring it "more important than the Civil
War" in its comprehensive impact on the region.[22]

More attention to the war years as precedent setting for the modern civil rights movement soon followed, extending much of what Tindall and Myrdal had argued. Richard Dalfiume labeled the period the "Forgotten Years of the Negro Revolution" (1968).[23] Dalfiume saw in the March on Washington movement and the refusal of black press editors to adopt the "close the ranks" strategy as evidence of World War II's unique importance as a precursor to the civil rights movement of the 1950s–1960s. Most importantly, black citizens themselves, including those in the South, used the war to directly challenge the racial status quo: "a mass militancy became characteristic of the American Negro in World War II." And though they did not initially succeed, these efforts trained a generation of black civil rights leaders.[24] Thus, Dalfiume argues, the war had worked a "revolution" in race relations that bore fruit in modern civil rights protests. In this sense, Dalfiume proclaimed to have recovered the black militancy of the 1940s from the dustbin of history.

Similar analyses followed—notably by Harvard Sitkoff, Neil Wynn, and Stephen Lawson[25]—but it was Lee Finkle who most countered this "revolutionary" reading of the war era. Between them, Finkle and Dalfiume established an axis of continuity and change, respectively, that has consistently defined this historiography in one way or another to the present day. In "The Conservative Aims of Militant Rhetoric" (1973), Finkle questioned the actual militancy of the wartime black press.[26] He countered Dalfiume, Sitkoff, Tindall, and even Myrdal in defining black press editors and leaders as gung-ho advocates for immediate racial change. Rather, he argued, they adopted a militant *rhetoric* that trumpeted a "Double V" for victory, but actually enlisted it to contain the frustration, anger, and cynicism of the black masses (i.e., workers), who were increasingly bitter during the war in the face of continued discrimination. As Finkle pointed out, promising to fight for racial change at home as the price of black support for the war effort sounded inspirational and even radical. But it actually aimed to keep the black working class channeled into support for the war effort, regardless of the limits of federal actions against discrimination.[27] In like fashion, though, Finkle also identified the destabilizing impact of the war on race relations, and the emergence of black protest as important. Sitkoff followed Finkle's example in pointing to the role of the Detroit race riot of 1943 in quelling the appetites of black leaders and white liberals for immediate racial change. The so-called Double V campaign, Sitkoff argued, became much more of a retreat into gradualism once racial violence erupted at home during the war.[28]

Other works addressing World War II and racial change in the South appeared in subsequent decades of the civil rights era, but none departed significantly from the patterns established by Tindall, Dalfiume, Finkle, and Sitkoff.[29] Soon, however, the volume of works assessing the home front impact of the Second World War ballooned as important anniversaries of the war arrived.

COMMEMORATIVE ERA

The 1990s marked the official era of remembrance for the Second World War, initiating a series of fiftieth anniversary events commemorating the war's milestones, from Pearl Harbor and the Normandy invasion to V-E and V-J days and the bombings of Hiroshima and Nagasaki. Naturally, the decade witnessed a spike in publications on the impact of the war in the South.[30] The commemorative-era literature explored what effect the war had on local communities caught up in the turbulent wartime milieu. Understanding the complicated matrix of racial change in the South became part of a broader effort to assess the emergence of the modern Sunbelt South, as well as part of the effort to extend the timeline of the modern civil rights movement.

The diversity of southern experience in the war—whether measured by class, race, subregion, gender, urban or rural location, or economic sectors—became more evident in the commemorative-era literature. Within that diversity, the pattern of weighing change versus continuity in regard to the war's racial impact remained consistent. Some scholars continued to advocate the thesis of the war as an engine of racial change in the Jim Crow South, while others took a more cautious approach, emphasizing continued obstacles and limited outcomes.

Those on the latter side pointed to the enduring strength of the southern planter elite, who proved adept at withstanding the currents of change or even managed to advance their power.[31] Continuity scholars also noted the less-than-militant activism of black leadership against Jim Crow once the Japanese bombed Pearl Harbor, which changed the context for American entry into the war.[32] In many respects, the "limited change" thesis made considerable sense, given the chronological distance between 1945 and 1965, and the obvious question of why a black civil rights movement did not happen until the 1950s and 1960s if World War II had truly been a racial watershed. Sitkoff concluded that African American militancy against discrimination crested prior to Pearl Harbor and subsided thereafter; even fairly militant black leaders, including A. Philip Randolph, joined the war effort, and labeled black conscientious objectors as a "lunatic fringe." Moreover, he noted, blacks readily volunteered for military service. Thus, he argued, "the notion that blacks would gain from the war, not as a gift of goodwill but because the nation needed the loyalty and manpower of African Americans . . . continued to reverberate throughout World War II."[33] Nonetheless, one's perspective on the meaning of World War II for southern racial change depends upon whom, what, or where one is looking. Even as Sitkoff defined the limits of black wartime militancy, another scholar simultaneously drew on anthropologist James C. Scott to offer an entirely different understanding of the southern African American experience.[34]

Adopting Scott's notion of "infrapolitics," Robin Kelley eschewed the major civil rights organizations and leaders on which Sitkoff focused to consider instead the individual acts of resistance waged daily among black southerners as evidence of the instability of white supremacy.[35] In this view, the refusal of an African American soldier to change seats on a segregated bus in the Deep South ranked as just as significant as A. Philip Randolph's threat of an organized mass march on Washington. From this perspective, the southern black populace began to look far less quiescent during the war, even as the outcomes of organized actions, such as the FEPC, proved less than anticipated.[36]

Historians such as Kelley found that shifting focus away from the middle class and to the black working class revealed the war as a signal step in the journey toward comprehensive racial change for the region. Even in the restrictive environs of southern agriculture and rural labor relations, the war's racial impact registered. As Pete Daniel noted, labor competition emboldened black workers, who "either demanded higher wages or left rural areas for better opportunities." In Mississippi, some planters even agreed to raise wages in order to keep cotton-pickers on hand. Thus, "the people left behind in rural areas during the war sensed in this conflict important changes that would alter southern culture. . . . Indeed, race relations became the most visible elements of conflict and change."[37]

Expanding the definition of "political" beyond mainstream notions of electoral competitions and polling places underscored the role of the black working class in forging biracial coalitions of activists against Jim Crow. This focus, in fact, merged nicely with the efforts of civil rights historians in the 1990s to lengthen the chronology of the movement to encompass eras prior to 1954. Thus there emerged in the commemorative era several works examining organized labor in the wartime South through the activities of black workers determined to enlist both industrial unionism and wartime exigencies to advance the cause of civil and economic equality. At the tail end of the civil-rights era literature, in "Opportunities Found and Lost" (1988), Robert Korstad and Nelson Lichtenstein had identified the development of biracial coalitions rooted in the Congress of Industrial Organizations (CIO) as a critical development—and their demise under the weight of Cold War conservatism as a lost opportunity—for progressive racial reform. Commemorative era historians quickly followed suit. Perhaps the most important contribution of the commemorative era scholars thus lay in identifying "civil rights unionism" as a bridge between the activism of the New Deal era and the later movement of the 1950s and 1960s. In *Speak Now against the Day: The Generation before the Civil Rights Movement* (1995), John Egerton explored the southern popular front during World War II as a coalition of black-white, labor-liberal activists dedicated to fighting Jim Crow.[38] And from the tire factories of Memphis, Tennessee, to the tobacco mills of Winston-Salem, North Carolina, to the shipyards of Mobile, Alabama, and elsewhere, the South's black working class expressed heightened expectations for first-class citizenship during the war, and a willingness to join the National Association for the Advancement of Colored People (NAACP) or the CIO, and even to mount individual battles for the cause of racial equality.[39] Such resistance and assertiveness, for many scholars, testified to the inherently destabilizing racial impact of the Second World War.

The strength of southern white backlash and resistance, empowered by political expediency in Washington, however, cannot be denied, as several scholars have noted; ultimately, racial change was only incrementally achieved (according to some) or outright delayed (according to others) in the 1940s. In comparison to the 1930s and the 1960s, for example, according to Harvard Sitkoff, "blacks in World War II faced greater resistance to change, in a milieu less hospitable to disruptive protests, with reduced internal wherewithal and external support." As a result, although change occurred, it did so "in a limited manner."[40] But, taking an opposite view, Tim Tyson concluded that the "war against fascism brought African Americans their first viable opportunities to break the confines of . . . civility and challenge . . . 'our little Hitlers here in America.'" Conceding the moderation of black middle-class leaders, and that "the wartime struggle did not end segregation," Tyson nonetheless found that the Second World War was no less a racial watershed, when African Americans "launched the decades of political activism that would win back their full citizenship during the 1960s."[41]

MILLENNIAL ERA

The notion of "the more things change, the more they stay the same" has continued to mark this historiography into the next millennium. Indeed, with the twenty-first century, interpretations of the war's impact on southern race relations have not departed significantly from earlier historiographical eras. However, millennial scholars do expand the horizon on the landscape of racial change in the 1940s-era South, thereby deepening our understanding of the complexities of the war's impact. Among other trends, these historians often deemphasize World War II itself as the pivotal moment, pointing toward the later civil rights movement. They also bring "new" players to the debate, such as Latinos, Asians, nonsoutherners, and segregationists. And finally, millennial scholars consider the war's racial impact in a global context, not just as an impetus for regional or national change. The sharpest departure from all prior interpretations, however, questions the entire framework of connecting a devastating war to any real progress on civil rights.

As in earlier eras of historiography, scholars of the early twenty-first century have perpetuated the change-versus-continuity debate on the war's southern impact. On one side are those historians who emphasize the war's role in generating increased economic opportunities for blacks as well as heightened expectations and frustrations with the Jim Crow obstacles that remained. Like Dalfiume and others previously, scholars such as Robin Kelley opened the century asserting the war's primacy as the incubator of the modern civil rights movement, identifying the war as a critical turning point in the nation's journey to Selma and Montgomery. Specifically— and quite contrary to the continuarian view—Kelley and Earl Lewis have argued that "the 'Double V' campaign for victory at home and abroad, the March on Washington Movement, and the growing use of the federal government to secure their aims helped to write a new chapter in the history of African Americans and set the stage for the modern civil rights movement of the postwar years."[42] Other millennial scholars have agreed, finding that the war's racial legacy lay in its topsy-turvy impact on racial, economic, and political tradition; the arrival of widespread federal intervention in economic and social life; the migration of millions of southerners from countryside to city; the transition from civilian to soldier and sailor; and the intellectual and moral implications of the war against racially imbued fascism.[43]

Yet, on balance, millennial scholars have adopted a more cautious approach in labeling the war as a racial watershed. The excellent volume of essays, *The Fog of War: The Second World War and the Civil Rights Movement* (2012), brought many millennial trends together. Edited by historians Kevin Kruse and Stephen Tuck, the essays consider the broader historical impact of the racial turmoil induced by the war, and they do not confine their assessments to the South or even to the United States. James Sparrow considers the political economy of wartime mobilization that "politicized consumption," while Thomas Sugrue examines the "global vision" of civil rights activists in Hillburn, New York. Jason Ward offers the white supremacist version of a "Double V" campaign to preserve Jim Crow; Jane Dailey considers how the sexual politics of racial change undermined the fortitude of southern white liberals during the war; and Penny Von Eschen traces the ways that "race and racism were made and remade during and after the war" in the global colonial context.[44]

In assessing the various topics covered in the volume, editors Kruse and Tuck conclude that overall the war had a deeply destabilizing impact on American race relations, but the result was often contradictory and always ambiguous, obscuring the clarity of any line drawn between the war years and the black freedom struggle of the 1950s and 1960s. For each piece of evidence that linked the war's impact to real racial change—such as the establishment of the FEPC, for example—there existed an equally compelling case of the real limits to what people of color could achieve in the South, the United States, and the colonized world abroad. Yet, the instability and turmoil of the war years had an "undeniable" impact on the "idea of race" and on racism, Kruse and Tuck argue, slowly altering the social, cultural, and political milieu from which the modern phase of the civil rights movement emerged.[45]

Viewing the glass of civil rights progress during the war as half full or half empty has had much to do with where a scholar has looked. Historians such as Lichtenstein, Kelley, and Korstad, for example, have focused on urban and industrial spaces.[46] They have noted expanded industrial employment for black men and women; the assertiveness of black workers in pursuing civil rights equality through organized labor; and voter registration campaigns linked to earlier eras but energized anew in the 1940s. Other historians, however, have examined the small-town and rural South, where the story is much different. Even as thousands of black southerners flocked to urban areas, creating new turmoil for Jim Crow, the small-town and rural South sustained the racial, economic, and political hierarchies of white supremacy, despite the challenges presented by the war. Echoing James C. Cobb's analysis of the planters of the Mississippi Delta, J. Mills Thornton recently pointed out that, at least in Alabama, neither state nor federal policy, nor the war itself, really intruded much on black Alabamians' daily lives, which remained dominated by white supremacy.[47] Most importantly, Thornton points out, the racial impact of the war was so defined by locality that a broader historical pattern is hard to discern. Diversity was the rule. Thus, Thornton could find in small-town Alabama significant limits to the war's role in helping generate the "early phase" of the modern civil rights movement, whereas Kelley identified a restive and increasingly assertive urban black working class in Birmingham.[48] Indeed, Greta de Jong agrees, emphasizing a broader era of change in rural Louisiana from the 1930s through the postwar 1940s that produced an independent black middle class out of the ashes of southern agriculture. This group originated in the prewar organizing of the 1930s, coalesced in the 1940s, and emerged as indigenous civil rights leaders *after* World War II to welcome the national Congress of Racial Equality (CORE) activists in the 1960s.[49]

Other important trends in the millennial literature have been to connect the war's racial impact to events in the rest of the world—before, during, and after the war—and to widen the lens to include people of color other than African Americans. Historians have long pointed to the war's role in altering the dialogue of racial ideology as the world's western democracies ostensibly lined up against the racial intolerance and militarism of the Axis powers.[50] Like Gunnar Myrdal in 1944, and many since, millennial era historians have also widely noted how World War II altered the intellectual context in the United States on matters of race. However, several scholars in the twenty-first century take this matter much further, emphasizing the war's disruption of racial imperialism and connecting this American "seedtime of the modern civil rights movement" with popular reactions against colonialism worldwide.[51] Representative of this trend is Gary Gerstle's article, "The Crucial Decade" (2006). Gerstle transnationalizes the question of racial change and the South during World War II, defining the war as a period of *global* upheaval in race relations and placing wartime events on the Jim Crow home front in that context, not simply as a regional or national response to the war.[52]

Thomas Guglielmo, to cite another example, examined the fight of Mexican Americans in Texas during World War II for equality and for recognition as "Caucasians," a struggle that earned the support of the Mexican government.[53] Similarly, in "'No Jap Crow'" (2007), Jason Morgan Ward explored how the war's global dimensions complicated the South's black/white racial binary through the prism of Japanese American internment. Betrayed by their own government, displaced from their homes in California, and relocated to the Arkansas Delta, Japanese Americans "confounded the color line in the Jim Crow South," Ward finds, and "rejected the rules of segregated society, while others actively rebelled against discrimination." Alarmed southern whites thought they saw the influence of "Tokyo" on the home front; however, as Ward found, it was "the growing impatience of southern blacks and Japanese Americans with second class citizenship (that) spurred homegrown resistance."[54]

Other examples in this vein include John Howard's *Concentration Camps on the Home Front* (2008) and Thomas Guglielmo's article "Red Cross, Double Cross: Race and America's World War II-Era Blood Donor Service" (2010).[55] In the latter, Guglielmo examines the race-based prejudice and discrimination that characterized the Red Cross blood donor service during the war. Like other millennial authors, Guglielmo finds even more evidence of civil rights activism energized by the war, as contesting "blood" segregation became "one of the war's great civil rights causes and flashpoints for debates on race."[56] Ultimately, however, Guglielmo identifies further limits to what activists achieved. Racial thinking among American segregationist whites evolved during the war to create a "multiracial messiness" of "state-sanctioned color lines."[57]

Providing a final note on the millennial era is Kim Phillips's contrarian *War! What Is It Good For?* (2012). In this provocative, if sometimes speculative, account, Phillips rejects outright the assumed logic that more freedom can be won through the use of modern warfare. Phillips thus offers the most direct challenge to the notion of the Second World War as expanding racial equality, directly or indirectly. In evaluating black participation in the U.S. military from World War II through the Vietnam conflict, Phillips concludes that long wars, by their very nature, tend to harden racial ideologies and hierarchies, not weaken or eradicate them. Even with the desegregation of the U.S. armed forces in 1948, Phillips argues, the American military perpetuated its discriminatory racial practices wherever it went. Service in the military tended to be a disillusioning experience for African Americans, if they survived it. Phillips finds black intellectuals in the 1940s to be acutely aware of this contradiction, as black troops labored globally on behalf of the imperial goals of a nation that sustained their second-class citizenship in the military and at home. The military's "systematic use of violence against civilians" politicized African American GIs, who ultimately interpreted World War II (and the Korean and Vietnam conflicts) as damaging to the black freedom struggle.[58] Thus, Phillips offers an interpretation of the war's racial impact that is distinctly contrary to all previous ones. Most scholars, while noting the problems of service in a Jim Crow military, have still tended to identify that service as ultimately generating heightened expectations and hopes for change as much as disillusionment among black GIs.[59]

As the range of scholarship in each era demonstrates, no definitive interpretation of World War II and racial change in the South has emerged, even among the plethora of excellent, complex, and nuanced studies that exist. Scholars agree that the war shaped the events that followed it, but they still do not agree on the extent to which World War II accelerated preexisting trends, established new foundations upon which racial change was built, or created daunting obstacles that complicated or delayed the achievement of racial reform. Nonetheless, the historiography of each era has made an important contribution to understanding the impact of this war on southern society. Civil rights era scholars, from as early as Myrdal and Tindall, rightly drew attention to the war years as critical to understanding the contradictory evolution of the modern South. The commemorative era scholars identified both the real militancy of the war years in the black working class and the strength of southern white resistance to racial change and the dampening effect of the developing Cold War. Finally, as millennial scholars have noted, the true meaning of events in the wartime South may, in fact, be most apparent when adopting a broader global perspective, placing the American black freedom struggle in the context of a worldwide revolt against racial imperialism, one rooted in earlier decades, but accelerated during World War II and ultimately blossoming in the decades thereafter. All the scholars do agree that the war mattered. And our attempts to keep exploring its impact on southern race relations will continue to complicate and enrich our understanding of the South, the nation, and the world.

NOTES

1. For a thorough consideration of this historiographical trend in civil rights literature, see Jacquelyn Dowd Hall, "The Long Civil Rights Movement and the Political Uses of the Past," *Journal of American History* 91 (Mar. 2005): 1233-63.

2. See, for example, Neil McMillen, ed., *Remaking Dixie: The Impact of World War II on the American South* (Oxford: Univ. Press of Mississippi, 1997).

3. Rayford Logan, ed., *What the Negro Wants* (Chapel Hill: Univ. of North Carolina Press, 1944). For an excellent discussion of the writings of Zora Neale Hurston, William Faulkner, Ralph Ellison, Langston Hughes, Lillian Smith, and Katherine Dupree Lumpkin during World War II, and reactions to them, see James C. Cobb, *Away Down South: A History of Southern Identity* (New York: Oxford Univ. Press, 2005), 185-211; for later assessments of this literature, see Glenda Gilmore, *Defying Dixie: The Radical Roots of Civil Rights, 1919-1950* (New York: W. W. Norton and Co., 2008); Bryant Simon, "Introduction to the 1997 Edition," in *Race and Rumors of Race: The American South in the Early Forties,* by Howard Odum (1943; repr., Baltimore: Johns Hopkins

Univ. Press, 1997); John Egerton, *Speak Now against the Day: The Generation before the Civil Rights Movement in the South* (Chapel Hill: Univ. of North Carolina Press, 1995); Patricia Sullivan, *Days of Hope: Race and Democracy in the New Deal Era* (Chapel Hill: Univ. of North Carolina Press, 1996).

4. Odum, *Race and Rumors of Race.*

5. Gunnar Myrdal, *An American Dilemma: The Negro Problem and Modern Democracy,* 9th ed. (1944; repr., New York: Harper and Row, 1962).

6. Sullivan, *Days of Hope,* 135.

7. Myrdal, *American Dilemma,* 1005.

8. Ibid., 1006.

9. Ibid., quoted from *The Nation,* Sept. 26, 1942, 68.

10. Odum, *Race and Rumors of Race.*

11. An excellent discussion of the many implications of a changed labor market for the World War II-era South may be found in Charles D. Chamberlain, *Victory at Home: Manpower and Race in the American South during World War II* (Athens: Univ. of Georgia Press, 2003).

12. Myrdal, *American Dilemma,* 1007.

13. Ibid., 1014.

14. On the racial violence of the war years, see Harvard Sitkoff, "Racial Militancy and Interracial Violence in the Second World War," *Journal of American History* 58 (1971): 661-81.

15. See, for example, Jennifer E. Brooks, "Winning the Peace: Georgia Veterans and the Struggle to Define the Political Legacy of World War II," *Journal of Southern History* 66 (Aug. 2000): 563-604.

16. For early treatments of the impact of World War II on the U.S. home front generally, see Richard Polenberg, *War and Society: The United States, 1941-1945* (New York: Greenwood Press, 1973); Polenberg, *One Nation, Divisible: Class, Race, and Ethnicity in the United States since 1938* (New York: Viking Press, 1980); J. Morton Blum, *V Was for Victory: Politics and American Culture during World War II* (New York: Putnum Publishers, 1976).

17. For an assessment of the Cold War's impact on the civil rights movement, see Mary Dudziak, *Cold War Civil Rights: Race and the Image of American Democracy* (Princeton, N.J.: Princeton Univ. Press, 2000).

18. See, for example, Howell Raines, *My Soul Is Rested: The Story of the Civil Rights Movement in the Deep South* (1977; repr., New York: Penguin Books, 1983).

19. George Brown Tindall, *The Emergence of the New South, 1913-1945* (Baton Rouge: Louisiana State Univ. Press, 1967).

20. Originating in Texas and decided by the U.S. Supreme Court in 1944, the *Smith* case invalidated the common practice among southern Democrats of prohibiting black participation in Democratic electoral primaries, even as the party was deeply embedded within state electoral structures. For more on the all-white primary and southern Democratic efforts to evade implementa-

tion of the *Smith* decision, see V. O. Key, *Southern Politics in State and Nation* (New York: Alfred A. Knopf, 1950), 619-44; J. Morgan Kousser, *The Shaping of Southern Politics: Suffrage Restriction and the Establishment of the One-Party South, 1880-1910* (Hartford, Conn.: Yale Univ. Press, 1974); Jennifer E. Brooks, *Defining the Peace: World War II Veterans, Race, and the Remaking of Southern Political Tradition* (Chapel Hill: Univ. of North Carolina Press, 2004), 26-27.

21. Tindall, *Emergence of the New South,* 727, quoted from H. Clarence Nixon, "The South after the War," *Virginia Quarterly Review* 20 (Summer 1944): 321-34.

22. Morton Sosna, "More Important Than the Civil War? The Impact of World War II on the South," in *Perspectives on the American South: An Annual Review of Society, Politics, and Culture,* vol. 4, ed. James C. Cobb and Charles R. Wilson (New York: Gordon and Breach, 1987).

23. Richard M. Dalfiume, "The Forgotten Years of the Negro Revolution," *Journal of American History* 55 (June 1968): 90-106.

24. Ibid., 102-6. Also see Richard Dalfiume, *Desegregation of the U.S. Armed Forces: Fighting on Two Fronts, 1939-1953* (Columbia: Univ. of Missouri Press, 1969).

25. Sitkoff, "Racial Militancy and Interracial Violence"; Neil A. Wynn, "The Impact of the Second World War on the American Negro," *Journal of Contemporary History* 6, no. 2 (1971): 42-53; Steven Lawson, *Black Ballots: Voting Rights in the American South, 1944-1969* (New York: Columbia Univ. Press, 1976).

26. Lee Finkle, "The Conservative Aims of Militant Rhetoric: Black Protest during World War II," *Journal of American History* 60 (Dec. 1973): 692-713.

27. Ibid., 700.

28. Sitkoff, "Racial Militancy and Interracial Violence."

29. Many good older treatments of the home-front impact of the Second World War, in addition to those already cited, include Louis Ruchames, *Race, Jobs, and Politics: The Story of the FEPC* (New York: Columbia Univ. Press, 1953); Morton Sosna, *In Search of the Silent South: Southern Liberals and the Race Issue* (New York: Columbia Univ. Press, 1977); Jonathan M. Wiener, "Class Structure and Economic Development in the American South, 1865-1955," *American Historical Review* 84 (Oct. 1979): 970-92; Harvard Sitkoff, *The Struggle for Black Equality, 1954-1980* (New York: Hill and Wang, 1981); Karen Tucker Anderson, "Last Hired, First Fired: Black Women Workers During World War II," *Journal of American History* 69 (June 1982): 82-97; Karen Hartmann, *The Homefront and Beyond: American Women in the 1940s* (Boston: Twayne Publishers, 1982); Catherine Ann Barnes, *Journey from Jim Crow: The Desegregation of Southern Transit* (New York: Columbia Univ. Press, 1983); Phillip McGuire, *Taps for a Jim Crow Army: Letters from Black Soldiers in World War II* (New York: ABC-Clio, 1983); Robert J. Norrell, *Reaping the Whirlwind: The Civil Rights Movement in Tuskegee* (New York: Knopf, 1985); Robert

Korstad and Nelson Lichtenstein, "Opportunities Found and Lost: Labor, Radicals, and the Early Civil Rights Movement," *Journal of American History* 75 (Dec. 1988): 786-811.

30. One example is McMillen, *Remaking Dixie*.

31. James C. Cobb, *The Most Southern Place on Earth: The Mississippi Delta and the Roots of Regional Identity* (Oxford: Oxford Univ. Press, 1992), 184, 199, 203, 207; Patricia Sullivan, *Days of Hope: Race and Democracy in the New Deal Era* (Chapel Hill: Univ. of North Carolina Press, 1996).

32. Harvard Sitkoff, "African American Militancy in the World War II South," in McMillen, *Remaking Dixie*, 71.

33. Ibid., 74.

34. Historians have drawn particularly on Scott's ideas put forth in each of the following: *Weapons of the Weak: Everyday Forms of Peasant Resistance* (Hartford, Conn.: Yale Univ. Press, 1985); *Domination and the Arts of Resistance: Hidden Transcripts* (Hartford, Conn.: Yale Univ. Press, 1990); *Seeing Like a State: How Certain Schemes to Improve the Human Condition Have Failed* (Hartford, Conn.: Yale Univ. Press, 1998).

35. Robin D. G. Kelley, *Race Rebels: Culture, Politics, and the Black Working Class* (New York: Free Press, 1994).

36. Kelley develops and applies Scott's notion of "infrapolitics" to the black working class experience most explicitly in "We Are Not What We Seem: Rethinking Black Working Class Opposition in the Jim Crow South," *Journal of American History* 80 (June 1993): 75-112, but his book, *Race Rebels*, deals more extensively with the black experience during World War II.

37. Pete Daniel, "Going among Strangers: Southern Reactions to World War II," *Journal of American History* 77 (Dec. 1990): 892.

38. John Egerton, *Speak Now against the Day: The Generation before the Civil Rights Movement in the South* (Chapel Hill: Univ. of North Carolina Press, 1995).

39. See, for example, Michael K. Honey, *Southern Labor and Black Civil Rights: Organizing Memphis Workers* (Urbana: Univ. of Illinois Press, 1994); Bruce Nelson, "Organized Labor and the Struggle for Black Equality in Mobile during World War II," *Journal of American History* 80 (Dec. 1993): 952-88. Robert Korstad produced the most detailed and comprehensive assessment of civil rights unionism in *Civil Rights Unionism: Tobacco Workers and the Struggle for Democracy in the Mid-Twentieth Century South* (Chapel Hill: Univ. of North Carolina Press, 2003), which actually appeared during the millennial era but had been underway throughout the commemorative era.

40. Sitkoff, "African American Militancy," 88-91.

41. Timothy Tyson, ed., *Democracy Betrayed: The Wilmington Race Riot and Its Legacy* (Chapel Hill: Univ. of North Carolina Press, 1998), 9-10.

42. Robin Kelley and Earl Lewis, *To Make Our World Anew: A History of African Americans* (Oxford: Oxford Univ. Press, 2000), 444.

43. See, for example, Bryant Simon, "Race Reactions: African American Organizing, Liberalism, and White Working Class Politics in Postwar South Carolina," in *Jumpin' Jim Crow: Southern Politics from Civil War to Civil Rights,* ed. Jane Dailey, Glenda Gilmore, and Simon (Princeton, N.J.: Princeton Univ. Press, 2000); Simon, "Fearing Eleanor: Racial Anxieties and Wartime Rumors in the American South, 1940-1945," in *Labor in the Modern South,* ed. Glenn Eskew (Athens: Univ. of Georgia Press, 2001); Alex Lichtenstein, "Exclusion, Fair Employment, or Interracial Unionism: Race Relations in Florida's Shipyards during World War II," in Eskew, *Labor in the Modern South;* Stephen G. N. Tuck, *Beyond Atlanta: The Struggle for Racial Equality in Georgia, 1940-1980* (Athens: Univ. of Georgia Press, 2001); Chamberlain, *Victory at Home;* Brooks, *Defining the Peace;* Robert J. Norrell, *The House I Live In: Race in the American Century* (London: Oxford Univ. Press, 2005).

44. All of these essays may be found in *The Fog of War: The Second World War and the Civil Rights Movement,* ed. Kevin Kruse and Stephen Tuck (New York: Oxford Univ. Press, 2012), quotation, 173. See also Jason Morgan Ward, *Defending White Democracy: The Making of a Segregationist Movement and the Remaking of Racial Politics, 1936-1965* (Chapel Hill: Univ. of North Carolina Press, 2011).

45. Kruse and Tuck, *Fog of War,* introduction.

46. Lichtenstein, "Exclusion, Fair Employment, or Interracial Unionism"; Kelley, *Race Rebels;* Korstad, *Civil Rights Unionism.*

47. James C. Cobb, *The Most Southern Place on Earth: The Mississippi Delta and the Roots of Regional Identity* (Oxford: Oxford Univ. Press, 1992); J. Mills Thornton, "Segregation and the City: White Supremacy in the Mid-Twentieth Century," in Kruse and Tuck, *Fog of War.*

48. Kelley, *Race Rebels.*

49. Greta de Jong, *A Different Day: African American Struggles for Justice in Rural Louisiana, 1900-1970* (Chapel Hill: Univ. of North Carolina Press, 2002).

50. See, for example, Myrdal, *American Dilemma,* 1004; Tyson, "Wars for Democracy: African American Militancy and Interracial Violence in North Carolina during World War II," in Tyson, *Democracy Betrayed;* Steven Lawson, "The Long Origins of the Short Civil Rights Movement, 1954-1968," in *Freedom Rights: New Perspectives on the Civil Rights Movement,* ed. Danielle L. McGuire and John Dittmer (Lexington: Univ. Press of Kentucky, 2011).

51. This phrase comes from Merl Reed, *Seedtime for the Modern Civil Rights Movement: The President's Committee on Fair Employment Practice, 1941-1946* (Baton Rouge: Louisiana State Univ. Press, 1991).

52. Gary Gerstle, "The Crucial Decade: The 1940s and Beyond," *Journal of American History* 92 (Mar. 2006): 1292-99.

53. Thomas A. Guglielmo, "Fighting for Caucasian Rights: Mexicans, Mexican-Americans, and the Transnational Struggle for Civil Rights in World War II Texas," *Journal of American History* 92 (Mar. 2006): 1212-37.

54. Jason Morgan Ward, "'No Jap Crow': Japanese Americans Encounter the World War II South," *Journal of Southern History* 73, no. 1 (Feb. 2007): 75-104.

55. John Howard, *Concentration Camps on the Home Front: Japanese Americans in the House of Jim Crow* (Chicago: Univ. of Chicago, 2008); Thomas Guglielmo, "Red Cross, Double Cross: Race and America's World War II-Era Blood Donor Service," *Journal of American History* 97, no. 1 (June 2010): 63-90.

56. Guglielmo, "Red Cross, Double Cross," 64.

57. Ibid., 67.

58. Kim Phillips, *War! What Is It Good For? Black Freedom Struggles and the U.S. Military from World War II to Iraq* (Chapel Hill: Univ. of North Carolina Press, 2012).

59. See, for example, Brooks, *Defining the Peace.*

CHAPTER NINE

To Redeem the Soul of Dixie

On the Second Reconstruction and the New South

MICHAEL T. BERTRAND

Nearly a quarter of a century ago, historian Adam Fairclough put forth this inquiry: "What was the civil rights movement? When did it begin and end, and what did it achieve?"[1] Fairclough poses a set of questions regarding a transformative moment that until recently has generated a fairly straightforward set of answers. Three successive and overlapping waves of scholarship on the subject have produced studies that focus on change as it flowed downward through national organizations, the federal government, and the courts; upward by way of grassroots activism, local movements, and direct action campaigns; and, finally, in both directions simultaneously, via an interactive dynamic that combined elements of each. In this chapter, we will examine how this dialectic has shaped the historiography of the civil rights movement. It is a body of literature that is distinctive. Unlike most historical problems or issues, those associated with civil rights generally engage scholars who all reside on the same side and are sympathetic to the forces that attempted to right what appeared to be so blatantly wrong. While some disagreements have occurred, such differences are based less on substantive disputes than they are on the prominence given particular subjects. Despite this diversity of emphasis, a consensus nevertheless emerges that the civil rights movement represented the most significant undertaking of domestic reform in the twentieth century.

At the very least, it dismantled a regionally distinctive segregationist system that for three generations had not only deprived African American women and men of equality under the law, but also endeavored to steal their dignity. Not unimportantly, the restoration of long-denied rights to black citizens allowed the South between 1954 and 1965 to free itself from a burdensome history that stretched back some seventy years. It was a past that had long prohibited the region from joining the national mainstream and truly inaugurating a new era.[2]

Racism in the United States, of course, knows no chronological or spatial boundaries. It is an ongoing national affliction that can be traced to the country's origins. Correspondingly, challenges to racial discrimination also are timeless and wide-ranging, existing wherever they are roused in both the past and the present. Indeed, recent scholarship on what is termed the "long civil rights movement" acknowledges this reality. Looking outward, proponents of this view operate from a new and broader interpretative model that places the South and race relations in a global context. These historians minimize the exceptional nature of the region, while locating structural and cultural traits that are universal. Specifically, they focus more on the affliction than on the host or locality. In addressing Fairclough's questions, therefore, they declare that the answers should be open-ended; the struggle, after all, is not yet concluded, the sickness remains rife. Previous reform drives represent phases in a larger and continuous crusade against oppression that is multidimensional in its color, class, and gender construction and application. The implication is clear: In diagnosing the illness, adherents of the long civil rights movement believe that past remedies treated the symptoms but did not cure the disease. Much work, obviously, remains to be done.[3]

The insights provided by proponents of the long civil rights movement are invaluable. They help sharpen historical scrutiny and widen the investigative field. They force scholars to revisit with a new set of lenses the so-called master narrative of the civil rights movement. What promises to come from this fresh examination is a recognition that history never stands still. Revision is the bedrock of historical thought.

Another anchor, though, is the habit of historians to distinguish one era from those that precede and follow it. Certainly what happened in the South between 1954 and 1965 signified merely one component in a long-term and wider push for black liberation, as revisionists claim. Nevertheless, what occurred there at that time was distinctive and deserves to be assessed on its own terms. Patricia Sullivan and Armstead Robinson skillfully captured this duality in a statement that arguably describes both the "classical phase" and the evolving historical interpretations that address it: The moment represents "a transformative event, one which constantly created and recreated itself. That brief and fragile coming together during the *Brown* decade should be understood as part of a long-term, dynamic, and multifaceted process."[4]

Sullivan and Robinson's reference to *Brown v. Board of Education* (1954) is significant. Although historians from a late twentieth and early twenty-first century vantage point have viewed it in a wider context, guided by advances in long-view scholarship, contemporaries witnessed the Supreme Court decision in a daily milieu informed by media headlines. Given *Brown*'s exclusive focus on southern public-school desegregation and the former Confederate states' highly publicized resistance to the decision, journalists writing the "first draft" of movement history inevitably established a framework that concentrated on racial turmoil below the Mason–Dixon line. Formulating the term "Second Reconstruction," historian C. Vann Woodward, who along with colleague John Hope Franklin had supplied scholarly sustenance to Thurgood Marshall's legal brief for *Brown,* contributed to the emergent civil rights narrative and honed its analysis. By drawing comparisons with the South's first proposed makeover—a post-Civil War experiment that historian Eric Foner later tabbed an "unfinished revolution"—Woodward defined the era as bounded by the *Brown* decision in 1954 and the Voting Rights Act of 1965 (later scholars extended the closing year to 1968, following the death of Martin Luther King Jr.); these are generally the parameters that scholars evaluating the civil rights movement have since followed. Restoring legal and racial reforms initiated by Republicans and their African American collaborators in the 1860s and 1870s, which Democratic-controlled southern state and local governments later disavowed, the civil rights movement of the 1950s and 1960s at last brought closure. It fulfilled a promise that the original New South had long ago abdicated. In short, the Woodwardian model convincingly connected the history of racial progress to that of regional progression. The story of one necessarily paralleled and validated that of the other.[5]

The Reconstruction analogy provided an intriguing historiographical orientation. It definitely carried historical baggage for southerners, both black and white. If ever William Faulkner's adage that the "past is never dead, it is not even past" has applied, it did so for a region that could not forget Reconstruction. Later, Glenn Feldman would refer to a "Reconstruction syndrome" as a means to understand southern white resistance to centralized authority, outside influence, and social change, especially in relation to the issue of race. Complicating the reaction was a widely held belief in a nineteenth-century Reconstruction myth characterized by unbridled political corruption, "Yankee" coercion, and "Negro" misrule. Seemingly trapped in this Faulknerian loop, southern whites, at the slightest hint of a threat to the status quo, would drag out and dust off the dubious subjugation storyline, modify it for current circumstances, and mount the barricades. On the other hand, references to Reconstruction also could bring to mind positive images that conveyed the potential for progress, particularly as they harkened to the era's passage of the Thirteenth, Fourteenth, and Fifteenth amendments to the U.S. Constitution. The past in this case provided the legal artifacts that would fuel a movement attempting to restore equality under the law. Popular memories or perceptions of Reconstruction, therefore, established a familiar plotline that stressed the dual nature of the modern movement: the rise of black expectations and white responses to them.[6]

To tell this story of reform and resistance, historians initially relied upon journalistic accounts and the memoirs of movement participants or those who had actively supported it from the side-lines. Interestingly, the early autobiographical statements of such activists as Daisy Bates, Anne Moody, and James Foreman merged with those of scholars such as August Meier and Howard Zinn, two professional historians who joined students and others in direct-action protests and demonstrations. Other historians also placed themselves on the southern front lines during the *Brown* decade. Several, like Harvard Sitkoff, Clayborne Carson, and John Dittmer, later would distill their experiences into studies that examined various aspects of the civil rights movement. From the outset, it was evident that personal investment in the struggle would define early academic interpretations of it, setting a sympathetic course that would characterize the historical literature well into the new millennium.[7]

The first scholarly treatments of the movement, however, dealt with the segregationist opposition to racial integration. Appearing in the late 1960s and early 1970s, the works of Neil McMillen, Hugh Davis Graham, Idus A. Newby, and Numan Bartley examined such facets as the White Citizens' Councils, grassroots hostility toward public school desegregation, the intellectual rationale behind racial segregation, and a state-by-state portrayal of massive resistance. Their studies reiterated that the story taking shape would address both black and white and race and region.[8]

Following this preliminary surge, professional academics then engaged in what became the first wave of civil rights–movement scholarship, one that adhered to a hierarchical orientation. By the mid-1970s, historians and others in academe produced studies that benefited from the mining of newly available government and organization archives. The resulting monographs conveyed a traditional "top-down" perspective that described and analyzed civil rights policies and practices of presidential administrations from Franklin Roosevelt through Lyndon Johnson. Such institutional and political studies put a great emphasis on individual leaders; federal courts, departments, and agencies; and national organizations. The works of Harvard Sitkoff, Darlene Clark Hine, William C. Berman, Robert F. Burk, Carl M. Brauer, and James C. Harvey established the format for this particular genre.[9]

As for civil rights organizational studies that followed a "top-down" model informed by archival research, journalists Pat Watters and Reece Cleghorn set the tone with *Climbing Jacob's Ladder,* a 1967 work that relied on the files of the Voter Education Project (VEP). Significantly, the Kennedy administration, preferring voter registration to direct-action campaigns, bestowed encouragement upon the VEP. Run through the moderate Southern Regional Council, the VEP also obtained monetary support from several nonprofit foundations. By 1973, August Meier and Elliott Rudwick produced the first historical interpretation of a major civil rights organization, the Congress of Racial Equality (CORE). A year later, Nancy Weiss addressed the National Urban League. The Student Nonviolent Co-ordinating Committee (SNCC) had received an early and on-the-ground treatment by the activist-historian Howard Zinn, *SNCC: The New Abolitionists* (1964); Clayborne Carson's archives-bound history, *In Struggle: SNCC and the Black Awakening of the 1960s* (1981), became the definitive volume. Over a quarter of a century later, Patricia Sullivan wrote the first comprehensive history of the National Association for the Advancement of Colored People (NAACP). Her book, *Lift Every Voice: The NAACP and the Making of the Civil Rights Movement* (2009), extensively utilized the NAACP Records, the single largest collection of archival materials on the civil rights movement.[10]

The NAACP was decisive in assaulting segregation through litigation and was successful on several fronts, including politics, *Smith v. Allwright* (1944); interstate transportation, *Morgan v. Commonwealth of Virginia* (1946); and housing, *Shelley v. Kraemer* (1948). It garnered its greatest victories, however, in the field of public education. Following a successful run of victories between 1938 and 1950—*Missouri ex rel. Gaines v. Canada* (1938), *Sipuel v. Oklahoma State Board of Regents* (1948), *McLaurin v. Oklahoma State Regents* (1950), and *Sweatt v. Painter* (1950)—the NAACP made its most significant and symbolic stand in 1954 with the *Brown* case. The authoritative history of the lawsuit and the successful litigation that preceded it still can be found in Richard Kluger's *Simple Justice* (1975). A relatively recent interpretative model challenges the positive significance attributed to *Brown*. Michael Klarman has argued that the decision actually created a white backlash that could have been avoided. Claiming that school desegregation was too sensitive an area for reform, Klarman maintains it unnecessarily crippled the moderate response within the white South. His argument, of course, assumes that there was little or no resistance to previous and "less controversial" attempts at racial change. Considering the depth and duration of southern white racial antipathy, this is a big assumption. Nevertheless, at least for black southerners, *Brown* suggested that a favorable transition was imminent; for the NAACP, it was a victory which implied that protest and change could be limited to the courtroom—the ultimate "top-down" mechanism.[11]

Brown's elevated status, however, did not ensure that the NAACP as an organization would garner the most attention over the course of the movement's "classical phase." That honor went to a relative newcomer on the scene. Because it served as the vehicle for the charismatic Martin Luther King Jr., the Southern Christian Leadership Conference (SCLC) stands apart. To the chagrin of the older and more venerable NAACP, as well as other less-celebrated peers, the SCLC received the era's widest national and media exposure, a factor that directly impacted efforts at fundraising. In assessing SCLC's significance (it remains active into the second decade of the twenty-first century), prominent studies have tended to conflate its impact with that of its founder. Adam Fairclough's *To Redeem the Soul of America,* published in 1987, fits this characterization, as does David J. Garrow's Pulitzer Prize-winning *Bearing the Cross,* published a year earlier. Both of these studies obviously influenced the framework for the highly popular three-volume life of King written by journalist Taylor Branch. The first book, *Parting the Waters,* published in 1988, also won the Pulitzer Prize. More importantly, perhaps, Branch's work linked the story of civil rights to its most recognized leader.[12]

Prominent in the first wave of civil rights-movement scholarship and never truly diminishing in popularity, the biographical format has become a cornerstone of the "top-down" approach to understanding social and racial change. King, of course, has been at the center of this emphasis. David Levering Lewis produced the first scholarly biography of King in 1970. Stephen Oates followed a decade later, setting the stage for the works by Garrow, Fairclough, and Branch. A virtual cottage industry, the biographical King has endured well into the twenty-first century. King's own writings—ghostwriters helped him produce several books during his lifetime—continue to be reprinted and also provide insight. Likewise invaluable are the King papers being processed at Stanford University. Former activist-turned-historian Clayborne Carson is the editor of the project and since 1992 has overseen the publication of numerous volumes. During the same span, various writers have charted a direction that compares and contrasts King with his contemporary Malcolm X. This twofold approach, as with most King biographies, accentuates his identification with nonviolent social protest. Interestingly, this attention on the civil-disobedience aspect of his public persona has caused some historians to note that such methods went against the southern rural culture from which many activists emerged. As they maintain, the opposite tendency—armed self-defense—characterized the region historically. Indeed, Timothy Tyson, whose account of the gun-toting NAACP organizer Robert F. Williams of North Carolina provides a stark contrast to King, suggests that the civil rights movement did not necessarily have to follow the course that it did.[13]

Other biographies written since the 1970s also highlight figures other than the Atlanta-born minister, theologian, and Nobel Peace laureate. There are excellent and probing works (sometimes multiple) on Bob Moses, Ella Baker, A. Philip Randolph, Fannie Lou Hamer, Thurgood Marshall, Rosa Parks, Stokely Carmichael, Pauli Murray, Malcolm X, Daisy Bates, Bayard Rustin, Septima Clark, and Medgar Evers. Such a sampling, which does not include numerous autobiographies by notables like Roy Wilkins, John Lewis, Melba Pattillo, and James Farmer, among others, indicates the multifaceted nature of the movement. Still, it is difficult to imagine social change occurring without King. In the minds of many, he became synonymous with the nonviolent, direct-action protests that characterized the 1950s and 1960s. King, whose campaigns at Birmingham and Selma helped bring about federal legislation, understood the crusade as a religious one, and undoubtedly helped shape it to fit what he imagined. He ardently believed that his insistence on redeeming souls and creating beloved communities coincided with an evangelical Protestantism that burned inside the majority of southerners, black and white, even as the flames of racial intolerance often consumed all appearances of Christian charity. It obviously conveyed a powerful message. As David Chappell, a recent biographer, has argued in *Waking from the Dream* (2014), King's life and vision still dominate the discussion.[14]

Nevertheless, it was the attempt to get out from under King's shadow that at least partly motivated the second wave of civil rights-movement scholarship, with its emphasis on grassroots and local organizing. William Chafe, in *Civilities and Civil Rights* (1980), inaugurated a "bottom-up" approach to assess the crusade for racial change and initiated the genre of community studies. He demonstrated that local groups and events were not necessarily dependent on national leaders, organizations, or trends. More significant was the interplay between various indigenous entities. Particularly perceptive is Chafe's ability, through extensive oral interviews, to trace racial reform efforts back several decades. In short, black activism and white resistance—at least in Chafe's subject region of Greensboro, North Carolina, and other places as traced by other scholars—did not commence overnight at a downtown lunch counter. Chafe's methods and point of view influenced similar investigations, notably Robert Norrell's case study of grassroots engagement in Tuskegee, Alabama, and David Colburn's examination of similar activity in St. Augustine, Florida. Each of these studies illustrate that national leaders and organizations existed on the periphery; these were communities in which local dynamics prevailed, in conversation with both the present and the past.[15]

No community symbolized a grassroots approach to change more than Montgomery, Alabama. When Rosa Parks refused to give up a seat on a city bus because she was tired of a status quo that demeaned all African Americans, it led to a boycott informed by a cooperative spirit traceable to various sources, present and past. Individuals such as E. D. Nixon, who belonged to the Brotherhood of Sleeping Car Porters, for instance, counted on guidance and in-spiration from A. Philip Randolph, while Jo Ann Gibson Robinson, a professor at Alabama State College, canvassed fellow members of the Women's Political Council. Both stirred and organized or-dinary and otherwise anonymous people to take a stand. What resulted proved to be as important as the attorney-driven *Brown* decision. Along with Robinson's memoir, *The Montgomery Bus Boy-cott and the Women Who Started It,* the work of J. Mills Thornton III emphasizes the significance of grassroots protest to the larger movement. Indeed, although it ultimately propelled Martin Luther King Jr. into the national spotlight, scholarship from the second wave reveals that multiple strands coalesced as the driving force behind the boycott and all that followed.[16]

Often, to reach those involved in such "bottom-up" episodes, scholars had to employ methods that went beyond traditional ar-chival research. Oral history thus became a necessary tool to exca-vate local stories. Not surprisingly, journalists were the first to use this method extensively. In a 1977 monograph, for example, How-ell Raines of the *New York Times* captured the recollections of those who fought for and against civil rights. In 1984, sociologist Aldon Morris focused more on the freedom fighters in a pathbreaking study, *The Origins of the Civil Rights Movement.* Seeking further to create an oral and video history archive, filmmaker Henry Hamp-ton in 1987 produced a six-hour documentary entitled *Eyes on the Prize.* Although on the surface it appears to follow the older "top-down" model of civil rights-movement narrative, reminiscent of chronicles such as Harvard Sitkoff's *The Struggle for Black Equal-ity* (1980), its inclusion of a wide variety of oral accounts captures the movement's grassroots character. Hampton and Steve Fayer's *Voices of Freedom,* which includes over 1,000 interviews, supple-ments the film and reiterates the importance of oral history to the telling of the civil rights-movement story.[17]

Oral history represented one of the new avenues explored as scholars moved away from a King-centric and ministerial focus. An-other involved the belated inclusion of women in the movement's master narrative, an integrative corrective that owed much to trends that had been developing in social history. Their exclusion had been odd, as Steven Lawson noted, since film footage from the *Eyes on the Prize* documentary revealed that women maintained a pervasive presence in all of the televised episodes. Evident in the visual evidence, women, who had been instrumental throughout the "classical phase," finally began to be recognized in the scholarly literature. As part of the second wave, *Women in the Civil Rights Movement* (1990), a major collection of biographical essays edited by Barbara Woods, Jacqueline Rouse, and Vicki Crawford set the standard. Other anthologies, such as Lynne Olson's *Freedom's Daughters* (2001), Bettye Thomas and V. P. Franklin's *Sisters in the Struggle* (2001), and Houck and Dixon's *Women and the Civil Rights Movement, 1954-1965* continue the tradition of stretching chronological and topical boundaries. The years after 1980 also witnessed the publication of a number of biographical monographs on figures such as Ella Baker, Rosa Parks, Fannie Lou Hamer, and Ruby Doris Smith Robinson.[18]

Sara Evans in 1979 created controversy when she pointed to the experiences of white females within the SNCC as a catalyst to the rise of the women's liberation movement. Her book, *Personal Politics,* identified the committee's commitment to equality, local autonomy, female activism, and male chauvinism as vital in awakening feminist consciousness. Evans's argument that the men in the group treated women as second-class citizens suggested that movement politics were complex and often bound by cultural conventions, although it did provoke a terse rejoinder of denial from SNCC staffer Mary King in *Freedom Song* (1987). Nevertheless, the debate encouraged future analysis concerning sexual and gender tensions that paralleled racial ones in the freedom struggle. Several scholars since have approached the multifaceted issue, including Belinda Robnett, Deborah Gray White, Danielle McGuire, and Paula Giddings. Further explorations along similar lines are evident in Steve Estes's *I Am a Man!* (2005) and Peter Ling's *Gender and the Civil Rights Movement* (2004).[19]

The activities of SNCC, including the numerous internal difficulties that developed involving racial, gender, generational, and regional issues—the Freedom Summer participation of transitory nonsouthern white students frequently created intragroup tension—reveal the complexities associated with collective efforts to bring about meaningful change. Dissimilar leadership styles and organizing strategies, sexual and class divisions, capricious interactions between the powerful and the powerless, astounding victories followed by abysmal defeats and disillusionment, and continual harassment and oppression by the guardians of the status quo were just a few of the factors that both drove and frustrated activists in the 1960s. The third wave of civil rights-movement scholarship addressed these realities. In adhering to a more holistic approach, it combined "top-down" and "bottom-up" perspectives and focused on locating links between various entities—local, national, and international; state and federal; intentional and unintentional; and social and political. Interestingly, two books associated with this more collaborative methodology, John Dittmer's *Local People* (1994) and Charles Payne's *I've Got the Light of Freedom* (1995), direct much of their attention on the work of SNCC. More importantly, they brought a new sense of sophistication and inclusion to civil rights-movement studies. In short, they signaled that the scholarship had matured.[20]

Analyses from the twentieth century's last years represented the initial surge of this third wave, one that makes connections between subjects that both encompass and transcend the 1954–65/68 period. Works such as Doug McAdam's *Political Process and the Development of Black Insurgency, 1930–1970* (1982), Manning Marable's *Race, Reform, and Rebellion* (1984), and Jack Bloom's *Race, Class, and the Civil Rights Movement* (1987) led this tide. Consequently, since the late 1990s, the range of scholarship has expanded greatly. As the new millennium enters its second decade, third-wave scholars are blazing trails into uncharted frontiers while bringing fresh insights to those areas considered familiar. Biographies of movement participants (King and others) continue to predominate, as do community and local or state studies. Historians also have maintained their focus on the prominence of women within a grassroots framework, while new examinations of the federal government's role seem to follow hard on the heels of various anniversaries of important Supreme Court cases and landmark pieces of legislation.[21]

Likewise, investigations that identify the historical context and prehistory of the "classical phase" also have flourished. They include assessments of the long-term outlook of the NAACP, the economic and ideological impact of the New Deal and World War II, organizational tendencies rooted in church and trade unions, white supremacy's long tentacles, and the economic forces that eroded the South's isolation and brought the region into the national mainstream. Particularly astute have been works that place the modern civil rights movement in a global setting. This includes appraisals that concentrate on foreign affairs—in particular, nuanced readings of the Cold War and the decolonization of the African continent. The international scope of black liberation was not lost on younger activists working in seemingly remote southern locales. Black Power advocates were just as likely to emerge from Mississippi or Alabama as they were from Los Angeles or Detroit. As recent scholars of mass media have demonstrated, newspapers, magazines, radio, television, and popular music also played a key role in breaking down previous forms of isolation and stirring a consciousness conducive to social change.[22]

This latest wave segued rather smoothly into the aforementioned emphasis on a "long civil rights movement." Venturing down an alternate path, scholars of the long civil rights movement seem to undermine the triumphant and dominant account that has classically described the southern struggle to eradicate legislative segregation. *Freedom North* (2003) by Jeanne F. Theoharis and Komozi Woodard heralded this new direction. A gentler assessment, perhaps, is that these scholars seek to lengthen and complicate the conventional story line. In short, the 1950s-1960s assault against and eventual demise of Jane and Jim Crow signaled neither the commencement nor the conclusion of the fight against racial discrimination; on the contrary, the hard-fought battles and ultimate triumph simply closed one (and not the first) chapter and launched another, a new and more onerous installment that involves unceasing efforts to define and apply on a daily basis the fruits of those victories.[23]

Yet, according to Jacqueline Dowd Hall, a leading advocate for extending traditional period and spatial parameters, the civil rights saga in popular memory has digressed into a static, one-dimensional chronicle that reflexively celebrates American progress, pioneers, and individualism while avoiding any reference to the national persistence of structural inequality (a tale, not coincidently, that is readily appropriated by some with agendas that arguably do not match those of the individuals being honored). It is not difficult to view the commemoration of Rosa Parks—whether in the U.S. Capitol's Statuary Hall or in popular media, as simply an exhausted domestic worker too tired to leave her bus seat—as substantiating Hall's argument. The same might be said for a frozen-in-time Martin Luther King Jr., whose purportedly color-blind "I Have a Dream" speech is ensconced in collective consciousness with little recollection that the 1963 setting of the oration on racial justice was the "March on Washington *for Jobs and Freedom.*" As activists well understood, economic and racial justice have always been linked.[24]

Scholars who call for a liberality in periodization and subject matter argue that the economic issues inherent to the 1963 march and the overall civil rights crusade are easier to discern and more difficult to ignore within a framework that speaks to a long movement (the same holds true for the activist background of Parks, whose actions, like those of many of her contemporaries, were far from spontaneous). Utilizing a perspective that travels both backward and forward from the 1954-65/68 era, they demonstrate that the issues of race and class were and are inextricable. Connecting the efforts of activists from the 1930s to those of the late 1960s and beyond, they likewise suggest the continuity of collective, strategic, and radical activism. The classical ("southern") and Black Power (presumably "northern") phases of the movement, for example, were not, as is customarily assumed, mutually exclusive; the latter did not maliciously derail or hijack the former. They shared a past that linked them equally to the present and to the future: the black freedom struggle, waging war on racial oppression, is a fight that knows no chronological, spatial, political, or taxonomical boundaries.[25]

Acknowledging the seemingly incessant and pervasive battles against racism, a long view serves to enhance our understanding of what did or did not happen in the South between 1954 and 1965/68.

For instance, long-view scholars lament that domestic containment quashed the potentially liberating activities (e.g., civil rights unionism, the black popular front, the labor feminism of the Congress of American Women, National Negro Congress programs, Highlander Folk School workshops, Congress of Industrial Organizations operations) in which the Communist Party and left-leaning unions within and without Dixie had been engaged during the 1930s and 1940s. Pointing to the "lost opportunities thesis" propagated by labor historians such as Nelson Lichtenstein, Robert Korstad, and Michael Honey, they maintain that McCarthyism and the second Red Scare emboldened southern white oligarchs to repel radical measures that could have eradicated regional forms of racial and class oppression. Focusing on what could have been, however, is a tricky maneuver, particularly when assessing activities that cut so deeply against the cultural grain. Yet even if it sometimes betrays a tendency to romanticize or exaggerate Communist and leftist contributions or advances—after all, anticommunism and conservatism were entrenched on each side of both the color line and the class divide—the long-view reading of the Cold War climate nevertheless helps to explain how and why the "classical phase" of the movement may have proceeded down a relatively conservative path.[26]

Nevertheless, despite the various nuances and insights offered by a view of the long civil rights movement, this seemingly elevated vantage point needs to be approached cautiously; it is not without its drawbacks. In intimating an intellectual connection to the black liberation movement (BLM) that followed the Second Reconstruction, it often comes very close to conflating time periods, places, motives, and actions. Potentially lost in such an approach is the South's distinctiveness during an era that truly represented a regional and cultural watershed. This is not to exaggerate or sentimentalize post–World War II southern exceptionality. But there is a reason that natives, non-natives, political operatives, the national media, and civil rights-movement participants focused on Dixie. Despite its own internal variations, the South as an entity was different from the rest of the United States. Its economic, political, social, cultural, and institutional structures and traditions diverged from those elsewhere, even if only by degree. These disparities necessitated an undertaking that was of a particular place and time. Various events and people no doubt influenced the reform narrative that unfolded. To combine all pieces of the prewar black freedom struggle and the postwar black liberation movement as one and dissolve their dissimilarities rightly focuses on what remains to be achieved. In doing so, however, it threatens to distort or overlook the real gains that were made in the land of cotton and segregation. That racial oppression and discrimination remain steadfast is without question; to believe that they remain unchanged or impervious to change, however, goes against the historical record. It also tears out a significant page from southern history. The South in the second decade of the twenty-first century is not the same as it was at the midpoint of the twentieth. Much of the transformation can be attributed to the changes brought on by the civil rights movement.[27]

For change did come to "Uncle Sam's Other Province." Over the course of more than a decade, numerous people and forces collaborated to transform the South's racial landscape, culminating in the passage of the Civil Rights Act of 1964 and the Voting Rights Act of 1965. With these legislative achievements, the "classical phase" of the modern civil rights movement came to a close. In renewing the sanctity of equality under the law below the Mason-Dixon line, much had been accomplished. Much, of course, was left for another day. Economic inequality, genuine public school desegregation, and institutionalized racism along national rather than regional lines, for instance, were not sufficiently addressed. Much, too, can be asked of change that is perhaps associated more with the pocketbook than with principle. Still, the Second Reconstruction without doubt succeeded where the initial Reconstruction had not. Having failed at its first shot at redemption following the Civil War, the South seemed to get it right the second time around. No longer limited by isolation, poverty, and dependency (and seemingly illimitable in its ability to advance and participate within a consumer-driven global economy), the South discovered that state-mandated racial segregation, like its other discarded historical baggage, did not relate to modern life. Yet it was a hard-won discovery that materialized only after countless numbers of people had engaged in over eleven years of struggle and protest.[28]

This brings us back to Adam Fairclough's original questions: "What was the civil rights movement? When did it begin and end, and what did it achieve?" Any response to such inquiries, of course, must go beyond a recitation of the historical literature. It also must recall the moving anthem, "We Shall Overcome," which in turn prompts another question, one more complex than it may initially appear: Overcome what?

The answer is history. As C. Vann Woodward noted at the outset of the civil rights movement, although the careers of Jane and Jim Crow may not have been of a long duration, they gave the impression of being timeless, of being historical. Southerners who came of age in the two decades bracketing the turn of the twentieth century belonged to a generation whose shadow would darken their region well into the 1950s and 1960s. Theirs represented a defining moment, an age whose dusky outline later inhabitants would find difficult to escape. For in addressing what superseded all others as the most important issue of the day—that of race—they invented a tradition that stopped time, a feat that was ill-fated and tragic.[29]

Accordingly, the post-Reconstruction era beheld the advent of segregation by statute, black disfranchisement, and an inconceivable rise in racial violence. Melding together the spheres of economics, politics, and race relations and the fears encompassed by each, the turn to racial exclusion undoubtedly represented the culmination of trends that had been evolving for some time; their implementation at this specific juncture occurred with an intensity and ferocity that suggested nothing less than a complete "capitulation to racism." The rationalization for such surrender, historian Leon Litwack declared, demonstrated that the generation which reached maturity during this era stood apart, if only by degree, from its predecessors: "Whether described by a 'moderate' or an 'extremist,' by political rhetoric or by popular culture, black people [were] reduced to something less than human."[30]

Apprehensive about a presumably irrepressible generation of African Americans unaffiliated directly with the institution of slavery, southern whites brought to life Jane and Jim Crow, a pair fashioned to restore racial order and ensure that white forever prevailed over black. In short, they invented tradition. From lynchings to "separate but equal" and grandfather clauses to "All Coons Look Alike to Me," the message was clear: "The past was never dead. It was not even past."[31]

As Faulkner implied, southerners had stopped time. Race relations in the South of 1950 too closely resembled those of 1890. In response, the Second Reconstruction witnessed a black minority, seeking victory over a decades-old oppressive racial system, and a white majority, struggling to redefine an identity historically given meaning by its attachment to that same system. Under attack was a Jane and Jim Crow arrangement that allowed people to share a culture but prohibited them from truly getting to know one another across the color line. Yet also in the crosshairs was a past that needed to die. Writing in the midst of the civil rights storm, James Baldwin hoped that black and white southerners together could lay those olden times to rest, forever: "They are, in effect, still trapped in a history which they do not understand; and until they understand it, they cannot be released from it. . . . We cannot be free until they are free."[32]

Such was the burden of a generation of southerners who arose in the 1950s and 1960s to challenge the region's racial past, a generation that nevertheless looked with confidence toward the future. The world they aspired to create would not come easy; the journey to get there would be hindered and impeded by obstacles that most could not have foreseen or imagined. The task would be difficult and dangerous, the outcomes frequently less than perfect. Yet unlike their predecessors who came of age in the 1890s, these southerners built a world based on hope, not fear. Significantly, this generation sought to overcome history, not continuously engage in repeating it.[33]

And that, Mr. Fairclough, was the civil rights movement.

NOTES

1. Adam Fairclough, "Historians and the Civil Rights Movement," *Journal of American Studies* 24 (Dec. 1990): 387.

2. Excellent historiographical surveys of the civil rights movement include Charles W. Eagles, *The Price of Defiance: James Meredith and the Integration of Ole Miss* (Chapel Hill: Univ. of North Carolina Press, 2009); Fairclough, "Historians and the Civil Rights Movement"; Kevin K. Gaines, "The Civil Rights Movement in World Perspective," *OAH Magazine of History* 21 (2007): 57-64; several works by Steven F. Lawson, notably "Long Origins of the Short Civil Rights Movement, 1954-1968," in *Freedom Rights: New Perspectives on the Civil Rights Movement,* ed. Danielle L. McGuire and John Dittmer (Lexington: Univ. Press of Kentucky, 2011), and others listed in the bibliography; Charles M. Payne, *I've Got the Light of Freedom: The Organizing Tradition and the Mississippi Freedom Struggle* (Berkeley: Univ. of California Press, 1995).

3. For an interesting online resource on this topic, visit the "Long Civil Rights Movement Project" at the Southern Oral History Program of the Center for the Study of the American South, University of North Carolina-Chapel Hill. A description of the initiative can be found at http://sohp.org/research/the-long-civil-rights-movement-initiative/ (accessed April 27, 2017).

4. Patricia Sullivan and Armstead Robinson, "Introduction: Reassessing the History of the Civil Rights Movement," in *New Directions in Civil Rights Studies,* ed. Sullivan and Robinson (Charlottesville: Univ. Press of Virginia, 1991), quotation, 6. It was organizer Bayard Rustin who characterized the eleven-year period of civil rights reform as the "classical phase." See Rustin, *Down the Line: The Colored Writings of Bayard Rustin* (Chicago: Quadrangle Books, 1971), 111-22.

5. For a "retrospective" sampling of the "first draft" of movement history by journalists, see John Bartlow Martin, *The Deep South Says "Never!"* (New York: Ballantine Books, 1957); Anthony Lewis, *Portrait of a Decade: The Second American Revolution* (New York: Random House, 1964); Charles E. Silberman, *Crisis in Black and White* (New York: Random House, 1964); Michael Dorman, *We Shall Overcome: A Reporter's Eyewitness Account of the Year of Racial Strife and Triumph* (New York: Dell Publishing, 1965). For the phrase "Second Reconstruction," see C. Vann Woodward, *The Strange Career of Jim Crow* (New York: Oxford Univ. Press, 1955); Woodward, "From the First Reconstruction to the Second," *Harper's* 230 (April 1965): 127-33.

6. Faulkner is quoted from *Requiem for a Nun* (New York: Random House, 1950), 73. The "Reconstruction syndrome" can be found in Glenn Feldman, *Reading Southern History: Essays on Interpreters and Interpretations* (Tuscaloosa: Univ. of Alabama Press, 2001).

7. Daisy Bates, *The Long Shadow of Little Rock: A Memoir* (1962; repr., Baton Rouge: Louisiana State Univ. Press, 1990); Anne Moody, *Coming of Age in*

Mississippi (New York: Dial Press, 1968); James Foreman, *The Making of Black Revolutionaries* (New York: MacMillan, 1972); August Meier, *A White Scholar and the Black Community, 1945-1965: Essays and Reflections* (Amherst: Univ. of Massachusetts Press, 1992); Howard Zinn, *You Can't Be Neutral on a Moving Train: A Personal History of Our Times* (Boston: Beacon Press, 1994). For the recollections of historians who participated in the movement, see Paul A. Cimbala and Robert F. Himmelberg, eds., *Historians and Race: Autobiography and the Writing of History* (Bloomington: Indiana Univ. Press, 1996); Walter Johnson, "Historians Join the March on Montgomery," *South Atlantic Quarterly* 74 (Spring 1980): 158-74.

8. See especially Neil McMillen, *The Citizens' Council: Organized Resistance to the Second Reconstruction, 1954-1964* (Urbana: Univ. of Illinois Press, 1971); Hugh Davis Graham, *Crisis in Print: Desegregation and the Press in Tennessee* (Nashville: Vanderbilt Univ. Press, 1967); Idus A. Newby, *Challenge to the Court: Social Scientists and the Defense of Segregation, 1954-1966* (Baton Rouge: Louisiana State Univ. Press, 1967); Numan Bartley, *The Rise of Massive Resistance: Race and Politics in the South during the 1950s* (Baton Rouge: Louisiana State Univ. Press, 1969).

9. See especially Harvard Sitkoff, *A New Deal for Blacks: The Emergence of Civil Rights as a National Issue* (New York: Oxford Univ. Press, 1978); Darlene Clark Hine, *Black Victory: The Rise and Fall of the White Primary in Texas* (Millwood, N.Y.: KTP Press, 1979); William C. Berman, *The Politics of Civil Rights in the Truman Administration* (Columbus: Ohio State Univ. Press, 1970); Robert F. Burk, *The Eisenhower Administration and Black Civil Rights* (Knoxville: Univ. of Tennessee Press, 1984); Carl M. Brauer, *John F. Kennedy and the Second Reconstruction* (New York: Columbia Univ. Press, 1977); James C. Harvey, *Black Civil Rights during the Johnson Administration* (Jackson: Univ. and College Press of Mississippi, 1973). Later scholars have widened and deepened the analysis; for example, see works by Steve Fraser and Gary Gerstle, Nancy J. Weiss, Lauren Rebecca Sklaroff, Michael Gardner, Merl Reed, Kari Frederickson, Joseph E. Lowndes, Garth E. Pauley, Michael R. Belknap, David A. Nichols, and Dan T. Carter.

10. Pat Watters, *Down to Now: Reflections on the Southern Civil Rights Movement* (New York: Pantheon, 1971); Watters and Reece Cleghorn, *Climbing Jacob's Ladder: The Arrival of Negroes in Southern Politics* (New York: Harcourt, Brace and World, 1967); August Meier and Elliot Rudwick, *CORE: A Study in the Civil Rights Movement, 1942-1968* (New York: Oxford Univ. Press, 1973); Nancy Weiss, *The National Urban League, 1910-1940* (New York: Oxford Univ. Press, 1974); Howard Zinn, *SNCC: The New Abolitionists* (Boston: Beacon Press, 1964); Clayborne Carson, *In Struggle: SNCC and the Black Awakening of the 1960s* (Cambridge, Mass.: Harvard Univ. Press, 1981); Patricia Sullivan, *Lift Every Voice and Sing: The NAACP and the Making of the Civil Rights Movement* (New York: The New Press, 2009). The NAACP Records are available at

the Library of Congress, https://www.loc.gov/loc/lcib/1003/collection.html (accessed April 2, 2017).

11. Richard Kluger, *Simple Justice: The History of Brown v. Board of Education and Black America's Struggle for Equality,* rev. ed. (New York: Knopf, 2004); Michael J. Klarman, *From Jim Crow to Civil Rights: The Supreme Court and the Struggle for Racial Equality* (New York: Oxford Univ. Press, 2004). On the NAACP and the court-oriented strategy, see James T. Patterson, *Brown v. Board of Education: A Civil Rights Milestone and its Troubled Legacy* (New York: Oxford Univ. Press, 2001); Mark V. Tushnet, *The NAACP's Legal Strategy against Segregated Education, 1925-1950* (Chapel Hill: Univ. of North Carolina Press, 1987); Genna Rae McNeil, *Groundwork: Charles Hamilton Houston and the Struggle for Civil Rights* (Philadelphia: Univ. of Pennsylvania Press, 1983); Gary M. Lavergne, *Before Brown: Herman Marion Sweatt, Thurgood Marshall and the Long Road to Justice* (Austin: Univ. of Texas Press, 2010). On recent work dealing with white resistance in its various forms, see Clive Webb, ed., *Massive Resistance: Southern Opposition to the Second Reconstruction* (New York: Oxford Univ. Press, 2005); Brian Ward, "Racial Politics, Culture and the Cole Incident of 1956," in *Race and Class in the American South since 1890,* ed. Melvyn Stokes and Rick Halpern (Providence, R.I.: Berg Publishers, 1994), 181-208. For an even longer view, see David Goldfield, *Still Fighting the Civil War: The American South and Southern History* (Baton Rouge: Louisiana State Univ. Press, 2002).

12. Adam Fairclough, *To Redeem the Soul of America: The Southern Christian Leadership Conference and Martin Luther King, Jr.* (Athens: Univ. of Georgia Press, 1987); David J. Garrow, *Bearing the Cross: Martin Luther King, Jr., and the Southern Christian Leadership Conference* (New York: W. Morrow, 1986); Taylor Branch, *Parting the Waters: America in the King Years, 1954-1963* (New York: Simon and Schuster, 1988). See also the subsequent books in Branch's life of King: *Pillar of Fire, 1963-1965* (New York: Simon and Schuster, 1998), and *At Canaan's Edge, 1965-1968* (New York: Simon and Schuster, 2006).

13. David Levering Lewis, *King: A Biography* (Urbana: Univ. of Illinois Press, 1970); Stephen B. Oates, *Let the Trumpet Sound: The Life of Martin Luther King, Jr.* (New York: New American Library, 1982). King's autobiographical works include *Strength to Love* (New York: Harper and Row, 1963); *Stride towards Freedom: The Montgomery Story* (New York: Harper and Brothers, 1958); *The Trumpet of Conscience* (New York: Harper and Row, 1967); *Where Do We Go from Here: Chaos or Community?* (New York: Harper and Row, 1967); *Why We Can't Wait* (New York: HarperCollins, 1963). Also see Clayborne Carson, ed., *The Papers of Martin Luther King, Jr.,* 6 vols (Berkeley: Univ. of California Press, 1992-2007). For the King Papers Project at Stanford University, see https://kinginstitute.stanford.edu/king-papers/about-papers-project (accessed April 2, 2017). For the southern emphasis on armed self-defense: Timothy B. Tyson, *Radio Free Dixie: Robert F. Williams and the Roots of Black Power* (Chapel Hill: Univ. of North Carolina Press, 1999). See

also Rebecca N. Hill, *Men, Mobs, and Law: Anti-Lynching and Labor Defense in U.S. Radical History* (Durham, N.C.: Duke Univ. Press, 2008); Akinyele Omowale Umoja, *We Will Shoot Back: Armed Resistance in the Mississippi Freedom Movement* (New York: New York Univ. Press, 2013); Charles E. Cobb, *This Nonviolent Stuff'll Get You Killed: How Guns Made the Civil Rights Movement Possible* (New York: Basic Books, 2014). These works represent a recent trend in excavating an alternative vision to that of King's nonviolence.

14. David Chappell, *Waking from the Dream: The Struggle for Civil Rights in the Shadow of Martin Luther King, Jr.* (New York: Random House, 2014). For a sampling of biographies devoted to those associated with the civil rights movement—among others included in the bibliography—see Eric Burner, *And Gently He Shall Lead Them: Robert Parris Moses and Civil Rights in Mississippi* (New York: New York Univ. Press, 1994); Barbara Ransby, *Ella Baker and the Black Freedom Movement: A Radical Democratic Vision* (Chapel Hill: Univ. of North Carolina Press, 2003); Manning Marable, *Malcolm X: A Life of Reinvention* (New York: Viking, 2011); Pauli Murray, *Song in a Weary Throat: An American Pilgrimage* (New York: Harper and Row, 1987); Jerald Podair, *Bayard Rustin: American Dreamer* (Lanham, Md.: Rowman and Littlefield, 2009); Septima Clark, *Echo in My Soul* (New York: E. P. Dutton, 1962). Retrospective memoirs of activists include Roy Wilkins, *Standing Fast: The Autobiography of Roy Wilkins* (New York: Viking, 1982); John Lewis, *Walking with the Wind: A Memoir of the Movement* (New York: Simon and Schuster, 1998); Melba Pattillo Beals, *Warriors Don't Cry: A Searing Memoir of the Battle to Integrate Little Rock's Central High* (New York: Washington Square Books, 1994); James Farmer, *Lay Bare the Heart: An Autobiography of the Civil Rights Movement* (New York: Arbor House, 1985).

15. William Chafe, *Civilities and Civil Rights: Greensboro, North Carolina and the Black Freedom Struggle* (New York: Oxford Univ. Press, 1980); Robert Norrell, "Caste in Steel: Jim Crow Careers in Birmingham, Alabama," *Journal of American History* 73, no. 3 (Dec. 1986): 669-94; David R. Colburn, *Racial Change and Community Crisis: St. Augustine, Florida, 1877-1980* (New York: Columbia Univ. Press, 1985).

16. Jo Ann Robinson, *The Montgomery Bus Boycott and the Women Who Started It* (Knoxville: Univ. of Tennessee Press, 1987); J. Mills Thornton III, *Dividing Lines: Municipal Politics and the Struggle for Civil Rights in Montgomery, Birmingham, and Selma* (Tuscaloosa: Univ. of Alabama Press, 2002). For a recent appraisal of Rosa Parks, see Jeanne Theoharis, *The Rebellious Life of Mrs. Rosa Parks* (Boston: Beacon Press, 2013).

17. Howell Raines, *My Soul is Rested: Movement Days in the Deep South Remembered* (New York: G. P. Putnam's Sons, 1977); Aldon Morris, *The Origins of the Civil Rights Movement: Black Communities Organizing for Change* (New York: The Free Press, 1984); *Eyes on the Prize: America's Civil Rights Years, 1954-1965,* DVD, produced by Henry Hampton (Boston: Blackside, 1986); Harvard Sitkoff, *The Struggle for Black Equality, 1945-1980* (New York: Hill

and Wang, 1981). In 1990, Hampton produced a sequel to the original video series, entitled *Eyes on the Prize II, 1965-1985,* DVD (Boston: Blackside, 1990). In addition, see the *Eyes on the Prize* companion volumes: Juan Williams, *Eyes on the Prize: America's Civil Rights Years, 1954-1965* (New York: Viking, 1987); and Henry Hampton and Steve Fayer, eds., *Voices of Freedom: An Oral History of the Civil Rights Movement from the 1950s through the 1980s* (New York: Bantam Books, 1990), which collected written transcripts from the oral histories produced for the films.

18. The insight about the role of women as seen on video can be found in Steven F. Lawson, "Freedom Then, Freedom Now: The Historiography of the Civil Rights Movement," *American Historical Review* 96 (Apr. 1991): 468. Barbara Woods, Jacqueline Anne Rouse, and Vicki L. Crawford, *Women in the Civil Rights: Movement Trailblazers and Torchbearers, 1941-1965* (New York: Carlson Publishing, 1990); Lynne Olson, *Freedom's Daughters: The Unsung Heroines of the Civil Rights Movement from 1830 to 1970* (New York: Scribners, 2001); Bettye Thomas and V. P. Franklin, eds., *Sisters in the Struggle: African-American Women in the Civil Rights-Black Power Movement* (New York: New York Univ. Press, 2001); Davis W. Houck and David E. Dixon, eds., *Women and the Civil Rights Movement, 1954-1965* (Jackson: Univ. Press of Mississippi, 2009); Ransby, *Ella Baker;* Theoharis, *The Rebellious Life of Mrs. Rosa Parks;* Chana Kai Lee, *For Freedom's Sake: The Life of Fannie Lou Hamer* (Champaign: Univ. of Illinois Press, 1999); Cynthia G. Fleming, *Soon We Will Not Cry: The Liberation of Ruby Doris Smith Robinson* (Lanham, Md.: Rowman and Littlefield, 1998).

19. Sara Evans, *Personal Politics: The Roots of Women's Liberation in the Civil Rights Movement and the New Left* (New York: Alfred A. Knopf, 1980); Mary King, *Freedom Song: A Personal Story of the Civil Rights Movement* (New York: William Morrow and Company, 1987); Belinda Robnett, *How Long? How Long? African American Women in the Struggle for Civil Rights* (New York: Oxford Univ. Press, 1997); Deborah Gray White, *Too Heavy a Load: Black Women in Defense of Themselves, 1894-1994* (New York: W. W. Norton, 1999); Danielle L. McGuire, *At the Dark End of the Street: Black Women, Rape, and Resistance—A New History of the Civil Rights Movement from Rosa Parks to the Rise of Black Power* (New York: Knopf, 2010); Paula Giddings, *When and Where I Enter: The Impact of Black Women on Race and Sex in America* (New York: Bantam Books, 1984); Steve Estes, *I Am a Man! Race, Manhood, and the Civil Rights Movement* (Chapel Hill: Univ. of North Carolina Press, 2005); Peter Ling, *Gender and the Civil Rights Movement* (Piscataway, N.J.: Rutgers Univ. Press, 2004).

20. John Dittmer, *Local People: The Struggle for Civil Rights in Mississippi* (Champaign: Univ. of Illinois Press, 1995); Payne, *I've Got the Light of Freedom.* Additional books in this genre include Adam Fairclough, *Race and Democracy: The Civil Rights Struggle in Louisiana, 1915-1972* (Athens: Univ. of Georgia Press, 1995); Glenn Eskew, *But for Birmingham: The Local and National Movements in the Civil Rights Struggles* (Chapel Hill: Univ. of North Carolina, 1997); Elizabeth Jacoway, *Turn Away Thy Son: Little Rock, the Crisis That*

Shocked the Nation (Fayetteville: Univ. of Arkansas Press, 2008); Robin D. G. Kelley, *Race Rebels: Culture, Politics, and the Black Working Class* (New York: The Free Press, 1994); Eagles, *Price of Defiance;* Raymond Arsenault, *Freedom Riders: 1961 and the Struggle for Racial Justice* (New York: Oxford Univ. Press, 2006); Bruce Watson, *Freedom Summer: The Savage Season of 1964 That Made Mississippi Burn and Made America a Democracy* (New York: Viking, 2010).

21. Doug McAdam, *Political Process and the Development of Black Insurgency, 1930-1970* (Chicago: Univ. of Chicago Press, 1982); Manning Marable, *Race, Reform, and Rebellion: The Second Reconstruction in Black America, 1945-1982* (Jackson: Univ. Press of Mississippi, 1984); Jack Bloom, *Race, Class, and the Civil Rights Movement: The Changing Political Economy of Southern Racism* (Bloomington: Indiana Univ. Press, 1987).

22. Particularly see Patricia Sullivan, *Days of Hope: Race and Democracy in the New Deal Era* (Chapel Hill: Univ. of North Carolina Press, 1996); Glenda Gilmore, *Defying Dixie: The Radical Roots of the Civil Rights Movement, 1919-1950* (New York: W. W. Norton, 2008). An analysis of the impact of foreign affairs on the civil rights movement must begin with World War II. For this, see Kevin Kruse and Stephen Tuck, eds., *The Fog of War: The Second World War and the Civil Rights Movement* (New York: Oxford Univ. Press, 2012). On civil rights and foreign affairs, see Thomas Borstelmann, *The Cold War and the Color Line: American Race Relations in the Global Arena* (Cambridge, Mass.: Harvard Univ. Press, 2001); Mary L. Dudziak, *Cold War Civil Rights: Race and the Image of American Democracy* (Princeton, N.J.: Princeton Univ. Press, 2000). On various aspects of the media and civil rights, see Gene Roberts, *The Race Beat: The Press, the Civil Rights Struggle, and the Awakening of a Nation* (New York: Knopf, 2006); Jannette L. Dates and William Barlow, eds., *Split Image: African Americans in the Mass Media* (Washington, D.C.: Howard Univ. Press, 1990). On the significance of black-oriented radio, see Brian Ward, *Radio and the Struggle for Civil Rights in the South* (Gainesville: Univ. Press of Florida, 2006). On popular music and civil rights, refer to Ward, *Just My Soul Responding: Rhythm and Blues, Black Consciousness, and Race Relations* (Berkeley: Univ. of California Press, 1998); Craig Werner, *A Change is Gonna Come: Music, Race, and the Soul of America* (Ann Arbor: Univ. of Michigan Press, 2006); Michael T. Bertrand, *Race, Rock, and Elvis* (Urbana: Univ. of Illinois Press, 2000). On sports and civil rights, particularly baseball, see Jules Tygiel, *Baseball's Great Experiment: Jackie Robinson and His Legacy* (New York: Oxford Univ. Press, 1983).

23. Jeanne Theoharis and Komozi Woodard, eds., *Freedom North: Black Freedom Struggles outside the South, 1940-1980* (New York: Palgrave MacMillan, 2003); Thomas Sugrue, *Sweet Land of Liberty: The Forgotten Struggle for Civil Rights in the North* (New York: Random House, 2008); Jeanne Theoharis and Komozi Woodard, eds., *Groundwork: Local Black Freedom Movements in America* (New York: New York Univ. Press, 2005); Emilye Crosby, ed., *Civil Rights History from the Ground Up: Local Struggles, a National Movement* (Athens:

Univ. of Georgia Press, 2011); Clarence Taylor, *Civil Rights in New York City: From World War II to the Giuliani Era* (New York: Fordham Univ. Press, 2011).

24. For the most comprehensive approach to this new path of scholarship, see Jacquelyn Dowd Hall, "The Long Civil Rights Movement and the Political Uses of the Past," *Journal of American History* 91 (Mar. 2005): 1233-63. This perspective can be found in recent scholarship, including Tracy K'Meyer, *Civil Rights in the Gateway to the South: Louisville, Kentucky, 1945-1980* (Lexington: Univ. Press of Kentucky, 2009); Robert R. Korstad and James L. Leloudis, *To Right These Wrongs: The North Carolina Fund and the Battle to End Poverty and Inequality in 1960s America* (Chapel Hill: Univ. of North Carolina Press, 2010); Karen Kruse Thomas, *Deluxe Jim Crow: Civil Rights and American Health Policy, 1935-1954* (Athens: Univ. of Georgia Press, 2011); Barbara Harris Combs, *From Selma to Montgomery: The Long March to Freedom* (New York: Routledge, 2013); Eben Miller, *Born along the Color Line: The 1933 Amenia Conference and the Rise of a National Civil Rights Movement* (New York: Oxford Univ. Press, 2012); Gordon Mantler, *Power to the Poor: Black-Brown Coalition and the Fight for Economic Justice, 1960-1974* (Chapel Hill: Univ. of North Carolina Press, 2015); Mark Brilliant, *The Color of America Has Changed: How Racial Diversity Shaped Civil Rights Reform in California, 1941-1978* (New York: Oxford Univ. Press, 2010).

25. The phrase "black freedom struggle" seems to have originated in print with Pauli Murray, *States' Laws on Race and Color: Studies in the Legal History of the South* (Cincinnati: Women's Division of Christian Service [Board of Missions and Church Extension, Methodist Church], 1950), xvi, xxii.

26. For the "lost opportunities thesis," see Robert Korstad and Nelson Lichtenstein, "Opportunities Found and Lost: Labor, Radicals, and the Early Civil Rights Movement," *Journal of American History* 75 (1988): 786-811. See also Michael Honey, *Southern Labor and Black Civil Rights: Organizing Memphis Workers* (Urbana: Univ. of Illinois Press, 1993).

27. On the black liberation movement, see Jeanne Theoharis and Komozi Woodard, eds., *Groundwork: Local Black Liberation Movements in America* (New York: New York Univ. Press, 2005); Cedric Johnson, *Revolutionaries to Race Leaders: Black Power and the Making of African American Politics* (Minneapolis: Univ. of Minnesota Press, 2007). For a powerful critique of the "long civil rights movement" perspective, see Sundiata Keita Cha-Jua and Clarence Lang, "The 'Long Movement' as Vampire: Temporal and Spatial Fallacies in Recent Black Freedom Studies," *Journal of African American History* 92 (Spring 2007): 265-88. Also see Eric Arnesen, "Reconsidering the 'Long Civil Rights Movement,'" *Historically Speaking* 10 (Apr. 2009): 31-34.

28. Interestingly, Allen Tate used the term "Uncle Sam's Other Province" at a time when it seemed the rest of the world was watching the civil rights movement unfold on the nightly news. The images generally were not favorable to the South. See Allen Tate, "Faulkner's 'Sanctuary' and the Southern

Myth," *Virginia Quarterly Review* 44 (1968): 418-27. An excellent overview of the South's development from the end of World War II through the Sunbelt era is found in Numan Bartley, *The New South, 1945-1980: The Story of the South's Modernization* (Baton Rouge: Louisiana State Univ. Press, 1995).

29. My interpretation of the "New South" era is based heavily on C. Vann Woodward, *The Origins of the New South, 1877-1913* (Baton Rouge: Louisiana State Univ. Press, 1951); Edward L. Ayers, *The Promise of the New South: Life after Reconstruction* (New York: Oxford Univ. Press, 1992); Leon Litwack, *Trouble in Mind: Black Southerners in the Age of Jim Crow* (New York: Knopf, 1998).

30. "Capitulation to racism" is in reference to the title of chapter 3 in C. Vann Woodward, *The Strange Career of Jim Crow* (1955; repr., New York: Oxford Univ. Press, 2002). For the longer quotation, see Litwack, *Trouble in Mind,* 246.

31. "All Coons Look Alike to Me" is a reference to the 1896 song penned by Ernest Hogan. The William Faulkner quotation ending the paragraph was cited in note 6.

32. The quotation is from James Baldwin, *The Fire Next Time* (New York: Dial Press, 1963), 8-10.

33. The civil rights movement may have been the twentieth century's greatest push toward reform, but it must be remembered that it occurred in a region that also was undergoing change. The term "bulldozer revolution," which was coined by C. Vann Woodward, refers to this relatively dramatic regional transformation. Such impersonal or economic forces did have an impact on race relations. See C. Vann Woodward, "The Search for Southern Identity," *The Burden of Southern History* (Baton Rouge: Louisiana State Univ. Press, 1960), 6. On a related note, also see Neil R. McMillen, ed., *Remaking Dixie: The Impact of World War II on the American South.* The "bulldozer revolution" apparently led to the creation of the "Sunbelt South." See Bruce J. Schulman, *From Cotton Belt to Sunbelt: Federal Policy, Economic Development, and the Transformation of the South, 1938-1980* (New York: Oxford Univ. Press, 1991). For a recent synthesis on the civil rights movement, which incorporates much of what has been stated in this essay, see Stephen Tuck, *We Ain't What We Ought To Be: The Black Freedom Struggle from Emancipation to Obama* (Cambridge, Mass.: Belknap Press of Harvard Univ. Press, 2010).

CHAPTER TEN

Realigning the Base

The Republican Party in the Postwar South

MICHAEL BOWEN

In recent years, the political history of the post–World War II South has drawn the attention of scholars and general audiences alike. In thirty-five years, the Democratic "Solid South" became the cornerstone of the Republican Party, a process that had clear ramifications for the nation as a whole, given the success of the GOP since the 1980s. Historians and social scientists generally attribute the transformation of the South to four trends: demographic changes, economic growth, the legacy of white supremacy, and evangelical religion. At the national level, a number of influential scholars have argued that today's conservatism evolved from the South's distinctive political culture, especially its populist tradition and the remnants of the Jim Crow system. Regardless of the causes and the ramifications, recent debates on the growth of southern Republicanism have generated a vibrant, contested scholarship and created a subfield of southern history that has asked many questions but answered few.

Writing as contemporary observers, political scientists were the first to survey the virtually nonexistent southern GOP. In his landmark *Southern Politics in State and Nation* (1949), V. O. Key examined the eleven states of the Confederacy and sketched a detailed overview of Democratic dominance. While cognizant of each state's unique qualities, he attributed the one-party phenomenon to white supremacy, going as far to say, "In its grand outlines, the politics of the South revolves around the position of the Negro."[1] Though Key found functioning Republican organizations in Tennessee, Virginia, and North Carolina, these were isolated remnants of antiplanter populism in the mountain regions and provided little more than token opposition at the state level. Elsewhere, Democrats had no competition. The power of white elites in the Black Belt region of Mississippi, Alabama, Georgia, and South Carolina tended to dominate the southern political landscape and exaggerate race as a political factor, leaving an indelible impression in the mind of northerners, who saw the South as a backward but coherent whole. Key's study would be authoritative for the next two decades.[2]

In the 1950s and 1960s the South's economic and urban growth made conditions more favorable to Republicans, but the civil rights movement overshadowed these developments. The Dixie electorate generally supported the Democratic politicians who led the massive resistance campaign against federal civil rights programs, but their hatred for the Republican Party began to fade as 1964 GOP nominee Barry Goldwater made his vote against that year's landmark Civil Rights Act into a campaign issue. While scholarship on the Jim Crow system dominated the field at this time, some writers looked for the political connections between the South and the rest of the country through the so-called Conservative Coalition of southern Democrats and Republicans in Congress. Though Key had claimed that little cohesiveness existed between the two parties, in 1967 political scientist John Robert Moore used newer statistical techniques and found that the conservatives did indeed work together frequently in the 1930s to block New Deal legislation.[3] James T. Patterson's *Congressional Conservatism and the New Deal* (1967) provided a historical treatment of this alliance in the Senate. He argued that a solid conservative core existed, but that ideological and partisan differences prevented it from operating effectively most of the time. Congress did block a number of Franklin D. Roosevelt's major projects in the late 1930s, but southerners only voted in lockstep on racial issues. Patterson concluded that the Conservative Coalition did indeed exist, but it was not as monolithic as many suggested.[4]

Five of the six states Goldwater carried in 1964 were former Confederate states. In 1968 Richard Nixon and Alabama governor George Wallace, running as an independent, split ten of eleven southern states and prompted political scientists and campaign operatives to reexamine the growth of southern Republicanism.[5] In 1969 Nixon staffer Kevin Phillips justified the Republican "southern strategy" in *The Emerging Republican Majority*. Making no effort to be humble or nonpartisan, Phillips proclaimed that Nixon's victory signaled a complete realignment of the American political system. Since 1945, the GOP had slowly built a new base on the growing population and economic development of the South and West and on white southern disaffection with the Democratic civil rights program. While Phillips did not believe that race was the prime factor in this shift, he conceded that the Voting Rights Act of 1965 had given African Americans more prominence within the Democratic Party and pushed southern whites into the GOP.[6] Political scientists Richard Scammon and Ben Wattenberg rejected Phillips's argument in their 1970 book *The Real Majority*. They predicted that the increasing clout of both the "Wallaceites" and "Radical Left" would alienate voters, especially given the "middle-class, middle-aged, middle-minded, unyoung, unpoor, unblack nature of the electorate."[7] Republicans could capitalize in all regions, the authors claimed, if they rejected extremism and governed from the center.

Both the Phillips and the Scammon-Wattenberg theses fit with a broader cultural narrative best articulated by journalist John Egerton. In his 1974 book, *The Americanization of Dixie,* the writer chronicled the disappearance of regional differences between the North and South. Rather than seeing this as a step forward for Dixie, Egerton feared that the rest of the nation was adopting the South's worst traits, including the racial character of its politics. Egerton concluded that, without the intervening Watergate scandal, Nixon's southern strategy would have remade the GOP in his image.[8] Through the remainder of the 1970s, scholars merged the "southernization" idea with the Phillips and Scammon-Wattenberg theses. Kirkpatrick Sale's *Power Shift* (1975) echoed Phillips, albeit in a much less partisan fashion, when it regarded the growth of the "Southern

Rim" since the end of World War II as a challenge to the northeastern hegemony in the United States.[9] A year later, journalists Jack Bass and Walter De Vries published *The Transformation of Southern Politics*. After acknowledging the legacy of Jim Crow, they argued that urbanization, the opening of two-party competition, and increased voting rights for African Americans had moderated the region's politics. The success of New South governors like Reuben Askew and Jimmy Carter, as well as Carter's 1976 presidential nomination, underscored the idea that the South was becoming less distinctive and reactionary.[10] By the late 1970s the consensus held that the South was beginning to resemble the rest of the nation, but the ramifications of that metamorphosis were not abundantly clear.

In the early 1980s, as Ronald Reagan ran strong in the South and Republicans began to reliably win down-ballot races in the region, it certainly appeared that Phillips's 1969 prediction of a new Republican majority based in the South had been prescient. Political scientists were the first to address these changing dynamics. Alexander Lamis's *The Two-Party South* was published in 1984 and contended that, by the mid-1970s, the racial issues of the civil rights era had dissipated to the point that Democrats could build successful biracial coalitions. He attributed Alabama governor George Wallace's 1982 resurgence to African American support and implied that Wallace's evolution from race-baiting demagogue to New South moderate signaled the end of the politics of white supremacy.[11] Three years later, brothers Earl and Merle Black produced *Politics and Society in the South*. An impeccably researched study, the authors explored the demographic, economic, and cultural changes since World War II and found that the interests of middle-class whites had displaced those of the rural, Black Belt politicians who built the Jim Crow system. The Black brothers predicted that race would remain a political issue, but that the economic individualism of the middle-class would be the prime concern for the region going forward and could benefit both Republicans and Democrats.[12]

The White Backlash Thesis

Lamis and the Black brothers made convincing arguments, but others were unwilling to completely disregard the lasting impact of segregation on the region. In 1988, Dewey Grantham's *Life and Death of the Solid South* conceded that urbanization, economic diversification, and shifting demography made the South more electorally competitive in the 1970s and 1980s, but he saw the reactionary response to the civil rights movement as the most potent political force. Unlike Lamis, who saw Wallace as emblematic of the declining importance of race, Grantham regarded the Alabamian as a modern-day populist, a crusader for traditional, rural values that the national Democratic Party had jettisoned during its quest for racial equality. Wallace made a strong showing in the South during the 1968 campaign, thanks to the "white backlash," the shorthand moniker for the exodus of the white working class from the Democratic Party. Grantham believed that both Wallace's and Nixon's southern strategy pushed the Republicans, both in the South and nationally, toward the former's position on race. Southern Democrats responded with a move to the center-left to remain viable in the face of a shifting electorate. Doing so fulfilled the Scammon-Wattenberg thesis and pushed a host of centrist leaders like Bill Clinton and Bob Graham into governorships. Though he gives short shrift to the fiscal conservatism of the Boll Weevils, the southern Democrats who supported Ronald Reagan's fiscal policy in the 1980s, Grantham concluded his analysis with the Solid South ruined and two-party competition seemingly imminent.[13]

By the mid-1990s, historians were ready to join the discussion. Numan Bartley's synthetic *The New South, 1945–1980* argued that the political changes were closely tied to economic gains and the decline of white supremacy. He bridged the gap between the civil rights movement and the Reagan revolution of 1980, finding that the unrest of the 1960s and 1970s made lower-class whites socially conservative while the economic boom of the Sunbelt South made the upper-middle class fiscally conservative. Reagan's policies appealed to both groups and finally eroded the Democratic Solid South once and for all.[14]

As political scientists and historians ruminated on the place of race in southern politics and conservatism remained strong nationally, historians and pundits developed the connections between the two trends. Much of the early scholarship on the Reagan Administration continued the "southernization" thesis and firmly ensconced race as the key to Republican success in presidential elections. In 1992, journalist Thomas Edsall and his wife, Mary, published *Chain Reaction: The Impact of Race, Rights, and Taxes on American Politics,* a survey of the previous twenty-five years of American politics aimed for a general readership. The Edsalls argued that in 1968 and 1972 George Wallace and Richard Nixon utilized a racially coded language to capitalize on discontent among blue-collar workers and separate them from the Democratic Party. While Wallace was more aggressive, Nixon co-opted Wallace's populism through his calls for law and order and his attention to the South, essentially making race-based appeals without being overtly racist. The Edsalls claimed that this laid the groundwork for the conservative takeover of the GOP. In the 1970s, as the Democratic Party fostered deeper ties with disaffected groups such as homosexuals, prisoners, and minority groups, the white working class came to believe that the party no longer represented their interests. According to these voters, rather than promoting economic opportunity for the worker as it had since the 1930s, the Democratic Party had become a "give-away" organization, raising taxes on the working and middle classes to fund programs that benefited other groups. The "have-nots" that drove the economic populism of the New Deal coalition were now the "haves" of the white working class who cast their lot with Ronald Reagan and the Republicans. *Chain Reaction* is not a work devoted specifically to southern politics, but its reliance on race as the primary dividing line between the parties extends the southern turn to the GOP in the 1960s and 1970s to the rest of the nation.[15]

Dan T. Carter furthered the case that modern conservatism was a direct outgrowth of southern politics in two works. His

Politics of Rage (1995) is a meticulously researched biography of George Wallace that traces the governor's rise from Clio, Alabama, through Montgomery, and onto the national stage. The book is solid throughout, but it shines in its treatment of Wallace's 1968 and 1972 presidential campaigns. Carter deftly shows how Wallace used economic populism to appeal to blue-collar whites in the North, anticipating and fueling the white backlash in earnest in the early 1970s. Carter rejects that idea put forth by Lamis and others that Wallace's outreach to the African American community following his 1972 shooting symbolized a softening of the racial issue in the South. Instead, Carter argues that Wallace, as one of the first to understand the shifting landscape of post-civil rights America, drew the blueprint for making racially coded language acceptable. He stoked the white backlash to the benefit of both himself and Nixon. In the process, according to Carter, Wallace became "the most influential loser in twentieth-century American politics."[16] Carter's second book, *From George Wallace to Newt Gingrich* (1996), expanded his argument through the 1990s, tracing the evolution of the racially based appeal from Wallace through Nixon, Ronald Reagan, George H. W. Bush, and finally Newt Gingrich. Like the Edsalls, Carter emphasized the linkage between racial and economic conservatism and illustrated how, by the Reagan era, Republican politicians utilized symbols like the "welfare queen" to activate the racial sensibilities of the electorate.[17]

The white-backlash thesis was the accepted interpretation for the recent growth of conservatism, but scholars soon looked past its simplicity and its top-down emphasis for a deeper explanation for Republican power in the once "solid" South. In *The Rise of Southern Republicans* (2002), Earl and Merle Black expanded on their previous work and made a compelling argument that race was still an overarching concern, although no longer the sole determinant of southern political behavior. Through an examination of Republican gains in the House of Representatives and Senate between 1960 and 2002, they demonstrate that a lingering distrust of the GOP and the advantages of Democratic incumbency stymied the growth of the two-party system until the 1980s. In the peripheral South, younger

Democratic politicians built biracial coalitions by moving to the left and representing the interests of all of their constituents, black and white. In the Deep South, conservative Democrats held on by espousing positions that were to the right of their national party but popular with whites at the local level. It was not until the 1980s, when Ronald Reagan made Republicanism "respectable," that the southern GOP achieved a critical mass of supporters. Due to the incredibly high cohesion of African Americans voters to the Democratic Party, Republicans had to build their majorities among whites who, by default, were not necessarily conservative or inclined to vote Republican. Breaking down the electorate by class, religious affiliation, race, and gender, the Black brothers show that upper-income whites and more religiously oriented whites of all economic classes tended to vote conservative and made up the new Republican base. To carry Dixie with this political calculus, the Republicans pushed socially conservative issues and Reagan's economic program. Where the Edsalls saw these policies as driven by race, the Blacks contend that these were separate issues that became intertwined on the campaign trail. This formula succeeded in the 1994 midterm elections, when the GOP won control of the House for the first time since 1954.[18]

A number of historians likewise rejected the idea that the racial feelings of the white backlash were unique to the 1960s. Kari Frederickson's comprehensive treatment of the 1948 Dixiecrat campaign, led at the top of the ticket by South Carolina governor Strom Thurmond, argued that the act of rebellion from the national Democratic Party started the process that led to the dissolution of the Solid South in 1968.[19] Both Glenn Feldman's anthology *Before Brown* (2004) and Joseph Lowndes's *From the New Deal to the New Right* (2008) contend that the move toward the Republican Party began as early as the 1940s, well before the civil rights movement began in earnest; they reject the idea that the South suddenly turned Republican following the civil rights movement. According to Feldman, "there is much to suggest that modern Republican dominance of the South—and, by extension, the nation—has been built on the back of white supremacy, racism, and emotional intolerance."[20] Lowndes takes a less polemical approach in his book, which traces the intellectual and political connections between the white supremacist positions of the Dixiecrats and northern conservatives. His book makes a strong case that the construction of a conservative worldview evolved from openly racist positions to the color-blind, populist language of the Nixon and Reagan campaigns.[21] Michael J. Klarman's *From Jim Crow to Civil Rights* (2004) examines the backlash thesis in the context of the Supreme Court, adding another nuance to the discussion beyond simple partisan politics.[22]

The Suburban School

As the white backlash thesis came under fire, a group of young scholars looked beyond the massive resistance campaigns of the 1950s and 1960s to interactions between working-class whites, African Americans, and politicians at the grassroots level. Where previous scholars posited that resistance to civil rights drove southern politics from the top down, the new "suburban school" emulated Thomas Sugrue's Bancroft Prize-winning *Origins of the Urban Crisis* (1996) and examined how segregationists and moderates shaped conservative politics from the bottom up.[23] Kevin Kruse's *White Flight* (2005), an examination of postwar Atlanta, argued that the process of white flight, the exodus of upper- and middle-class white residents to the suburbs, transformed this one-time bastion of moderation into an archetype of the new southern conservatism.[24] Atlanta provides fertile ground for study, having well-defined moderate business and political organizations, a strong black community, and a vocal, aggressive white minority. Housing patterns locked African Americans into certain neighborhoods but, as upward mobility and overcrowding pushed many to expand beyond the accepted boundaries, they met white resistance. Mayor William Hartsfield and his associates reached temporary accommodations with African American leaders to manage the transition, but as events moved beyond their control, white homeowners and parents largely eschewed violence and rallied behind the concept of "freedom of association." They argued that they had the right to choose whom they sold their homes to and where their children went to school, making an expansion of African American civil rights into a reduction of their own liberty. When their pleas fell on deaf ears, those who could afford to simply fled to the more affluent, largely white suburbs. Kruse contends that the rhetoric around "freedom of association" served as the blueprint for modern conservatism; unlike Carter and the Edsalls, Kruse sees this as stemming from local activists, not from political leaders like George Wallace or Ronald Reagan.[25]

Taking a broader view, while covering some of the same ground, Matthew Lassiter's *Silent Majority* (2006) contends that the suburban policies of the Nixon Administration, rather than its southern strategy, made the South go Republican. Lassiter places the suburbs at the center of the New South, noting their importance in the region's economic growth following World War II. Federal housing and transportation subsidies developed new neighborhoods and affluent whites settled them, creating a system of structural inequality that manifested in housing and school segregation in the urban core. These new suburbanites based their worldview on three distinct roles: taxpayer, homeowner, and school parent. As Lassiter details the desegregation campaigns in Atlanta and Charlotte, he illustrates how these three identities coalesced into a color-blind ideology that accepted equal opportunities, but firmly rejected any kind of remedial affirmative action or busing policy. When a federal judge mandated the busing of public school students to achieve desegregation in *Swann v. Charlotte-Mecklenburg Board of Education* (1971), suburban whites felt victimized. Many of them had worked to afford a home near a "good" school and transporting their child to an "inferior" city school violated all three tenets of their civic identity. In his final three chapters, Lassiter argues that Richard Nixon's appeal to Sunbelt suburbanites was more important in pushing the South into the Republican column than the racially coded politics depicted by Carter and the Edsalls.[26]

Though not without its critics, the emergence of the suburban school and its emphasis on local happenings indicate that the most fruitful areas for further research likely will be at the subregional level.[27] In the past several years, a number of books have looked at the growth of southern Republicanism in particular states and further discredited the white backlash thesis. Joseph Crespino's *In Search of Another Country* (2007) examined Mississippi and found a great deal of continuity between rural politics of the planter elite and the more individualistic ideology of modern conservatism. As the events of the civil rights movement overtook Mississippi, elites connected white supremacy to broader Right-wing concerns such as anticommunism and constitutionalism. In response to state events, they adopted color-blind rhetoric and promoted the concept of the white backlash well before 1968. Race is the motivating factor in this analysis, but Crespino is also sensitive to changes in religion. In the late 1970s, the Internal Revenue Service struck the tax exemption of segregated Christian schools and caused a vehement reaction from southern whites, who now saw their rights as parents *and* as Christians under attack. The issue of tax exemption, more than any other, helped bridge the gap between the racial and social conservatism of the region.[28] Tim S. R. Boyd's examination of Georgia Democrats argued that a top-down, white backlash did not occur in Georgia and attributes the rise of Republicanism to an inability of Georgia Democrats to maintain their power in the midst of a factional conflict.[29] Other state-level studies have addressed the political culture of South Carolina, Alabama, and Texas in recent years, all contributing to an emerging historiography of a South in transition.[30]

RELIGION

With the emergence of the religious Right as a key component of the Republican coalition, the role of organized religion in southern politics has emerged recently as a fruitful area of study. In the 1970s, evangelical denominations such as the Southern Baptists and the Church of Christ grew in size, popularity, and political activism. The presidential election of Jimmy Carter, a Sunday school-teaching Baptist from Plains, Georgia, piqued scholarly interest, but the growth of socially conservative pressure groups like the Moral Majority and the Christian Coalition in the late 1970s and 1980s attracted the most scrutiny. These groups aligned with the Republican Party and pushed social issues such as opposition to abortion and homosexual rights with such intensity that, by 1988, the "culture war" was fully ensconced in the political lexicon. Many scholars believed this trend was an outgrowth of the growing strength of southern Republicanism.[31]

The earliest examinations of the religious Right treated the movement as an anomaly. Noted religious scholar Samuel S. Hill found that the evangelical doctrine had historically kept most southern clergy focused on saving souls and away from political controversies. He wrote in 1985 that "although considerable grassroots religious-political conservatism lives in the South, much of the force of that movement is attributable to the symbolic leadership of President Reagan."[32] He predicted that, once Reagan and individuals like North Carolina senator Jesse Helms left office, evangelicals would lose much of their newfound importance. By the mid-1990s, it was evident that this was wide of the mark, and political scientists rushed to the fore with analyses of the phenomenon. The editors of *God at the Grass Roots, 1996* (1997) surveyed fourteen states and found the religious Right strongest in the six southern states they sampled.[33] Work specifically on the South highlighted the role of evangelicals in strengthening the Republican Party. In his institutional analysis of state parties, Joseph Aistrup gave evangelicals credit for organizing voters at the grassroots level in the South, something the Republican Party failed to do in the 1970s and 1980s as its reputation grew among white voters.[34] Examinations of the Southern Baptist Convention found that the organization had been taken over by Right-leaning activists, with one scholar arguing that the organization "has become a barometer of Southern culture and politics by . . . adopting . . . a militant 'go for the jugular' two-party Republican conservatism."[35]

The debates among historians of the religious Right have developed over two major questions: When did the movement begin?

And how southern was it? The first question is a matter of continuity between nineteenth- and early twentieth-century evangelical movements and the "new Christian Right." Numerous individuals, including many of the political scientists cited above, claimed that the movement began in earnest in the 1970s as a response to a disparate group of social issues, including the elimination of prayer in public schools, less-restrictive abortion policies, and a culture of openness stemming from the 1960s. In the most authoritative account of evangelical politicization, Daniel K. Williams argued that individuals and denominations had been politically active since the 1920s, but they became more partisan in reaction to the civil rights movement and the social issues of the 1970s. Though the book is not exclusively focused on the South, many of Williams's characters hail from Dixie.[36] Steven P. Miller's biography of Billy Graham contended that, though Graham criticized groups like the Moral Majority in the late 1970s and early 1980s, his political brand of evangelicalism in the 1950s and 1960s paved the way for the explosion of the religious Right and hastened the South's shift to the Republican Party.[37]

Miller makes Graham's southern identity one of the minister's defining characteristics. Scholars looking at the national growth of the religious Right have likewise traced the roots of the movement to Dixie. Bethany Moreton's *To Serve God and Wal-Mart* (2009) places the construction of Christian free enterprise, a blending of evangelical Christianity and laissez-faire economics, within the distinctive culture of the Ozark Mountains of Arkansas.[38] Barclay Key found southern religious colleges to be an especially effective vehicle for converting students to the Republican Party.[39] Darren Dochuk argued that southern California became the epicenter of the postwar religious Right thanks to southern migrants who populated the area looking for work, bringing their evangelicalism and conservatism with them.[40] Glenn Feldman linked the peculiarities of southern religion and its Jim Crow past to make the case that that modern conservatism was a continuation of the region's politics of hate. Most recently, however, Kevin Kruse has disputed the centrality of the South and has claimed that that the movement has broader origins and contemporaneous parallels in the North.[41]

As connections between the South, the Republican Party, and the conservative movement become clearer—and as contemporary events lead to new questions—the postwar southern GOP will continue to be a popular topic for historians and political scientists. Currently the suburban school is under review due to both attacks from critics and new interpretations from its proponents. In *The Myth of Southern Exceptionalism,* editors Matthew Lassiter and Joseph Crespino evolve the suburban school into a broader framework for analyzing the South and its history. In their co-authored introduction to their anthology, they argue that scholars and the media have overdrawn the distinctions between the North and the South, making regional differences a permanent part of our public and political memory while obscuring similarities in culture, economics, and politics. The South has often been regarded as a backward, inferior "other"; in this conception the southern position was always a "worst-case scenario." When it came to social progress, as long as the North took a more enlightened, more defensible position than the South, northerners were satisfied with their efforts. This was especially true in their treatment of African Americans. Lassiter, for example, contends that a half-hearted commitment to fair housing in the North was sufficient because it was more fair-minded than those of hard-line segregationists in Mississippi or Alabama. The politics of race are the foundation of modern conservatism, they argue, but not as a uniquely southern phenomenon. After all, the three aspects of suburban identity that Lassiter laid out in the *Silent Majority* were not specific to the South. Lassiter, Crespino, and many of the contributing authors argue that the false dichotomy has led many to misdiagnose the cause of the nation's ills and forgive the North for its weak efforts to solve the problems of inequality.[42]

Glenn Feldman responded with a fiery review in the *Journal of Southern History,* rejecting Lassiter and Crespino's broader contentions and accusing them of parroting apologies "for a white supremacist South that George C. Wallace and Henry W. Grady have already made."[43] He was willing to accept some of their points, but believed that they had drawn artificial distinctions between policies and programs to mute some aspects of conservatism that he found to be distinctly southern. In the conclusion to his latest edited volume, *Painting Dixie Red* (2011), Feldman expands his denunciation of the suburban school. Though he includes a number of different views in the volume (including one from this author), he clearly sees distinctive brands of southern racism and evangelicalism as the reason for recent Republican success across the country. "Perhaps the greatest surprise . . . is the assumption of many that the South's worst traits (a kind of anti-intellectual religious and free-market fundamentalism, bigotry, intolerance, anti-unionism, and others) would gradually be ameliorated by southern integration into the American mainstream. Obviously this has not turned out to be the case."[44]

As Feldman's criticism makes clear, the roots, meaning, and implications of postwar southern Republicanism are still unsettled topics. This fact was apparent during the 2012 election cycle. As Barack Obama was campaigning for reelection, Democrats and journalists accused the Republican Party and its "super-PAC" allies of once again using racially coded language. As Sally Kohn stated on Salon.com, "Today, despite the fact that most people on welfare are white, most Americans think the majority of welfare recipients are black. So when Newt Gingrich called President Obama the 'food stamp president,' the implicit story he was telling was that the nation's first black president was giving handouts to other black people."[45] Conservatives forcefully pushed back against the charges in numerous articles, including one from pundit Michelle Malkin, who listed twelve terms the Democrats had deemed racist, including "Chicago" and "golf."[46] Both the immediacy and the polarizing nature of the controversy, and of the election itself, ensure that southern Republicanism, and what it says about the nation as a whole, will be a matter of controversy for some time.

NOTES

1. V. O. Key Jr., *Southern Politics in State and Nation* (New York: Vintage Books 1949), 5.

2. Ibid.

3. Ibid., 346-68; John Robert Moore, "The Conservative Coalition in the United States Senate, 1942-1945," *Journal of Southern History* 33, no. 3 (Aug. 1967): 368-76.

4. James T. Patterson, *Congressional Conservatism and the New Deal: The Growth of the Conservative Coalition in Congress, 1933-1939* (Lexington: Univ. Press of Kentucky, 1967). Patterson also found that Democrats from rural districts were more likely to vote against FDR than their urban colleagues, but he hedged a bit and contended that the votes should be read in the context of an institution reasserting its independence as a co-equal branch of government.

5. Alabama governor George Wallace carried another five states, with the Democrat Hubert Humphrey carrying only Texas.

6. Phillips explicitly states that the Republicans should push for expanded African American voting rights so the Democratic Party will not "remain viable as spokesmen for Deep Southern conservatism." He attributed Nixon's victory to "a shift away from the sociological jurisprudence, more permissiveness, experimental residential, welfare and educational programming and massive federal spending" of the Democratic Party. Kevin Phillips, *The Emerging Republican Majority* (New Rochelle, N.Y.: Arlington House 1969), quotations, 287, 471.

7. Richard M. Scammon and Ben J. Wattenberg, *The Real Majority* (New York: Coward-McCann, 1970), quotation, 279.

8. John Egerton, *The Americanization of Dixie: The Southernization of America* (New York: Harper's Magazine Press, 1974). Egerton's analysis held a great deal of explanatory power beyond politics as well. For an economic assessment, see Stephen O. Cummings, *The Dixification of America: The American Odyssey into the Conservative Economic Trap* (Westport, Conn.: Praeger, 1998).

9. Kirkpatrick Sale, *Power Shift: The Rise of the Southern Rim and Its Challenge to the Eastern Establishment* (New York: Vintage Books, 1975).

10. Jack Bass and Walter De Vries, *The Transformation of Southern Politics: Social Change and Political Consequence since 1945* (Athens: Univ. of Georgia Press, 1995).

11. Alexander Lamis, *The Two Party South,* 2nd expanded ed. (1984; New York: Oxford Univ. Press, 1990). Lamis's conclusion seems strange given

subsequent events; however, to his credit, in later editions he revised his findings and predicted the continued importance of the white vote for Republicans.

12. Earl Black and Merle Black, *Politics and Society in the South* (Cambridge, Mass.: Harvard Univ. Press, 1987). See also Black and Black, *The Vital South: How Presidents Are Elected* (Cambridge, Mass.: Harvard Univ. Press, 1992).

13. Dewey Grantham, *The Life and Death of the Solid South: A Political History* (Lexington: Univ. Press of Kentucky Press, 1988). For a more recent treatment on a state-by-state basis, see Charles S. Bullock III and Mark J. Rozell, eds., *The New Politics of the Old South: An Introduction to Southern Politics* (Lanham, Mass.: Rowman and Littlefield, 1998).

14. Numan V. Bartley, *The New South, 1945-1980* (Baton Rouge: Louisiana State Univ. Press, 1995). For more on the economic development of the South, see James C. Cobb, *The Selling of the South* (Champaign: Univ. of Illinois Press, 1993); Bruce J. Schulman, *From Cotton Belt to Sunbelt: Federal Policy, Economic Development, and the Transformation of the South, 1938-1980* (New York: Oxford Univ. Press, 1991).

15. Thomas Byrne Edsall and Mary Edsall, *Chain Reaction: The Impact of Race, Rights, and Taxes on American Politics* (New York: W. W. Norton and Company, 1991).

16. Dan T. Carter, *Politics of Rage: George Wallace, the Origins of the New Conservatism, and the Transformation of American Politics* (New York: Simon and Schuster, 1995), quotation, 468.

17. Dan T. Carter, *From George Wallace to Newt Gingrich: Race and the Conservative Counterrevolution, 1964-1994* (Baton Rouge: Louisiana State Univ. Press, 1996). For a more contemporaneous account of the Wallace phenomenon, see Numan V. Bartley, *From Thurmond to Wallace: Political Tendencies in Georgia, 1948-1968* (Baltimore: Johns Hopkins Univ. Press, 1970).

18. Earl Black and Merle Black, *The Rise of Southern Republicans* (Cambridge, Mass.: The Belknap Press of Harvard Univ. Press, 2002). In 2004, political scientist David Lubin argued that the South became solidly Republican due to a mix of racial and economic concerns, but forecast a Democratic resurgence driven by growing African American and Hispanic populations. Writing two years later, Byron Shafer and Richard Johnston declared the Republican Party the majority party of the South. They noted that race was still "hugely consequential," but a class-based dichotomy was nearly as strong. As they put it, "Where once there was a minority party based on concentrations of poor whites plus blacks everywhere, there was *still* a minority party based on concentrations of poor whites plus blacks everywhere. It was just that once this party had been the Republicans, and now it was the Democrats." See Lubin, *The Republican South: Democratization and Partisan Change* (Princeton, N.J.: Princeton Univ. Press, 2004); Shafer and Johnston, *The End of Southern Exceptionalism: Class, Race, and Partisan Change in the Postwar South* (Cambridge, Mass.: Harvard Univ. Press, 2006).

19. Kari Frederickson, *The Dixiecrat Revolt and the End of the Solid South, 1932-1968* (Chapel Hill: Univ. of North Carolina Press, 2001). For more on Thurmond, see Jack Bass and Marilyn W. Thompson, *Ol' Strom: An Unauthorized Biography of Strom Thurmond* (Columbia: Univ. of South Carolina Press, 2003); Joseph Crespino, *Strom Thurmond's America* (New York: Hill and Wang, 2012).

20. Glenn Feldman, ed., *Before Brown: Civil Rights and White Backlash in the Modern South* (Tuscaloosa: Univ. of Alabama Press, 2004), quotation, 307.

21. Joseph E. Lowndes, *From the New Deal to the New Right: Race and the Southern Origins of Modern Conservatism* (New Haven, Conn.: Yale Univ. Press, 2008).

22. Michael J. Klarman, *From Jim Crow to Civil Rights: The Supreme Court and the Struggle for Racial Equality* (New York: Oxford Univ. Press, 2004).

23. Thomas J. Sugrue, *The Origins of the Urban Crisis: Race and Inequality in Postwar Detroit* (Princeton, N.J.: Princeton Univ. Press, 1996).

24. Kevin Kruse, *White Flight: Atlanta and the Making of Modern Conservatism* (Princeton, N.J.: Princeton Univ. Press, 2005). Kruse's book was the first monograph to take this approach. Earlier, *The Moderate's Dilemma* had looked at the role of moderate whites in school desegregation cases previously, and there were a handful of local case studies on desegregation, but Kruse's book was the first single-volume to take the suburban approach. See Matthew J. Lassiter and Andrew Lewis, *The Moderate's Dilemma: Massive Resistance to School Desegregation in Virginia* (Charlottesville: Univ. Press of Virginia, 1998); William Henry Kellar, *Make Hast Slowly: Moderates, Conservatives, and School Desegregation in Houston* (College Station: Texas A&M Press, 1999).

25. Kruse, *White Flight*.

26. Matthew Lassiter, *The Silent Majority: Suburban Politics in the Sunbelt South* (Princeton, N.J.: Princeton Univ. Press, 2006).

27. Jeff Norrell attacked the suburban school for placing too much emphasis on race and isolating events in the South from the broader changes in conservative intellectual and political thought. See Norrell, "Modern Conservatism and the Consequences of Its Ideas," *Reviews in American History* 36, no. 3 (Sept. 2008): 456-67.

28. Joseph Crespino, *In Search of Another Country: Mississippi and the Conservative Counterrevolution* (Princeton, N.J.: Princeton Univ. Press, 2007). For a distilled account of the outcry against the IRS, see Crespino, "Civil Rights and the Religious Right," in *Rightward Bound: Making America Conservative in the 1970s,* ed. Bruce Schulman and Julian Zelizer (Cambridge, Mass.: Harvard Univ. Press, 2008).

29. Timothy S. R. Boyd, *Georgia Democrats, the Civil Rights Movement, and the Shaping of the New South* (Gainesville: Univ. Press of Florida, 2012).

30. Bruce H. Kalk, *The Origins of the Southern Strategy: Two-Party Competition in South Carolina, 1950-1972* (Lanham, Mass.: Lexington Books, 2001); Sean Cunningham, *Cowboy Conservatism: Texas and the Rise of the Modern*

Right (Lexington: Univ. Press of Kentucky, 2010); Allen Tullos, *Alabama Getaway: The Political Imaginary and the Heart of Dixie* (Athens: Univ. of Georgia Press, 2011).

31. Much of the scholarly debate on Southern religion and political culture is beyond the scope of this chapter. For a good introduction to the topic, see Walter H. Cosner Jr. and Rodger M. Payne, eds., *Southern Crossroads: Perspectives on Religion and Culture* (Lexington: Univ. Press of Kentucky, 2008); Paul Harvey, *Freedom's Coming: Religious Culture and the Shaping of the South from the Civil War through the Civil Rights Era* (Chapel Hill: Univ. of North Carolina Press, 2005).

32. Samuel S. Hill, "Religion and Politics in the South," in *Religion in the South,* ed. Charles Reagan Wilson (Jackson: Univ. Press of Mississippi, 1985), 139–54; quotation, 153.

33. Mark J. Rozell and Clyde Wilcox, *God at the Grass Roots, 1996: The Christian Right in the American Elections* (Lanham, Mass.: Rowman and Littlefield, 1997). Since the mid-1990s, there has been an outpouring of work on the religious conservatives. See also Bruce Nesmith, *The New Republican Coalition: The Reagan Campaign and White Evangelicals* (New York: Peter Lang, 1994); William Martin, *With God on Our Side: The Rise of the Religious Right in America* (New York: Broadway Books, 1996).

34. Joseph Aistrup, *The Southern Strategy Revisited: Republican Top-Down Advancement in the South* (Lexington: Univ. Press of Kentucky, 1996).

35. James L. Guth, "Southern Baptist Clergy, the Christian Right, and Political Activism in the South," in *Politics and Religion in the White South,* ed. Glenn Feldman (Lexington: Univ. Press of Kentucky, 2005), 187–214; Oran P. Smith, *The Rise of Baptist Republicanism* (New York: New York Univ. Press, 1997), quotation, 22.

36. Daniel K. Williams, *God's Own Party: The Making of the Christian Right* (New York: Oxford Univ. Press, 2010). He emphasizes the southern character of the evangelical movement in Williams, "Voting for God and the GOP: The Role of Evangelical Religion in the Emergence of the Republican South," in *Painting Dixie Red: When, Where, Why, and How the South Became Republican,* ed. Glenn Feldman (Gainesville: Univ. Press of Florida, 2011), 21–37.

37. Steven P. Miller, *Billy Graham and the Rise of the Republican South* (Philadelphia: Univ. of Pennsylvania Press, 2009).

38. Bethany Moreton, *To Serve God and Wal-Mart: The Making of Christian Free Enterprise* (Cambridge, Mass.: Harvard Univ. Press, 2009).

39. Barclay Key, "'Out-Democratin' the Democrats': Religious Colleges and the Rise of the Republican Party in the South—A Case Study," in *Painting Dixie Red: When, Where, Why, and How the South Became Republican,* ed. Glenn Feldman (Gainesville: Univ. Press of Florida, 2011), 38–54.

40. Darren Dochuk, *From Bible Belt to Sunbelt: Plain-Folk Religion, Grassroots Politics, and the Rise of Evangelical Conservatism* (New York: W. W. Norton, 2010). For more on the Sunbelt and religious Right, see John G. Turner, *Bill*

Bright and Campus Crusade for Christ: The Renewal of Evangelicalism in Postwar America (Chapel Hill: Univ. of North Carolina Press, 2008).

41. Glenn Feldman, "The Status Quo Society, the Rope of Religion, and the New Racism," in *Politics and Religion in the White South,* ed. Glenn Feldman (Lexington: Univ. Press of Kentucky, 2005); Kevin Kruse, "Beyond the Southern Cross: The National Origins of the Religious Right," in *The Myth of Southern Exceptionalism,* ed. Matthew D. Lassiter and Joseph Crespino (New York: Oxford Univ. Press, 2010), 286-307.

42. Matthew D. Lassiter and Joseph Crespino, "The End of Southern History," in *The Myth of Southern Exceptionalism,* ed. Matthew D. Lassiter and Joseph Crespino (New York: Oxford Univ. Press, 2010), 286-307.

43. Glenn Feldman, "The Myth of Southern Exceptionalism," review of *The Myth of Southern Exceptionalism,* ed. Matthew D. Lassiter and Joseph Crespino, *Journal of Southern History* 77, no. 3 (Aug. 2011): 783-86.

44. Glenn Feldman, "America's Appointment with Destiny—A Cautionary Tale," in *Painting Dixie Red: When, Where, Why, and How the South Became Republican,* ed. Glenn Feldman (Gainesville: Univ. Press of Florida, 2011), 314-60; quotation, 326.

45. Sally Kohn, "Race Baiting at the RNC," Salon.com, http://www.salon.com/2012/08/29/race_baiting_at_the_rnc/ (accessed Aug. 31, 2012).

46. Michelle Malkin, "That's Racist! A Guide to What's Off-Limits," National Review Online, http://www.nationalreview.com/articles/315564/s-racist-michelle-malkin?pg=1 (accessed Sept. 5, 2012).

CHAPTER ELEVEN

The New South and the Natural World

MARK D. HERSEY AND JAMES C. GIESEN

It has become something of a cliché to bemoan the comparative underdevelopment of southern environmental history.[1] To be sure, such complaints are not entirely without grounding. Historians of the American South warmed to environmental history later than historians of other regions, while environmental historians all but ignored the South until the mid-1990s. Even now, comparatively few southern historians identify themselves as environmental historians. Of those who do, most received their formal training in only one of the two disciplines and followed a meandering path in drifting toward the other.[2] Others seem to have awoken one day and declared, "I am an environmental historian," with apparently little cause.

Even so, self-consciously environmental histories of the South have proliferated over the past two decades, and a small handful of history departments in the region have begun emphasizing the field in their graduate programs. One telling indication of its growth might be seen in the fact that that the Southern Historical Association has established a biennial article prize for southern agricultural or environmental history, and it recently awarded its major book and article prizes to environmental histories.[3] Thus, if southern environmental history has not fully arrived, it has clearly gained a substantial footing in southern history generally and is rapidly working its way from the periphery to the center. For that matter, the annual meetings of the American Society for Environmental History have lately featured southern U.S. panels, and more and more articles about the South have appeared between the covers of *Environmental History* in recent years.

This emergent southern environmental history has drawn on, engaged, and benefited from a long-standing historiographical thread in southern history that acknowledged the importance of the natural world. Southern historians have debated the influence of the region's climate in shaping the southern experience for generations and, given the centrality of agriculture to the South's past, have emphasized crop production and related phenomena like soil erosion. Prior to the 1990s, however, they seldom accounted for local ecologies, often painted the natural world with a broad (sometimes determinative) brush, and tended to posit a relatively fixed natural world that served as an important *backdrop,* rather than as an actor involved in a dialectical process with people jointly shaping the past. Nevertheless, it is true that for more than a century southern historians have proven comparatively sensitive to environmental forces.

While this essay concentrates on scholarship about the post-Civil War South, it is hardly surprising that this historiographical tradition emerged out of a focus on the South's prewar plantation economy. The most famous of its foundational works—Avery O. Craven's *Soil Exhaustion as a Factor in the Agricultural History of Virginia and Maryland, 1606-1860* (1925), Lewis C. Gray's *History of Agriculture in the Southern United States to 1860* (1933), and Ulrich B. Phillips's *Life and Labor in the Old South* (1929) among them—focused on the antebellum era.[4] Even as Craven, Gray, and Phillips were writing, however, sociologists like Rupert Vance, Howard W. Odum, Arthur Raper, and Charles S. Johnson had begun to frame the myriad problems facing impoverished tenants in the Depression-era South's plantation districts in historical terms.[5] In drawing connections between the debilitating poverty of the region and its denuded agro-ecosystems, these sociologists developed an important scholarly tradition that environmental historians would later expand. At the time, however, historians proved reluctant to join sociologists in connecting the exploitation of labor with the environment. As late as 1947, Francis Butler Simkins could suggest that the shortcomings of the crop-lien system might be explained by the fact that "Southern agricultural laborers were among the most improvident of Americans."[6]

As it did with virtually every facet of the region's historiography, the publication of C. Vann Woodward's masterful *Origins of the New South* (1951) changed the terms of the debate. Although Woodward did not place the environment at the forefront of his study, he did highlight the exploitative nature of the crop-lien system and of southern industry writ large. Lamenting, for instance, that timber companies had brushed aside "warnings against denuded forests and irreparable waste . . . as 'immeasurably stupid,'" he pointed out that lumbering proved typical of the New South's economy insofar as it required cheap, comparatively unskilled labor, "added the lowest value of product per wage earner," and had its social costs "charged up to 'progress.'"[7] *Origins of the New South,* of course, set the tone for much of the scholarship that followed, even for those challenging aspects of Woodward's discontinuity thesis. George Brown Tindall, for example, found at least a thread of continuity connecting the New South Progressives and the antebellum Bourbons. Nevertheless, in his 1967 classic *The Emergence of the New South, 1913-1945,* he followed Woodward in acknowledging the environmental costs that the social exploitation of labor entailed, even if his focus was on the latter.[8]

Woodward and Tindall each recognized that World War II changed both the South and southern historiography. In its wake, the civil rights movement helped usher in the New Social History, which privileged questions of race, class, and gender—all of which undeniably proved germane to the southern experience. The "holy trinity" of race, class, and gender dominated historians' perspectives on the region; so when environmental history began to coalesce nationally as a discipline during the 1970s, it appeared by contrast to be of little relevance to the history of the South. As Mart Stewart has pointed out, the nascent field's focus on wilderness, conservation, and the frontier seemed unimportant to a region that had few swaths of wilderness, but numerous, often painful reminders of a society rent by class, gender, and especially racial tensions.[9]

This is not to say southern historians did not take any notice of the new discipline. In 1983, for instance, Albert Cowdrey published *This Land, This South: An Environmental History,* which offered a first stab at laying out an overarching environmental history of the region.[10] Unsurprisingly, given the state of the field at the time, it proved considerably stronger in some areas than others. Nevertheless, the fact that the first book-length work of southern history to frame itself as an environmental history proved essentially synthetic offers a telling indication of southern history's long tradition of accounting in one fashion or another for the natural world.

Cowdrey's work notwithstanding, environmental history remained well outside the main currents of southern historiography. Indeed, the collective indifference of southern historians to environmental history over the course of the 1970s and 1980s fostered a misguided impression by nonsouthern specialists that the natural world was of little importance in the region's historiographical tradition—an impression that lingers in many quarters. However, as Barbara Fields pointed out in the 1990s, the germination of a self-consciously southern environmental history over the previous decade represented a return to a "*temporarily* neglected line of inquiry rather than [the initiation of] a new one."[11] Indeed, the natural world was a central force in a great deal of the history of the New South written in the twentieth century.

The 1980s saw a boom in writing about the rural South since the Civil War. Though nearly all of this scholarship came from historians trained in southern history, from this work there emerged a new intellectual thread, a series of ideas that would come to be known as southern environmental history. It is safe to say that the bulk of the scholarship about the South's natural environment published between World War II and 2000 focused on agriculture. Indeed, much of the most important work on southern history broadly was work that centered on the experiences of the region's farmers and the land on which they worked. One of the most interesting facets of southern environmental history is in fact the way that this scholarship morphed from something called "agricultural history" into "environmental history."

The undisputed king of southern farm history written in this era, in terms of output and influence, is Pete Daniel. Trained at Wake Forest University and the University of Maryland, Daniel grew up in Spring Hope, North Carolina, surrounded by tobacco culture.[12] Taken together, his seven books not only make important insights into the region's environmental history, they also make a case for the importance of rural people to southern history writ large. In other words, every scholar interested in southern history, not just agricultural or environmental history, reads Daniel's work. Daniel himself, over the course of his long career, made the transition from calling himself an agricultural historian to an environmental historian.[13]

Probably the most influential of Pete Daniel's books is *Breaking the Land: The Transformation of Cotton, Tobacco, and Rice Cultures since 1880* (1986), which was the first and most successful attempt to describe the sea change to southern agriculture in the long New South period. The book centers on the three most important crops to the southern economy and culture—cotton, tobacco, and rice—but its strength is its focus as much on the people growing, tending, and picking the plants as on the crops themselves. As a result, *Breaking the Land* makes the transformation of the southern landscape a human story as much or more than an environmental or agricultural one. Readers have lauded its ability to explain arcane federal farm policy through the lens of the region's poor, often uneducated, farmers, but its greatest insights revolve around race and class.[14]

Making the southern environmental story one about people allowed Daniel to extend an argument that he had begun with his first book, *The Shadow of Slavery: Peonage in the South, 1901-1969* (1972), and would continue to make through his six later books.[15] Simply stated, that argument is that the political, economic, and agricultural realities of rural southern life since the Civil War served to reinforce racism and classism. For Daniel, the mechanism of change on the land is the force of capitalism. His overarching argument has not been that environmental control meant social control per se, but rather that racial and class oppression served as key pillars of increasingly capitalistic agricultural and rural industrial systems. For Daniel, the changing economic landscape of the South—the rise of corporate-owned farms, the diversification of southern economies, the economic pressures exerted by state policies, the near absence of labor unions, and the entrenched legal and extralegal economic realities of Jim Crowism—drove changes on the southern landscape. Put too baldly: money moved the dirt and water; people suffered. In each of his powerful and important books, rural southerners, white and black, felt this economic force most keenly.

Daniel reserves his most pointed criticism for the role of the state, both in terms of its reaction to environmental change, like its response to the infamous 1927 Mississippi River flood, and in terms of its role forcing environmental change. New Deal agencies, state cooperative extension services, land-grant colleges, and the U.S. Department of Agriculture (USDA), attract most of his attention—and indeed he makes a compelling case that these institutions fostered changes to agriculture and the natural world that unnecessarily hurt the lives of millions of rural southerners. For instance, in *Toxic Drift* (2005), Daniel points to a number of cases where the USDA and state agencies allowed deadly pesticides to be sprayed where tenant farmers and laborers lived and worked.[16] Even more convincing is his demonstration in *Dispossession* (2013) of case after case of discrimination by state extension services against African American employees and farmers.[17]

Pete Daniel rose in the 1980s as the leading historian of the southern countryside, but he did so among a throng of other historians suddenly paying new attention to the subject. As Wayne Flynt wrote in 1986, Daniel's work was but one of the "historical torrents" that had begun raining down on the field after a "long and inexplicable drought."[18] Mart Stewart and Jack Temple Kirby joined Daniel in this movement to write about the post-Civil War South as a rural world first and foremost. Indeed, it was Stewart and Kirby who first began using the term "environment," though not at first claiming their own work as "environmental history."[19]

Southern historians did not know what to make of Stewart's enormously influential *What Nature Suffers to Groe: Life, Labor,*

and Landscape on the Georgia Coast, 1680-1920 when it appeared in
1996.[20] A westerner by birth, Stewart has always been somewhat
of an outsider to southern history, even though he earned a Ph.D.
from Emory University in Atlanta. Indeed, in 2012, Stewart told a
panel at the Agricultural History Society meeting that most southern historians either misunderstood or simply ignored his inter-
disciplinary approach to history. His book, however, convincingly
connected human relationships with the environment of the Georgia coast to over two centuries of social, political, and labor developments there. While most of the work deals with the pre-Civil
War period, its long temporal scope is actually part of its argument.
The Civil War did not fundamentally change the human relationship with the environment, Stewart argues, though labor changes
brought with emancipation had natural repercussions.

Jack Temple Kirby's career, more than Stewart's, followed the
rise of a self-conscious southern environmental history. He was
already a credentialed southern historian with several important
books, including an influential history of the culture of the rural
South, before he started thinking and writing about the natural
world as a principal actor in the region's past. In *Poquosin: A Study
of Rural Landscape and Society* (1995) Kirby waits only one sentence
before claiming that the book "is an 'environmental' history."[21]
The scare quotes reveal both the newness of the field and Kirby's
self-consciousness in claiming it as his territory. Indeed, others
struggled too. In the *Journal of Southern History,* Albert Cowdrey
noted that Kirby's book "defies easy classification."[22] But *Poquosin is*
environmental history. It is the long-view of a place—the swamps
and lowlands of Virginia and North Carolina between the James
River and Albemarle Sound—that demonstrates the environmental
constraints on political and cultural development over hundreds
of years. For Kirby, then, the natural world is a boundary and an
actor. The people of the Great Dismal Swamp and its surrounding areas had to make choices about politics, labor, and economics
only after considering immediate environmental factors.

A talented prose stylist, Kirby fashioned himself as raconteur,
which makes for compelling and persuasive reading, but his works

proved to be unusable as models for others trying to break in to the field. Thus, when he followed up *Poquosin* with the Bancroft-winning *Mockingbird Song: Ecological Landscapes of the South* (2006), southern and environmental historians were waiting anxiously. The sprawling, often-unfocused book was intended as an update of Cowdrey's *This Land, This South,* and it appeared at just the right moment. In the *Journal of American History,* Mart Stewart called it a "grand synthesis with perfect timing."[23] The book's strength is its refusal to present the environmental history of the South with a single theme or even argument. While much of the book focuses on the region's plantation past, Kirby weaves in and out various locales over more than three centuries. Despite an undeniable and provocative brilliance, it proved as idiosyncratic as its predecessor. Even so, it was through Kirby as much as anyone that environmental history began to enter the southern history mainstream, as is evident from the fact that the annual award presented by the Southern Historical Association (SHA) for the best article in agricultural or environmental history bears his name. Indeed, when Kirby's life was tragically cut short in 2009, he was serving as president of the SHA.

There were, of course, larger historiographical trends happening that impacted the production and reception of this scholarship. The 1980s and 1990s was the heyday of American environmental history. Donald Worster and William Cronon had won Bancrofts and were training a generation of environmental historians who would write the great second wave of histories. The great majority of this work, however, focused on the Northeast and American West or on the modern environmental movement and its antecedents. Thus, if southern historians were slow to come to environmental history, it is equally true that environmental historians came to questions of race and class comparatively late. Indeed, environmental historians spent much of the 1990s collectively flagellating themselves for the delay.[24]

This is also the twenty years that saw the greatest expansion of the population and economy of the Sunbelt. This explosive and apparently uncontrolled growth seemed to test the environment itself in new ways; to many outside observers, the region seemed unwilling and unprepared to deal with its problems. It is no surprise then that in 2000 Otis Graham could ask in the pages of *Southern Cultures,* if the South was "again the backward region," since it was failing to deal with the "ecological crisis" at hand and, to top it off, did not have any institutions that were actively fostering and teaching environmental history. "The South lags far behind the West in writing and graduate training in environmental history today," he wrote.[25]

It was this lag Kirby had in mind when he quipped that the group photo of southern environmental historians might be taken with all of the players seated on a single park bench.[26] It is probably worth noting here that Kirby was *not* contending that southern historians were ignoring the region's environmental degradation altogether. He was well aware, for instance, that several historians of the Sunbelt South had pointed out that the region's lax environmental legislation played a role in attracting industry, and that scarred and polluted landscapes represented a significant price of southern economic progress. But environmental exploitation in such accounts seldom figured prominently (in either their narratives or analyses), and tended to remain something of an abstraction, as it was seldom detailed to a significant degree.[27] Kirby was thus thinking of the relative dearth of self-conscious environmental historians, those committed to examining the nexus of the natural world and southern culture.

Even measured in those more specific terms, however, by the time Kirby began writing *Mockingbird Song,* the field of southern environmental history was beginning to bloom. To be sure, if Daniel, Stewart, and Kirby led the way in framing a field centered on questions of the natural world's connections to race and class, they had not been alone in writing about the South's environment. A slew of articles and books published by historians, geographers, and anthropologists appeared in 1980s and 1990s that in retrospect clearly reflected a growing interest in the intersection of nature and culture in the New South. At the time, that interest was obscured to some degree by their topically and theoretically diffuse approaches. Even so, scholars like Ray Arsenault, Carville Earle, Thomas D. Clark, Stanley Trimble,

Tamara Miner Haygood, Harvey Jackson, and Jeffrey Stine explored a broad range of subjects across the diverse region—from farming, to huge state-funded earthmoving projects, to air conditioning.[28]

What's more, social and political historians of the region occasionally took the environment seriously. Steven Hahn's "Hunting, Fishing, and Foraging: Common Rights and Class Relations in the Postbellum South" (1982) stands out as an exemplar of such studies, hearkening back in some ways to the New Deal-era sociologists in connecting social and environmental exploitation. In essence, Hahn argued that elite whites reinforced the dependence of poor whites and African Americans by altering the laws that governed access to land use. By closing the commons and cutting off a traditional means of supplementing family incomes in the decades following the Civil War, planters managed to secure a cheap, malleable agricultural labor force, even as they laid an important foundation for the agrarian discontent that would culminate in the Populist movement.[29]

These previously discrete strands began to merge in the late 1990s and early 2000s, as the field witnessed a veritable explosion of studies that spoke in one fashion or another to the environmental history of the New South. While this burgeoning scholarship proved scattershot in many regards, it increasingly sought to engage both southern and environmental historians. Given environmental history's long connection with scenic landscapes and national parks, it is not entirely surprising that the mountain South proved to be among the first areas to witness a flowering. Ronald Lewis led the way with *Transforming the Appalachian Countryside: Railroads, Deforestation, and Social Change in West Virginia, 1880-1920* (1998). While Lewis's monograph pulled no punches in tracing the ugly environmental and social consequences attending the collapse of a forest-based, livestock agriculture under the pressure of industrial timbering, it was only incidentally an environmental history. His chief intervention rested in his appraisal of the economic orientation of backcountry Appalachians, and the book was aimed more clearly at scholars of the Appalachian experience than at environmental or even southern historians.[30]

Donald Davis and Margaret Brown, by contrast, both published books on the heels of *Transforming the Appalachian Countryside* that proved more explicitly environmental in their orientation. In examining "the southern core of Appalachia," Davis's *Where There Are Mountains* (2000) sought to frame the arc of the region's environmental history as something more than a simplistic declension narrative.[31] He posited instead a syncretic model that saw nature and culture shaping and reshaping each other as successive cultures manipulated the environment to different degrees and for different purposes, with the environment responding by opening and foreclosing economic options as a consequence. In the end, *Where There Are Mountains* proved somewhat declensionist anyway, not least because the advent of industrial capitalism in Appalachia proved as profoundly undemocratic as it did environmentally catastrophic.[32] Still, Davis's fine study added an important voice to the growing effort to self-consciously integrate the fields of southern and environmental history.

Margaret Brown's *The Wild East: A Biography of the Great Smoky Mountains* (2001) offered a similarly self-conscious intervention. The title of the book not only played on one of the perceived reasons for environmental historians' early neglect of the South, but also captured a core argument insofar as Brown highlighted the manifold issues that attended the National Park Service's efforts to transpose its policies from national parks in the West to a much more densely inhabited place, one with a longstanding tradition of use. Blending the themes emphasized by Stewart, Daniel, and Kirby with a conventional subject of environmental history, Brown argued, in short, that the southern experience proved different. The Great Smoky forests had long been a commons, and efforts to cut off traditional access to that commons undercut the sustenance of vulnerable populations (including African Americans) and the wellbeing (the viability, even) of local communities.[33]

Chad Montrie similarly sought to engage both southern and environmental historians in *To Save the Land and People* (2003). At its heart, Montrie's story is one of failure—a familiar motif in both southern and environmental history—as the coal industry generally managed to thwart efforts to regulate its activities in the Appalachians effectively. But in highlighting the grassroots opposition to strip mining, the degree to which local farmers not only sabotaged the coal companies but invoked the protection of natural resources as a federal trust in the legal fight to regulate the industry, Montrie called attention to a conservation impulse often overlooked by southern historians. At the same time, he complicated a conventional narrative in environmental history that privileged the role of middle-class professionals in framing environmental policy.[34]

Perhaps the most important of the Appalachian studies came the same year, with Timothy Silver's *Mount Mitchell and the Black Mountains* (2003), an uncommonly compelling study of the highest peaks east of the Mississippi River. Already a leader in the field—his first book, *A New Face on the Countryside* (1990), charted landscape change in the colonial Southeast and represented the first *monograph* deliberately situated at the nexus of southern and environmental history—Silver aimed his second book at both scholars and a popular audience, interspersing journal entries that follow his own experiences in the North Carolina range through the course of a year. Destabilizing the notion of a static, Edenic landscape by beginning with the region's geological past, Silver adroitly traced the intersections of nature and culture in the Black Mountains through the twentieth century. Perhaps unavoidably, *Mount Mitchell and the Black Mountains* amounts to something of a declension narrative, but in Silver's layered and elegantly crafted telling the nuances often proved surprising. Moreover, Silver's prize-winning book emphasized the role of the natural world in shaping human history in the region to a greater degree than any other study of the southern Appalachians.[35]

Silver's relatively local focus made it something of an anomaly among Appalachian studies, but it typified the general historiographical trend of southern environmental histories, which often examined a particular place from the deep past to the near present. Mikko Saikku, for instance, a talented Finnish environmental historian, adopted a "bioregional approach" in *This Delta, This Land: An Environmental History of the Yazoo-Mississippi Floodplain* (2005).

An older-style environmental history, Saikku's book emphasized the hydrological and ecological processes that established both limits and possibilities for agriculture and forestry in the Delta, and traced human-induced landscape change from the time of the paleo-Indians through the more or less permanent destruction of its mosaic forest that attended the rise and fall of the cotton kingdom. Few places, of course, have attracted as much attention from southern historians as the Delta; while Saikku's study might have engaged those scholars more completely, he argues convincingly that natural processes mattered a great deal in shaping the experience of one of the most iconic southern places.[36]

Megan Kate Nelson's study of Georgia's Okefenokee Swamp, *Trembling Earth* (2006), took a similar track—albeit one with a greater emphasis on the social consequences of environmental transformation—embracing an "ecolocal" view in which the analysis hinged on the competing visions of how the famous swamp might best be turned to human ends.[37] Even those books with a shorter chronological scope, such as Tycho de Boer's provocative *Nature, Business, and Community in North Carolina's Green Swamp* (2008), tended to examine particular locales.[38] For that matter, several excellent Appalachian studies followed Silver's lead in taking a more local view. Sara Gregg's *Managing the Mountains* (2010), for example, offered a comparative study of federal land-use planning in Virginia and Vermont, while Kathryn Newfont's *Blue Ridge Commons* (2012) looked at grassroots environmental activism in western North Carolina.[39]

Of course, historians produced broader studies as well. Robert Outland's prize-winning *Tapping the Pines: The Naval Stores Industry in the American South* (2004) examined the once-vital industry that took advantage of the roughly ninety million acres of longleaf forest, stretching from southern Virginia to Texas.[40] In *Hunting and Fishing in the New South: Black Labor and White Leisure after the Civil War* (2008), Scott Giltner offered a fascinating account of the ways in which African American men sought to leverage their environmental knowledge into economic opportunity, while elite white hunters sought out black guides to recapitulate Old South mythologies and reinforce their standing in society.[41] And Joshua Blu Buhs's *The*

Fire Ant Wars: Nature, Science, and Public Policy in Twentieth-Century America (2004) focused on scientific and policy debates that followed the spread of the invasive *Solenopsis invicta* across the South, and transformed the fire ant into one of the insects most readily associated with the region.[42]

Insofar as he blended the history of science with environmental history, Buhs highlighted another avenue through which environmental history has been obliquely encountered in the historiography of the New South. Trained as a historian of science at Johns Hopkins, for instance, Christine Keiner produced what is to-date the most important environmental history of the Chesapeake Bay, with the publication of her prize-winning *The Oyster Question: Scientists, Watermen, and the Maryland Chesapeake Bay since 1880* (2009).[43] Still others have followed a similar line from the history of medicine. Diseases like pellagra, hookworm, malaria, and yellow fever, of course, have long commanded the attention of southern historians, but perhaps none of the recent works published in this vein has attracted more attention than Jim Downs's *Sick from Freedom* (2012).[44] In highlighting the widespread, unwelcome, and often overlooked medical consequences of emancipation, Downs made a powerful and explicit historiographical intervention that has already reshaped to some degree the conventional understanding of this pivotal moment in southern history.

Another burgeoning line of enquiry in the New South's environmental historiography approached African American health from a rather different perspective, that of environmental justice. Some of the foundational work in the field was done by sociologists like Robert Bullard, whose *Dumping in Dixie: Race, Class, and Environmental Quality* (1990) has become something of a classic.[45] Probably the most important study in terms of building on and historicizing the framework laid out by Bullard and others is Eileen McGurty's *Transforming Environmentalism: Warren County, PCBs, and the Origins of Environmental Justice* (2007), which argues that opposition to the relocation of soil contaminated with PCBs to Warren County, North Carolina, touched off a series of events that fundamentally altered the framework of regional environmentalist thought.[46]

Much of southern environmental history's meandering path from the 1980s into the twenty-first century, including its failure to coalesce even as its bibliography grew, was due to simple institutional reasons. No graduate programs taught it. The leading authors, including Tim Silver, Mart Stewart, Jack Temple Kirby, Pete Daniel, Albert Cowdrey, and Mikko Saikku, worked at institutions without Ph.D. programs.[47] Meanwhile the best environmental history programs (California-Berkeley, Kansas, and Wisconsin) were located far from the South, making it less likely that students there would choose a southern topic. Where was one to go to learn it?

This institutional dilemma changed in 2002 when Paul Sutter, an assistant professor who had trained with Donald Worster at the University of Kansas, arrived in the history department at the University of Georgia. In less than ten years, Sutter had built the leading program for southern environmental history, despite the fact that he did not publish a monograph about the South while working there. His success might be measured in any number of ways, however, including the awards garnered by his students. Between 2010 and 2014, his advisees won the top dissertation prizes from the Southern Historical Association, the Agricultural History Society, the American Society for Environmental History, and the Society for American Historians.[48] In addition to training students, Sutter was the founding editor of the University of Georgia Press's "Environmental History and the American South" book series, which quickly became the leading imprint for books in the field.[49]

Though Sutter's influence proved real, by the time he left Athens for the University of Colorado in 2010, southern environmental history had gained sufficient momentum to overcome his departure. Mississippi State University, for instance, had already begun building a research cluster in the field, hiring two southern environmental historians (the authors of this chapter), founding the Center for the History of Agriculture, Science, and the Environment of the South (CHASES), and initiating the now annual Southern Forum on Agricultural, Rural, and Environmental History. Thus, when Sutter stepped down as the editor of the University of Georgia Press series, Mississippi State's James C. Giesen—whose *Boll Weevil Blues: Cotton,*

Myth, and Power in the American South (2011) was a self-consciously southern environmental history that reframed the historic significance of that notorious cotton pest—stepped in to replace him.[50]

To be sure, the emergence of institutions committed to training southern environmental historians reflected the field's drift toward the main currents of southern history. Perhaps even more telling, however, has been a reconceptualization of the field by its second-generation practitioners. If the first generation of writers attempted to define the field of southern environmental history against environmental history broadly, Sutter and the group of historians he trained and mentored put their trust in the development of a southern environmental history apart from its kin in other parts of the world. While Stewart had rightly argued in his classic essay "If John Muir Had Been an Agrarian" that southern environmental history suffered in comparison to the West because the regional subjects that mattered were different, by the end of the first decade of the twenty-first century, the comparison with the West seemed less important with each new book released. The field has developed on its own, blending its long-standing tradition with insights and methodologies pulled from environmental histories elsewhere.

A number of works published in recent years illumine this trend. Albert G. Way's *Conserving Southern Longleaf: Herbert Stoddard and the Rise of Ecological Land Management* (2011), for instance, enriched a subject familiar to environmental historians (conservation biology) by embedding it in a southern context, emphasizing among other things the importance of long-standing folk practices and the ironic contributions of racialized landscapes to the emergence of an ecologically sensitive science of land management.[51] In *Remaking Wormsloe Plantation,* Drew Swanson accomplished a similar feat, by taking the subject of historical memory (a familiar one to southern historians) and placing it in an environmental context. Tracing the landscape history of one of Georgia's most iconic places from the colonial era through the end of the twentieth century, Swanson explained how the proprietors of Wormsloe had manipulated its landscape to accentuate certain aspects of its past and obscure others.[52]

The "Georgia school" (both Way and Swanson were trained by Sutter) was hardly the only group producing southern environmental histories.[53] Trained as an environmental historian at the University of Kansas, for instance, Mark Hersey turned to the South for his dissertation, one he revised and published as *My Work Is That of Conservation: An Environmental Biography of George Washington Carver* (2011).[54] Hersey used Carver's claim that he should be remembered as a conservationist as a point of entry, and highlighted the degree to which Progressive-era conservation looked different in the South. Hersey showed how Carver's conservation was agricultural in focus and hardly lily-white—two differences with historians' consensus on the conservation movement—and pointed out that African American farmers in the post–Civil War South experienced their second-class citizenship as an environmental predicament, one that circumscribed their choices to be sure, but one that could be (and was in fact) creatively engaged.

Christopher Morris and Jack Davis, by contrast, were prize-winning southern historians in their own right before self-consciously lending their work an environmental focus. Though Morris's *The Big Muddy* (2012) offered a sweeping examination of the transformation of the lower Mississippi River valley from the pre-Columbian era to the present, the heart of the book centered on the transformations that followed the Civil War. The realization of long-standing dreams to separate water and earth, Morris argued, facilitated the triumph of the cotton kingdom in the region, but at an environmental cost that would periodically (indeed, inevitably) become evident, as it did with the flooding of New Orleans after Hurricane Katrina.[55]

Davis, a professor of history at the University of Florida, had already edited a collection of essays on Florida's environmental history when he published *An Everglades Providence: Marjory Stoneman Douglas and the American Environmental Century* (2012). A thoroughly impressive biography, Davis's book did more than trace the long life of Douglas, who died in 1998 at the age of 108 and who more than anyone else came to be associated with the preservation of the Everglades. It integrated Douglas's life into the history of the Everglades, and in so doing offered a persuasive argument that the South provided as clear a lens as any region into the emergence and maturation of American environmentalism in the twentieth century.[56]

Scholars' attention has most recently turned to the Piedmont, a subregion of the South that has undergone perhaps the most striking environmental changes since the Civil War. Two books on tobacco, by Barbara Hahn and Drew Swanson, reveal that crop's lasting legacy on the Piedmont, through Swanson pays more attention to the environmental components of the weed's rise and fall. Paul Sutter's *Let Us Now Praise Famous Gullies: Providence Canyon and the Soils of the South* (2015) artfully explores the meaning of Providence Canyon, a state park in southwest Georgia that locals marketed as "the Little Grand Canyon." Rather than a relic of a former geologic epoch, however, the canyon is the product of twentieth-century soil erosion. Sutter uses the gully to uncover the long history of soil science in the United States and more importantly to suggest the ways that this seemingly ironic site is actually the logical outgrowth of an unknowable tension between human decision and natural capacity.[57]

This recent flurry of scholarship appears to be merely the tip of the spear. Every indication suggests that the field's continued drift toward the main currents of southern history shows no sign of slowing. In fact, it has been bolstered by environmental history's shift toward the kinds of studies connecting social and cultural history through hybrid landscapes to which the South is particularly suited. Indeed, these works put environmental history closer—if not yet in the middle—of mainstream southern history.

To be sure, much work remains to be done. The urban South, for instance, has received comparatively scant treatment; substantial swaths of the South remain underdeveloped as topics; and the importance of the natural world is only beginning to be reflected in textbook treatments of the New South. Even so, southern historians now accept that the New South's history cannot be understood apart from its environmental context. Much of what shaped the economy and culture of the South was tied to environmental transformation, from the deforestation and tenant landscapes that marked the late nineteenth and early twentieth centuries to toxic waste sites, loblolly pine plantations, tourist-trap beaches, golf courses, and well-maintained yards of the modern suburban South. With a distinctive southern environmental history now on firm footing, studies examining the place of the natural world in the New South seem sure to proliferate in the coming years.

NOTES

1. See, for instance, Otis L. Graham, "Again the Backward Region? Environmental History in and of the American South," *Southern Cultures* 6 (2000): 50-72; Christopher Morris, "A More Southern Environmental History," *Journal of Southern History* 75 (2009): 581-98; Shane Hamilton, "Poisons in the Land," *Reviews in American History* 34 (2006): 65. For other historiographical treatments of southern environmental history, see Mart A. Stewart, "Southern Environmental History," in *A Companion to the American South,* ed. John B. Boles (John Wiley and Sons, 2008), 409-23; Stewart, "If John Muir Had Been an Agrarian: American Environmental History West and South," *Environment and History* 11, no. 2 (May 2005): 139-62; Paul Sutter, "Introduction: 'No More the Backward Region: Southern Environmental History Comes of Age,'" in *Environmental History and the American South: A Reader,* ed. Paul S. Sutter and Christopher J. Manganiello (Athens: Univ. of Georgia Press, 2009); Mark D. Hersey, review of Sutter and Manganiello, *Environmental History and the American South, Organization and Environment* 23, no. 2 (2010): 240-42; Ellen Griffith Spears, "Landscapes and Ecologies of the U.S. South: Essays in Eco-Cultural History," Feb. 18, 2013, Southern Spaces, https://southernspaces.org/2013/landscapes-and-ecologies-us-south-essays-eco-cultural-history (accessed April 10, 2017).

2. The two authors of this piece offer a case in point. Hersey trained with Donald Worster at the University of Kansas in its environmental history program. Giesen trained with James C. Cobb in the southern history program at the University of Georgia.

3. The biennial Jack Temple Kirby Award was established following Kirby's death in 2009, and first awarded in 2011. In 2012, the SHA awarded its biennial Fletcher M. Green and Charles W. Ramsdell Award, for the best article published in that journal, to Paul S. Sutter, "What Gullies Mean: Georgia's 'Little Grand Canyon' and Southern Environmental History," *Journal of Southern History* 76 (Aug. 2010): 579-616. In 2013, the SHA awarded its biennial Frances Simkins Award, for the best first book on southern history, to James C. Giesen, *Boll Weevil Blues: Cotton, Myth, and Power in the American South* (Chicago: Univ. of Chicago Press, 2011).

4. Avery Craven, *Soil Exhaustion as a Factor in the Agricultural History of Virginia and Maryland, 1606-1860* (Urbana: Univ. of Illinois Press, 1925);

Lewis Cecil Gray, *History of Agriculture in the Southern United States to 1860*, 2 vols. (Washington, D.C.: Carnegie Institution of Washington, 1933); Ulrich Bonnell Phillips, *Life and Labor in the Old South* (New York: Little, Brown, and Co., 1929).

5. Rupert Bayless Vance, *Human Factors in Cotton Culture: A Study in the Social Geography of the American South* (Chapel Hill: Univ. of North Carolina Press, 1929); Vance, *Human Geography of the South: A Study in Regional Resources and Human Adequacy* (Chapel Hill: Univ. of North Carolina Press, 1932); Howard Washington Odum, *Race and Rumors of Race: Challenge to American Crisis* (Chapel Hill: Univ. of North Carolina Press, 1943); Odum, *The Way of the South: Toward the Regional Balance of America* (New York: Macmillan Co., 1947); Arthur Raper, *Preface to Peasantry: A Tale of Two Black Belt Counties* (Chapel Hill: Univ. of North Carolina Press, 1936); Charles Spurgeon Johnson, *Shadow of the Plantation* (Chicago: Univ. of Chicago Press, 1934).

6. Francis Butler Simkins, *A History of the South* (1947; repr., New York: Alfred Knopf, 1961), 342.

7. C. Vann Woodward, *Origins of the New South, 1877-1913* (1951; repr., Baton Rouge: Louisiana State Univ. Press, 1997), 118, 310.

8. George Brown Tindall, *The Emergence of the New South, 1913-1945* (Baton Rouge: Louisiana State Univ. Press, 1967). Jonathan M. Wiener similarly argued that there was a greater continuity among the planter class between the Old South and New South than Woodward suggested; however, in tracing the ways the planters sought to undercut industrial development, he also acknowledged significant environmental damage done by industrialists and plantations. Jonathan M. Wiener, *Social Origins of the New South: Alabama, 1860-1885* (Baton Rouge: Louisiana State Univ. Press, 1978).

9. Stewart, "If John Muir Had Been an Agrarian." The fact that environmental historians effectively ignored the region suggests an implicit agreement with southern historians' conclusion that the South's environmental scars mattered less than its social ones.

10. Albert E. Cowdrey, *This Land, This South: An Environmental History* (1983; repr., Lexington: Univ. Press of Kentucky, 1996).

11. Barbara J. Fields, "Commentary on Jack Temple Kirby's Paper 'Bioregionalism: Landscape and Culture in the South Atlantic,'" in *The New Regionalism: Essays and Commentaries,* ed. Robert L. Dorman and Charles Reagan Wilson (Jackson: Univ. Press of Mississippi, 1998), 38, as cited in Spears, "Landscapes and Ecologies of the U.S. South."

12. Pete Daniel, "Accidental Historian," in *Shapers of Southern History: Autobiographical Reflections,* ed. John B. Boles (Athens: Univ. of Georgia Press, 2004), 164-86.

13. Pete Daniel, *The Shadow of Slavery: Peonage in the South, 1901-1969* (Urbana: Univ. of Illinois Press, 1972); Daniel, *Deep'n as It Come: The 1927 Mississippi River Flood* (New York: Oxford Univ. Press, 1977); Daniel, *Breaking the*

Land: The Transformation of Cotton, Tobacco, and Rice Cultures since 1880 (Urbana: Univ. of Illinois Press, 1986); Daniel, *Standing at the Crossroads: Southern Life in the Twentieth Century* (New York: Hill and Wang, 1986); Daniel, *Lost Revolutions: The South in the 1950s* (Chapel Hill: Univ. of North Carolina Press, for the Smithsonian National Museum of American History, Washington, D.C., 2000); Daniel, *Toxic Drift: Pesticides and Health in the post-World War II South* (Baton Rouge: Louisiana State Univ. Press, in association with the Smithsonian Institution, Washington, D.C., 2005); Daniel, *Dispossession: Discrimination against African American Farmers in the Age of Civil Rights* (Chapel Hill: Univ. of North Carolina Press, 2013).

14. Daniel, *Breaking the Land.*

15. Daniel, *Shadow of Slavery.*

16. Daniel, *Toxic Drift.*

17. Daniel, *Dispossession.*

18. Wayne Flynt, review of Daniel, *Breaking the Land, Journal of Southern History* 52 (Aug. 1986): 475.

19. Mart A. Stewart, *What Nature Suffers to Groe: Life, Labor, and Landscape on the Georgia Coast, 1680-1920* (Athens: Univ. of Georgia Press, 1996); Jack Temple Kirby, *Darkness at the Dawning: Race and Reform in the Progressive South* (Philadelphia: Lippincott, 1972); Kirby, *Media-Made Dixie: The South in the American Imagination* (Baton Rouge: Louisiana State Univ. Press, 1978); Kirby, *Rural Worlds Lost: The American South, 1920-1960* (Baton Rouge: Louisiana State Univ. Press, 1987); Kirby, *Poquosin: A Study of Rural Landscape and Society* (Chapel Hill: Univ. of North Carolina Press, 1995); Kirby, *Mockingbird Song: Ecological Landscapes of the South* (Chapel Hill: Univ. of North Carolina Press, 2006). The following two works offer other examples of rural histories that foreground the experience of southerners grappling with the natural world, though neither is an environmental history: Charles S. Aiken, *The Cotton Plantation South since the Civil War* (Baltimore: Johns Hopkins Univ. Press, 1998); Gilbert Courtland Fite, *Cotton Fields No More: Southern Agriculture, 1865-1980* (Lexington: Univ. Press of Kentucky, 1984).

20. Stewart, *What Nature Suffers to Groe.*

21. Kirby, *Poquosin.*

22. Albert E. Cowdrey, review of Kirby, *Poquosin, Journal of Southern History* 63 (Feb. 1997): 147.

23. Mart Stewart, review of Kirby, *Mockingbird Song, Journal of American History* 94 (Mar. 2008): 1280.

24. Donald Worster, *Dust Bowl: The Southern Plains in the 1930s* (New York: Oxford Univ. Press, 1979); William Cronon, *Nature's Metropolis: Chicago and the Great West* (New York: W. W. Norton and Co., 1991). Mart A. Stewart emerged in the 1990s and early 2000s as the most potent and influential thinker on the field itself. He published a number of historiographical essays, the most frequently cited of which is "If John Muir Had Been an Agrarian."

25. Graham, "Again the Backward Region?," 59.

26. Kirby had in mind himself, Tim Silver, Mart Stewart, and Albert Cowdrey. Timothy Silver, email message to Mark Hersey, March 2, 2014.

27. Typical studies of this sort would include David Goldfield, *Promised Land: The South since 1945* (Wheeling, Ill.: Harlan Davidson, 1987); James C. Cobb, *The Selling of the South: The Southern Crusade for Industrial Development* (Baton Rouge: Louisiana State Univ. Press, 1982). Not all studies of the Sunbelt South, however, so much as acknowledged the environmental consequences of economic development. Bruce Schulman, for instance, essentially ignored the environment in his now-classic *From Cotton Belt to Sunbelt*. Indeed, the word "environment" generally appears modified by words like "labor," "political," and "anti-union." See Bruce J. Schulman, *From Cotton Belt to Sunbelt: Federal Policy, Economic Development, and the Transformation of the South, 1938-1980* (Durham, N.C.: Duke Univ. Press, 1994), 118, 163, 264. The degree to which the region's economic development has been abstracted from its environmental consequences in the main currents of southern history can be seen in the fact that the word "pollution" doesn't so much as appear in the index to the volume dedicated to agriculture and industry for the *New Encyclopedia of Southern Culture*. See James C. Cobb and Melissa Walker, eds., *The New Encyclopedia of Southern Culture: Agriculture and Industry* (Chapel Hill: Univ. of North Carolina Press, 2008), 349.

28. Raymond Arsenault, "The End of the Long Hot Summer: The Air Conditioner and Southern Culture," *Journal of Southern History* 50 (Nov. 1984): 597-628; Carville Earle, "The Myth of the Southern Soil Miner: Macrohistory, Agricultural Innovation, and Environmental Change," in *The Ends of the Earth: Perspectives on Modern Environmental History*, ed. Donald Worster (New York: Cambridge Univ. Press, 1988): 175-210; Thomas Dionysius Clark, *The Greening of the South: The Recovery of Land and Forest* (1984; repr., Lexington: Univ. Press of Kentucky, 2004); Stanley W. Trimble, *Man-Induced Soil Erosion on the Southern Piedmont, 1700-1970*, enhanced ed. (1974; repr., Ankeny, Iowa: Soil and Water Conservation Agency, 2008); Tamara Miner Haygood, "Cows, Ticks, and Disease: A Medical Interpretation of the Southern Cattle Industry," *Journal of Southern History* 52 (Nov. 1986): 551-64; Harvey H. Jackson, *Rivers of History: Life on the Coosa, Tallapoosa, Cahaba, and Alabama* (Tuscaloosa: Univ. of Alabama Press, 1995); Jeffrey K. Stine, *Mixing the Waters: Environment, Politics, and the Building of the Tennessee-Tombigbee Waterway* (Akron, Ohio: Univ. of Akron Press, 1993).

29. Steven Hahn, "Hunting, Fishing, and Foraging: Common Rights and Class Relations in the Postbellum South," *Radical History Review* 26 (Oct. 1982): 37-64. See also Forrest McDonald and Grady McWhiney, "The South from Self-sufficiency to Peonage: An Interpretation," *American Historical Review* (Dec. 1980): 1095-1118.

30. Ronald L. Lewis, *Transforming the Appalachian Countryside: Railroads,*

Deforestation, and Social Change in West Virginia, 1880-1920 (Chapel Hill: Univ. of North Carolina Press, 1998).

31. Donald Edward Davis, *Where There Are Mountains: An Environmental History of the Southern Appalachians* (Athens: Univ. of Georgia Press, 2000), 7. Davis framed his narrative in part to engage a debate over the relative merits of wilderness that had attracted a good deal of attention among environmental historians during the 1990s.

32. Davis would go on to serve as the lead author for a collection published by ABC-CLIO that traced the South's environmental history from the Pleistocene into the early twenty-first century. See Donald Davis, Craig Colten, Megan Kate Nelson, Barbara Allen, and Mikko Saikku, *Southern United States: An Environmental History* (Santa Barbara, Calif.: ABC-CLIO, 2006).

33. Margaret Lynn Brown, *The Wild East: A Biography of the Great Smoky Mountains* (Gainesville: Univ. Press of Florida, 2001).

34. Chad Montrie, *To Save the Land and People: A History of Opposition to Surface Coal Mining in Appalachia* (Chapel Hill: Univ. of North Carolina Press, 2003).

35. Timothy Silver, *A New Face on the Countryside: Indians, Colonists, and Slaves in South Atlantic Forests, 1500-1800* (New York: Cambridge Univ. Press, 1990); Silver, *Mount Mitchell and the Black Mountains: An Environmental History of the Highest Peaks in Eastern America* (Chapel Hill: Univ. of North Carolina Press, 2003).

36. Mikko Saikku, *This Delta, This Land: An Environmental History of the Yazoo-Mississippi Floodplain* (Athens: Univ. of Georgia Press, 2005).

37. Although it includes antebellum material, the heart of Nelson's analysis rests in the competing visions of the New South. Predictably, by the middle of the twentieth century, industrial lumber interests had triumphed over the small-scale use of local "swampers," but Nelson presented a considerably more complicated story, highlighting the ironies and ambivalences that attended that triumph. Swampers, for instance, often found employment with lumber companies, and found their way of life permanently undercut as much by environmentalists pushing for the preservation of the Okefenokee as by the timber interests bent on exploiting it. Megan Kate Nelson, *Trembling Earth: A Cultural History of the Okefenokee Swamp* (Athens: Univ. of Georgia Press, 2005).

38. Tycho de Boer, *Nature, Business, and Community in North Carolina's Green Swamp* (Gainesville: Univ. Press of Florida, 2008).

39. Sara M. Gregg, *Managing the Mountains: Land Use Planning, the New Deal, and the Creation of a Federal Landscape in Appalachia* (New Haven, Conn.: Yale Univ. Press, 2010); Kathryn Newfont, *Blue Ridge Commons: Environmental Activism and Forest History in Western North Carolina* (Athens: Univ. of Georgia Press, 2012). See also Sara M. Gregg, "Uncovering the Subsistence Economy in the Twentieth-Century South: Blue Ridge Mountain Farms,"

Agricultural History 78 (Autumn 2004): 417-37; Ralph H. Lutts, "Like Manna from God: The American Chestnut Trade in Southwestern Virginia," *Environmental History* 9 (July 2004): 497-525; Sarah Middlefehldt, *Tangled Roots: The Appalachian Trail and American Environmental Politics* (Seattle: Univ. of Washington Press, 2013); Daniel S. Pierce, *The Great Smokies: From Natural Habitat to Natural Park* (Knoxville: Univ. of Tennessee Press, 2000); Randal Hall, *Mountains on the Market: Industry, the Environment, and the South* (Lexington: Univ. Press of Kentucky). Overlapping (but not entirely confined to) this Appalachian history is a history of tourism in the South. See, for example, Anne Mitchell Whisnant, *Super-Scenic Motorway: A Blue Ridge Parkway History* (Chapel Hill: Univ. of North Carolina Press, 2006); Richard Starnes, *Southern Journeys: Tourism, History, and Culture in the Modern South* (Tuscaloosa: Univ. of Alabama Press, 2003).

40. Robert B. Outland, *Tapping the Pines: The Naval Stores Industry in the American South* (Baton Rouge: Louisiana State Univ. Press, 2004). Outland's book was joined the same year by Lawrence Earley's *Looking for Longleaf: The Fall and Rise of An America Forest* (Chapel Hill: Univ. of North Carolina Press, 2004). An impressive introduction to longleaf forests generally—and so, after a fashion, an important work in southern environmental history—Earley's book, by his own admission, was the work of a passionate longleaf advocate rather than a history proper. He was "neither a historian, forester, or ecologist" (ix).

41. Scott E. Giltner, *Hunting and Fishing in the New South: Black Labor and White Leisure after the Civil War* (Baltimore: Johns Hopkins Univ. Press, 2008). It's probably worth noting that the ostensible scope of both Outland's and Giltner's books was extrapolated from comparatively local evidence.

42. Joshua Blu Buhs, *The Fire Ant Wars: Nature, Science, and Public Policy in Twentieth-Century America* (Chicago: Univ. of Chicago Press, 2004).

43. Christine Keiner, *The Oyster Question: Scientists, Watermen, and the Maryland Chesapeake Bay since 1880* (Athens: Univ. of Georgia Press, 2009).

44. Jim Downs, *Sick from Freedom: African-American Illness and Suffering during the Civil War and Reconstruction* (New York: Oxford Univ. Press, 2012). A brief list of the classics in southern history of disease includes John Hubert Ellis, *Yellow Fever and Public Health in the New South* (Lexington: Univ. Press of Kentucky, 1992); Margaret Humphreys, *Yellow Fever and the South* (Baltimore: Johns Hopkins Univ. Press, 1999); Todd L. Savitt and James Harvey Young, *Disease and Distinctiveness in the American South* (Knoxville: Univ. of Tennessee Press, 1991); Edward J. Blum, "The Crucible of Disease: Trauma, Memory, and National Reconciliation during the Yellow Fever Epidemic of 1878," *Journal of Southern History* 69 (Nov. 2003): 791-820; Frederick R. Davis, *The Man Who Saved Sea Turtles: Archie Carr and the Origins of Conservation Biology* (New York: Oxford Univ. Press, 2007). Some recent additions to the field, like those of Conevery Bolton Valencius, were not produced by scholars who would self-identify as southern historians. Valencius's prize-

winning first book, *The Health of the Country* (2002), and her recent New Madrid book are both antebellum in focus. See Valencius, *The Health of the Country: How American Settlers Understood Themselves and Their Land* (New York: Basic Books, 2003); Valencius, *The Lost History of the New Madrid Earthquakes* (Chicago: Univ. of Chicago Press, 2013).

45. Robert D. Bullard, *Dumping in Dixie: Race, Class, and Environmental Quality* (Boulder, Colo.: Westview Press, 1990).

46. Eileen Maura McGurty, *Transforming Environmentalism: Warren County, PCBs, and the Origins of Environmental Justice* (New Brunswick, N.J.: Rutgers Univ. Press, 2007). See also McGurty, "From NIMBY to Civil Rights: The Origins of the Environmental Justice Movement," *Environmental History* 2 (July 1997): 301-23; Ellen Spears, *Baptized in PCBs: Race, Pollution, and Justice in an All-American Town* (Chapel Hill: Univ. of North Carolina Press, 2014).

47. Jack Temple Kirby retired from Miami University in 2002 and died three years after the publication of *Mockingbird Song* in 2006. Miami had shuttered its Ph.D. program in the early 1990s.

48. In 2010, the American Society for Environmental History awarded the Rachel Carson Prize, for the best dissertation in environmental history, to Christopher Manganiello, "Dam Crazy with Wild Consequences: Artificial Lakes and Natural Rivers in the American South, 1845-1990" (Ph.D. diss., Univ. of Georgia, 2010). In 2011, the Southern Historical Association awarded the C. Vann Woodward Dissertation Prize to Drew Swanson, "Land of the Bright Leaf: Yellow Tobacco, Environment, and Culture along the Border of Virginia and North Carolina," (Ph.D. diss., Univ. of Georgia, 2010). In 2013, the Society of American Historians awarded the Allan Nevins Dissertation Prize to W. Tom Okie, "'Everything is Peaches Down in Georgia': Culture and Agriculture in the American South" (Ph.D. diss., Univ. of Georgia, 2012); Okie's dissertation also won the Southern Historical Association's Woodward Prize and the Agricultural History Society's Gilbert Fite Dissertation Prize. It was revised and published as William Thomas Okie, *The Georgia Peach: Culture, Agriculture, and Environment in the American South* (New York: Cambridge Univ. Press, 2016).

49. One of the series' first books was *Environmental History and the American South: A Reader*. Editors Sutter and Manganiello pulled together articles previously published in a range of places in the decades prior, including many discussed above. It was intended to be a kind of grab-and-go introduction to the field, and as such it was successful. In the event, however, by the time it was released it almost seemed out-of-date since there was a wave of new work that appeared right around this time. Paul Sutter and Christopher J. Manganiello, *Environmental History and the American South: A Reader* (Athens: Univ. of Georgia Press, 2009).

50. Giesen, *Boll Weevil Blues*.

51. Albert G. Way, *Conserving Southern Longleaf: Herbert Stoddard and the Rise of Ecological Land Management* (Athens: Univ. of Georgia Press, 2011).

52. Drew A. Swanson, *Remaking Wormsloe Plantation: The Environmental History of a Lowcountry Landscape* (Athens: Univ. of Georgia Press, 2012).

53. Other notable books from the Georgia school would include Christopher Manganiello's excellent *Southern Water, Southern Power: How the Politics of Cheap Energy and Water Scarcity Shaped a Region* (Chapel Hill: Univ. of North Carolina Press, 2015), and Drew Swanson's prize-winning *A Golden Weed: Tobacco and Environment in the Piedmont South* (New Haven, Conn.: Yale Univ. Press, 2014).

54. Mark D. Hersey, *My Work Is That of Conservation: An Environmental Biography of George Washington Carver* (Athens: Univ. of Georgia Press, 2011).

55. Christopher Morris, *The Big Muddy: An Environmental History of the Mississippi and Its Peoples from Hernando de Soto to Hurricane Katrina* (New York: Oxford Univ. Press, 2012).

56. Jack E. Davis, *An Everglades Providence: Marjory Stoneman Douglas and the American Environmental Century* (Athens: Univ. of Georgia Press, 2009).

57. Barbara Hahn, *Making Tobacco Bright: Creating an American Economy* (Baltimore: Johns Hopkins Univ. Press, 2011); Drew Swanson, *Golden Weed;* Paul S. Sutter, *Let Us Now Praise Famous Gullies: Providence Canyon and the Soils of the South* (Athens: Univ. of Georgia Press, 2015). Other works that appeared in the twenty-first century as "new" southern environmental histories include Duncan Maysilles, *Ducktown Smoke: The Southern Appalachian Story of the Supreme Court's First Air Pollution Case* (Chapel Hill: Univ. of North Carolina Press, 2011); Torben Huus Larsen, *Enduring Pastoral: Recycling the Middle Landscape Ideal in the Tennessee Valley* (Amsterdam: Rodopi, 2010); Andrew W. Kahrl, *The Land Was Ours: African American Beaches from Jim Crow to the Sunbelt South* (Cambridge, Mass.: Harvard Univ. Press, 2012); Ari Kelman, *A River and Its City: The Nature of Landscape in New Orleans* (Berkeley: Univ. of California Press, 2003); Craig E. Colten, *An Unnatural Metropolis: Wresting New Orleans from Nature* (Baton Rouge: Louisiana State Univ. Press, 2006).

Bibliography

PRIMARY SOURCES

Francis Butler Simkins Papers. Special Collections, Greenwood Library, Longwood Univ. Farmville, Va.

"Long Civil Rights Movement Project." Southern Oral History Program, Center for the Study of the American South, University of North Carolina-Chapel Hill (accessed April 27, 2017).

The NAACP Records. Library of Congress, Washington, D.C. https://www.loc.gov/loc/lcib/1003/collection.html (accessed April 2, 2017).

United Faculty of Florida (UFF) Collection. Samuel Proctor Oral History Program. Univ. of Florida, Gainesville, Fla.

SECONDARY SOURCES

Abernathy, Ralph D. *And the Walls Came Tumbling Down.* New York: Harper and Row, 1989.

Acker, James R. *Scottsboro and Its Legacy: The Case That Challenged American Legal and Social Justice.* Westport, Conn.: Praeger, 2008.

Adams, Thomas Jessen. "Walmart and the Making of 'Postindustrial Society.'" *Labor: Studies in the Working-Class History of the Americas* 8, no. 1 (Spring 2011): 117-25.

Adeleke, Tunde. *UnAfrican Americans: Nineteenth-Century Black Nationalists and the Civilizing Mission.* Lexington: Univ. Press of Kentucky, 1998.

Agee, James, and Walker Evans. *Let Us Now Praise Famous Men.* Boston: Houghton Mifflin Company, 1941.

Aiken, Charles S. *The Cotton Plantation South since the Civil War.* Baltimore: Johns Hopkins Univ. Press, 1998.

Aistrup, Joseph. *The Southern Strategy Revisited: Republican Top-Down Advancement in the South.* Lexington: Univ. of Kentucky Press, 1996.

Akers, Monte. *Flames after Midnight: Murder, Vengeance, and the Desolation of a Texas Community.* Austin: Univ. of Texas Press, 1999.

Alexander, Michelle. *The New Jim Crow: Mass Incarceration in the Age of Colorblindness.* New York: New Press, 2010.

Ali, Omar H. *In the Lion's Mouth: Black Populism in the New South, 1886-1900*. Jackson: Univ. Press of Mississippi, 2010.

———. "Reconceptualizing Black Populism in the New South." In *Populism in the South Revisited: New Interpretations and New Departures*, ed. James M. Beeby, 128-44. Jackson: Univ. Press of Mississippi, 2012.

Allen, James, et al. *Without Sanctuary: Lynching Photography in America*. Santa Fe, N.M.: Twin Palms, 2000.

Anderson, Carol. *Eyes off the Prize: The United Nations and the African American Struggle for Human Rights, 1944-1955*. Cambridge: Cambridge Univ. Press, 2007.

Anderson, Devery S. *Emmett Till: The Murder That Shocked the World and Propelled the Civil Rights Movement*. Jackson: Univ. Press of Mississippi, 2015.

Anderson, Karen Tucker. "Last Hired, First Fired: Black Women Workers during World War II." *Journal of American History* 69 (June 1982): 82-97.

Apel, Dora. *Imagery of Lynching: Black Men, White Women, and the Mob*. New Brunswick, N.J.: Rutgers Univ. Press, 2004.

———. "On Looking: Lynching Photographs and Legacies of Lynching after 9/11." *American Quarterly* 55, no. 3 (Sept. 2003): 457-78.

———, and Shawn Michelle Smith. *Lynching Photographs*. Berkeley: Univ. of California Press, 2007.

Arellano, Lisa. *Vigilantes and Lynch Mobs: Narratives of Community and Nation*. Philadelphia: Temple Univ. Press, 2012.

Argersinger, Peter H. *The Limits of Agrarian Radicalism: Western Populism and American Politics*. Lawrence: Univ. Press of Kansas, 1995.

Armstrong, Julie Buckner. *Mary Turner and the Memory of Lynching*. Athens: Univ. of Georgia Press, 2011.

Arnesen, Eric. *Brotherhoods of Color: Black Railroad Workers and the Struggle for Equality*. Cambridge, Mass.: Harvard Univ. Press, 2001.

———. "'Like Banquo's Ghost, It Will Not Down': The Race Question and the American Railroad Brotherhoods, 1880-1920." *American Historical Review* 99, no. 5 (Dec. 1994): 1601-33.

———. "Reconsidering the 'Long Civil Rights Movement.'" *Historically Speaking* 10 (2009): 31-34.

———. *Waterfront Workers of New Orleans: Race, Class, and Politics, 1863-1923*. Illini Books. 1991. Reprint, Urbana: Univ. of Illinois Press, 1994.

———. "Whiteness and the Historians' Imagination." *International Labor and Working-Class History* no. 60 (2001): 3-32.

Arsenault, Raymond. "The End of the Long Hot Summer: The Air Conditioner and Southern Culture." *Journal of Southern History* 50, no. 4 (Nov. 1984): 597-628.

———. *Freedom Riders: 1961 and the Struggle for Racial Justice*. New York: Oxford Univ. Press, 2006.

Ashworth, John. *Slavery, Capitalism, and Politics in the Antebellum Republic*. 2 vols. 1995. Reprint, Cambridge: Cambridge Univ. Press, 2007.

———. "Towards a Bourgeois Revolution? Explaining the American Civil War." *Historical Materialism* 19 (2011): 193-205.

Avirett, James B. *The Memoirs of General Turner Ashby and His Compeers*. Baltimore: Shelby and Dulany, 1867.

Ayers, Edward L. *The Promise of the New South: Life after Reconstruction.* New York: Oxford Univ. Press, 1992.

Azaransky, Sarah. *The Dream Is Freedom: Pauli Murray and American Democratic Faith.* New York: Oxford Univ. Press, 2011.

Badger, Anthony J. *New Deal/New South: An Anthony J. Badger Reader.* Fayetteville: Univ. of Arkansas Press, 2007.

———, and Brian Ward, eds. *The Making of Martin Luther King and the Civil Rights Movement.* New York: New York Univ. Press, 1996.

Bailey, Amy Kate, and Stewart E. Tolnay. *Lynched: The Victims of Southern Mob Violence.* Chapel Hill: Univ. of North Carolina Press, 2015.

Baker, Bruce E. *This Mob Will Surely Take My Life: Lynchings in the Carolinas, 1871-1947.* New York: Continuum, 2008.

Barlow, William, and Janette L. Dates. *Split Image: African Americans in the Mass Media.* Washington, D.C.: Howard Univ. Press, 1993.

Barnes, Catherine Ann. *Journey from Jim Crow: the Desegregation of Southern Transit.* New York: Columbia Univ. Press, 1983.

Barthelme, Marion K. *Women in the Texas Populist Movement: Letters to the* Southern Mercury. College Station: Texas A&M Univ. Press, 1997.

Bartley, Numan V. *From Thurmond to Wallace: Political Tendencies in Georgia, 1948-1968.* Baltimore: Johns Hopkins Univ. Press, 1970.

———. *The New South, 1945-1980: The Story of the South's Modernization.* Baton Rouge: Louisiana State Univ. Press, 1995.

———. *The Rise of Massive Resistance: Race and Politics in the South during the 1950s.* Baton Rouge: Louisiana State Univ. Press, 1969.

Basler, Roy P., ed. *The Collected Works of Abraham Lincoln.* 8 vols. New Brunswick, N.J.: Rutgers Univ. Press, 1953.

Bass, Jack, and Marilyn W. Thompson. *Ol' Strom: An Unauthorized Biography of Strom Thurmond.* Columbia: Univ. of South Carolina Press, 2003.

Bass, Jack, and Walter De Vries. *The Transformation of Southern Politics: Social Change and Political Consequence since 1945.* Athens: Univ. of Georgia Press, 1995.

Bass, S. Jonathan. *Blessed Are the Peacemakers: Martin Luther King, Jr., Eight White Religious Leaders, and the "Letter from Birmingham Jail."* Baton Rouge: Louisiana State Univ. Press, 2001.

Bates, Daisy. *The Long Shadow of Little Rock: A Memoir.* 1962. Reprint, Baton Rouge: Louisiana State Univ. Press, 1990.

Bauerlein, Mark. *Negrophobia: A Race Riot in Atlanta, 1906.* San Francisco: Encounter Books, 2001.

Bay, Mia. *To Tell the Truth Freely: The Life of Ida B. Wells.* New York: Hill and Wang, 2009.

Beals, Melba Pattillo. *Warriors Don't Cry: A Searing Memoir of the Battle to Integrate Little Rock's Central High.* New York: Washington Square Books, 1994.

Beckert, Sven. "Emancipation and Empire: Reconstructing the Worldwide Web of Cotton Production in the Age of the American Civil War." *American Historical Review* 109 (2004): 1405-38.

———. *Empire of Cotton: A Global History.* New York: Alfred A. Knopf, 2014.

———. *The Monied Metropolis: New York City and the Consolidation of the American Bourgeoisie, 1850-1896.* Cambridge: Cambridge Univ. Press, 2001.

Beeby, James M. "'[T]he Angels from Heaven Had Come Down and Wiped Their Names off the Registration Books': The Demise of Grassroots Populism in North Carolina." In *Populism in the South Revisited: New Interpretations and New Departures,* ed. James M. Beeby, 177-98. Jackson: Univ. Press of Mississippi, 2012.

———. *Revolt of the Tar Heels: The North Carolina Populist Movement, 1890-1901.* Jackson: Univ. Press of Mississippi, 2008.

Belknap, Michael R. *Federal Law and Southern Order: Racial Violence and Constitutional Conflict in the Post-Brown South.* Athens: Univ. of Georgia Press, 1987.

Benjamin, Robert C. O. *Southern Outrages: A Statistical Record of Lawless Doings.* N.p., 1894.

Bennett Jr., Lerone. *Before the Mayflower: A History of Black America.* New York: Viking Penguin, 1984.

Berg, Manfred. *Popular Justice: A History of Lynching in America.* Chicago: Ivan R. Dee, 2011.

———, and Simon Wendt. *Globalizing Lynching History: Vigilantism and Extralegal Punishment from an International Perspective.* New York: Palgrave Macmillan, 2011.

Berlin, Ira, and Herbert G. Gutman. "Natives and Immigrants, Free Men and Slaves: Urban Workingmen in the Antebellum American South." *The American Historical Review* 88 (1983): 1175-1200.

Berman, William C. *The Politics of Civil Rights in the Truman Administration.* Columbus: Ohio State Univ. Press, 1970.

Bernstein, Patricia. *The First Waco Horror: The Lynching of Jesse Washington and the Rise of the NAACP.* College Station: Texas A&M Univ. Press, 2005.

Bertrand, Michael T. *Race, Rock, and Elvis.* Urbana: Univ. of Illinois Press, 2000.

Bess, Michael K. "Obreros in the Peach State: The Growth of Georgia's Working-Class Mexican Immigrant Communities from a Transnational Perspective." In *Life and Labor in the New New South,* ed. Robert H. Zieger, 214-35. Gainesville: Univ. Press of Florida, 2012.

Bevacqua, Maria. *Rape on the Public Agenda: Feminism and the Politics of Sexual Assault.* Boston: Northeastern Univ. Press, 2000.

Biegert, M. Langley. "Legacy of Resistance: Uncovering the History of Collective Action by Black Agricultural Workers in Central East Arkansas from the 1860s to the 1930s." *Journal of Social History* 32, no. 1 (Fall 1998): 73-100.

Biles, Roger. *The South and the New Deal.* Lexington: Univ. Press of Kentucky, 1994.

Billington, Monroe Lee. *The Political South in the Twentieth Century.* New York: Charles Scribner's Sons, 1975.

Bingham, Emily S., and Thomas A. Underwood, eds. *The Southern Agrarians and the New Deal: Essays after* I'll Take My Stand. Charlottesville: Univ. Press of Virginia, 2001.

Black, Earl, and Merle Black. *Politics and Society in the South.* Cambridge, Mass.: Harvard Univ. Press, 1987.

———. *The Rise of Southern Republicans.* Cambridge, Mass.: The Belknap Press of Harvard Univ. Press, 2002.

————. *The Vital South: How Presidents Are Elected.* Cambridge, Mass.: Harvard Univ. Press, 1992.

Blackburn, Robin. *An Unfinished Revolution: Karl Marx and Abraham Lincoln.* London: Verso, 2011.

Blackett, R. J. M. *Divided Hearts: Britain and the American Civil War.* Baton Rouge: Louisiana State Univ. Press, 2001.

————. "Martin R. Delany and Robert Campbell: Black Americans in Search of an African Colony." *Journal of Negro History* 62 (1977): 1-25.

Blackmon, Douglas A. *Slavery by Another Name: The Re-enslavement of Black Americans from the Civil War to World War II.* Duxford, Cambridgeshire: Icon Books, 2012.

Blakeslee, George H. "Introduction." *Journal of Race Development* 1 (1910-11): 1-4.

Blight, David W. *Race and Reunion: The Civil War in American Memory.* Cambridge, Mass.: Harvard Univ. Press, 2001.

Bloom, Jack. *Class, Race, and the Civil Rights Movement: The Changing Political Economy of Southern Racism.* Bloomington: Indiana Univ. Press, 1987.

Blum, Edward J. "The Crucible of Disease: Trauma, Memory, and National Reconciliation during the Yellow Fever Epidemic of 1878." *Journal of Southern History* 69, no. 4 (Nov. 2003): 791-820.

Blum, J. Morton. *V Was for Victory: Politics and American Culture during World War II.* New York: Putnam Publishers, 1976.

Bodroghkozy, Aniko. *Equal Time: Television and the Civil Rights Movement.* Champaign: Univ. of Illinois Press, 2012.

Boer, Tycho de. *Nature, Business, and Community in North Carolina's Green Swamp.* Gainesville: Univ. Press of Florida, 2008.

Boles, John B. *A Companion to the American South.* New York: John Wiley and Sons, 2008.

————, ed. *Shapers of Southern History: Autobiographical Reflections.* Athens: Univ. of Georgia Press, 2004.

Borders, Gary B. *A Hanging in Nacogdoches: Murder, Race, Politics, and Polemics in Texas's Oldest Town, 1870-1916.* Austin: Univ. of Texas Press, 2006.

Borstelmann, Thomas. *The Cold War and the Color Line: American Race Relations in the Global Arena.* Cambridge, Mass.: Harvard Univ. Press, 2001.

Boyd, Timothy S. R. *Georgia Democrats, the Civil Rights Movement, and the Shaping of the New South.* Gainesville: Univ. Press of Florida, 2012.

Boyle, Kevin. "Labor, the Left, and the Long Civil Rights Movement." *Social History* 30 (2005): 366-72.

Boyte, Harry. "The Textile Industry: Keel of Southern Industrialization." *Radical America* 6 (Mar.-Apr. 1972): 4-49.

Brady, Lisa M. *War upon the Land: Military Strategy and the Transformation of Southern Landscapes during the American Civil War.* Athens: Univ. of Georgia Press, 2012.

Branch, Taylor. *At Canaan's Edge, 1965-1968.* New York: Simon and Schuster, 2006.

————. *Parting the Waters: America in the King Years.* New York: Simon and Schuster, 1988.

————. *Pillar of Fire, 1963-1965.* New York: New York: Simon and Schuster, 1998.

Brattain, Michelle. *The Politics of Whiteness: Race, Workers, and Culture in the Modern South.* Princeton, N.J.: Princeton Univ. Press, 2001.

———. "The Pursuits of Post-exceptionalism: Race, Gender, Class, and Politics in the New Southern Labor History." In *Labor in the Modern South,* ed. Glenn T. Eskew, 1-46. Athens: Univ. of Georgia Press, 2001.

Brauer, Carl. *John F. Kennedy and the Second Reconstruction.* New York: Columbia Univ. Press, 1977.

Brilliant, Mark. *The Color of America Has Changed: How Racial Diversity Shaped Civil Rights Reform in California, 1941-1978.* New York: Oxford Univ. Press, 2010.

Brinkley, Alan. *Liberalism and Its Discontents.* Cambridge, Mass.: Harvard Univ. Press, 1998.

———. *Voices of Protest: Huey Long, Father Coughlin, and the Great Depression.* New York: Alfred A. Knopf, 1982.

Brooks, Jennifer E. *Defining the Peace: World War II Veterans, Race, and the Remaking of Southern Political Tradition.* Chapel Hill: Univ. of North Carolina Press, 2004.

———. "Winning the Peace: Georgia Veterans and the Struggle to Define the Political Legacy of World War II." *Journal of Southern History* 66 (Aug. 2000): 563-604.

Brophy, Alfred L. *Reconstructing the Dreamland: The Tulsa Riot of 1921.* New York: Oxford Univ. Press, 2002.

Brown, Edwin L., and Colin J. Davis. *It Is Union and Liberty: Alabama Coal Miners and the UMW.* Tuscaloosa: Univ. of Alabama Press, 1999.

Brown, Elsa Barkley. "To Catch the Vision of Freedom: Reconstructing Southern Black Women's Political History, 1865-1880." In *African American Women and the Vote, 1837-1965,* ed. Ann D. Gordon et al., 66-99. Amherst: Univ. of Massachusetts Press, 1997.

Brown, Margaret Lynn. *The Wild East: A Biography of the Great Smoky Mountains.* Gainesville: Univ. Press of Florida, 2001.

Brown, Thomas J. "Negotiating and Transforming the Public Sphere: African American Political Life in the Transition from Slavery to Freedom." In *Women Transforming Politics: An Alternative Reader,* ed. Cathy J. Cohen, Kathleen B. Jones, and Joan C. Tronto, 343-76. New York: New York Univ. Press, 1997.

———, ed. *Reconstructions: New Perspectives on the Postbellum United States.* New York: Oxford Univ. Press, 2006.

Brundage, W. Fitzhugh. *Lynching in the New South: Georgia and Virginia, 1880-1930.* Urbana: Univ. of Illinois Press, 1993.

Buhs, Joshua Blu. *The Fire Ant Wars: Nature, Science, and Public Policy in Twentieth-Century America.* Chicago: Univ. of Chicago Press, 2004.

Bullard, Robert D. *Dumping in Dixie: Race, Class, and Environmental Quality.* Boulder, Colo.: Westview Press, 1990.

Bullock III, Charles S., and Mark J. Rozell, eds. *The New Politics of the Old South: An Introduction to Southern Politics.* Lanham, Md.: Rowman and Littlefield, 1998.

Burgess, John W. "The American Commonwealth: Changes in Its Relation to the Nation." *Political Science Quarterly* 1 (1886): 9-35.

Burin, Eric. *Slavery and the Peculiar Solution: A History of the American Colonization Society.* Gainesville: Univ. Press of Florida, 2005.

Burk, Robert F. *The Eisenhower Administration and Civil Rights.* Knoxville: Univ. of Tennessee Press, 1984.

Burner, Eric. *And Gently He Shall Lead Them: Robert Parris Moses and Civil Rights in Mississippi.* New York: New York Univ. Press, 1994.

Bynum, Cornelius A. *Philip Randolph and the Struggle for Civil Rights.* Urbana: Univ. of Illinois Press, 2010.

Callahan, North. *TVA: Bridge over Troubled Waters.* South Brunswick, N.J.: A. S. Barnes and Company, 1980.

Campbell, Charles Soutter. *The Transformation of American Foreign Relations, 1865-1900.* New York: Harper and Row, 1976.

Campbell, James T. "Redeeming the Race: Martin Delany and the Niger Valley Exploring Party, 1859-60." *New Formations* 45 (Winter 2001-2002): 125-49.

Campbell, James T. *Middle Passages: African American Journeys to Africa, 1787-2005.* New York: Penguin, 2006.

———. *Songs of Zion: The African Methodist Episcopal Church in the United States and South Africa.* New York: Oxford Univ. Press, 1995.

Campney, Brent M. S. "'Light Is Bursting Upon the World!': White Supremacy and Racist Violence against Blacks in Reconstruction Kansas." *Western Historical Quarterly* 41, no. 2 (Summer 2010): 171-94.

———. *This Is Not Dixie: Racist Violence in Kansas, 1861-1927.* Urbana: Univ. of Illinois Press, 2015.

Capeci Jr., Dominic J. *The Lynching of Cleo Wright.* Lexington: Univ. Press of Kentucky, 1998.

Carlson, Shirley J. "Black Ideals of Womanhood in the Late Victorian Era." *Journal of Negro History* 77 (Spring 1992): 61-73.

Carmichael, Stokely, and Charles V. Hamilton. *Black Power: The Politics of Liberation in America.* New York: Random House, 1967.

Carr, Cynthia. *Our Town: A Heartland Lynching, a Haunted Town, and the Hidden History of White America.* New York: Crown Publishers, 2006.

Carrigan, William D. *The Making of a Lynching Culture: Violence and Vigilantism in Central Texas, 1836-1916.* Urbana: Univ. of Illinois Press, 2004.

———, and Christopher Waldrep, eds. *Swift to Wrath: Lynching in Global Perspective.* Charlottesville: Univ. of Virginia Press, 2013.

———, and Clive Webb. *Forgotten Dead: Mob Violence against Mexicans in the United States, 1848-1928.* New York: Oxford Univ. Press, 2013.

Carson, Clayborn. *In Struggle: SNCC and the Black Awakening of the 1960s.* Cambridge, Mass.: Harvard Univ. Press, 1981.

———, et al., eds. *Eyes on the Prize: America's Civil Rights Years: A Reader and Guide.* New York: Penguin Books, 1987.

Carter, Dan T. *From George Wallace to Newt Gingrich: Race and the Conservative Counterrevolution, 1964-1994.* Baton Rouge: Louisiana State Univ. Press, 1996.

———. "From Segregation to Integration." In *Interpreting Southern History: Historiographical Essays in Honor of Sanford W. Higginbotham,* ed. John B. Boles and Evelyn Thomas Nolen, 408-33. Baton Rouge: Louisiana State Univ. Press, 1987.

———. *Politics of Rage: George Wallace, the Origins of the New Conservatism, and the Transformation of American Politics.* New York: Simon and Schuster, 1995.

———. *Scottsboro: A Tragedy of the American South.* 1969. Rev. ed. Baton Rouge: Louisiana State Univ. Press, 2007.

Cash, W. J. *The Mind of the South.* 1941. Reprint, New York: Vintage Books, 1991.

Cecelski, David S., and Timothy B. Tyson, eds. *Democracy Betrayed: The Wilmington Race Riot of 1898 and Its Legacy.* Chapel Hill: Univ. of North Carolina Press, 1998.

Censer, Jane Turner. *The Reconstruction of White Southern Womanhood, 1865-1895.* Baton Rouge: Louisiana State Univ. Press, 2003.

Chadbourn, James Harmon. *Lynching and the Law.* Chapel Hill: Univ. of North Carolina Press, 1933.

Chafe, William H. *Civilities and Civil Rights: Greensboro, North Carolina, and the Black Struggle for Freedom.* New York: Oxford Univ. Press, 1980.

————, Raymond Gavins, and Robert Rodgers Korstad, eds. *Remembering Jim Crow: African Americans Tell about Life in the Segregated South.* New York: New Press, in association with Lyndhurst Books of the Center for Documentary Studies of Duke Univ., 2001.

Cha-Jua, Sundiata Keita, and Clarence Lang. "The 'Long Movement' as Vampire: Temporal and Spatial Fallacies in Recent Black Freedom Studies." *Journal of African American History* 92 (2007): 265-88.

Chamberlain, Charles D. *Victory at Home: Manpower and Race in the American South during World War II.* Athens: Univ. of Georgia Press, 2003.

Chandler, Alfred D. *The Visible Hand: The Managerial Revolution in American Business.* Cambridge, Mass.: Harvard Univ. Press, 1977.

Chapman, Anne W. "William Dunning." In *Dictionary of Literary Biography: Twentieth Century-American Historians,* ed. Clyde Wilson, 17:148-54. Detroit: Gale Research, 1983.

Chappell, David L. *Waking from the Dream: The Struggle for Civil Rights in the Shadow of Martin Luther King, Jr.* New York: Random House, 2014.

Chesnut, Mary Boykin Miller. *A Diary from Dixie.* New York: D. Appleton and Company, 1905.

Chirhart, Ann Short. *Torches of Light: Georgia Teachers and the Coming of the Modern South.* Athens: Univ. of Georgia Press, 2005.

Cimbala, Paul A., and Robert F. Himmelberg, eds. *Historians and Race: Autobiography and the Writing of History.* Bloomington: Indiana Univ. Press, 1996.

Clark, Anna. *The Struggle for the Breeches: Gender and the Making of the British Working Class.* Berkeley: Univ. of California Press, 1995.

Clark, Daniel. *Like Night and Day: Unionization in a Southern Mill Town.* Chapel Hill: Univ. of North Carolina Press, 1997.

Clark, Septima. *Echo in My Soul.* New York: E. P. Dutton, 1962.

Clark, Thomas D. *The Greening of the South: The Recovery of Land and Forest.* Lexington: Univ. Press of Kentucky, 2004.

————, and Albert D. Kirwan. *The South since Appomattox: A Century of Regional Change.* New York: Oxford Univ. Press, 1967.

Clegg III, Claude A. *Troubled Ground: A Tale of Murder, Lynching, and Reckoning in the New South.* Urbana: Univ. of Illinois Press, 2010.

Cobb, Charles E. *This Nonviolent Stuff'll Get You Killed: How Guns Made the Civil Rights Movement Possible.* New York: Basic Books, 2014.

Cobb, James C. *Away down South: A History of Southern Identity.* New York: Oxford Univ. Press, 2005.

————. *The Most Southern Place on Earth: The Mississippi Delta and the Roots of Regional Identity.* Oxford: Oxford Univ. Press, 1992.

————. *The Selling of the South.* Champaign: Univ. of Illinois Press, 1993.

————, and Michael V. Namorato, eds. *The New Deal and the South.* Jackson: Univ. Press of Mississippi, 1984.

————, and William Stueck, eds. *Globalization and the American South.* Athens: Univ. of Georgia Press, 2005.

————, and Charles R. Wilson, eds. *Perspectives on the American South: An Annual Review of Society, Politics, and Culture.* Vol. 4. New York: Gordon and Breach, 1987.

Cohen, Nancy. *The Reconstruction of American Liberalism, 1865-1914.* Chapel Hill: Univ. of North Carolina Press, 2002.

Cohn, David Lewis. *The Mississippi Delta and the World: The Memoirs of David L. Cohn.* Baton Rouge: Louisiana State Univ. Press, 1995.

Colburn, David R. *Racial Change and Community Crisis: St. Augustine, Florida, 1877-1980.* New York: Columbia Univ. Press, 1985.

————, and Elizabeth Jacoway, eds. *Southern Businessmen and Desegregation.* Baton Rouge: Louisiana State Univ. Press, 1982.

Collier-Thomas, Bettye, and V. P. Franklin, eds. *Sisters in the Struggle: African American Women in the Civil Rights-Black Power Movement.* New York: New York Univ. Press, 2001.

Collins, Ann V. *All Hell Broke Loose: American Race Riots from the Progressive Era through World War II.* Santa Barbara, Calif.: Praeger, 2012.

Collins, Winfield H. *The Truth about Lynching and the Negro in the South: In Which the Author Pleads That the South Be Made Safe for the White Race.* New York: Neale, 1918.

Colten, Craig E. *An Unnatural Metropolis: Wresting New Orleans from Nature.* Baton Rouge: Louisiana State Univ. Press, 2006.

Combs, Barbara Harris. *From Selma to Montgomery: The Long March to Freedom.* New York: Routledge, 2013.

Cook, Lisa D. "Converging to a National Lynching Database: Recent Developments." *Historical Methods* 45 (Apr.-June 2012): 55-63.

Cooper, Frederick, Thomas C. Holt, and Rebecca J. Scott. *Beyond Slavery: Explorations of Race, Labor, and Citizenship in Postemancipation Societies.* Chapel Hill: Univ. of North Carolina Press, 2000.

Cortner, Richard C. *A "Scottsboro" Case in Mississippi: The Supreme Court and Brown v. Mississippi.* Jackson: Univ. Press of Mississippi, 1986.

Cosner Jr., Walter H., and Rodger M. Payne, eds. *Southern Crossroads: Perspectives on Religion and Culture.* Lexington: Univ. Press of Kentucky, 2008.

Countryman, Matthew J. *Up South: Civil Rights and Black Power in Philadelphia.* Philadelphia: Univ. of Pennsylvania Press, 2007.

Cowdrey, Albert E. Review of *Poquosin: A Study of Rural Landscape and Society,* by Jack Temple Kirby. *Journal of Southern History* 63, no. 1 (Feb. 1997): 147-48.

————. *This Land, This South: An Environmental History.* Lexington: Univ. Press of Kentucky, 1996.

Cowie, Jefferson. *Capital Moves: RCA's Seventy-Year Quest for Cheap Labor.* Ithaca, N.Y.: Cornell Univ. Press, 1999.

Cox Richardson, Heather. *The Death of Reconstruction: Race, Labor, and Politics in the Post-Civil War North, 1865-1901.* Cambridge, Mass.: Harvard Univ. Press, 2001.

Cox, Karen L. *Dixie's Daughters: The United Daughters of the Confederacy and the Preservation of Confederate Culture.* Gainesville: Univ. Press of Florida, 2003.

Craven, Avery. *Soil Exhaustion as a Factor in the Agricultural History of Virginia and Maryland, 1606-1860.* Washington, D.C.: Carnegie Institution, 1933.

Craven, Paul, and Douglas Hay, eds. *Masters, Servants, and Magistrates in Britain and the Empire, 1562-1955.* Chapel Hill: Univ. of North Carolina Press, 2004.

Crawford, Vicki L., Jacqueline Rouse, and Barbara Woods, eds. *Women in the Civil Rights Movement: Trailblazers and Touchbearers, 1941-1965.* Bloomington: Indiana Univ. Press, 1993.

Creech, Joe. *Righteous Indignation: Religion and the Populist Revolution.* Urbana: Univ. of Illinois Press, 2006.

Crespino, Joseph. *In Search of Another Country: Mississippi and the Conservative Counterrevolution.* Princeton, N.J.: Princeton Univ. Press, 2007.

——. *Strom Thurmond's America.* New York: Hill and Wang, 2012.

Cronon, William. *Nature's Metropolis: Chicago and the Great West.* New York: W. W. Norton, 1991.

Crosby, Emilye, ed. *Civil Rights History from the Ground Up: Local Struggles, a National Movement.* Athens: Univ. of Georgia Press, 2011.

Cummings, Stephen O. *The Dixification of America: The American Odyssey into the Conservative Economic Trap.* Westport, Conn.: Praeger, 1998.

Cunliffe, Marcus. *Chattel Slavery and Wage Slavery: The Anglo-American Context, 1830-1860.* Athens: Univ. of Georgia Press, 1979.

Cunningham, Raymond J. "Herbert Baxter Adams." In *Dictionary of Literary Biography: American Historians, 1866-1912,* ed. Clyde N. Wilson, 47:20-34. Detroit: Gale Research, 1983.

Cunningham, Sean. *Cowboy Conservatism: Texas and the Rise of the Modern Right.* Lexington: Univ. Press of Kentucky, 2010.

Curry, Constance, et al., eds. *Deep in Our Hearts: Nine Women in the Freedom Movement.* Athens: Univ. of Georgia Press, 2000.

Curtin, Mary Ellen. *Black Prisoners and Their World.* Charlottesville: Univ. of Virginia Press, 2000.

Curtin, Philip D. *The Rise and Fall of the Plantation Complex: Essays in Atlantic History.* New York: Cambridge Univ. Press, 1990.

Cutler, James Elbert. *Lynch-Law: An Investigation into the History of Lynching in the United States.* London: Longmans, Green, and Co., 1905.

Dailey, Jane, Glenda Elizabeth Gilmore, and Bryant Simon, eds. *Jumpin' Jim Crow: Southern Politics from Civil War to Civil Rights.* Princeton, N.J.: Princeton Univ. Press, 2000.

Dal Lago, Enrico. *American Slavery, Atlantic Slavery, and Beyond: The U.S. "Peculiar Institution" in International Perspective.* Boulder, Colo.: Paradigm Publishers, 2012.

Dalfiume, Richard M. *Desegregation of the U.S. Armed Forces: Fighting on Two Fronts, 1939-1953.* Columbia: Univ. of Missouri Press, 1969.

——. "The Forgotten Years of the Negro Revolution." *Journal of American History* 55 (June 1968): 90-106.

Dallek, Robert. *Flawed Giant: Lyndon Johnson and His Times, 1961-1973.* New York: Oxford Univ. Press, 1998.

———. *Lone Star Rising: Lyndon Johnson and His Times, 1908-1960.* New York: Oxford Univ. Press, 1991.

Daniel, Clete. *Culture of Misfortune: An Interpretive History of Textile Unionism in the United States.* Ithaca, N.Y.: ILR Press/Cornell Univ. Press, 2001.

Daniel, Pete. "Accidental Historian." In *Shapers of Southern History: Autobiographical Reflections,* ed. John B. Boles, 164-86. Athens: Univ. of Georgia Press, 2004.

———. *Breaking the Land: The Transformation of Cotton, Tobacco, and Rice Cultures since 1880.* Urbana: Univ. of Illinois Press, 1985.

———. *Deep'n as It Come: The 1927 Mississippi River Flood.* New York: Oxford Univ. Press, 1977.

———. *Dispossession: Discrimination against African American Farmers in the Age of Civil Rights.* Chapel Hill: Univ. of North Carolina Press, 2013.

———. "Going among Strangers: Southern Reactions to World War II." *Journal of American History* 77 (Dec. 1990): 886-911.

———. *Lost Revolutions: The South in the 1950s.* Chapel Hill: Univ. of North Carolina Press, for the Smithsonian National Museum of American History, Washington, D.C., 2000.

———. *The Shadow of Slavery: Peonage in the South, 1901-1969.* Urbana: Univ. of Illinois Press, 1972, 1990.

———. *Standing at the Crossroads: Southern Life since 1900.* New York: Hill and Wang, 1986.

———. *Toxic Drift: Pesticides and Health in the Post-World War II South.* Baton Rouge: Louisiana State Univ. Press, in association with Smithsonian Institution, Washington, D.C., 2005.

Dates, Jannette L., and William Barlow, eds. *Split Image: African Americans in the Mass Media.* Washington, D.C.: Howard Univ. Press, 1990.

Davidson, James West. *"They Say": Ida B. Wells and the Reconstruction of Race.* New York: Oxford Univ. Press, 2009.

Davis, Donald Edward. *Where There Are Mountains: An Environmental History of the Southern Appalachians.* Athens: Univ. of Georgia Press, 2000.

Davis, Frederick Rowe. *The Man Who Saved Sea Turtles: Archie Carr and the Origins of Conservation Biology.* New York: Oxford Univ. Press, 2007.

Davis, Jack E. *An Everglades Providence: Marjory Stoneman Douglas and the American Environmental Century.* Athens: Univ. of Georgia Press, 2009.

Davis, Jefferson. *The Rise and Fall of the Confederate Government.* New York: D. Appleton and Company, 1881.

Davis, Mike. *Late Victorian Holocausts: El Niño Famines and the Making of the Third World.* London: Verso, 2001.

Davis, William W. *The Civil War and Reconstruction in Florida.* New York: Columbia Univ. Press, 1913.

Diggs, Annie L. "The Women in the Alliance Movement." *The Arena* 6 (July 1892): 161-79.

Dillon, Merton L. *Ulrich Bonnell Phillips: Historian of the Old South.* Southern Biography Series. Baton Rouge: Louisiana State Univ. Press, 1985.

Dittmer, John. *Local People: The Struggle for Civil Rights in Mississippi.* Champaign: Univ. of Illinois Press, 1995.

Dochuk, Darren. *From Bible Belt to Sunbelt: Plain-Folk Religion, Grassroots Politics, and the Rise of Evangelical Conservatism.* New York: W. W. Norton, 2010.

Dorman, Michael. *We Shall Overcome: A Reporter's Eyewitness Account of the Year of Racial Strife and Triumph.* New York: Dell Publishing, 1965.

Dorr, Lisa Lindquist. *White Women, Rape, and the Power of Race in Virginia, 1900-1960.* Chapel Hill: Univ. of North Carolina Press, 2004.

Dowden-White, Priscilla A. "To See Past the Differences to the Fundamentals: Racial Coalition within the League of Women Voters of St. Louis, 1920-1946." In *Women Shaping the South: Creating and Confronting Change,* ed. Angela Boswell and Judith N. McArthur, 174-203. Columbia: Univ. of Missouri Press, 2006.

Downey, Dennis B., and Raymond M. Hyser. *No Crooked Death: Coatesville, Pennsylvania and the Lynching of Zachariah Walker.* Urbana: Univ. of Illinois Press, 1991.

Downs, Jim. *Sick from Freedom: African-American Illness and Suffering during the Civil War and Reconstruction.* New York: Oxford Univ. Press, 2012.

Drake, Richard B. *A History of Appalachia.* Lexington: Univ. of Kentucky Press, 2001.

Draper, Alan. *Conflict of Interests: Organized Labor and the Civil Rights Movement in the South, 1954-1968.* Ithaca, N.Y.: ILR Press, 1994.

———. "The New Southern Labor History Revisited: The Success of the Mine, Mill and Smelter Workers Union in Birmingham, 1934-1938." *Journal of Southern History* 62, no. 1 (Feb. 1996): 87-108.

Dray, Philip. *At the Hands of Persons Unknown: The Lynching of Black America.* New York: Random House, 2002.

Drescher, Seymour. *The Mighty Experiment: Free Labor vs. Slavery in British Emancipation.* New York: Oxford Univ. Press, 2002.

Du Bois, W. E. B. *An ABC of Color: Selections Chosen by the Author from over a Half Century of His Writings.* New York: International Publishers, 1969.

———. *Black Reconstruction: An Essay toward a History of the Part Which Black Folk Played in the Attempt to Reconstruct Democracy in America, 1860-1880.* 1935. Reprint, New York: Free Press, 1998.

Du Pre Lumpkin, Katherine. *The Making of a Southerner.* New York: Alfred A. Knopf, 1946.

Dubois, Laurent. *Avengers of the New World: The Story of the Haitian Revolution.* Cambridge, Mass.: Harvard Univ. Press, 2004.

Dudziak, Mary L. *Cold War Civil Rights: Race and the Image of American Democracy.* Princeton, N.J.: Princeton Univ. Press, 2000.

Dunning, N. A. *The Farmers' Alliance History and Agricultural Digest.* Washington, D.C.: Farmers'Alliance, 1889.

Dunning, William Archibald. "The Process of Reconstruction." In *Essays on the Civil War and Reconstruction and Related Topics,* 176-252. New York: The Macmillan Company, 1898.

DuRocher, Kristina. *Raising Racists: The Socialization of White Children in the Jim Crow South.* Lexington: Univ. Press of Kentucky, 2011.

Durr, Virginia Foster. *Outside the Magic Circle: The Autobiography of Virginia Foster Durr.* Ed. Hollinger F. Barnard. Tuscaloosa: Univ. of Alabama Press, 1985.

Eagles, Charles W. *The Price of Defiance: James Meredith and the Integration of Ole Miss.* Chapel Hill: Univ. of North Carolina Press, 2009.

———. "Toward New Histories of the Civil Rights Era." *Journal of Southern History* 66 (Nov. 2000): 815-48.

Earle, Carville. "The Myth of the Southern Soil Miner: Macrohistory, Agricultural Innovation, and Environmental Change." In *The Ends of the Earth: Perspectives on Modern Environmental History,* ed. Donald Worster, 175-210. New York: Cambridge Univ. Press, 1988.

Earle, Jonathan H. *Jacksonian Antislavery and the Politics of Free Soil, 1824-1854.* Chapel Hill: Univ. of North Carolina Press, 2004.

Earley, Lawrence. *Looking for Longleaf: The Fall and Rise of an America Forest.* Chapel Hill: Univ. of North Carolina Press, 2004.

Egerton, John. *The Americanization of Dixie: The Southernization of America.* New York: Harper's Magazine Press, 1974.

———. *Speak Now against the Day: The Generation before the Civil Rights Movement in the South.* New York: Alfred A. Knopf, 1994.

Edsall, Thomas Byrne, and Mary Edsall. *Chain Reaction: The Impact of Race, Rights, and Taxes on American Politics.* New York: W. W. Norton and Company, 1991.

Efford, Alison Clark. *German Immigrants, Race, and Citizenship in the Civil War Era.* Cambridge: Cambridge Univ. Press, 2013.

Eley, Geoff. *Forging Democracy: The History of the Left in Europe, 1850-2000.* New York: Oxford Univ. Press, 2002.

Eller, Ronald D. *Uneven Ground: Appalachian since 1945.* Lexington: Univ. Press of Kentucky, 2008.

Ellis, John Hubert. *Yellow Fever and Public Health in the New South.* Lexington: Univ. Press of Kentucky, 1992.

Ellsworth, Scott. *Death in a Promised Land: The Tulsa Race Riot of 1921.* Baton Rouge: Louisiana State Univ. Press, 1984.

Emberton, Carole. *Beyond Redemption: Race, Violence, and the American South after the Civil War.* Chicago: Univ. of Chicago Press, 2013.

Enstam, Elizabeth York. *Women and the Creation of Urban Life: Dallas, Texas, 1843-1920.* College Station: Texas A&M Univ. Press, 1998.

Eskew, Glenn T., ed. *Labor in the Modern South.* Athens: Univ. of Georgia Press, 2001.

———. *But for Birmingham: The Local and National Movements in the Civil Rights Struggles.* Chapel Hill: Univ. of North Carolina, 1997.

Estes, Steve. *I Am a Man! Race, Manhood, and the Civil Rights Movement.* Chapel Hill: Univ. of North Carolina Press, 2005.

Eyes on the Prize: America's Civil Rights Years, 1954-1965. DVD. Produced by Henry Hampton. Boston: Blackside, 1986.

Eyes on the Prize II: America at the Racial Crossroads, 1965-1985. DVD. Produced by Henry Hampton. Boston: Blackside, 1990.

Evans, Ivan Thomas. *Cultures of Violence: Lynching and Racial Killing in South Africa and the American South.* Manchester, U.K.: Manchester Univ. Press, 2009.

Evans, Sara. *Personal Politics: The Roots of Women's Liberation in the Civil Rights Movement and the New Left.* New York: Alfred A. Knopf, 1980.

Fairclough, Adam. "Historians and the Civil Rights Movement." *Journal of American Studies* 24 (Dec. 1990): 387-98.

———. *Martin Luther King, Jr.* Athens: Univ. of Georgia Press, 1995.

———. *Race and Democracy: The Civil Rights Struggle in Louisiana, 1915-1972.* Athens: Univ. of Georgia Press, 1995.

———. *To Redeem the Soul of America: The Southern Christian Leadership Conference and Martin Luther King, Jr.* Athens: Univ. of Georgia Press, 1987.

Fannin, Mark. *Labor's Promised Land: Radical Visions of Gender, Race, and Religion in the South.* Knoxville: Univ. of Tennessee Press, 2003.

Farmer, James. *Freedom—When?* New York: Random House, 1965.

———. *Lay Bare the Heart: An Autobiography of the Civil Rights Movement.* New York: Arbor House, 1985.

Farnham, Christine Anne. *The Education of the Southern Belle: Higher Education and Student Socialization in the Antebellum South.* New York: New York Univ. Press, 1995.

Farrell, Harry. *Swift Justice: Murder and Vengeance in a California Town.* New York: St. Martin's, 1992.

Fedo, Michael W. *The Lynchings in Duluth.* St. Paul: Minnesota Historical Society Press, 2000.

Feimster, Crystal N. *Southern Horrors: Women and the Politics of Rape and Lynching.* Cambridge, Mass.: Harvard Univ. Press, 2009.

Feldman, Glenn, ed. *Before Brown: Civil Rights and White Backlash in the Modern South.* Tuscaloosa: Univ. of Alabama Press, 2004.

———. "The Myth of Southern Exceptionalism." Review of *The Myth of Southern Exceptionalism,* ed. Matthew D. Lassiter and Joseph Crespino. *Journal of Southern History* 77, no. 3 (Aug. 2011): 783-86.

———. *Painting Dixie Red: When, Where, Why, and How the South Became Republican.* Gainesville: Univ. Press of Florida, 2011.

———. *Politics and Religion in the White South.* Lexington: Univ. Press of Kentucky, 2005.

———. *Reading Southern History: Essays on Interpreters and Interpretations.* Tuscaloosa: Univ. of Alabama Press, 2001.

Fernbach, David, ed. *Marx's Political Writings.* Vol. 3, *The First International and After.* 1973. Reprint, London: Verso, 2010.

Fick, Carolyn. "Emancipation in Haiti: From Plantation Labour to Peasant Proprietorship." *Slavery and Abolition* 21 (2000): 11-40.

Fields, Barbara J. "Commentary on Jack Temple Kirby's paper 'Bioregionalism: Landscape and Culture in the South Atlantic.'" In *The New Regionalism: Essays and Commentaries,* ed. Robert L. Dorman and Charles Reagan Wilson, 19-44. Jackson: Univ. Press of Mississippi, 1998.

———. *Slavery and Freedom on the Middle Ground: Maryland during the Nineteenth Century.* New Haven, Conn.: Yale Univ. Press, 1985.

Fink, Leon. *The Maya of Morganton: Work and Community in the Nuevo New South.* Chapel Hill: Univ. of North Carolina Press, 2003.

———, and Brian Greenberg. *Upheaval in the Quiet Zone: A History of Hospital Workers' Union Local 1199.* Urbana: Univ. of Illinois Press, 1989.

Finkle, Lee. "The Conservative Aims of Militant Rhetoric: Black Protest during World War II." *Journal of American History* 60 (Dec. 1973): 692-713.

Finnegan, Terence. *A Deed So Accursed: Lynching in Mississippi and South Carolina, 1881-1940.* Charlottesville: Univ. of Virginia Press, 2013.

Fite, Gilbert Courtland. *Cotton Fields No More: Southern Agriculture, 1865-1980.* Lexington: Univ. Press of Kentucky, 1984.

Flamming, Douglas. *Creating the Modern South: Millhands and Managers in Dalton, Georgia, 1884-1984.* Chapel Hill: Univ. of North Carolina Press, 1992.

Fleming, Cynthia G. *Soon We Will Not Cry: The Liberation of Ruby Doris Smith Robinson.* Lanham, Md.: Rowman and Littlefield, 1998.

Flynt, Wayne. Review of *Breaking the Land: The Transformation of Cotton, Tobacco, and Rice Cultures since 1880,* by Pete Daniel. *Journal of Southern History* 52, no. 3 (Aug. 1986): 475-76.

Foner, Eric. *Free Soil, Free Labor, Free Men: The Ideology of the Republican Party before the Civil War.* New York: Oxford Univ. Press, 1970.

———. *Nothing but Freedom: Emancipation and Its Legacy.* Baton Rouge: Louisiana State Univ. Press, 1983.

———. *Reconstruction: America's Unfinished Revolution, 1863-1877.* New York: Harper and Row, 1988.

———. "Why Is There No Socialism in the United States?" *History Workshop* no. 17 (Spring 1984): 57-80.

Fones-Wolf, Elizabeth, and Ken Fones-Wolf. "Sanctifying the Southern Organizing Campaign: Protestant Activists in the CIO's Operation Dixie." *Labor: Studies in Working-Class History of the Americas* 6, no. 1 (Spring 2009): 5-32.

Foreman, James *The Making of Black Revolutionaries.* New York: MacMillan, 1972.

Fosl, Catherine. *Subversive Southerner: Anne Braden and the Struggle for Racial Justice in the Cold War South.* New York: Palgrave Macmillan, 2002.

Foster, Gaines M. *Ghosts of the Confederacy: Defeat, the Lost Cause, and the Emergence of the New South, 1865 to 1913.* New York: Oxford Univ. Press, 1985.

Fox-Genovese, Elizabeth, and Eugene D. Genovese. *Slavery in White and Black: Class and Race in the Southern Slaveholders' New World Order.* Cambridge: Cambridge Univ. Press, 2008.

Franklin, John Hope. "Demagoguery—Southern Style." Review of *Pitchfork Ben Tillman, South Carolinian,* by Francis Butler Simkins. *Journal of Negro Education* 15 (Autumn 1946): 654-55.

———. *From Slavery to Freedom: A History of Negro Americans.* New York: Alfred A. Knopf, 1947.

———. *Reconstruction after the Civil War.* Chicago: Univ. of Chicago Press, 1961.

———, and Alfred A. Moss Jr. *From Slavery to Freedom: A History of African Americans.* New York: McGraw Hill, 1994.

Fraser, Steve, and Gary Gerstle, eds. *The Rise and Fall of the New Deal Order, 1930-1980.* Princeton: N.J.: Princeton Univ. Press, 1989.

Frederickson, Kari. *The Dixiecrat Revolt and the End of the Solid South, 1932-1968.* Chapel Hill: Univ. of North Carolina Press, 2001.

Frederickson, Mary. "Heroines and Girl Strikers: Gender Issues and Organized Labor in the Twentieth-Century American South." In *Organized Labor in the*

Twentieth-Century South, ed. Robert H. Zieger, 84-112. Knoxville: Univ. of Tennessee Press, 1991.

———. "'I Know Which Side I'm on': Southern Women in the Labor Movement in the Twentieth Century." In *Women, Work and Protest: A Century of U.S. Women's Labor History,* ed. Ruth Milkman, 156-80. Boston: Routledge and Kegan Paul, 1985.

Fredrickson, George M. *The Black Image in the White Mind: The Debate on Afro-American Character and Destiny, 1817-1914.* 1st ed. New York: Harper and Row, 1971.

———. *White Supremacy: A Comparative Study in American and South African History.* New York: Oxford Univ. Press, 1981.

Freedman, Estelle B. *Redefining Rape: Sexual Violence in the Era of Suffrage and Segregation.* Cambridge, Mass.: Harvard Univ. Press, 2013.

Freidel, Frank. *Franklin D. Roosevelt: A Rendezvous with Destiny.* Boston: Little, Brown and Company, 1990.

Friedman, Tami J. "'How Can Greenville Get New Industry to Come Here If We Get the Label of a C.I.O. Town': Capital Migration and the Limits of Unionism in the Postwar South." In *Life and Labor in the New New South: Essays in Southern Labor History since 1950,* ed. Robert H. Zieger, 16-44. Gainesville: Univ. Press of Florida, 2012.

Fuller, Paul E. *Laura Clay and the Woman's Rights Movement.* Lexington: Univ. Press of Kentucky, 1975.

Gaines, Kevin K. "The Civil Rights Movement in World Perspective." *OAH Magazine of History* 21 (2007): 57-64.

———. "The Historiography of the Struggle for Black Equality since 1945." In *A Companion to Post-1945 America,* ed. Jean-Christophe Agnew and Ray Rosenzweig, 211-34. Malden, Mass.: Wiley-Blackwell, 2002.

———. *Uplifting the Race: Black Leadership, Politics, and Culture in the Twentieth Century.* Chapel Hill: Univ. of North Carolina Press, 1996.

Gaither, Gerald H. *Blacks and the Populist Revolt: Ballots and Bigotry in the "New South."* Tuscaloosa: Univ. of Alabama Press, 1977.

Gardner, Michael. *Harry Truman and Civil Rights: Moral Courage and Political Risks.* Carbondale: Southern Illinois Univ. Press, 2002.

Gardner, Sarah E. *Blood and Irony: Southern White Women's Narratives of the Civil War, 1861-1937.* Chapel Hill: Univ. of North Carolina Press, 2004.

Garner, James W. *Reconstruction in Mississippi.* New York: Macmillan, 1901.

Garrow, David J. *Bearing the Cross: Martin Luther King, Jr., and the Southern Christian Leadership Conference.* New York: W. Morrow, 1986.

Gary, Brett. *The Nervous Liberals: Propaganda Anxieties from World War I to the Cold War.* New York: Columbia Univ. Press, 1999.

Gass, W. Conrad. "Franklin L. Riley and The Historical Renaissance In Mississippi, 1897-1914." *Journal of Mississippi History* 32 (May 1970): 195-227.

Gaston, Paul M. *The New South Creed: A Study in Southern Mythmaking.* New York: Alfred A. Knopf, 1970.

Geiss, Imanuel. *The Pan-African Movement: A History of Pan-Africanism in America, Europe, and Africa.* New York: Africana Pub. Co., 1974.

Gellman, Erik S., and Jarod Roll. *The Gospel of the Working Class: Labor's Southern Prophets in New Deal America*. Urbana: Univ. of Illinois Press, 2011.

Gerstle, Gary. "The Crucial Decade: The 1940s and Beyond." *Journal of American History* 92 (Mar. 2006): 1292-99.

Giddings, Paula. *Ida: A Sword among Lions*. New York: Amistad, 2008.

———. *When and Where I Enter: The Impact of Black Women on Race and Sex in America*. New York: Bantam Books, 1984.

Giesen, James C. *Boll Weevil Blues: Cotton, Myth, and Power in the American South*. Chicago: Univ. of Chicago Press, 2011.

———. "'The Truth about the Boll Weevil': The Nature of Planter Power in the Mississippi Delta." *Environmental History* 14, no. 4 (Oct. 2009): 683-704.

Gilmore, Glenda E. *Defying Dixie: The Radical Roots of Civil Rights, 1929-1950*. New York: W. W. Norton, 2008.

———. *Gender and Jim Crow: Women and the Politics of White Supremacy in North Carolina, 1896-1920*. Chapel Hill: Univ. of North Carolina Press, 1996.

Giltner, Scott E. *Hunting and Fishing in the New South: Black Labor and White Leisure after the Civil War*. Baltimore: Johns Hopkins Univ. Press, 2010.

Glymph, Thavolia, and John J. Kushma, eds. *Essays on the Postbellum Southern Economy*. College Station: Texas A&M Univ. Press, 1985.

Godoy, Angelina Snodgrass. *Popular Injustice: Violence, Community, and Law in Latin America*. Stanford, Calif.: Stanford Univ. Press, 2006.

Godshalk, David F. *Veiled Visions: The 1906 Atlanta Race Riot and the Reshaping of American Race Relations*. Chapel Hill: Univ. of North Carolina Press, 2005.

———. "William J. Northen's Public and Personal Struggles against Lynching." In *Jumpin' Jim Crow: Southern Politics from Civil War to Civil Rights*, ed. Jane Dailey, Glenda Elizabeth Gilmore, and Bryant Simon, 140-61. Princeton, N.J.: Princeton Univ. Press, 2000.

Goldberg, David Theo. *The Racial State*. Malden, Mass: Blackwell Publishers, 2002.

Goldfield, David R. *Black, White, and Southern: Race Relations and Southern Culture, 1940 to the Present*. Baton Rouge: Louisiana State Univ. Press, 1990.

———. *Still Fighting the Civil War: The American South and Southern History*. Baton Rouge: Louisiana State Univ. Press, 2002.

Goldfield, Michael. *The Decline of Organized Labor in the United States*. Chicago: Univ. of Chicago Press, 1987.

———. "Was There a Golden Age of the CIO? Race, Solidarity, and Union Growth during the 1930s and 1940s." In *Trade Union Politics: American Unions and Economic Change, 1960s-1990s*, ed. Glenn Perusek and Kent Worcester, 78-110. Atlantic Highlands, N.J.: Humanities Press, 1995.

Goldsby, Jacqueline. *A Spectacular Secret: Lynching in American Life and Literature*. Chicago: Univ. of Chicago Press, 2006.

Golston, Robert. *The Great Depression: The United States in the Thirties*. Indianapolis: Bobbs-Merrill Company, 1968.

Goluboff, Risa Lauren. *The Lost Promise of Civil Rights*. Cambridge, Mass.: Harvard Univ. Press, 2007.

Gonzales-Day, Ken. *Lynching in the West, 1850-1935.* Durham, N.C.: Duke Univ. Press, 2006.

Goode, Richard C. "The Godly Insurrection in Limestone County: Social Gospel, Populism, and Southern Culture in the Late Nineteenth Century." *Religion and Culture* (1992): 155-69.

Goodman, James. *Stories of Scottsboro.* New York: Pantheon Books, 1994.

Goodman, Paul. *Of One Blood: Abolitionism and the Origins of Racial Equality.* Berkeley: Univ. of California Press, 1998.

Goodwyn, Lawrence. *Democratic Promise: The Populist Moment in America.* New York: Oxford Univ. Press, 1976.

Gordon, Ann D., et al., eds. *African American Women and the Vote, 1837-1965.* Amherst: Univ. of Massachusetts Press, 1997.

Gordon, John B. *Reminiscences of the Civil War.* New York: Charles Scribner's Sons, 1903.

Graham, Hugh Davis. *Crisis in Print: Desegregation and the Press in Tennessee.* Nashville: Vanderbilt Univ. Press, 1967.

Graham, Otis L. "Again the Backward Region? Environmental History in and of the American South." *Southern Cultures* 6, no. 2 (2000): 50-72. doi:10.1353scu.2000.0000.

Grandin, Greg. *Fordlandia: The Rise and Fall of Henry Ford's Forgotten Jungle City.* New York: Metropolitan Books, 2009.

Grant, Kevin. *A Civilised Savagery: Britain and the New Slaveries in Africa, 1884-1926.* New York: Routledge, 2005.

Grantham, Dewey. *The Life and Death of the Solid South: A Political History.* Lexington: Univ. of Kentucky Press, 1988.

Gray, Lewis Cecil. *History of Agriculture in the Southern United States to 1860.* Washington, D.C.: Carnegie Institution of Washington, 1933.

Green, Elna C. *Southern Strategies: Southern Women and the Woman Suffrage Question.* Chapel Hill: Univ. of North Carolina Press, 1997.

Green, James R. *Grass-Roots Socialism: Radical Movements in the Southwest, 1895-1943.* Baton Rouge: Louisiana State Univ. Press, 1978.

Greenberg, Stanley B. *Race and State in Capitalist Development: Comparative Perspectives.* New Haven, Conn.: Yale Univ. Press, 1980.

Greene, Julie. *The Canal Builders: Making America's Empire at the Panama Canal.* New York: Penguin Press, 2009.

Gregg, Sara M. *Managing the Mountains: Land Use Planning, the New Deal, and the Creation of a Federal Landscape in Appalachia.* New Haven, Conn.: Yale Univ. Press, 2010.

———. "Uncovering the Subsistence Economy in the Twentieth-Century South: Blue Ridge Mountain Farms." *Agricultural History* 78, no. 4 (2004): 417-37.

Griffith, Barbara S. *The Crisis of American Labor: Operation Dixie and the Defeat of the CIO.* Philadelphia: Temple Univ. Press, 1988.

Grubbs, Donald H. *Cry from the Cotton: The Southern Tenant Farmers' Union and the New Deal.* Chapel Hill: Univ. of North Carolina Press, 1971.

Guglielmo, Thomas A. "Fighting for Caucasian Rights: Mexicans, Mexican-Americans, and the Transnational Struggle for Civil Rights in World War II Texas." *Journal of American History* 92 (Mar. 2006): 1212-37.

————. "Red Cross, Double Cross: Race and America's World War II-Era Blood Donor Service." *Journal of American History* 97, no. 1 (June 2010): 63-90.

Gunning, Sandra. *Race, Rape, and Lynching: The Red Record of American Literature, 1890-1912.* New York: Oxford Univ. Press, 1996.

Guridy, Frank Andre. *Forging Diaspora: Afro-Cubans and African Americans in a World of Empire and Jim Crow.* Chapel Hill: Univ. of North Carolina Press, 2010.

Gutman, Herbert G. "The Negro and the United Mine Workers of America." In *The Negro and the American Labor Movement,* ed. Julius Jacobson, 49-127. Garden City, N.Y.: Anchor Books, 1968.

Gwin, Minrose. *Remembering Medgar Evers: Writing the Long Civil Rights Movement.* Athens: Univ. of Georgia Press, 2013.

Haberland, Michelle. "After the Wives Went to Work: Organizing Women in the Southern Apparel Industry." In *"Lives Full of Struggle and Triumph": Southern Women, Their Institutions, and Their Communities,* ed. Bruce L. Clayton and John A. Salmond, 283-302. Gainesville: Univ. Press of Florida, 2003.

————. "'It Takes a Special Kind of Woman to Work Up There': Race, Gender and the Impact of the Apparel Industry on Clarke County, Alabama, 1937-1980." In *Work, Family and Faith: Rural Southern Women in the Twentieth Century,* ed. Melissa Walker and Rebecca Sharpless, 257-82. Columbia: Univ. of Missouri Press, 2006.

————. "Look for the Union Label: Organizing Women Workers and Women Consumers in the Southern Apparel Industry." In *Entering the Fray: Gender, Politics, and Culture in the New South,* ed. Jonathan Daniel Wells and Sheila R. Phipps, 184-202. Columbia: Univ. of Missouri Press, 2010.

Hackney, Sheldon. *Populism to Progressivism in Alabama.* Princeton, N.J.: Princeton Univ. Press, 1969.

Hagood, Margaret Jarmon. *Mothers of the South.* New York: W. W. Norton and Company, 1977.

Hahamovitch, Cindy. *The Fruits of Their Labor: Atlantic Coast Farmworkers and the Making of Migrant Poverty, 1870-1945.* Chapel Hill: Univ. of North Carolina Press, 1997.

————. *No Man's Land: Jamaican Guestworkers in America and the Global Economy.* Princeton, N.J.: Princeton Univ. Press, 2011.

————. "Standing Idly By: 'Organized' Farmworkers in South Florida during the Depression and World War II." In *Southern Labor in Transition,* ed. Robert H. Zieger, 15-36. Knoxville: Univ. of Tennessee Press, 1997.

Hahn, Steven. "Hunting, Fishing, and Foraging: Common Rights and Class Relations in the Postbellum South." *Radical History Review* 26 (1982): 37-64.

————. *A Nation under Our Feet: Black Political Struggles in the Rural South from Slavery to the Great Migration.* Cambridge, Mass.: Harvard Univ. Press, 2003.

————. *A Nation without Borders: The United States and Its World in an Age of Civil Wars, 1830-1910.* New York: Viking, 2016.

————. *The Roots of Southern Populism: Yeoman Farmers and the Transformation of the Georgia Upcountry, 1850-1890.* New York: Oxford Univ. Press, 1985.

Halberstam, David. *The Children.* New York: Random House, 1988.

Hale, Grace Elizabeth. *Making Whiteness: The Culture of Segregation in the South, 1890-1940.* New York: Pantheon, 1998.

Hall, Jacquelyn Dowd. "Disorderly Women: Gender and Labor Militancy in the Appalachian South." *Journal of American History* 73, no. 2 (Sept. 1986): 354-82.

———. "The Long Civil Rights Movement and the Political Uses of the Past." *Journal of American History* 91 (Mar. 2005): 1233-63.

———. *Revolt against Chivalry: Jessie Daniel Ames and the Women's Campaign against Lynching.* New York: Columbia Univ. Press, 1979.

———, Robert Korstad, and James Leloudis. "Cotton Mill People: Work, Community, and Protest in the Textile South, 1880-1940." *American Historical Review* 91, no. 2 (Apr. 1986): 245-86.

———, James Leloudis, Robert Korstad, Mary Murphy, Lu Ann Jones, and Christopher B. Daly. *Like a Family: The Making of a Southern Cotton Mill World.* Chapel Hill: Univ. of North Carolina Press, 1987.

Halpern, Rick. "The CIO and the Limits of Labor-Based Civil Rights Activism: The Case of Louisiana's Sugar Workers, 1947-1966." In *Southern Labor in Transition,* ed. Robert H. Zieger, 86-112. Knoxville: Univ. of Tennessee Press, 1997.

———. "Interracial Unionism in the Southwest: Fort Worth's Packinghouse Workers, 1937-1954." In *Organized Labor in the Twentieth-Century South,* ed. Robert H. Zieger, 158-82. Knoxville: Univ. of Tennessee Press, 1991.

Hamilton, David E., ed. *The New Deal.* Boston: Houghton Mifflin Company, 1999.

Hamilton, Joseph Gregoire de Roulhac. *Reconstruction in North Carolina.* Gloucester, Mass.: Smith, 1914.

Hamilton, Shane. "Poisons in the Land." *Reviews in American History* 34, no. 1 (2006): 64-71.

Hampton, Henry, and Steve Fraser, eds. *Voices of Freedom: An Oral History of the Civil Rights Movement from the 1950s through the 1980s.* New York: Bantam Books, 1990.

Hanson, Joyce A. *Mary McLeod Bethune and Black Women's Political Activism.* Columbia: Univ. of Missouri Press, 2003.

Harding, Vincent. *There Is a River: The Black Struggle for Freedom in America.* New York: Harcourt, Brace and Co., 1981.

Harper, Kimberly. *White Man's Heaven: The Lynching and Expulsion of Blacks in the Southern Ozarks, 1894-1909.* Fayetteville: Univ. of Arkansas Press, 2010.

Harris, Trudier. *Exorcising Blackness: Historical and Literary Lynching and Burning Rituals.* Bloomington: Indiana Univ. Press, 1984.

Hartmann, Susan M. *The Homefront and Beyond: American Women in the 1940s.* Boston: Twayne Pubs., 1982.

Harvey, James C. *Black Civil Rights during the Johnson Administration.* Jackson: Univ. and College Press of Mississippi, 1973.

Harvey, Paul. *Freedom's Coming: Religious Culture and the Shaping of the South from the Civil War through the Civil Rights Era.* Chapel Hill: Univ. of North Carolina Press, 2005.

Hay, Melba Porter. *Madeline McDowell Breckinridge and the Battle for a New South.* Foreword by Marjorie Julian Spruill. Lexington: Univ. Press of Kentucky, 2009.

Haygood, Tamara Miner. "Cows, Ticks, and Disease: A Medical Interpretation of the Southern Cattle Industry." *Journal of Southern History* 52, no. 4 (Nov. 1986): 551-64.

Henderson, Harry L., and David B. Woolner. *FDR and the Environment.* New York: Palgrave Macmillan, 2005.

Hersey, Mark D. Review of *Environmental History and the American South: A Reader,* ed. Paul S. Sutter and Christopher J. Manganiello. *Organization and Environment* 23, no. 2 (2010): 240-42.

———. *My Work Is That of Conservation: An Environmental Biography of George Washington Carver.* Athens: Univ. of Georgia Press, 2011.

Hesseltine, William B. Review of *Origins of the New South, 1877-1913,* by C. Vann Woodward. *American Historical Review* 57 (July 1952): 993-94.

Hewitt, Nancy A. *Southern Discomfort: Women's Activism in Tampa, Florida, 1880s-1920s.* Urbana: Univ. of Illinois Press, 2001.

Hickey, Georgina. *Hope and Danger in the New South City: Working-Class Women and Urban Development in Atlanta, 1890-1940.* Athens: Univ. of Georgia Press, 2003.

Hicks, John D. *The Populist Revolt: The Farmers' Alliance and the People's Party.* Minneapolis: Univ. of Minnesota Press, 1931.

Higginbotham, Evelyn Brooks. *Righteous Discontent: The Women's Movement in the Black Baptist Church, 1880-1920.* Cambridge, Mass.: Harvard Univ. Press, 1993.

Hild, Matthew. *Greenbackers, Knights of Labor, and Populists: Farmer-Labor Insurgency in the Late-Nineteenth Century South.* Athens: Univ. of Georgia Press, 2007.

Hill, Lance. *The Deacons for Defense: Armed Resistance and the Civil Rights Movement.* Chapel Hill: Univ. of North Carolina Press, 2004.

Hill, Rebecca N. *Men, Mobs, and Law: Anti-Lynching and Labor Defense in U.S. Radical History.* Durham, N.C.: Duke Univ. Press, 2008.

———. "Men, Mobs, and Law: Defense Campaigns and U.S. Radical History." Ph.D. diss., Univ. of Minnesota, 2000.

Hine, Darlene Clark. *Black Victory: The Rise and Fall of the White Primary in Texas.* Millwood, N.Y.: KTP Press, 1979.

———. "Rape and the Inner Lives of Southern Black Women: Thoughts on the Culture of Dissemblance." In *Southern Women: Histories and Identities,* ed. Virginia Bernhard, Betty Brandon, Elizabeth Fox-Genovese, and Theda Perdue, 177-189. Columbia: Univ. of Missouri Press, 1992.

———, and Christie Anne Farnham. "Black Women's Culture of Resistance and the Right to Vote." In *Women of the American South: A Multicultural Reader,* ed. Christie Anne Farnham, 204-219. New York: New York Univ. Press, 1997.

"Historical News." *North Carolina Historical Review* 9 (Apr. 1932): 220.

Hobsbawm, Eric J. *The Age of Capital: 1848-1875.* 1962. Reprint, New York: Vintage, 1996.

Hodes, Martha Elizabeth. *White Women, Black Men: Illicit Sex in the Nineteenth-Century South.* New Haven, Conn.: Yale Univ. Press, 1997.

Hodges, James A. *New Deal Labor Policy and the Southern Cotton Textile Industry, 1933-1941.* Knoxville: Univ. of Tennessee Press, 1986.

Hofstadter, Richard. *The Age of Reform: From Bryan to FDR.* New York: Vintage, 1955.

Hollars, B. J. *Thirteen Loops: Race, Violence, and the Last Lynching in America.* Tuscaloosa: Univ. of Alabama Press, 2011.

Holley, Donald. *Uncle Sam's Farmers: The New Deal Communities in the Lower Mississippi Valley.* Urbana: Univ. of Illinois Press, 1975.

Holley, William C., Ellen Winston, and T. J. Woofter Jr. *The Plantation South, 1934-1937*. Research Monograph XXII, Division of Research, Federal Works Agency, Works Progress Administration. Washington, D.C.: GPO, 1940.

Holmes, William F. "Populism in Search of Context." *Agricultural History* 64 (Fall 1990): 26-58.

Holt, Marilyn Irvin. *Linoleum, Better Babies, and the Modern Farm Woman, 1890-1930*. Lincoln: Univ. of Nebraska Press, 2006.

Holt, Thomas C. *The Problem of Freedom: Race, Labor, and Politics in Jamaica and Britain, 1832-1938*. Baltimore: Johns Hopkins Univ. Press, 1992.

Honeck, Mischa. *We Are the Revolutionists: German-Speaking Immigrants and American Abolitionists after 1848*. Athens: Univ. of Georgia Press, 2011.

Honey, Michael K. *Going down Jericho Road: The Memphis Strike, Martin Luther King's Last Campaign*. New York: W. W. Norton, 2007.

———. "Martin Luther King, Jr., the Crisis of the Black Working Class, and the Memphis Sanitation Strike." In *Southern Labor in Transition, 1940-1995*, ed. Robert H, Zieger, 146-75. Knoxville: Univ. of Tennessee Press, 1997.

———. *Southern Labor and Black Civil Rights: Organizing Memphis Workers*. Urbana: Univ. of Illinois Press, 1993.

———, and Solomon Barkin. "'Operation Dixie': Two Views." *Labor History* 31, no. 3 (Summer 1990): 373-85.

Horne, Gerald. *Communist Front? The Civil Rights Congress, 1946-1956*. Rutherford, N.J.: Fairleigh Dickinson Univ. Press, 1988.

Houck, Davis W., and David E. Dixon, eds. *Women and the Civil Rights Movement, 1954-1965*. Jackson: Univ. Press of Mississippi, 2009.

Howard, John. *Concentration Camps on the Home Front: Japanese Americans in the House of Jim Crow*. Chicago: Univ. of Chicago Press, 2008.

Howard, Walter T. *Lynchings: Extralegal Violence in Florida during the 1930s*. Selinsgrove, Pa.: Susquehanna Univ. Press, 1995.

Howe, Daniel Walker. *What Hath God Wrought: The Transformation of America, 1815-1848*. New York: Oxford Univ. Press, 2007.

Hulsemann, Karsten. "Greenfields in the Heart of Dixie: How the American Auto Industry Discovered the South." In *The Second Wave: Southern Industrialization from the 1940s to the 1970s*, ed. Philip Scranton, 219-54. Athens: Univ. of Georgia Press.

Humphreys, James S. *Francis Butler Simkins: A Life*. Gainesville: Univ. Press of Florida, 2008.

———. "William Archibald Dunning: Flawed Colossus of American Letters." In *The Dunning School: Historians, Race, and the Meaning of Reconstruction*, ed. John David Smith and J. Vincent Lowery, 77-105. Lexington: Univ. Press of Kentucky, 2013.

Humphreys, Margaret. *Yellow Fever and the South*. Baltimore: Johns Hopkins Univ. Press, 1999.

Hunt, James L. *Marion Butler and American Populism*. Chapel Hill: Univ. of North Carolina Press, 2003.

Hunter, Tera W. "Domination and Resistance: The Politics of Wage Household Labor in New South Atlanta." *Labor History* 34, no. 2-3 (Spring-Summer 1993): 205-20.

———. *To 'Joy My Freedom: Southern Black Women's Lives and Labors after the Civil War.* Cambridge, Mass.: Harvard Univ. Press, 1997.

———. "'Work That Body': African-American Women, Work, and Leisure in Atlanta and the New South." In *Labor Histories: Class, Politics, and the Working-Class Experience,* ed. Eric Arnesen, Julie Green, and Bruce Laurie, 153-74. Urbana: Univ. of Illinois Press, 1998.

Huntley, Horace. "The Red Scare and Black Workers in Alabama: The International Union of Mine, Mill, and Smelter Workers, 1945-53." In *Labor Divided: Race and Ethnicity in United States Labor Struggles, 1835-1960,* ed. Robert Asher and Charles Stephenson, 129-45. Albany: State Univ. of New York Press, 1990.

Ifill, Sherrilyn A. *On the Courthouse Lawn: Confronting the Legacy of Lynching in the Twenty-first Century.* Boston: Beacon Press, 2007.

Ignatiev, Noel. *How the Irish Became White.* 1995. Reprint, New York: Routledge, 2009.

Irons, Janet. *Testing the New Deal: The General Textile Strike of 1934 in the American South.* Urbana: Univ. of Illinois Press, 2000.

Isaacman, Allen, and Richard Roberts, eds. *Cotton, Colonialism, and Social History in Sub-Saharan Africa.* Portsmouth, N.H.: Heinemann, 1995.

Jabour, Anya. *Scarlett's Sisters: Young Women in the Old South.* Chapel Hill: Univ. of North Carolina Press, 2007.

Jackson, Harvey H. *Rivers of History: Life on the Coosa, Tallapoosa, Cahaba, and Alabama.* Tuscaloosa: Univ. of Alabama Press, 1995.

Jacobson, Matthew Frye. *Barbarian Virtues: The United States Encounters Foreign Peoples at Home and Abroad, 1876-1917.* New York: Hill and Wang, 2000.

Jacoway, Elizabeth. *Turn Away Thy Son: Little Rock, the Crisis That Shocked the Nation.* Fayetteville: Univ. of Arkansas Press, 2008.

———, and C. Fred Williams, eds. *Understanding the Little Rock Crisis: An Exercise in Remembrance and Reconciliation.* Fayetteville: Univ. of Arkansas Press, 1982.

James, C. L. R. *The Black Jacobins: Toussaint L'Ouverture and the San Domingo Revolution,* 2nd ed. 1938. Reprint, New York: Vintage, 1989.

Janiewski, Dolores E. *Sisterhood Denied: Race, Gender, and Class in a New South Community.* Philadelphia: Temple Univ. Press, 1985.

Janney, Caroline E. *Burying the Dead but Not the Past: Ladies' Memorial Associations and the Lost Cause.* Chapel Hill: Univ. of North Carolina Press, 2008.

Jaspin, Elliott. *Buried in Bitter Waters: The Hidden History of Racial Cleansing in America.* New York: Basic Books, 2007.

Jeffrey, Julie Roy. "The Women in the Southern Farmers' Alliance: A Reconsideration of Their Role and Status in the Late Nineteenth-Century South." *Feminist Studies* 3 (1975): 72-91.

Jenkins, William S. *Pro-Slavery Thought in the Old South.* Chapel Hill: Univ. of North Carolina Press, 1935.

Jenness, Valerie, and Ryken Grattet. *Making Hate a Crime: From Social Movement to Law Enforcement.* New York: Russell Sage Foundation, 2001.

Johnson, Cedric. *Revolutionaries to Race Leaders: Black Power and the Making of African American Politics.* Minneapolis: Univ. of Minnesota Press, 2007.

Johnson, Charles Spurgeon. *Shadow of the Plantation.* Chicago: Univ. of Chicago Press, 1934.

Johnson, Guion Griffis. *A Social History of the Sea Islands of South Carolina and Georgia with Special Reference to St. Helena, South Carolina.* Chapel Hill: Univ. of North Carolina Press, 1930.

Johnson, Guy Benton, and Guion Griffis Johnson. *Research in Service to Society: The First Fifty Years of the Institute for Research in Social Science at the Univ. of North Carolina.* Chapel Hill: Univ. of North Carolina Press, 1980.

Johnson, Joan Marie. *Southern Women at the Seven Sisters Colleges: Feminist Values and Social Activism, 1875-1915.* Athens: Univ. of Georgia Press, 2008.

Johnson, Walter. "Historians Join the March on Montgomery." *South Atlantic Quarterly* 74 (Spring 1980): 158-74.

———. *Southern Ladies, New Women: Race, Region, and Clubwomen in South Carolina, 1890-1930.* Gainesville: Univ. Press of Florida, 2004.

———. *Southern Women at Vassar: The Poppenheim Family Letters, 1882-1916.* Columbia: Univ. of South Carolina Press, 2002.

Jonas, Gilbert. *Freedom's Sword: The NAACP and the Struggle against Racism in America, 1909-1969.* New York: Routledge, 2005.

Jones, Jacqueline. *American Work: Four Centuries of Black and White Labor.* New York: W. W. Norton, 1998.

———. *Labor of Love, Labor of Sorrow: Black Women, Work, and the Family, from Slavery to the Present.* New York: Basic Books, 1985.

Jones, Lu Ann. *Mama Learned Us to Work: Farm Women in the New South.* Chapel Hill: Univ. of North Carolina Press, 2002.

Jones, William P. *The Tribe of Black Ulysses: African American Lumber Workers in the Jim Crow South.* Urbana: Univ. of Illinois Press, 2005.

Jong, Greta de. *A Different Day: African American Struggles for Justice in Rural Louisiana, 1900-1970.* Chapel Hill: Univ. of North Carolina Press, 2002.

———. "'With the Aid of God and the F.S.A.': The Louisiana Farmers' Union and the African America Freedom Struggle in the New Deal Era." *Journal of Social History* 34, no. 1 (2000): 105-39.

Joseph, Peniel E. *The Black Power Movement: Rethinking the Civil Rights-Black Power Era.* New York: Routledge, 2006.

Jung, Moon-Ho. *Coolies and Cane: Race, Labor, and Sugar in the Age of Emancipation.* Baltimore: Johns Hopkins Univ. Press, 2006.

Kahrl, Andrew W. *The Land Was Ours: African American Beaches from Jim Crow to the Sunbelt South.* Cambridge, Mass.: Harvard Univ. Press, 2012.

Kalk, Bruce H. *The Origins of the Southern Strategy: Two-Party Competition in South Carolina, 1950-1972.* Lanham, Mass.: Lexington Books, 2001.

Kaplan, Amy. *The Anarchy of Empire in the Making of U.S. Culture.* Cambridge, Mass.: Harvard Univ. Press, 2002.

Katz, Philip M. *From Appomattox to Montmartre: Americans and the Paris Commune.* Cambridge, Mass.: Harvard Univ. Press, 1998.

Kaufman, Bruce E. "The Emergence and Growth of a Nonunion Sector in the Southern Paper Industry." In *Southern Labor in Transition,* ed. Robert H. Zieger, 295-329. Knoxville: Univ. of Tennessee Press, 1997.

Kaye, Anthony E. "The Second Slavery: Modernity in the Nineteenth-Century South and the Atlantic World." *Journal of Southern History* 75 (2009): 627-50.

Kazin, Michael. *The Populist Persuasion: An American History.* New York: Basic Books, 1995.

Keiner, Christine. *The Oyster Question: Scientists, Watermen, and the Maryland Chesapeake Bay Since 1880.* Athens: Univ. of Georgia Press, 2010.

Kellar, William Henry. *Make Haste Slowly: Moderates, Conservatives, and School Desegregation in Houston.* College Station: Texas A&M Univ. Press, 1999.

Kelley, Brian. *Race, Class, and Power in the Alabama Coalfields, 1908-21.* Urbana: Univ. of Illinois Press, 2001.

Kelley, Robin D. G. *Hammer and Hoe: Alabama Communists during the Great Depression.* Chapel Hill: Univ. of North Carolina Press, 1990.

———. *Race Rebels: Culture, Politics, and the Black Working Class.* New York: The Free Press, 1994.

———. "We Are Not What We Seem: Rethinking Black Working Class Opposition in the Jim Crow South." *Journal of American History* 80 (June 1993): 75-112.

———, and Earl Lewis. *To Make Our World Anew: A History of African Americans.* Oxford: Oxford Univ. Press, 2000.

Kelman, Ari. *A River and Its City: The Nature of Landscape in New Orleans.* Oakland: Univ. of California Press, 2003.

Key Jr., V. O. *Southern Politics in State and Nation.* New York: Vintage Books, 1949.

King Jr., Martin Luther. *The Papers of Martin Luther King, Jr.* Ed. Clayborne Carson. 6 vols. Berkeley: Univ. of California Press, 1992-2007.

———. *Strength to Love.* New York: Harper and Row, 1963.

———. *Stride Towards Freedom: The Montgomery Story.* New York: Harper and Brothers, 1958.

———. *The Trumpet of Conscience.* New York: Harper and Row, 1967.

———. *Where Do We Go From Here: Chaos or Community?* New York: Harper and Row, 1967.

———. *Why We Can't Wait.* New York: HarperCollins, 1963.

———. *Why We Can't Wait.* New York: New American Library, 1964.

King, Mary. *Freedom Song: A Personal Story of the Civil Rights Movement.* New York: William Morrow and Company, 1987.

Kinshasa, Kwando Mbiassi. *Black Resistance to the Ku Klux Klan in the Wake of the Civil War.* Jefferson, N.C.: McFarland, 2006.

Kirby, Jack Temple. *The Countercultural South.* Athens: Univ. of Georgia Press, 1995.

———. *Darkness at the Dawning: Race and Reform in the Progressive South.* Philadelphia: Lippincott, 1972.

———. *Media-Made Dixie: The South in the American Imagination.* Baton Rouge: Louisiana State Univ. Press, 1978.

———. *Mockingbird Song: Ecological Landscapes of the South.* Chapel Hill: Univ. of North Carolina Press, 2006.

———. *Poquosin: A Study of Rural Landscape and Society.* Chapel Hill: Univ. of North Carolina Press, 1995.

———. *Rural Worlds Lost: The American South, 1920-1960.* Baton Rouge: Louisiana State Univ. Press, 1987.

Klarman, Michael J. *From Jim Crow to Civil Rights: The Supreme Court and the Struggle for Racial Equality.* New York: Oxford Univ. Press, 2004.

Kluger, Richard. *Simple Justice: The History of Brown v. Board of Education and Black America's Struggle for Equality.* 1976. Rev. ed. New York: Knopf, 2004.

K'Meyer, Tracy. *Civil Rights in the Gateway to the South: Louisville, Kentucky, 1945-1980.* Lexington: Univ. Press of Kentucky, 2009.

Kohn, Sally. "Race Baiting at the RNC." Salon.com. http://www.salon.com/2012/08/29/race_baiting_at_the_rnc/ (accessed Aug. 31, 2012).

Kolchin, Peter. *A Sphinx on the American Land: The Nineteenth-Century South in Comparative Perspective.* Baton Rouge: Louisiana State Univ. Press, 2003.

Korstad, Robert R. *Civil Rights Unionism: Tobacco Workers and the Struggle for Democracy in the Mid-Twentieth Century South.* Chapel Hill: Univ. of North Carolina Press, 2003.

———, and James L. Leloudis. *To Right These Wrongs: The North Carolina Fund and the Battle to End Poverty and Inequality in 1960s America.* Chapel Hill: Univ. of North Carolina Press, 2010.

———, and Nelson Lichtenstein. "Opportunities Found and Lost: Labor, Radicals, and the Early Civil Rights Movement." *Journal of American History* 75 (Dec. 1988): 786-811.

Kotz, Nick. *Judgment Days: Lyndon Baines Johnson, Martin Luther King, Jr., and the Laws that Changed America.* New York: Houghton Mifflin, 2005.

Kousser, J. Morgan. *Colorblind Injustice: Minority Voting Rights and the Undoing of the Second Reconstruction.* Chapel Hill: Univ. of North Carolina Press, 1999.

———. *The Shaping of Southern Politics: Suffrage Restriction and the Establishment of the One-Party South, 1880-1910.* New Haven, Conn.: Yale Univ. Press, 1974.

Kramer, Paul A. *The Blood of Government: Race, Empire, the United States, and the Philippines.* Chapel Hill: Univ. of North Carolina Press, 2006.

Krochmal, Max. "An Unmistakably Working-Class Vision: Birmingham's Foot Soldiers and Their Civil Rights Movement." *Journal of Southern History* 76, no. 4 (Nov. 2010): 923-60.

———. "Chicano Labor and Multiracial Politics in Post-World War II Texas: Two Case Studies." In *Life and Labor in the New New South: Essays in Southern Labor History since 1950,* ed. Robert H. Zieger, 133-76. Gainesville: Univ. Press of Florida, 2012.

Kruse, Kevin. *White Flight: Atlanta and the Making of Modern Conservatism.* Princeton, N.J.: Princeton Univ. Press, 2005.

———, and Stephen Tuck, eds. *The Fog of War: The Second World War and the Civil Rights Movement.* New York: Oxford Univ. Press, 2012.

Lake, Marilyn, and Henry Reynolds. *Drawing the Global Colour Line: White Men's Countries and the International Challenge of Racial Equality.* Cambridge: Cambridge Univ. Press, 2008.

Lamis, Alexander. *The Two-Party South.* 2nd expanded ed. New York: Oxford Univ. Press, 1990.

Larsen, Torben Huus. *Enduring Pastoral: Recycling the Middle Landscape Ideal in the Tennessee Valley.* Atlanta: Rodopi, 2010.

Lassiter, Matthew D., and Joseph Crespino, eds. *The Myth of Southern Exceptionalism.* New York: Oxford Univ. Press, 2010.

———. "Introduction: The End of Southern History." In *The Myth of Southern Exceptionalism,* ed. Lassiter and Crespino, 3-22. New York: Oxford Univ. Press, 2010.

Lassiter, Matthew D., and Andrew Lewis. *The Moderate's Dilemma: Massive Resistance to School Desegregation in Virginia.* Charlottesville: Univ. Press of Virginia, 1998.

———. *The Silent Majority: Suburban Politics in the Sunbelt South.* Princeton, N.J.: Princeton Univ. Press, 2006.

Lavergne, Gary M. *Before Brown: Herman Marion Sweatt, Thurgood Marshall, and the Long Road to Justice.* Austin: Univ. of Texas Press, 2010.

Lawson, Steven F. *Black Ballots: Voting Rights in the American South, 1944-1969.* New York: Columbia Univ. Press, 1976.

———. "Freedom Then, Freedom Now: The Historiography of the Civil Rights Movement." *American Historical Review* 96 (Apr. 1991): 456-71.

———. "Freedom Then, Freedom Now." In *Civil Rights Crossroads: Nation, Community, and the Black Freedom Struggle,* 3-28. Lexington: Univ. Press of Kentucky, 2003.

———. "Long Origins of the Short Civil Rights Movement, 1954-1968." In *Freedom Rights: New Perspectives on the Civil Rights Movement,* ed. Danielle L. McGuire and John Dittmer, 9-37. Lexington: Univ. Press of Kentucky, 2011.

———, and Charles Payne, eds. *Debating the Civil Rights Movement, 1945-1968.* 2nd ed. Lanham, Md.: Rowman and Littlefield, 2006.

Lee, Chana Kai. *For Freedom's Sake: The Life of Fannie Lou Hamer.* Champaign: Univ. of Illinois Press, 1999.

Leiken, Steve. *The Practical Utopians: American Workers and the Cooperative Movement in the Gilded Age.* Detroit: Wayne State Univ. Press, 2005.

Leonard, Stephen. *Lynching in Colorado, 1859-1919.* Boulder: Univ. Press of Colorado, 2002.

Lerner, Gerda, ed. *Black Women in White America: A Documentary History.* New York: Pantheon Books, 1972.

———. *The Grimké Sisters of South Carolina: Pioneers for Women's Rights and Abolition.* New York: Oxford Univ. Press, 1998.

———. *The Grimkè Sisters of South Carolina: Rebels against Slavery.* Boston: Houghton Mifflin, 1967.

———. "Introduction." In *The Grimké Sisters from South Carolina: Pioneers for Women's Rights and Abolition,* xv-xix. Rev. and expanded ed. Chapel Hill: Univ. of North Carolina Press, 2004.

Lester, Connie L. "'Let Us Be Up and Doing': Women in the Tennessee Movements for Agrarian Reform, 1870-1892." *Tennessee Historical Quarterly* 54 (1995): 80-97.

———. *Up from the Mudsills of Hell: The Farmers' Alliance, Populism, and Progressive Agriculture in Tennessee, 1870-1915.* Athens: Univ. of Georgia Press, 2006.

Letwin, Daniel. *The Challenge of Interracial Unionism: Alabama Coal Miners, 1878-1921.* Chapel Hill: Univ. of North Carolina Press, 1998.

Levine, Bruce. *The Spirit of 1848: German Immigrants, Labor Conflict, and the Coming of the Civil War.* Urbana: Univ. of Illinois Press, 1992.

Lewis, Anthony. *Portrait of a Decade: The Second American Revolution.* New York: Random House, 1964.

Lewis, David Levering. *King: A Biography.* Urbana: Univ. of Illinois Press, 1970.

———. *King: A Critical Biography.* New York: Praeger, 1970.

———. *W. E. B. Du Bois: The Fight for Equality and the American Century 1919-1963.* New York: Henry Holt, 2000.

Lewis, John. *Walking with the Wind: A Memoir of the Movement.* New York: Simon and Schuster, 1998.

Lewis, Ronald L. *Transforming the Appalachian Countryside: Railroads, Deforestation, and Social Change in West Virginia, 1880-1920.* Chapel Hill: Univ. of North Carolina Press, 1998.

Lichtenstein, Alex. "Exclusion, Fair Employment, or Interracial Unionism: Race Relations in Florida's Shipyards during World War II." In *Life and Labor in the New New South: Essays in Southern Labor History since 1950,* ed. Robert H. Zieger, 135-57. Gainesville: Univ. Press of Florida, 2012.

———. "Racial Conflict and Solidarity in the Alabama Coal Strike of 1894: New Evidence in the Gutman-Hill Debate." *Labor History* 36, no. 1 (Winter 1995): 63-76.

———. *The Retail Revolution: How Wal-Mart Created a Brave New World of Business.* New York: Metropolitan Books/Henry Holt, 2009.

———. "'Scientific Unionism' and the 'Negro Question': Communists and the Transport Workers Union in Miami, 1947-1966." In *Southern Labor in Transition,* ed. Robert H. Zieger, 58-85. Knoxville: Univ. of Tennessee Press, 1997.

———. "'We at Last Are Industrializing the Whole Ding-busted Party': The Communist Party and Florida Workers in Depression and War." In *Florida's Working-Class Past: Current Perspectives on Labor, Race, and Gender from Spanish Florida to the New Immigration,* ed. Robert Cassanello and Melanie Shell-Weiss, 168-97. Gainesville: Univ. Press of Florida, 2009.

Lightweis-Goff, Jennie. *Blood at the Root: Lynching as American Cultural Nucleus.* Albany: State Univ. of New York Press, 2011.

Linebaugh, Peter, and Marcus Rediker. "The Many-Headed Hydra: Sailors, Slaves, and the Atlantic Working Class in the Eighteenth Century." *Journal of Historical Sociology* 3 (1990): 225-52.

Ling, Peter J. *Gender and the Civil Rights Movement.* Piscataway, N.J.: Rutgers Univ. Press, 2004.

Link, Arthur S., and Rembert W. Patrick, eds. *Writing Southern History: Essays in Historiography in Honor of Fletcher M. Green.* Baton Rouge: Louisiana State Univ. Press, 1965.

Litwack, Leon. *Trouble in Mind: Black Southerners in the Age of Jim Crow.* New York: Alfred A. Knopf, 1999.

Loewen, James W. *Sundown Towns: A Hidden Dimension of American Racism.* New York: New Press, 2005.

Logan, Rayford W. *The Negro in American Life and Thought: The Nadir, 1877-1901.* New York: The Dial Press, 1954.

———. *What the Negro Wants.* Chapel Hill: Univ. of North Carolina Press, 1944.

Long, Alecia P. *The Great Southern Babylon: Sex, Race, and Respectability in New Orleans, 1865-1920.* Baton Rouge: Louisiana State Univ. Press, 2004.

Long, David, and Brian C. Schmidt, eds. *Imperialism and Internationalism in the Discipline of International Relations.* Albany: State Univ. of New York Press, 2005.

Longstreet, James. *From Manassas to Appomattox.* Philadelphia: J. B. Lippincott Company, 1896.

Losurdo, Domenico. *Liberalism: A Counter-History.* Trans. Gregory Elliott. London: Verso Books, 2011.

Lott, Eric. *Love and Theft: Blackface Minstrelsy and the American Working Class.* New York: Oxford Univ. Press, 1993.

Louis Round Wilson Library Special Collection. "About the Southern Historical Collection." http//library.unc.edu/Wilson/shc/sbout/ (accessed January 31, 2016).

Love, Eric T. *Race over Empire: Racism and U.S. Imperialism, 1865-1900.* Chapel Hill: Univ. of North Carolina Press, 2004.

Lovejoy, Paul E. *Transformations in Slavery: A History of Slavery in Africa,* 2nd ed. Cambridge: Cambridge Univ. Press, 2000.

Lowndes, Joseph E. *From the New Deal to the New Right: Race and the Southern Origins of Modern Conservatism.* New Haven, Conn.: Yale Univ. Press, 2008.

Lubin, David. *The Republican South: Democratization and Partisan Change.* Princeton, N.J.: Princeton Univ. Press, 2004.

Lutts, Ralph H. "Like Manna from God: The American Chestnut Trade in Southwestern Virginia." *Environmental History* 9 (July 2004): 497-525.

Lynn, Martin. *Commerce and Economic Change in West Africa: The Palm Oil Trade in the Nineteenth Century.* Cambridge: Cambridge Univ. Press, 1997.

MacLean, Nancy. *Behind the Mask of Chivalry: The Making of the Second Ku Klux Klan.* New York: Oxford Univ. Press, 1994.

Maddex Jr., Jack P. *The Reconstruction of Edward A. Pollard: A Rebel's Conversion to Postbellum Unionism.* Chapel Hill: Univ. of North Carolina Press, 1974.

Madison, James H. *A Lynching in the Heartland: Race and Memory in America.* New York: St. Martin's Press, 2000.

Main, Gloria L. Review of *The Agrarian Origins of American Capitalism,* by Allan Kulikoff. *American Historical Review* 99, no. 1 (Feb. 1994): 293-94.

Malkin, Michelle. "That's Racist! A Guide to What's Off-Limits." National Review Online. http://www.nationalreview.com/articles/315564/s-racist-michelle-malkin?pg=1 (accessed September 5, 2012).

Manganiello, Christopher. "Dam Crazy with Wild Consequences: Artificial Lakes and Natural Rivers in the American South, 1845-1990." Ph.D. diss., Univ. of Georgia, 2010.

Mantler, Gordon. *Power to the Poor: Black-Brown Coalition and the Fight for Economic Justice, 1960-1974.* Chapel Hill: Univ. of North Carolina Press, 2015.

Marable, Manning. *Malcolm X: A Life of Reinvention.* New York: Viking, 2011.

———. *Race, Reform, and Rebellion: The Second Reconstruction in Black America, 1945-1982.* Jackson: Univ. Press of Mississippi, 1984.

Markovitz, Jonathan. *Legacies of Lynching: Racial Violence and Memory.* Minneapolis: Univ. of Minnesota Press, 2004.

Marshall, F. Ray. *Labor in the South.* Cambridge, Mass.: Harvard Univ. Press, 1967.

———. "Southern Unions: History and Prospects." In *Perspectives on the American South: An Annual Review of Society, Politics and Culture,* vol. 3, ed. James C. Cobb and Charles R. Wilson, 163-78. New York: Gordon and Breach Science Publishers, 1985.

Martin, John Bartlow. *The Deep South Says "Never!"* New York: Ballantine Books, 1957.

Martin, William. *With God on Our Side: The Rise of the Religious Right in America.* New York: Broadway Books, 1996.

Matory, J. Lorand. *Black Atlantic Religion: Tradition, Transnationalism, and Matriarchy in the Afro-Brazilian Candomblé.* Princeton, N.J.: Princeton Univ. Press, 2005.

Marx, Karl. *Capital.* Vol. 1. Trans. Ben Fowkes. 1867. Reprint, New York: Penguin Classics, 1976.

————, and Friedrich Engels. *The Civil War in the United States.* Ed. Andrew Zimmerman. New York: International Publishers, 2016.

Mayer, Gustav. "Die Trennung der proletarischen von der bürgerlichen Demokratie in Deutschland 1863-1870." In *Radikalismus, Sozialismus und bürgerliche Demokratie,* ed. Hans Ulrich Wehler, 108-78. Frankfurt am Main: Suhrkamp, 1969.

Mayhew, Anne. "A Reappraisal of the Causes of Farm Protest in the United States, 1870-1900." *Journal of Economic History* 61 (1972): 463-75.

Maysilles, Duncan. *Ducktown Smoke: The Southern Appalachian Story of the Supreme Court's First Air Pollution Case.* Chapel Hill: Univ. of North Carolina Press, 2011.

McAdam, Doug. *Political Process and the Development of Black Insurgency, 1930-1970.* Chicago: Univ. of Chicago Press, 1982.

McArthur, Judith N. *Creating the New Woman: The Rise of Southern Women's Progressive Culture in Texas, 1893-1918.* Urbana: Univ. of Illinois Press, 1998.

————, and Harold L. Smith. *Minnie Fisher Cunningham: A Suffragist's Life in Politics.* Oxford: Oxford Univ. Press, 2003.

McCandless, Amy T. *The Past in the Present: Women's Higher Education in the Twentieth-Century American South.* Tuscaloosa: Univ. of Alabama Press, 1999.

McClintock, Anne. *Imperial Leather: Race, Gender, and Sexuality in the Colonial Contest.* New York: Routledge, 1995.

McDonald, Forrest, and Grady McWhiney. "The South from Self-Sufficiency to Peonage: An Interpretation." *The American Historical Review* 85, no. 5 (Dec. 1980): 1095-1118.

McElhaney, Jacquelyn Masur. *Pauline Periwinkle and Progressive Reform in Dallas.* College Station: Texas A&M Univ. Press, 1998.

McElvaine, Robert S. *Down and Out in the Great Depression: Letters from the "Forgotten Man."* Chapel Hill: Univ. of North Carolina Press, 1983.

McGovern, James R. *Anatomy of a Lynching: The Killing of Claude Neal.* Baton Rouge: Louisiana State Univ. Press, 1982.

McGuire, Danielle L. *At the Dark End of the Street: Black Women, Rape, and Resistance—A New History of the Civil Rights Movement from Rosa Parks to the Rise of Black Power.* New York: Knopf, 2010.

————, and John Dittmer. *Freedom Rights: New Perspectives on the Civil Rights Movement.* Lexington: Univ. Press of Kentucky, 2011.

McGuire, Phillip. *Taps for a Jim Crow Army: Letters from Black Soldiers in World War II.* New York: ABC-CLIO, 1983.

McGurty, Eileen Maura. "From NIMBY to Civil Rights: The Origins of the Environmental Justice Movement." *Environmental History* 2, no. 3 (1997): 301-23.

———. *Transforming Environmentalism: Warren County, PCBs, and the Origins of Environmental Justice.* New Brunswick, N.J.: Rutgers Univ. Press, 2007.

McKitrick, Eric L. *Andrew Johnson and Reconstruction.* New York: Oxford Univ. Press, 1960.

McKiven Jr., Henry M. *Iron and Steel: Class, Race, and Community in Birmingham, Alabama, 1875-1920.* Chapel Hill: Univ. of North Carolina Press, 1995.

McLaurin, Melton A. *The Knights of Labor in the South.* Westport, Conn.: Greenwood Press, 1978.

———. *Paternalism and Protest: Southern Cotton Mill Workers and Organized Labor, 1875-1905.* Westport, Conn.: Greenwood Press, 1971.

McMath Jr., Robert C. *American Populism, A Social History: 1877-1898.* New York: Hill and Wang, 1993.

———. "Politics Matters: John D. Hicks and the History of Populism." *Agricultural History* 82, no. 1 (Winter 2008): 2-6.

———. *Populist Vanguard: A History of the Southern Farmers Alliance.* Chapel Hill: Univ. of North Carolina Press, 1975.

———, Peter H. Argersinger, Connie L. Lester, Michael F. Magliari, and Walter Nugent. "Agricultural History Roundtable on Populism." *Agricultural History* 82, no. 1 (Winter 2008): 1-35.

McMillen, Neil R. *The Citizens' Council: Organized Resistance to the Second Reconstruction, 1954-1964.* Urbana: Univ. of Illinois Press, 1971.

———, ed. *Remaking Dixie: The Impact of World War II on the American South.* Jackson: Univ. Press of Mississippi, 1997.

McMurry, Linda O. *To Keep the Waters Troubled: The Life of Ida B. Wells.* New York: Oxford Univ. Press, 1998.

McNeil, Genna Rae. *Groundwork: Charles Hamilton Houston and the Struggle for Civil Rights.* Philadelphia: Univ. of Pennsylvania Press, 1983.

McWhirter, Cameron. *Red Summer: The Summer of 1919 and the Awakening of Black America.* New York: Henry Holt, 2011.

McWhorter, Diane. *Carry Me Home: Birmingham, Alabama, the Climactic Battle of the Civil Rights Revolution.* New York: Simon and Schuster, 2001.

Mehta, Uday Singh. *Liberalism and Empire: A Study in Nineteenth-Century British Liberal Thought.* Chicago: Univ. of Chicago Press, 1999.

Meier, August. *A White Scholar and the Black Community, 1945-1965: Essays and Reflections.* Amherst: Univ. of Massachusetts Press, 1992.

———, and Elliott Rudwick. *CORE: A Study in the Civil Rights Movement, 1942-1968.* New York: Oxford Univ. Press, 1973.

Mertz, Paul E. *New Deal Policy and Southern Rural Poverty.* Baton Rouge: Louisiana State Univ. Press, 1978.

Messer-Kruse, Timothy. *The Yankee International: Marxism and the American Reform Tradition, 1848-1876.* Chapel Hill: Univ. of North Carolina Press, 1998.

Middlefehldt, Sarah. *Tangled Roots: The Appalachian Trail and American Environmental Politics.* Seattle: Univ. of Washington Press, 2013.

Miller, Eben. *Born along the Color Line: The 1933 Amenia Conference and the Rise of a National Civil Rights Movement.* New York: Oxford Univ. Press, 2012.

Miller, James A. *Remembering Scottsboro: The Legacy of an Infamous Trial.* Princeton, N.J.: Princeton Univ. Press, 2009.

Miller, Steven P. *Billy Graham and the Rise of the Republican South.* Philadelphia: Univ. of Pennsylvania Press, 2009.

Miller, Worth Robert. "A Centennial Historiography of American Populism." *Kansas History: A Journal of the Central Plains* 16 (Spring 1993): 54-69.

Mills, Cynthia J., and Pamela H. Simpson, eds. *Monuments to the Lost Cause: Women, Art, and the Landscapes of Southern Memory.* Knoxville: Univ. of Tennessee Press, 2003.

Mills, Kay. *This Little Light of Mine: The Life of Fannie Lou Hamer.* New York: Dutton Press, 1993.

Milton, George Fort. *Lynchings and What They Mean: General Findings of the Southern Commission for the Study of Lynching.* Atlanta: Southern Commission for the Study of Lynching, 1931.

Minchin, Timothy J. *The Color of Work: The Struggle for Civil Rights in the Southern Paper Industry, 1945-1980.* Chapel Hill: Univ. of North Carolina Press, 2001.

———. *"Don't Sleep with Stevens!" The J. P. Stevens Campaign and the Struggle to Organize the South, 1963-80.* Gainesville: Univ. Press of Florida, 2005.

———. *Empty Mills: The Fight against Imports and the Decline of the U.S. Textile Industry.* Lanham, Md.: Rowman and Littlefield, 2012.

———. *Fighting against the Odds: A History of Southern Labor since World War II.* Gainesville: Univ. Press of Florida, 2005.

———. *Hiring the Black Worker: The Racial Integration of the Southern Textile Industry, 1960-1980.* Chapel Hill: Univ. of North Carolina Press, 1999.

———. "'Just Like a Death': The Closing of the International Paper Company Mill in Mobile, Alabama, and the Deindustrialization of the South, 2000-2005." *Alabama Review* 59, no. 1 (Jan. 2006): 44-77.

———. "Shutdowns in the Sun Belt: The Decline of the Textile and Apparel Industry and the Deindustrialization in the South." In *Life and Labor in the New New South: Essays in Southern Labor History since 1950,* ed. Robert H. Zieger, 258-88. Gainesville: Univ. Press of Florida, 2012.

———. "Torn Apart: Permanent Replacements and the Crossett Strike of 1985." *Arkansas Historical Quarterly* 59, no. 1 (Spring 2000): 31-58.

———. *What Do We Need a Union For? The TWUA in the South, 1945-1955.* Chapel Hill: Univ. of North Carolina Press, 1997.

Minnen, Cornelis van, and Manfred Berg, eds. *The U.S. South and Europe: Transatlantic Relations in the Nineteenth and Twentieth Centuries.* Lexington: Univ. Press of Kentucky, 2013.

Mintz, Sidney W. *Sweetness and Power: The Place of Sugar in Modern History.* New York: Viking, 1985.

Mitchell, H. L. *Mean Things Happening in this Land: The Life and Times of H. L. Mitchell, Co-founder of the Southern Tenant Farmers Union.* Montclair, N.J.: Allanheld, Osmun and Company Publishers, 1979.

Mitchell, Koritha. *Living with Lynching: African American Lynching Plays, Performance, and Citizenship, 1890-1930.* Urbana: Univ. of Illinois Press, 2011.

Mitchell, Theodore R. *Political Education in the Southern Farmers' Alliance, 1877-1900.* Madison: Univ. of Wisconsin Press, 1987.

Mixon, Gregory. *The Atlanta Riot: Race, Class, and Violence in a New South City.* Gainsville: Univ. Press of Florida, 2005.

Mohl, Raymond A. "Latinos and Blacks in the Recent American South." In *Migration and Transformation of the Southern Workplace since 1945,* ed. Robert Cassanello and Colin J. Davis, 80-113. Gainesville: Univ. Press of Florida, 2009.

Montgomery, David. *Beyond Equality: Labor and the Radical Republicans, 1862-1872.* 1967. Reprint, Urbana: Univ. of Illinois Press, 1981.

————. *Workers Control in America: Studies in the History of Work, Technology, and Labor Struggles.* Cambridge: Cambridge Univ. Press, 1979.

Montgomery, Rebecca S. *The Politics of Education in the New South: Women and Reform in Georgia, 1890-1930.* Baton Rouge: Louisiana State Univ. Press, 2006.

Montrie, Chad. *To Save the Land and People: A History of Opposition to Surface Coal Mining in Appalachia.* Chapel Hill: Univ. of North Carolina Press, 2003.

Moody, Anne. *Coming of Age in Mississippi.* New York: Dial Press, 1968.

Moore, Barrington. *Social Origins of Dictatorship and Democracy: Lord and Peasant in the Making of the Modern World.* 1966. Reprint, Boston: Beacon Press, 1993.

Moore, John Hammond. *Carnival of Blood: Dueling, Lynching, and Murder in South Carolina, 1880-1920.* Columbia: Univ. of South Carolina Press, 2006.

Moore, John Robert. "The Conservative Coalition in the United States Senate, 1942-1945." *Journal of Southern History,* 33, no. 3 (Aug. 1967): 368-76.

Moreton, Bethany. *To Serve God and Wal-Mart: The Making of Christian Free Enterprise.* Cambridge, Mass.: Harvard Univ. Press, 2009.

Morgan, W. Scott. *History of the Wheel and Alliance and the Impending Revolution.* Hardy, Ark., 1889.

Mormino, Gary, and George E. Pozzetta. *The Immigrant World of Ybor City: Italians and Their Latin Neighbors in Tampa, 1885-1985.* Urbana: Univ. of Illinois Press, 1987.

Morris, Aldon D. *The Origins of the Civil Rights Movement: Black Communities Organizing for Change.* New York: The Free Press, 1984.

Morris, Christopher. "A More Southern Environmental History." *Journal of Southern History* 75, no. 3 (2009): 581-98.

————. *The Big Muddy: An Environmental History of the Mississippi and Its Peoples from Hernando de Soto to Hurricane Katrina.* New York: Oxford Univ. Press, 2012.

Morsman, Amy Feely. *The Big House after Slavery: Virginia Plantation Families and Their Postbellum Experiment.* Charlottesville: Univ. of Virginia Press, 2010.

Morton, Patricia. *Disfigured Images: The Historical Assault on Afro-American Women.* New York: Greenwood Press, 1991.

Muhammad, Khalil Gibran. *The Condemnation of Blackness: Race, Crime, and the Making of Modern Urban America.* Cambridge, Mass.: Harvard Univ. Press, 2010.

Murray, Pauli. *Song in a Weary Throat: An American Pilgrimage.* New York: Harper and Row, 1987.

———. *States' Laws on Race and Color: Studies in the Legal History of the South.* Cincinnati: Women's Division of Christian Service (Board of Missions and Church Extension, Methodist Church), 1950.

Myrdal, Gunnar. *An American Dilemma: The Negro Problem and Modern Democracy.* New York: Harper and Row, 1944.

Naison, Mark D. "The Southern Tenant Farmers' Union and the CIO." In *"We Are All Leaders": The Alternative Unionism of the Early 1930s,* ed. Staughton Lynd, 102-16. Urbana: Univ. of Illinois Press, 1996.

Namorato, Michael V., ed. *Have We Overcome? Race Relations Since Brown: Essays.* Jackson: Univ. Press of Mississippi, 1979.

National Association for the Advancement of Colored People (NAACP). "Lynching Goes Underground: A Report on a New Technique." New York: NAACP, 1940.

———. *Thirty Years of Lynching in the United States, 1889-1918.* New York: NAACP, 1919.

National Emergency Council. *The Report on Economic Conditions of the South.* Washington, D.C.: GPO, 1938.

Nelson, Bruce. "'CIO Meant One Thing for the Whites and Another Thing for Us': Steelworkers and Civil Rights, 1936-1974." In *Southern Labor in Transition,* ed. Robert H. Zieger, 113-45. Knoxville: Univ. of Tennessee Press, 1997.

———. "Class and Race in the Crescent City: The ILWU, from San Francisco to New Orleans." In *The CIO's Left-Led Unions,* ed. Steven Rosswurm, 19-45. New Brunswick, N.J.: Rutgers Univ. Press, 1992.

———. "Organized Labor and the Struggle for Black Equality in Mobile during World War II." *Journal of American History* 80, no. 3 (Dec. 1993): 952-88.

Nelson, Lynn A. *Pharsalia: An Environmental Biography of a Southern Plantation, 1780-1880.* Athens: Univ. of Georgia Press, 2009.

Nelson, Scott Reynolds. *A Nation of Deadbeats: An Uncommon History of America's Financial Disasters.* New York: Alfred A. Knopf, 2012.

Nelson, Megan Kate. *Trembling Earth: A Cultural History of the Okefenokee Swamp.* Athens: Univ. of Georgia Press, 2005.

Nesmith, Bruce. *The New Republican Coalition: The Reagan Campaign and White Evangelicals.* New York: Peter Lang, 1994.

Nevels, Cynthia Skove. *Lynching to Belong: Claiming Whiteness Through Racial Violence.* College Station: Texas A&M Univ. Press, 2007.

Neverdon-Morton, Cynthia. *Afro-American Women of the South and the Advancement of the Race, 1895-1925.* Knoxville: Univ. of Tennessee Press, 1989.

Newby, I. A. *Challenge to the Court: Social Scientists and the Defense of Segregation, 1954-1966.* Baton Rouge: Louisiana State Univ. Press, 1967.

———. *Jim Crow's Defense: Anti-Negro Thought in America.* Baton Rouge: Louisiana State Univ. Press, 1965.

———. *Plain Folk in the New South: Social Change and Cultural Persistence, 1880-1915.* Baton Rouge: Louisiana State Univ. Press, 1989.

Newfont, Kathryn. *Blue Ridge Commons: Environmental Activism and Forest History in Western North Carolina.* Athens: Univ. of Georgia Press, 2012.

Newman, Dale. "Work and Community in a Southern Textile Town." *Labor History* 19, no. 2 (Spring 1978): 204-25.

Nichols, David A. *A Matter of Justice: Eisenhower and the Beginning of the Civil Rights Revolution.* New York: Simon and Schuster, 2007.

Nissen, Bruce. "A Different Kind of Union: SEIU Healthcare Florida from the Mid-1990s through 2009." In *Life and Labor in the New New South,* ed. Robert H. Zieger, 289-313. Gainesville: Univ. Press of Florida, 2012.

Nixon, H. Clarence. "The South after the War." *Virginia Quarterly Review* 20 (Summer 1944): 321-44.

Norrell, Jeff. "Modern Conservatism and the Consequences of Its Ideas." In *Reviews in American History* 36, no. 3 (Sept. 2008): 456-67.

Norrell, Robert J. "Caste in Steel: Jim Crow Careers in Birmingham, Alabama." *Journal of American History* 73, no. 3 (Dec. 1986): 669-94.

———. *The House I Live In: Race in the American Century.* London: Oxford Univ. Press, 2005. Oxford: Univ. Press of Mississippi, 1997.

———. "Labor at the Ballot Box: Alabama Politics from the New Deal to the Dixiecrat Movement." *Journal of Southern History* 57, no. 2 (May 1991): 201-34.

———. "Labor Trouble: George Wallace and Union Politics in Alabama." In *Organized Labor in the Twentieth-Century South,* ed. Robert H. Zieger, 250-72. Knoxville: Univ. of Tennessee Press, 1991.

———. *Reaping the Whirlwind: the Civil Rights Movement in Tuskegee.* New York: Knopf, 1985.

Norwood, Stephen H. "Bogolusa Burning: The War against Biracial Unionism in the Deep South, 1919." *Journal of Southern History* 63, no. 3 (Aug. 1997): 591-628.

Novick, Peter. *That Noble Dream: The "Objectivity Question" and the American Historical Profession.* New York: Cambridge Univ. Press, 1988.

Oh Freedom After While: The Missouri Sharecroppers Strike of 1939. Film. Produced by Lynn Rubright, Candace O'Connor, and Steven John Ross. Narrated by Julian Bond. San Francisco: California Newsreel, 1999.

Oates, Stephen B. *Let the Trumpet Sound: The Life of Martin Luther King, Jr.* New York: New American Library, 1982.

O'Brien, Gayle Williams. *The Color of the Law: Race, Violence, and Justice in the Post-World War II South.* Chapel Hill: Univ. of North Carolina Press, 1999.

Odum, Howard W. *Race and Rumors of Race: The American South in the Early Forties.* 1943. Reprint, Baltimore: Johns Hopkins Univ. Press, 1997.

———. *The Way of the South; Toward the Regional Balance of America.* New York: Macmillan Co., 1947.

———, and Guy B. Johnson, *The Negro and His Songs.* Chapel Hill: Univ. of North Carolina Press, 1925.

———, and Guy B. Johnson. *Negro Workaday Songs.* Chapel Hill: Univ. of North Carolina Press, 1926.

Öfele, Martin W. *German-Speaking Officers in the United States Colored Troops, 1863-1867.* Gainesville: Univ. Press of Florida, 2004.

———. *True Sons of the Republic: European Immigrants in the Union Army.* Westport, Conn.: Praeger, 2008.

Okie, Tom W. "'Everything is Peaches Down in Georgia': Culture and Agriculture in the American South." Ph.D. diss., Univ. of Georgia, 2012.

Okihiro, Gary Y. *Pineapple Culture: A History of the Tropical and Temperate Zones.* Berkeley: Univ. of California Press, 2009.

Olson, Lynne. *Freedom's Daughters: The Unsung Heroines of the Civil Rights Movement from 1830 to 1970.* New York: Scribners, 2001.

Oney, Steve. *And the Dead Shall Rise: The Murder of Mary Phagan and the Lynching of Leo Frank.* New York: Pantheon Books, 2003.

Outland, Robert B. *Tapping the Pines: The Naval Stores Industry in the American South.* Baton Rouge: Louisiana State Univ. Press, 2004.

Palmer, Bruce. *"Man Over Money": The Southern Populist Critique of American Capitalism.* Chapel Hill: Univ. of North Carolina Press, 1980.

Palmié, Stephan. *Wizards and Scientists: Explorations in Afro-Cuban Modernity and Tradition.* Durham: Duke Univ. Press, 2002.

Parsons, Elaine Frantz. *Ku-Klux: The Birth of the Klan During Reconstruction.* Chapel Hill: Univ. of North Carolina Press, 2015.

Patterson, James T. *Brown v. Board of Education: A Civil Rights Milestone and Its Troubled Legacy.* New York: Oxford Univ. Press, 2001.

———. *Congressional Conservatism and the New Deal: The Growth of the Conservative Coalition in Congress, 1933-1939.* Lexington: Univ. of Kentucky Press, 1967.

Patterson, Orlando. *Rituals of Blood: Consequences of Slavery in Two American Centuries.* Washington, D.C.: Civitas Counterpoint, 1998.

Pauley, Garth E. *The Modern Presidency and Civil Rights: Rhetoric on Race from Roosevelt to Nixon.* College Station: Texas A&M Univ. Press, 2001.

Payne, Charles M. *I've Got the Light of Freedom: The Organizing Tradition and the Mississippi Freedom Struggle.* Berkeley: Univ. of California Press, 1995.

Peacock, James L., Harry L. Watson, and Carrie R. Matthews, eds. *The American South in the Global World.* Chapel Hill: Univ. of North Carolina Press, 2005.

Peffer, William A. *Populism: Its Rise and Fall.* 1899. Ed. Peter H. Argersinger. Lawrence: Univ. Press of Kansas, 1992.

Pember, Phoebe Yates. *A Southern Woman's Story.* New York: G. W. Carleton and Company, 1879.

Percy, William Alexander. *Lanterns on the Levee: Recollections of a Planters' Son.* 1941. Reprint, Baton Rouge: Louisiana State Univ. Press, 1994.

Perman, Michael. *Struggle for Mastery: Disenfranchisement in the South, 1888-1908.* Chapel Hill: Univ. of North Carolina Press, 2001.

Pfeffer, Paula F. *A. Philip Randolph, Pioneer of the Civil Rights Movement.* Baton Rouge: Louisiana State Univ. Press, 1990.

Pfeifer, Michael J. "At the Hands of Parties Unknown? The State of the Field of Lynching Scholarship." *Journal of American History* 101 (Dec. 2014): 832-46.

———, ed. *Lynching beyond Dixie: American Mob Violence outside the South.* Urbana: Univ. of Illinois Press, 2013.

———. *The Roots of Rough Justice: Origins of American Lynching.* Urbana: Univ. of Illinois Press, 2011.

———. *Rough Justice: Lynching and American Society, 1874-1947.* Urbana: Univ. of Illinois Press, 2004.

Phillips, Kevin. *The Emerging Republican Majority.* New Rochelle, N.Y.: Arlington House, 1969.

Phillips, Kimberly L. *War! What Is It Good For? Black Freedom Struggles and the U.S. Military from World War II to Iraq.* Chapel Hill: Univ. of North Carolina Press, 2012.

Phillips, Ulrich Bonnell. *Life and Labor in the Old South.* New York: Little, Brown, and Co., 1929.

The Plow That Broke the Plains. Film. Directed by Pare Lorentz. Washington, D.C.: U.S. Resettlement Administration/Farm Security Administration, 1936.

Plummer, Brenda Gayle. *Rising Wind: Black Americans and U.S. Foreign Affairs, 1935-1960.* Chapel Hill: Univ. of North Carolina Press, 1996.

Podair, Jerald. *Bayard Rustin: American Dreamer.* Lanham, Md.: Rowman and Littlefield, 2009.

Polenberg, Richard. *One Nation, Divisible: Class, Race, and Ethnicity in the United States since 1938.* New York: Viking Press, 1980.

———. *War and Society: The United States, 1941-1945.* New York: Greenwood Press, 1973.

Pollack, Norman. *The Humane Economy: Populism, Capitalism, and Democracy.* New Brunswick, N.J.: Rutgers Univ. Press, 1990.

Pollard, Edward A. *The Lost Cause: A New Southern History of the War of the Confederates: Compromising a Full and Authentic Account of the Rise and Progress of the Late Southern Confederacy—the Campaigns, Battles, Incidents, and Adventures of the Most Gigantic Struggle of the World's History.* New York: E. B. Treat and Company, 1866.

———. *The Lost Cause Regained.* New York: C. W. Carleton and Company, 1868.

Porter, Alexander E. *Military Memoirs of a Confederate.* New York: Charles Scribner's Sons, 1907.

Postel, Charles. *Populist Vision.* New York: Oxford Univ. Press, 2007.

Potter, David M. "The Emergence of the New South: An Essay Review." Review of *The Emergence of the New South, 1913-1945,* by George B. Tindall. *Journal of Southern History* 34 (Aug. 1968): 420-24.

Prather, H. Leon. *We Have Taken a City: Wilmington Racial Massacre and Coup of 1898.* Rutherford, N.J.: Fairleigh Dickinson Univ. Press, 1984.

Purcell, Aaron D. *White Collar Radicals: TVA's Knoxville Fifteen, the New Deal, and the McCarthy Era.* Knoxville: Univ. of Tennessee Press, 2009.

Raines, Howell. *My Soul Is Rested: Movement Days in the Deep South Remembered.* New York: G. P. Putnam's Sons, 1977.

Ramsdell, Charles W. *Reconstruction in Texas.* New York: Columbia Univ. Press, 1910.

Rancière, Jacques. *The Nights of Labor: The Workers' Dream in Nineteenth-Century France.* Philadelphia: Temple Univ. Press, 1989.

Ransby, Barbara. *Ella Baker and the Black Freedom Movement: A Radical Democratic Vision.* Chapel Hill: Univ. of North Carolina Press, 2003.

Ransom, Roger, and Richard Sutch. "Capitalists without Capital: The Burden of Slavery and the Impact of Emancipation." *Agricultural History* 62 (1988): 133-60.

———. "Debt Peonage in the Cotton South after the Civil War." *Journal of Economic History* 32 (1972): 641-99.

————. *One Kind of Freedom: The Economic Consequences of Emancipation.* Cambridge: Cambridge Univ. Press, 1977.

————. *One Kind of Freedom: The Economic Consequences of Emancipation,* 2nd ed. 1977. Reprint, Cambridge: Cambridge Univ. Press, 2001.

Raper, Arthur F. *Preface to Peasantry: A Tale of Two Black Belt Counties.* Chapel Hill: Univ. of North Carolina Press, 1936.

————. *The Tragedy of Lynching.* Chapel Hill: Univ. of North Carolina Press, 1933.

Rediker, Marcus. *The Many-Headed Hydra: Sailors, Slaves, Commoners, and the Hidden History of the Revolutionary Atlantic.* London: Verso Books, 2002.

Reed, Adolph. *Without Justice For All: The New Liberalism and Our Retreat from Racial Equality.* Boulder, Colo.: Westview Press, 1999.

Reed, Linda. *Simple Decency and Common Sense: The Southern Conference Movement, 1938-1963.* Bloomington: Indiana Univ. Press, 1991.

Reed, Merl. *Seedtime for the Modern Civil Rights Movement: The President's Committee on Fair Employment Practice, 1941-1946.* Baton Rouge: Louisiana State Univ. Press, 1991.

Reynolds, Katherine C., and Susan L. Schramm. *A Separate Sisterhood: Women Who Shaped Southern Education in the Progressive Era.* New York: Peter Lang, 2002.

Rhodes, James Ford. *History of the United States from the Compromise of 1850 to the End of the Roosevelt Administration.* 9 vols. New York: Macmillan Company, 1892-1912.

Ridge, Martin. "Populism Redux: John D. Hicks and the Populist Revolt." *Reviews in American History* 13 (Mar. 1985): 142-54.

Rimanelli, Marco, and Sheryl L. Postman, eds. *The 1891 New Orleans Lynching and U.S.-Italian Relations: A Look Back.* New York: Peter Lang, 1992.

Rise, Eric W. *The Martinsville Seven: Race, Rape, and Capital Punishment.* Charlottesville: Univ. of Virginia Press, 1995.

The River. Directed by Pare Lorentz. Washington, D.C.: Farm Security Administration, 1938.

Roberts, Gene. *The Race Beat: The Press, the Civil Rights Struggle, and the Awakening of a Nation.* New York: Knopf, 2006.

Robertson, Ben. *Red Hills and Cotton: An Upcountry Memoir.* New York: Alfred A. Knopf, 1942.

Robinson, Cedric J. *Black Marxism: The Making of the Black Radical Tradition.* 1983. Reprint, Chapel Hill: Univ. of North Carolina Press, 2000.

Robinson, Jo Ann. *The Montgomery Bus Boycott and the Women Who Started It.* Knoxville: Univ. of Tennessee Press, 1987.

Robinson, John L. *Living Hard: Southern Americans in the Great Depression.* Washington, D.C.: Univ. Press of America, 1981.

Robnett, Belinda. *How Long? How Long? African American Women in the Struggle for Civil Rights.* New York: Oxford Univ. Press, 1997.

Roediger, David R. *Seizing Freedom: Slave Emancipation and Liberty for All.* Brooklyn, N.Y.: Verso, 2014.

————. *The Wages of Whiteness: Race and the Making of the American Working Class.* Rev. ed. 1991. Reprint, London: Verso, 2007.

————, and Elizabeth D. Esch. *The Production of Difference: Race and the Management of Labor in U.S. History.* New York: Oxford Univ. Press, 2012.

Roll, Jarod. *Spirit of Rebellion: Labor and Religion in the New Cotton South.* Urbana: Univ. of Illinois Press, 2010.

Romano, Renee C., and Leigh Raiford, eds. *The Civil Rights Movement in American Memory.* Athens: Univ. of Georgia Press, 2006.

Roosevelt, Theodore. *The Winning of the West.* 4 vols. New York: G. P. Putnam's Sons, 1889-99.

Rose, Mariel. "Moving Capital, Moving Workers, and the Mountain Work Ethic." In *Migration and the Transformation of the Southern Workplace since 1945,* ed. Robert Cassanello and Colin J. Davis, 174-201. Gainesville: Univ. Press of Florida, 2009.

Rosen, Hannah. *Terror in the Heart of Freedom: Citizenship, Sexual Violence, and the Meaning of Race in Postemancipation America.* Chapel Hill: Univ. of North Carolina Press, 2009.

Rosenberg, Daniel. *New Orleans Dockworkers: Race, Labor, and Unionism, 1892-1923.* Albany: State Univ. of New York Press, 1988.

Rouse, Jacqueline Anne. *Lugenia Burns Hope: Black Southern Reformer.* Athens: Univ. of Georgia Press, 1989.

Rozell, Mark J., and Clyde Wilcox. *God at the Grass Roots, 1996: The Christian Right in the American Elections.* Lanham, Md.: Rowman and Littlefield, 1997.

Ruchames, Louis. *Race, Jobs, and Politics: the Story of the FEPC.* New York: Columbia Univ. Press, 1953.

Rugemer, Edward Bartlett. *The Problem of Emancipation: The Caribbean Roots of the American Civil War.* Baton Rouge: Louisiana State Univ. Press, 2008.

Rushdy, Ashraf H. A. *The End of American Lynching.* New Brunswick, N.J.: Rutgers Univ. Press, 2012.

Russ, Jonathan S. *Global Motivations: Honda, Toyota, and the Drive toward American Manufacturing.* Lanham, Md.: Univ. Press of America, 2008.

Rustin, Bayard. *Down the Line: The Colored Writings of Bayard Rustin.* Chicago: Quadrangle Books, 1971.

Saikku, Mikko. *This Delta, This Land: An Environmental History of the Yazoo-Mississippi Floodplain.* Athens: Univ. of Georgia Press, 2005.

Sale, Kirkpatrick. *Power Shift: The Rise of the Southern Rim and Its Challenge to the Eastern Establishment.* New York: Vintage Books, 1975.

Salmond, John A. *Gastonia, 1929: The Story of the Loray Mill Strike.* Chapel Hill: Univ. of North Carolina Press, 1995.

————. *The General Textile Strike of 1934: From Maine to Alabama.* Columbia: Univ. of Missouri Press, 2002.

————. *Southern Struggles: The Southern Labor Movement and the Civil Rights Struggle.* Gainesville: Univ. Press of Florida, 2004.

Sanders, Elizabeth. *Roots of Reform: Farmers, Workers, and the American State, 1877-1917.* Chicago: Univ. of Chicago Press, 1999.

Saunt, Claudio. "The Paradox of Freedom: Tribal Sovereignty and Emancipation during the Reconstruction of Indian Territory." *Journal of Southern History* 70, no. 1 (2004): 63-94.

Saville, Julie. *The Work of Reconstruction: From Slave to Wage Laborer in South Carolina, 1860-1870*. New York: Cambridge Univ. Press, 1994.

Savitt, Todd L., and James Harvey Young. *Disease and Distinctiveness in the American South*. Knoxville: Univ. of Tennessee Press, 1991.

Saxton, Alexander. *The Rise and Fall of the White Republic: Class Politics and Mass Culture in Nineteenth-Century America*. London: Verso, 2003.

Scammon, Richard M., and Ben J. Wattenberg. *The Real Majority*. New York: Coward-McCann, 1970.

Schechter, Patricia A. *Ida B. Wells-Barnett and American Reform, 1880-1930*. Chapel Hill: Univ. of North Carolina Press, 2001.

Schneider, Mary Beth, and Chris Sikich. "Indiana Becomes Rust Belt's First Right-to-Work State." *USA Today*, Feb. 20, 2012. http://usatoday30.usatoday.com/news/nation/story/2012-02-01/indiana-right-to-work-bill/52916356/1 (accessed Oct. 15, 2012).

Schulman, Bruce J. *From Cotton Belt to Sunbelt: Federal Policy, Economic Development, and the Transformation of the South, 1938-1980*. New York: Oxford Univ. Press, 1991.

———, and Julian Zelizer, eds. *Rightward Bound: Making America Conservative in the 1970s*. Cambridge, Mass.: Harvard Univ. Press, 2008.

Schuyler, Lorraine Gates. *The Weight of Their Votes: Southern Women and Political Leverage in the 1920s*. Chapel Hill: Univ. of North Carolina Press, 2006.

Schwartz, Stuart B. *Slaves, Peasants, and Rebels: Reconsidering Brazilian Slavery*. Urbana: Univ. of Illinois Press, 1992.

Scott, Anne Firor. *The Southern Lady: From Pedestal to Politics, 1830-1930*. Chicago: Univ. of Chicago Press, 1970.

Scott, James C. *Domination and the Arts of Resistance: Hidden Transcripts*. Hartford, Conn.: Yale Univ. Press, 1990.

———. *Seeing Like a State: How Certain Schemes to Improve the Human Condition Have Failed*. Hartford, Conn.: Yale Univ. Press, 1998.

———. *Weapons of the Weak: Everyday Forms of Peasant Resistance*. Hartford, Conn.: Yale Univ. Press, 1985.

Scott, Lawrence P. *Double V: The Civil Rights Struggle of the Tuskegee Airmen*. East Lansing: Michigan State Univ. Press, 1994.

Segrave, Kerry. *Lynchings of Women in the United States: The Recorded Cases, 1851-1946*. Jefferson, N.C.: McFarland, 2010.

Sellers, Charles. *The Market Revolution: Jacksonian America, 1815-1846*. New York: Oxford Univ. Press, 1991.

Sexton, Jay. *Debtor Diplomacy: Finance and American Foreign Relations in the Civil War Era, 1837-1873*, Oxford Historical Monographs. Oxford: Clarendon Press, 2005.

———. *The Monroe Doctrine: Empire and Nation in Nineteenth-Century America*. New York: Hill and Wang, 2011.

———. "Toward a Synthesis of Foreign Relations in the Civil War Era, 1848-77." *American Nineteenth Century History* 5, no. 3 (Fall 2004): 50-73.

Shafer, Byron, and Richard Johnston. *The End of Southern Exceptionalism: Class, Race, and Partisan Change in the Postwar South*. Cambridge, Mass.: Harvard Univ. Press, 2006.

Shapiro, Herbert. *White Violence and Black Response: From Reconstruction to Montgomery.* Amherst: Univ. of Massachusetts Press, 1988.

Shapiro, Karin A. *A New South Rebellion: The Battle against Convict Labor in the Tennessee Coalfields, 1871-1896.* Chapel Hill: Univ. of North Carolina Press, 1998.

Sharpless, Rebecca. *Cooking in Other Women's Kitchens: Domestic Workers in the South, 1860-1960.* Chapel Hill: Univ. of North Carolina Press, 2010.

———. *Fertile Ground, Narrow Choices: Women on Texas Cotton Farms, 1900-1940.* Chapel Hill: Univ. of North Carolina Press, 1999.

Shaw, Barton C. *The Wool-Hat Boys: Georgia's Populist Party.* Baton Rouge: Louisiana State Univ. Press, 1984.

Shaw, Stephanie J. *What a Woman Ought to Be and to Do: Black Professional Women Workers during the Jim Crow Era.* Chicago: Univ. of Chicago Press, 1996.

Shawhan, Dorothy S., and Martha H. Swain. *Lucy Somerville Howorth: New Deal Lawyer, Politician, and Feminist from the South.* Baton Rouge: Louisiana State Univ. Press, 2006.

Shell-Weiss, Melanie. "From Minority to Majority: The Latinization of Miami's Workforce, 1940-1980." In *Migration and the Transformation of the Southern Workplace since 1945,* ed. Robert Cassanello and Colin J. Davis, 13-33. Gainesville: Univ. Press of Florida, 2009.

———. "'I Dreamed I Went to Work': Expanding Southern Unionism in the Mid-Twentieth Century Lingerie Industry." In *Florida's Working-Class Past: Current Perspectives on Labor, Race, and Gender from Spanish Florida to the New Immigration,* ed. Robert Cassanello and Melanie Shell-Weiss, 227-56. Gainesville: Univ. Press of Florida, 2009.

Shugg, Roger W. Review of *Origins of the New South, 1877-1913,* by C. Vann Woodward, *Mississippi Valley Historical Review* 39 (June 1952): 141-42.

Shuler, Jack. *Blood and Bone: Truth and Reconciliation in a Southern Town.* Columbia: Univ. of South Carolina Press, 2012.

Silberman, Charles E. *Crisis in Black and White.* New York: Random House, 1964.

Silkenat, David. "'Hard Times is the Cry': Debt in Populist Thought in North Carolina." In *Populism in the South Revisited: New Interpretations and New Departures,* ed. James M. Beeby, 101-27. Jackson: Univ. Press of Mississippi, 2012.

Silkey, Sarah. *Black Woman Reformer: Ida B. Wells, Lynching, and Transatlantic Activism.* Athens: Univ. of Georgia Press, 2015.

Silver, Timothy. *A New Face on the Countryside: Indians, Colonists, and Slaves in South Atlantic Forests, 1500-1800.* New York: Cambridge Univ. Press, 1990.

———. *Mount Mitchell and the Black Mountains: An Environmental History of the Highest Peaks in Eastern America.* Chapel Hill: Univ. of North Carolina Press, 2003.

Simien, Evelyn E. *Gender and Lynching: The Politics of Memory.* New York: Palgrave Macmillan, 2011.

Simkins, Francis Butler. *A History of the South.* New York: Alfred Knopf, 1947.

———. "After Reconstruction." *Saturday Review.* Feb. 23, 1952.

———. *Pitchfork Ben Tillman, South Carolinian.* Baton Rouge: Louisiana State Univ. Press, 1944.

———. *The South, Old and New: A History.* New York: Alfred A. Knopf, 1947.

————, and Charles Pierce Roland. *A History of the South*. 4th ed. New York: Alfred A. Knopf, 1972.

————, and Robert Hilliard Woody. *South Carolina during Reconstruction*. Chapel Hill: Univ. of North Carolina Press, 1932.

Simon, Bryant. *A Fabric of Defeat: The Politics of South Carolina Millhands, 1910-1948*. Chapel Hill: Univ. of North Carolina Press, 1998.

————. "Introduction to the 1997 Edition." In Howard Odum, *Race and Rumors of Race: the American South in the Early Forties*. 1943. Reprint, Baltimore: Johns Hopkins Univ. Press, 1997.

————. "Rethinking Why There Are So Few Unions in the South." *Georgia Historical Quarterly* 81, no. 2 (Summer 1997): 465-84.

Simons, Lakisha Michelle. *Crescent City Girls: The Lives of Young Black Women in Segregated New Orleans*. Chapel Hill: Univ. of North Carolina Press, 2015.

Simpson, John A. *Edith D. Pope and Her Nashville Friends: Guardians of the Lost Cause in the Confederate Veteran*. Knoxville: Univ. of Tennessee Press, 2003.

Sims, Anastatia. *The Power of Femininity in the New South: Women's Organizations and Politics in North Carolina, 1880-1930*. Columbia: Univ. of South Carolina Press, 1997.

Singal, Daniel Joseph. *The War Within: From Victorian to Modernist Thought in the South, 1919-1945*. Chapel Hill: Univ. of North Carolina Press, 1982.

Sitkoff, Harvard. *A New Deal for Blacks: The Emergence of Civil Rights as a National Issue*. New York: Oxford Univ. Press, 1978.

————. "Racial Militancy and Interracial Violence in the Second World War." *Journal of American History* 58 (1971): 661-81.

————. *The Struggle for Black Equality, 1945-1980*. New York: Hill and Wang, 1981.

Sklaroff, Lauren Rebecca. *Black Culture and the New Deal: The Quest for Civil Rights in the Roosevelt Era*. Chapel Hill: Univ. of North Carolina Press, 2009.

Slap, Andrew L. *The Doom of Reconstruction: The Liberal Republicans in the Civil War Era*. New York: Fordham Univ. Press, 2006.

Smead, Howard. *Blood Justice: The Lynching of Mack Charles Parker*. New York: Oxford Univ. Press, 1986.

Smith, Douglas L. "The New Deal and the Urban South: The Advancement of a Southern Urban Consciousness during the Depression Decade." Ph.D. diss., Univ. of Southern Mississippi, 1978.

Smith, John David, and J. Vincent Lowery, eds. *The Dunning School: Historians, Race, and the Meaning of Reconstruction*. Lexington: Univ. Press of Kentucky, 2013.

————. *When Did Southern Segregation Begin?* New York: Bedford/St. Martin's, 2002.

Smith, Lillian. *Killers of the Dream*. New York: W. W. Norton, 1949.

Smith, Oran P. *The Rise of Baptist Republicanism*. New York: New York Univ. Press, 1997.

Sombart, Werner. *Warum gibt es in den Vereinigten Staaten keinen Sozialismus?* Tübingen: J.C.B. Mohr, 1906.

Sommerville, Diane Miller. *Rape and Race in the Nineteenth-Century South*. Chapel Hill: Univ. of North Carolina Press, 2004.

Sosna, Morton. *In Search of the Silent South: Southern Liberals and the Race Issue.* New York: Columbia Univ. Press, 1977.

Spears, Ellen Griffith. *Baptized in PCBs: Race, Pollution, and Justice in an All-American Town.* Chapel Hill: Univ. of North Carolina Press, 2014.

———. "Landscapes and Ecologies of the US South: Essays in Eco-Cultural History." Feb. 18, 2013. Southern Spaces, https://southernspaces.org/2013/landscapes-and-ecologies-us-south-essays-eco-cultural-history (accessed April 10, 2017).

Sproat, John G. *"The Best Men": Liberal Reformers in the Gilded Age.* New York: Oxford Univ. Press, 1968.

Stampp, Kenneth M. *The Era of Reconstruction 1865-1877.* New York: Vintage Books, 1965.

Stanley, Amy Dru. *From Bondage to Contract: Wage Labor, Marriage, and the Market in the Age of Slave Emancipation.* Cambridge: Cambridge Univ. Press, 1998.

Staples, Thomas Starling. *Reconstruction in Arkansas, 1862-1874.* New York: Columbia Univ. Press, 1923.

Stein, Judith. "Southern Workers in National Unions: Birmingham Steelworkers, 1936-1951." In *Organized Labor in the Twentieth-Century South,* ed. Robert H. Zieger, 183-222. Knoxville: Univ. of Tennessee Press, 1991.

Steinfeld, Robert J. *Coercion, Contract, and Free Labor in the Nineteenth Century.* Cambridge: Cambridge Univ. Press, 2001.

———. *The Invention of Free Labor: The Employment Relation in English and American Law and Culture, 1350-1870.* Chapel Hill: Univ. of North Carolina Press, 1991.

Stephenson, Wendell H. "A Half Century of Southern Historical Scholarship." *Journal of Southern History* 11 (Feb. 1945): 3-32.

Steward, Mart A. "Environmental History: Profile of a Developing Field." *The History Teacher* 31, no. 3 (1998): 351-68.

———. "If John Muir Had Been an Agrarian: American Environmental History West and South." *Environment and History* 11, no. 2 (2005): 139-62.

———. "'Let Us Begin with The Weather?' Climate, Race and Cultural Distinctiveness in the American South." In *Nature and Society in Historical Context,* ed. Mikulas Teich, Roy Porter, and Bo Gustafsson, 240-56. Cambridge: Cambridge Univ. Press, 1997.

———. Review of *Mockingbird Song: Ecological Landscapes of the South,* by Jack Temple Kirby. *Journal of American History* 94, no. 4 (Mar. 1, 2008): 1280.

———. "Southern Environmental History." In *A Companion to the American South,* ed. John B. Boles, 409-23. New York: John Wiley and Sons, 2008.

———. *What Nature Suffers to Groe: Life, Labor, and Landscape on the Georgia Coast, 1680-1920.* Athens: Univ. of Georgia Press, 1996.

———. *The World of Marcus Garvey: Race and Class in Modern Society.* Baton Rouge: Louisiana State Univ. Press, 1986.

Stine, Jeffrey K. *Mixing the Waters: Environment, Politics, and the Building of the Tennessee-Tombigbee Waterway.* Akron, Ohio: Univ. of Akron Press, 1993.

Stockley, Grif. *Daisy Bates: Civil Rights Crusader from Arkansas.* Jackson: Univ. Press of Mississippi, 2005.

Sugrue, Thomas J. *The Origins of the Urban Crisis: Race and Inequality in Postwar Detroit.* Princeton, N.J.: Princeton Univ. Press, 1996.

———. *Sweet Land of Liberty: The Forgotten Struggle for Civil Rights in the North.* New York: Random House, 2008.

———. "Workers' Paradise Lost." *New York Times,* Dec. 14, 2012.

Sullivan, James. "The Florida Teacher Walkout in the Political Transition of 1968." In *Southern Labor in Transition, 1940-1995,* ed. Robert H. Zieger, 205-29. Knoxville: Univ. of Tennessee Press, 1997.

Sullivan, Patricia. *Days of Hope: Race and Democracy in the New Deal Era.* Chapel Hill: Univ. of North Carolina Press, 1996.

———, and Armstead Robinson, eds. *New Directions in Civil Rights Studies.* Charlottesville: Univ. Press of Virginia, 1991.

———. *Lift Every Voice and Sing: The NAACP and the Making of the Civil Rights Movement.* New York: The New Press, 2009.

Sutter, Paul S. "No More the Backward Region: Southern Environmental History Comes of Age." *Environmental History and the American South: A Reader,* ed. Paul S. Sutter and Christopher J. Manganiello, 1-24. Athens: Univ. of Georgia Press, 2009.

———. "What Gullies Mean: Georgia's 'Little Grand Canyon' and Southern Environmental History." *Journal of Southern History* 76, no. 3 (2010): 579-616.

———. "The World with Us: The State of American Environmental History." *Journal of American History* 100, no. 1 (2013): 94-119.

———, and Christopher J. Manganiello. *Environmental History and the American South: A Reader.* Athens: Univ. of Georgia Press, 2009.

Swain, Martha H. *Pat Harrison: The New Deal Years.* Jackson: Univ. Press of Mississippi, 1978.

Swanson, Drew A. *Remaking Wormsloe Plantation: The Environmental History of a Lowcountry Landscape.* Athens: Univ. of Georgia Press, 2012.

Sweet, James H. *Domingos Álvares, African Healing, and the Intellectual History of the Atlantic World.* Chapel Hill: Univ. of North Carolina Press, 2011.

Tate, Allen. "Faulkner's 'Sanctuary' and the Southern Myth." *Virginia Quarterly Review* 44 (1968): 418-27.

Taylor, Clarence. *Civil Rights in New York City: From World War II to the Giuliani Era.* New York: Fordham Univ. Press, 2011.

Taylor, A. Elizabeth. *Citizens at Last: The Woman Suffrage Movement in Texas.* Ed. Ruth Winegarten and Judith N. McArthur, with foreword by Anne Firor Scott. Austin, Tex.: Ellen C. Temple, 1987.

———. "The Woman Suffrage Movement in Arkansas." *Arkansas Historical Quarterly* 15 (Spring 1956): 17-42.

———. "The Woman Suffrage Movement in Florida." *Florida Historical Quarterly* 36 (July 1957): 42-60.

———. "The Origin of the Woman Suffrage Movement in Georgia." *Georgia Historical Quarterly* 28 (June 1944): 63-79.

———. *The Woman Suffrage Movement in North Carolina.* Raleigh: N.C. State Department of Archives and History, 1961.

————. *The Woman Suffrage Movement in Tennessee.* 1957. Reprint, New York: Octagon Books, 1978.

Terborg-Penn, Rosalyn. *African American Women in the Struggle for the Vote, 1850-1920.* Bloomington: Indiana Univ. Press, 1998.

Terkel, Studs. *Hard Times: An Oral History of the Great Depression.* New York: Pantheon Books, 1970.

Terrill, Tom, and Jerrold Hirsch, eds. *Such as Us: Southern Voices of the Thirties.* Chapel Hill: Univ. of North Carolina Press, 1978.

Theoharis, Jeanne. "Black Freedom Struggles: Re-imagining and Redefining the Fundamentals." *History Compass* 4 (Feb. 2006): 348-67.

————. *The Rebellious Life of Mrs. Rosa Parks.* Boston: Beacon Press, 2013.

————, and Komozi Woodard, eds. *Freedom North: Black Freedom Struggles Outside the South, 1940-1980.* New York: Palgrave MacMillan, 2003.

————, and Komozi Woodard, eds. *Groundwork: Local Black Freedom Movements in America.* New York: New York Univ. Press, 2005.

Thomas, Bettye, and V. P. Franklin, eds. *Sisters in the Struggle: African-American Women in the Civil Rights-Black Power Movement.* New York: New York Univ. Press, 2001.

Thomas, Karen Kruse. *Deluxe Jim Crow: Civil Rights and American Health Policy, 1935-1954.* Athens: Univ. of Georgia Press, 2011.

Thomas, Mary Martha. *The New Woman in Alabama: Social Reforms and Suffrage, 1890-1920.* Tuscaloosa: Univ. of Alabama Press, 1992.

Thompson, C. Mildred. *Reconstruction in Georgia: Economic, Social, and Political, 1865-1877.* New York: Columbia Univ. Press, 1915.

Thompson, E. P. *The Making of the English Working Class.* 1964. Reprint, New York: Vintage, 1966.

Thompson, Mildred I. *Ida B. Wells-Barnett: An Exploratory Study of an American Black Woman, 1893-1930.* Brooklyn, N.Y.: Carlson Publishing, 1990.

Thornton III, J. Mills. *Dividing Lines: Municipal Politics and the Struggle for Civil Rights in Montgomery, Birmingham, and Selma.* Tuscaloosa: Univ. of Alabama Press, 2002.

Thornton, John. *Africa and Africans in the Making of the Atlantic World, 1400-1800.* 2nd ed. New York: Cambridge Univ. Press, 1998.

Thurston, Robert W. *Lynching: American Mob Murder in Global Perspective.* Burlington, Vt.: Ashgate, 2011.

Tindall, George Brown. *The Emergence of the New South, 1913-1945.* Baton Rouge: Louisiana State Univ. Press, 1967.

————. "Southern Negroes since Reconstruction: Dissolving the Static Image." In *Writing Southern History: Essays in Historiography in Honor of Fletcher M. Green,* ed. Arthur S. Link and Rembert W. Patrick, 337-61. Baton Rouge: Louisiana State Univ. Press, 1965.

Tolnay, Stewart, and E. M. Beck. *A Festival of Violence: An Analysis of Southern Lynchings, 1882-1930.* Urbana: Univ. of Illinois Press, 1995.

Torres, Sasha. *Black, White, and in Color: Television and Black Civil Rights.* Princeton, N.J.: Princeton Univ. Press, 2003.

Trelease, Allen W. *White Terror: The Ku Klux Klan Conspiracy and Southern Reconstruction*. New York: Harper and Row, 1971.

Trimble, Stanley W. "Man-Induced Soil Erosion on the Southern Piedmont." *Soil Conservation Society of America*. Univ. of Wisconsin Department of Geography, Milwaukee, WI, 1974. http://www.swcs.org/en/publications/man_induced_soil_erosion_on_the_southern_piedmont/ (accessed April 25, 2017).

Trotti, Michael Ayers. "What Counts: Trends in Racial Violence in the Postbellum South." *Journal of American History* 100 (Sept. 2013): 375-400.

Tuck, Stephen G. N. *Beyond Atlanta: The Struggle for Racial Equality in Georgia, 1940-1980*. Athens: Univ. of Georgia Press, 2001.

———. *We Ain't What We Ought to Be: The Black Freedom Struggle from Emancipation to Obama*. Cambridge, Mass.: Belknap Press of Harvard Univ. Press, 2010.

Tucker, Susan. *Telling Memories among Southern Women: Domestic Workers and Their Employers in the Segregated South*. Baton Rouge: Louisiana State Univ. Press, 1988.

Tullos, Allen. *Alabama Getaway: The Political Imaginary and the Heart of Dixie*. Athens: Univ. of Georgia Press, 2011.

Turner, Elizabeth Hayes. *Women, Culture, and Community: Religion and Reform in Galveston, 1880-1920*. New York: Oxford Univ. Press, 1997.

Turner, Jane. "Understanding Populists." *Journal of American History* 67 (1980): 354-73.

Turner, John G. *Bill Bright and Campus Crusade for Christ: The Renewal of Evangelicalism in Postwar America*. Chapel Hill: Univ. of North Carolina Press, 2008.

Turner, Mary, ed. *From Chattel Slaves to Wage Slaves: The Dynamics of Labour Bargaining in the Americas*. Bloomington: Indiana Univ. Press, 1995.

Tushnet, Mark V. *The NAACP's Legal Strategy against Segregated Education, 1925-1950*. Chapel Hill: Univ. of North Carolina Press, 1987.

Tuttle Jr., William M. *Race Riot: Chicago in the Red Summer of 1919*. New York: Atheneum, 1970.

Tygiel, Jules. *Baseball's Great Experiment: Jackie Robinson and His Legacy*. New York: Oxford Univ. Press, 1983.

Tyler, Pamela. *Silk Stockings and Ballot Boxes: Women and Politics in New Orleans, 1920-1963*. Athens: Univ. of Georgia Press, 1996.

Tyson, Timothy B. *Radio Free Dixie: Robert F. Williams and the Roots of Black Power*. Chapel Hill: Univ. of North Carolina Press, 1999.

Umoja, Akinyele Omowale. *We Will Shoot Back: Armed Resistance in the Mississippi Freedom Movement*. New York: New York Univ. Press, 2013.

Valencius, Conevery Bolton. *The Health of the Country: How American Settlers Understood Themselves and Their Land*. New York: Basic Books, 2003.

———. *The Lost History of the New Madrid Earthquakes*. Chicago: Univ. of Chicago Press, 2013.

Vance, Rupert Bayless. *Human Factors in Cotton Culture; a Study in the Social Geography of the American South*. Chapel Hill: Univ. of North Carolina Press, 1929.

———. *Human Geography of the South: A Study in Regional Resources and Human Adequacy*. Chapel Hill: Univ. of North Carolina Press, 1932.

Vandiver, Margaret. *Lethal Punishment: Lynchings and Legal Executions in the South.* New Brunswick, N.J.: Rutgers Univ. Press, 2006.

———. "Thoughts on Directions in Lynching Research." *Journal of American History* 101 (Dec. 2014): 854-55.

Vargas, Zaragosa. *Labor Rights Are Civil Rights: Mexican American Workers in Twentieth-Century America.* Princeton, N.J.: Princeton Univ. Press, 2005.

Vickers, Daniel. Review of *The Agrarian Origins of American Capitalism,* by Allan Kulikoff. *Journal of Southern History* 60, no. 2 (May 1994): 372-73.

Vitalis, Robert. "The Noble American Science of Imperial Relations and Its Laws of Race Development." *Comparative Studies in Society and History* 52 (2010): 909-38.

———. *White World Order, Black Power Politics: The Birth of American International Relations.* Ithaca, N.Y.: Cornell Univ. Press, 2015.

Vinson, Robert Trent. *The Americans Are Coming! Dreams of African American Liberation in Segregationist South Africa.* Athens: Ohio Univ. Press, 2012.

Von Eschen, Penny M. *Race against Empire: Black Americans and Anti-Colonialism, 1937-1957.* Ithaca, N.Y.: Cornell Univ. Press, 1996.

Waldrep, Christopher. *African Americans Confront Lynching: Strategies of Resistance from the Civil War to the Civil Rights Era.* Lanham, Md.: Rowman and Littlefield, 2009.

———, ed. *Lynching in America: A History in Documents.* New York: New York Univ. Press, 2006.

———. *The Many Faces of Judge Lynch: Extralegal Violence and Punishment in America.* New York: Palgrave MacMillan, 2002.

———. *Racial Violence on Trial.* Santa Barbara, Calif.: ABC-CLIO, 2001.

———. "'Raw, Quivering Flesh': John G. Cashman's 'Pornographic' Constitutionalism Designed to Produce an 'Aversion and Detestation,' 1883-1904." *American Nineteenth Century History* 6, no. 3 (Sept. 2005): 295-322.

———. "War of Words: The Controversy over the Definition of Lynching, 1899-1940." *Journal of Southern History* 66 (Feb. 2000): 75-100.

Waldschmidt-Nelson, Britta. *Dreams and Nightmares: Martin Luther King, Jr., Malcolm X, and the Struggle for Black Equality in America.* Gainesville: Univ. Press of Florida, 2012.

Walker, Melissa. *All We Knew Was to Farm: Rural Women in the Upcountry South, 1919-1941.* Baltimore: Johns Hopkins Univ. Press, 2000.

———, and Rebecca Sharpless, eds. *Work, Family, and Faith: Rural Southern Women in the Twentieth Century.* Columbia: Univ. of Missouri Press, 2006.

Wall, Bennett H. Review of *The Emergence of the New South, 1913-1945,* by George B. Tindall. *American Historical Review* 74 (June 1969): 1741-42.

Walton, Gary M., and Hugh Rockoff. *History of the American Economy.* Toronto: Nelson Thompson Learning, 2002.

Ward, Brian. *Just My Soul Responding: Rhythm and Blues, Black Consciousness, and Race Relations.* Berkeley: Univ. of California Press, 1998.

———, ed. *Media, Culture, and the Modern African American Freedom Struggle.* Gainesville: Univ. of Florida Press, 2001.

————. "Racial Politics, Culture and the Cole Incident of 1956." In *Race and Class in the American South since 1890*, ed. Melvyn Stokes and Rick Halpern, 181-208. Providence, R.I.: Berg Publishers, 1994.

————. *Radio and the Struggle for Civil Rights in the South*. Gainesville: Univ. Press of Florida, 2006.

————, Martyn Bone, and William A. Link, eds. *The American South and the Atlantic World*. Gainesville: Univ. Press of Florida, 2013.

Ward, Jason Morgan. *Defending White Democracy: The Making of a Segregationist Movement and the Remaking of Racial Politics, 1936-1965*. Chapel Hill: Univ. of North Carolina Press, 2011.

————. "'No Jap Crow': Japanese Americans Encounter the World War II South." *Journal of Southern History* 73, no. 1 (Feb. 2007): 75-104.

Ward, Robert Daniel, and William Warren Rogers. *Labor Revolt in Alabama: The Great Strike of 1894*. Tuscaloosa: Univ. of Alabama Press, 1965.

Watson, Bruce. *Freedom Summer: The Savage Season of 1964 That Made Mississippi Burn and Made America a Democracy*. New York: Viking, 2010.

Watters, Pat. *Down to Now: Reflections on the Southern Civil Rights Movement*. New York: Pantheon, 1971.

————, and Reese Cleghorn. *Climbing Jacob's Ladder: The Arrival of Negroes in Southern Politics*. New York: Harcourt, Brace and World, 1967.

Way, Albert G. *Conserving Southern Longleaf: Herbert Stoddard and the Rise of Ecological Land Management*. Athens: Univ. of Georgia Press, 2011.

Webb, Clive. "The Lynching of Sicilian Immigrants in the American South, 1886-1910." *American Nineteenth Century History* 3, no. 1 (Spring 2002): 45-76.

————, ed. *Massive Resistance: Southern Opposition to the Second Reconstruction*. New York: Oxford Univ. Press, 2005.

Webb, Samuel L. *Two-Party Politics in the One-Party South*. Tuscaloosa: Univ. of Alabama Press, 1997.

Weber, Max. *From Max Weber: Essays in Sociology*. Ed. H. H. Gerth and C. Wright Mills. London: Routledge, 1991.

Wedell, Marsha. *Elite Women and the Reform Impulse in Memphis, 1875-1915*. Knoxville: Univ. of Tennessee Press, 1991.

Weisbrot, Robert. *Freedom Bound: A History of America's Civil Rights Movement*. New York: W. W. Norton, 1990.

Weiss, Nancy J. *Farewell to the Party of Lincoln: Black Politics in the Age of FDR*. Princeton, N.J.: Princeton Univ. Press, 1983.

————. *The National Urban League, 1910-1940*. New York: Oxford Univ. Press, 1974.

————. *Whitney Young and the Struggle for Civil Rights*. Princeton, N.J.: Princeton Univ. Press, 1989.

Welke, Barbara Y. *Recasting American Liberty: Gender, Race, Law, and the Railroad Revolution, 1865-1920*. New York: Cambridge Univ. Press, 2001.

Wells, Ida B., ed. *The Reason Why the Colored American Is Not at the World's Columbian Exposition*. Chicago, 1893.

————. *A Red Record: Tabulated Statistics and Alleged Causes of Lynching in the United States*. Chicago: Donohue and Henneberry, 1895.

————. *Southern Horrors: Lynch Law in All its Phases*. [New York]: New York Age Print, 1892.

Wells-Barnett, Ida B. *Crusade for Justice: The Autobiography of Ida B. Wells*. Ed. Alfreda M. Duster. Chicago: Univ. of Chicago Press, 1970.

Werner, Craig. *A Change Is Gonna Come: Music, Race, and the Soul of America*. Ann Arbor: Univ. of Michigan Press, 2006.

Whayne, Jeannie M. *A New Plantation South: Land, Labor, and Federal Favor in Twentieth-Century Arkansas*. Charlottesville: Univ. Press of Virginia, 1996.

Wheeler, Marjorie Spruill. *New Women of the New South: The Leaders of the Woman Suffrage Movement in the Southern States*. New York: Oxford Univ. Press, 1993.

Whisnant, Anne Mitchell. *Super-Scenic Motorway: A Blue Ridge Parkway History*. Chapel Hill: Univ. of North Carolina Press, 2006.

Whitaker, Robert. *On the Laps of Gods: The Red Summer of 1919 and the Struggle for Justice That Remade a Nation*. New York: Crown Publishers, 2008.

White, Deborah Gray. *Too Heavy a Load: Black Women in Defense of Themselves, 1894-1994*. New York: W. W. Norton, 1999.

White, Walter Francis. *Rope and Faggot: A Biography of Judge Lynch*. New York: A. A. Knopf, 1929.

Whites, LeeAnn. *The Civil War as a Crisis in Gender: Augusta, Georgia, 1860-1890*. Athens: Univ. of Georgia Press, 1995.

————. "'Stand By Your Man': The Ladies Memorial Association and the Reconstruction of Southern White Manhood." In *Gender Matters: Civil War, Reconstruction, and the Making of the New South*, 85-94. New York: Palgrave Macmillan, 2005.

Whitfield, Stephen J. *A Death in the Delta: The Story of Emmett Till*. New York: Free Press, 1989.

Wiener, Jonathan M. "Class Structure and Economic Development in the American South, 1865-1955." *American Historical Review* 84 (Oct. 1979): 970-92.

————. *Social Origins of the New South: Alabama, 1860-1885*. Baton Rouge: Louisiana State Univ. Press, 1978.

Wilentz, Sean. *Chants Democratic: New York City and the Rise of the American Working Class, 1788-1850*. New York: Oxford Univ. Press, 1984.

Wilkens, Mark. "Gender, Race, Work Culture, and the Building of the Fire Fighters Union in Tampa, Florida, 1943-1985." In *Southern Labor in Transition, 1940-1995*, ed. Robert H, Zieger, 176-204. Knoxville: Univ. of Tennessee Press, 1997.

Wilkins, Roy. *Standing Fast: The Autobiography of Roy Wilkins*. New York: Viking, 1982.

Williams, Daniel K. *God's Own Party: The Making of the Christian Right*. New York: Oxford Univ. Press, 2010.

Williams, John Alexander. *Appalachia: A History*. Chapel Hill: Univ. of North Carolina Press, 2002.

Williams, Juan. *Eyes on the Prize: America's Civil Rights Years, 1954-1965*. New York: Viking, 1987.

————. *Thurgood Marshall: American Revolutionary*. New York: Times Books, 1998.

Williams, Kidada E. *They Left Great Marks on Me: African American Testimonies of*

Racial Violence from Emancipation to World War I. New York: New York Univ. Press, 2012.

Williams, Lee E., and Lee E. Williams II. *Anatomy of Four Race Riots: Racial Conflict in Knoxville, Elaine (Arkansas), Tulsa and Chicago, 1919-1921.* Jackson: Univ. Press of Mississippi, 1972.

Williams, T. Harry. *Huey Long.* New York: Alfred A. Knopf, 1969.

Williams, William Appleman. *The Tragedy of American Diplomacy.* 1959. New York: W. W. Norton, 2009.

Williamson, Joel. *The Crucible of Race: Black-White Relations in the American South since Emancipation.* New York: Oxford Univ. Press, 1984.

Wilson, Charles Reagan. *Baptized in Blood: The Religion of the Lost Cause, 1865-1920.* Athens: Univ. of Georgia Press, 1980.

———, ed. *Religion in the South.* Jackson: Univ. Press of Mississippi, 1985.

Wood, Amy Louise. *Lynching and Spectacle: Witnessing Racial Violence in America, 1890-1940.* Chapel Hill: Univ. of North Carolina Press, 2009.

Woodrum, Robert H. *"Everybody Was Black Down There": Race and Industrial Change in the Alabama Coalfields.* Athens: Univ. of Georgia Press, 2007.

Woods, Barbara, Jacqueline Anne Rouse, and Vicki L. Crawford. *Women in the Civil Rights Movement: Trailblazers and Torchbearers, 1941-1965.* New York: Carlson Publishing, 1990.

Woods, Randall B. *LBJ: Architect of American Ambition.* New York: The Free Press, 2006.

Woodward, C. Vann. "From the First Reconstruction to the Second." *Harper's* 230 (Apr. 1965): 127-33.

———. *Origins of the New South, 1877-1913.* Rev. ed. 1951. Reprint, Baton Rouge: Louisiana State Univ. Press, 1972.

———. "The Search for Southern Identity." *The Burden of Southern History.* Baton Rouge: Louisiana State Univ. Press, 1960.

———. *The Strange Career of Jim Crow.* Commemorative ed. 1955. New York: Oxford Univ. Press, 2002.

———. *Tom Watson, Agrarian Rebel.* New York: Macmillan, 1938.

Worster, Donald. "Transformations of the Earth: Toward an Agroecological Perspective in History." *Journal of American History* 76, no. 4 (Mar. 1990): 1087-1106.

Wright, Gavin. *Old South, New South: Revolutions in the Southern Economy since the Civil War.* New York: Basic Books, 1986.

Wright, George C. *Racial Violence in Kentucky, 1865-1940: Lynchings, Mob Rule, and "Legal Lynching."* Baton Rouge: Louisiana State Univ. Press, 1990.

Wynn, Neil A. "The Impact of the Second World War on the American Negro." *Journal of Contemporary History* 6, no. 2 (1971): 42-53.

Young, Andrew. *An Easy Burden: The Civil Rights Movement and the Transformation of America.* Waco, Tex.: Baylor Univ. Press, 2008.

Zamora, Emilio. *The World of the Mexican Worker in Texas.* College Station: Texas A&M Univ. Press, 1993.

Zangrando, Robert L. *The NAACP Crusade against Lynching, 1909-1950.* Philadelphia: Temple Univ. Press, 1980.

Zecker, Robert. "'Let Each Reader Judge': Lynching, Race, and Immigrant Newspapers." In *Swift to Wrath: Lynching in Global Perspective,* ed. William D. Carrigan and Christopher Waldrep, 137-59. Charlottesville: Univ. of Virginia Press, 2013.

Zieger, Robert H. "A Venture into Unplowed Fields: Daniel Powell and CIO Political Action in the Postwar South." In *Labor in the Modern South,* ed. Glenn T. Eskew, 158-81. Athens: Univ. of Georgia Press, 2001.

———. *The CIO, 1935-1955.* Chapel Hill: Univ. of North Carolina Press, 1995.

———. "Introduction: Southern Workers in a Changing Economy." In *Life and Labor in the New New South: Essays in Southern Labor History since 1950,* ed. Robert H. Zieger, 1-15. Gainesville: Univ. Press of Florida, 2012.

———. *For Jobs and Freedom: Race and Labor in America since 1865.* Lexington: Univ. Press of Kentucky, 2007.

———. "From Primordial Folk to Redundant Workers: Southern Textile Workers and Social Observers, 1920-1990." In *Southern Labor in Transition,* ed. Zieger, 273-94. Knoxville: Univ. of Tennessee Press, 1997.

———. *Rebuilding the Pulp and Paper Workers' Union, 1933-1941.* Knoxville: Univ. of Tennessee Press, 1984.

———. "Textile Workers and Historians." In *Organized Labor in the Twentieth-Century South,* ed. Zieger, 35-59. Knoxville: Univ. of Tennessee Press, 1991.

———. "The Union Comes to Covington: Virginia Paperworkers Organize, 1933-1952." *Proceedings of the American Philosophical Society* 126, no. 1 (Feb. 1982): 51-89.

———. "Walmart and the Broken Narrative of US Labor History." *Labor History* 52, no. 4 (Nov. 2011): 563-69.

Zimmerman, Andrew. *Alabama in Africa: Booker T. Washington, the German Empire, and the Globalization of the New South.* Princeton, N.J.: Princeton Univ. Press, 2010.

———. "From the Rhine to the Mississippi: Property, Democracy, and Socialism in the American Civil War." *Journal of the Civil War Era* 5, no.1 (Mar. 2015): 3-37.

Zimring, Franklin E. *The Contradictions of American Capital Punishment.* New York: Oxford Univ. Press, 2003.

Zinn, Howard. *SNCC: The New Abolitionists.* Boston: Beacon Press, 1964.

———. *The Southern Mystique.* New York: Alfred A. Knopf, 1964.

———. *You Can't Be Neutral on a Moving Train: A Personal History of Our Times.* Boston: Beacon Press, 1994.

Contributors

MICHAEL T. BERTRAND is an associate professor of history at Tennessee State University in Nashville, Tennessee, where he teaches courses on modern U.S., civil rights, and southern history. His research focuses on the relationship between popular culture, music, and social change in southern history. The author of *Race, Rock, and Elvis* (2004), Bertrand currently is working on a manuscript entitled *Remixing the Master/Reframing the Story: The Significance of Rock 'n' Roll in Southern History*. Bertrand holds a Ph.D. from the University of Mississippi.

MICHAEL BOWEN served as assistant director of the Bob Graham Center for Public Service at the University of Florida, where he completed a Ph.D. in history. He served as visiting assistant professor of history at Westminster College in New Wilmington, Pennsylvania, and John Carroll University in University Heights, Ohio. He is the author of *The Roots of Modern Conservatism: Dewey, Taft, and the Battle for the Soul of the Republican Party* (2011), published by the University of North Carolina Press.

JENNIFER E. BROOKS received her Ph.D. in history from the University of Tennessee in 1997. She is currently an associate professor of history at Auburn University. Her first book was published by the University of North Carolina Press in 2004, entitled *Defining the Peace: World War II Veterans, Race, and the Remaking of Southern Political Tradition*. Other work has appeared in the *Journal of Southern History, Labor: Studies in the Working Class History of the Americas,* and *Southern Cultures.* Her research on World War II veterans and the southern labor movement has also been curated as a traveling public history exhibit in Tennessee. She is the past president of the Southern Labor Studies Association, and is currently working on a book about the history of labor and immigration in Alabama.

STEPHANIE A. CARPENTER, who completed a Ph.D. at Iowa State University, serves as associate professor of history and chair of the History and Political Science Department at Andrews University in Berrien Springs, Michigan. She taught in the history department at Murray State University for sixteen years before going to Andrews. Carpenter is the author of *On the Farm Front: The Women's Land Army in World War II* (2003), published by the Northern Illinois University Press.

JAMES C. GIESEN earned a Ph.D. at the University of Georgia. He is a historian who specializes in the environmental and agricultural history of the American South. His book *Boll Weevil Blues: Cotton, Myth, and Power in the American South* (2011), published by the University of Chicago Press, was awarded the Deep South Book Prize and the Francis B. Simkins Award. In addition to serving as an associate professor of history at Mississippi State University, he is the executive secretary of the Agricultural History Society and editor of the "Environmental History and the American South" book series at the University of Georgia Press.

MARK D. HERSEY earned a Ph.D. from the University of Kansas and is now associate professor of history at Mississippi State University, where he directs the Center for the History of Agriculture, Science, and the Environment of the South (CHASES). Hersey is the author of *My Work Is That of Conservation: An Environmental Biography of George Washington Carver* (2011), published by the University of Georgia Press, as well as several articles and book chapters. He currently serves as an associate editor for the NEXUS: New Histories of Science, Technology, the Environment, Agriculture and Medicine series for the University of Alabama Press.

JAMES S. HUMPHREYS is a professor of history at Murray State University in Murray, Kentucky, where he specializes in the history of the American South. Humphreys completed a Ph.D. in history in 2005 at Mississippi State University. He is the author of *Francis Butler Simkins: A Life,* published by the University of Florida Press in 2008 in a book series titled "New Perspectives on the History of the South." Humphreys also serves as coeditor of the Interpreting American History series, published by Kent State University Press.

CONNIE L. LESTER is an associate professor in the Department of History at the University of Central Florida in Orlando. She is the editor of the *Florida Historical Quarterly* and the director of the Regional Initiative to Collect the History, Experiences, and Stories (RICHES) of the Central Florida digital project. She earned her Ph.D. at the University of Tennessee and is the author of *Up from the Mudsills of Hell: The Farmers' Alliance, Populism, and Progressive Agriculture in Tennessee, 1870-1915* (2011), published by the University of Georgia Press, and numerous articles and essays. She is currently working on two book projects, an edited Civil War diary titled *Yours Always: The Civil War Diaries of Lucy Virginia French, 1862-1865* and an economic history of twentieth-century Mississippi titled *Making Do: History, Poverty, and the Mississippi Economy in the Twentieth Century.*

REBECCA MONTGOMERY is associate professor of history at Texas State University in San Marcos, Texas. She completed a Ph.D. at the University of Missouri-Columbia and taught in Georgia and Mississippi before returning to her historical roots in Texas. Her first book, *The Politics of Education in the New South: Women and Reform in Georgia, 1890-1930* (2006), was published by Louisiana State University Press. She currently is completing a book-length biography of Celestia S. Parrish (1852-1918), an educator and women's rights advocate who was in the forefront of the progressive education movement in the South.

SARAH L. SILKEY is associate professor of history at Lycoming College in Williamsport, Pennsylvania. She received her Ph.D. from the University of East Anglia in Norwich, England. Her research examines cultural narratives of violence and transnational debates about American race relations. She is the author of *Black Woman Reformer: Ida B. Wells, Lynching, and Transatlantic Activism* (2015).

ROBERT H. ZIEGER, after completing a Ph.D at the University of Maryland, rose to be one of the great labor historians of the twentieth century. The last thirty years of his teaching and writing career were spent at the University of Florida. Zieger produced several books, numerous articles, and three edited studies. Among his works on labor history are *John L. Lewis: Labor Leader* (1988), published by Twayne Publishers, *The CIO, 1935-1955* (1995), published by the University of North Carolina Press, and *For Jobs and Freedom: Race and Labor in America since 1865* (2007), published by the University of Kentucky Press.

ANDREW ZIMMERMAN earned a Ph.D. from the University of California at San Diego and now serves as professor of history at The George Washington University. He is author of *Anthropology and Antihumanism in Imperial Germany* (2001) and *Alabama in Africa: Booker T. Washington, the German Empire, and the Globalization of the New South* (2010). He is also the editor of Karl Marx and Friedrich Engels, *The Civil War in the United States* (2016). Zimmerman is currently writing a history of the American Civil War as part of a transnational revolution against slave labor and wage labor.

Index

abolitionism, 9, 25, 51-52
Adams, Herbert Baxter, 12
Africa: colonial expansion in, 37, 51;
  colonization in, 51-52
African Americans: activism by, 11,
  52, 77, 175; efforts to control, 2, 21,
  85-86, 90; resistance by, 99-100, 137
African Americans, perceptions of,
  50, 235; criminality, 83, 85-86, 88,
  102; immorality, 120; inferiority,
  119-20; as rapists, 82-83
African Americans Confront Lynching
  (Waldrep), 100
The Age of Reform (Hofstadter), 65
Agee, James, 152-53
agrarian dissent, 63-64, 67; causes of,
  69-70, 250; influence of, 66, 75-76;
  participants in, 71-73
Agricultural Adjustment Administration (AAA), 154, 160-61, 167
agricultural labor, 67, 182, 250; race
  and ethnicity in, 137-38; shift to
  free, 37, 125; women's, 124-25
Agricultural Wheel, 65, 73
agriculture, 6, 28, 51, 245-46; becoming market-oriented, 65-70;
  changes in, 65, 245; conservation
  and, 257; crop-lien system in, 68,
  124, 243; diverse and subsistence,
  65-67; education through organizations of, 73; Farmers' Alliance
  advocating in, 63-64; globalization
  of, 51; in Great Depression, 157-58;
  natural world focused on, 242, 244-

45; poverty and debt in, 67, 152;
  as source of independence, 39-40;
  tenant farming in, 28, 152, 161, 167.
  See also agrarian dissent; plantation
  systems; sharecropping
Aiken, Charles S., 28-29
Aistrup, Joseph, 232
Alabama Department of Archives and
  History, 12
Alabama in Africa (Zimmerman), 30-31
Alexander, Michelle, 102-3
Ali, Omar H., 72
All We Knew Was to Farm (Walker), 27
Allen, James, 92-93
Allen, John R., 63
American Colonization Society (ACS),
  51
An American Dilemma (Myrdal), 4,
  174-77
American exceptionalism, 97-98
American Federation of Labor (AFL),
  131-32
American Historical Association
  (AHA), 10, 13, 15
American Society for Environmental
  History, 242
*The American South and the Atlantic
  World* (Ward, Bone, and Link), 31
The American South in the Global World
  (Peacock, Watson, and Matthews), 31
The Americanization of Dixie (Egerton),
  223
Ames, Jessie Daniel, 89, 119
Anatomy of a Lynching (McGovern), 90

Fite, Gilbert C., 28-29, 157
Fitzhugh, George, 113
Flamming, Douglas, 134
Fleming, Walter Lynwood, 12
Flynt, Wayne, 246
The Fog of War (Kruse and Tuck), 185
Foner, Eric, 24, 39, 46, 197
Foreign Affairs, 49
Foreman, James, 199
Forgotten Dead (Carrigan and Webb), 97
Fourteenth Amendment, 23-24, 47, 198
France, socialism in, 47
Franklin, John Hope, 19, 197
Franklin, V. P., 205
Frederickson, Kari, 228
Freedman, Estelle B., 99
freedom: economic, 42, 46-47; independence *vs.,* 39
Freedom North (Theoharis and Woodward), 207
freedom of association, 229-30
Freedom Song (King), 205
Freedom's Daughters (Olsen), 205
French Revolution, *vs.* Reconstruction, 49
From George Wallace to Newt Gringrich (Carter), 227
From Jim Crow to Civil Rights (Klarman), 229
From Manassas to Appomattox (Longstreet), 9
From Slavery to Freedom (Franklin), 19
From the New Deal to the New Right (Lowndes), 228-29
frontier thesis, 65, 82
Fuller, Paul, 114

Gaither, Gerald H., 72
Gardner, Sarah, 119
Garner, James W., 11
Garrow, David J., 201, 202
Garvey, Marcus, 52
Gaston, Paul, 22-23
Gellman, Erik S., 164, 167-68
Gender and the Civil Rights Movement (Ling), 205
gender discrimination, 123, 138

gender politics, in suffrage movement, 114
gender relations, 112, 115, 125; in civil rights organizations, 205-6; conservatism of, 117-19, 121
gender roles, influences on, 25-26, 125
The Georgia Peach (Okie), 265n48
"Georgia school," of environmental history, 255-57, 266n52
German Empire, 30
Gerstle, Gary, 187
Giddings, Paula, 205
Giesen, James C., 28, 255-56
Gilmore, Glenda, 122
Giltner, Scott, 253
Gingrich, Newt, 227, 235
global issues, 207; concurrent with Reconstruction, 37; race relations in, 184, 186-87, 189, 196; South's influence on, 30-31, 50
globalization, of agriculture, 51
God at the Grass Roots (Rozell and Wilcox), 232
A Golden Weed (Swanson), 266n52
Goldfield, Michael, 132
Goldwater, Barry, 222-23
Golston, Robert, 158
Gonzales-Day, Ken, 96-97
Goodman, Andrew, 101
Goodwyn, Lawrence, 65-66, 70, 73
Gordon, John B., 9
Gordon, Kate, 121
The Gospel of the Working Class (Gellman and Roll), 164, 167-68
government, federal, 15, 75, 245, 253; antilynching legislation by, 90, 98; civil rights legislation by, 199-200, 202-3; expansion of, 155, 184; imperialism and, 52-54; intervention in racial issues, 100, 178, 206; regulation by, 63-64, 252; relation to states, 156-57; rural populations and, 153-54, 166-67. *See also* New Deal
government, states, 11, 73, 75, 156-57, 246
Graham, Billy, 233
Graham, Bob, 225

public sector, unionism in, 133, 136, 149n34
Purcell, Aaron D., 164, 168

race, 37, 162, 248-49; colonialism based on South's, 48-50; divisions based on, 38, 132, 138, 158; in southern politics, 226, 235-36, 237n18; suffrage and, 3, 114, 121-22
Race, Class, and the Civil Rights Movement (Bloom), 206
Race, Reform, and Rebellion (Marable), 206
Race and Rumors of Race (Odum), 174, 176
race relations, 20, 22, 186; in civil rights organizations, 205-6; debate over improvement in, 23, 183, 211-12; global upheaval of, 187, 189, 196; inflaming of divide in, 16, 19; white backlash in, 178, 183, 201, 225-29, 231; WWII's influence on, 4, 17-18, 173-77, 179-81, 183-84, 188-89
race riots, 88-89, 180
racial attitudes, 72, 233-34
racial cooperation, 22; among farmers, 74-75; against Jim Crow, 182-83; women and, 115-16, 126
racial equality: in constitutional amendments, 198; disbelief in, 72; failed hopes for, 21; opposition to, 16, 49, 119
racial identity, 41, 50, 92, 187
racial issues: northern, 24, 234-35; political use of, 225-29, 235-36
racial uplift, 115, 120-21
racial violence, 18; black resistance to, 99-100; in civil rights movement, 101-2; effects of, 81-82, 119-20; forms of, 81, 95; hate crime legislation against, 101-2; to maintain white supremacy, 88, 96; responses to, 100-102; uses of, 81, 119-20. *See also* lynchings
racism, 16, 18, 48; antiracism and, 43, 53; colonization motivated by, 51; in criminal justice system, 102-3; decline of scientific, 17; fascism and, 17, 175; prevalence of, 24, 136,

196; rural life reinforcing classism and, 245-46; targets of, 30, 48, 187; as white response, 41, 45
Radical Reconstruction, 15, 23-24
Radical Republicans, 11
railroads, 68, 70
Randolph, A. Philip, 175, 181, 204
Ransom, Roger, 67-68
rape: of black women, 98-99; lynchings and, 82-84, 86, 92
Raper, Arthur F., 14, 86-87, 242
Reagan, Ronald, 224; conservatism of, 228, 232; southern support for, 225-26; use of racial language, 227, 229
The Real Majority (Scammon and Wattenberg), 223, 225
"Reappraisal of the Causes of Farm Protest in the United States" (Mayhew), 69
Reconstruction, 38, 52, 95; conflicting views on, 11, 119; effects of, 112, 198; myths about, 198; studies of, 10-11, 15; transnational perspective on, 1-2, 37, 49, 53-54
Reconstruction in Georgia (Thompson), 11
Reconstruction in Mississippi (Garner), 11
Reconstruction in North Carolina (Hamilton), 11, 14-15
"Red Cross, Double Cross" (Guglielmo), 187-88
Red Hills and Cotton (Robertson), 18-19
Redeemers, wealth of, 20-21
Redefining Rape (Freedman), 99
Rediker, Marcus, 39
reforms, 152, 168; civil rights movement as crucial, 195, 220n33; in Democratic Party, 177; gender relations and, 121, 126; New Deal, 156; Republicans', 74-75; third-party parties in, 66; women's activism in, 3, 72, 113-15, 123
regional differences: decline of, 223-24; overemphasis on, 233-35
religion, 203; all-black churches, 15; in colleges, 233; in Populism, 72-73; in Republican coalition, 231-34; revivals, 167; women's church-based organizations, 116-17

religious Right, in Republican politics, 231-34
Remaking Wormsloe Plantation (Swanson), 256
Reminiscences of the Civil War (Gordon), 9
The Report on Economic Conditions of the South (NEC), 154
Republican Party, 236n6; civil rights movement and, 228-29; growth of, 221, 223-24, 228-30, 235; influences on growth of, 5, 222, 237n18; race relations in, 88, 225-26; in reform efforts, 74-75; religious Right in, 231-34; use of racial language, 235-36
Resettlement Administration (RA), 153-54
revisionism, 21, 168, 197; on Great Depression, 159; in historiography, 164; on meaning of Civil War, 118; on Populism, 66
Revolt against Chivalry (Hall), 89
Rhodes, James Ford, 10
right-to-work legislation, 133, 149n34
Riley, Franklin L., 12
Rise, Eric W., 88
The Rise and Fall of the Confederate Government (Davis), 8
The Rise of Southern Republicans (Black and Black), 227-28
The River (film), 154
Robertson, Ben, 18-19
Robinson, Armstead, 197
Robinson, Jo Ann Gibson, 204
Robinson, John L., 161, 163
Robnett, Belinda, 205
Rodgers, Joe, 100-101
Roediger, David, 45
Roll, Jarod, 164, 167-68
Roosevelt, Franklin Delano, 2, 151, 159, 175; Democrats and, 154-55, 236n4; southern politicians distancing from, 157
Roosevelt, Theodore, 10
Roots of Reform (Sanders), 75-76
The Roots of Southern Populism (Hahn), 70

Rope and Faggot (White), 86
Rosen, Hannah, 99
Rosenberg, Daniel, 135
Ross, Steven John, 164, 166-67
Rouse, Jacqueline, 115, 205
Rubright, Lynn, 164, 166-67
Rudwick, Elliott, 200
rural life, 244; lack of progress in, 186, 245-46; women's, 27, 71-72
Rural Worlds Lost: The American South, 1920-1960 (Kirby), 29
Rushdy, Ashraf H. A., 95
Russia, 51

Saikku, Mikko, 252-53
Sale, Kirkpatrick, 223-24
Salmond, John, 134
Sanders, Elizabeth, 75-76
Santo Domingo (Dominican Republic), 53
Saunt, Claudio, 52-53
Scammon, Richard, 223, 225
Scarlett's Sisters: Young Women in the Old South (Jabour), 26-27
Schechter, Patricia, 120
Schuyler, Lorraine Gates, 122-23
Schwerner, Michael, 101
Scott, Anne Firor, 25-26, 112-14
Scott, James C., 181
"Scottsboro Boys," 87
Scramble for Africa, 51
Second Reconstruction, 209
"Second Reconstruction," 197-98
Segrave, Kerry, 98
segregation, 4, 22, 81; of blood, 187-88; effects of, 20, 211-12; ending, 101, 196; justifications for, 83, 89, 119; legislative, 200-201, 207, 210
Sellers, Charles, 56n12
separate but equal policies, 72
sexuality, 88, 120; abuse of black women, 98-99; racial limits on, 82-83; white men's double standard of, 113
The Shadow of Slavery (Daniel), 245-46
Shafer, Byron, 237n18
Shapiro, Herbert, 81
Shapiro, Karin, 135